Foundations of Robotics

Foundations of Robotics
Analysis and Control

Tsuneo Yoshikawa

The MIT Press
Cambridge, Massachusetts
London, England

This book was set in Times Roman by Asco Trade Typesetting Ltd. in Hong Kong and was printed and bound in the United States of America.

Library of Congress Cataloging-in-Publication Data

Yoshikawa, Tsuneo, 1941–
[Robotto seigyo kisoron. English]
Foundations of robotics: analysis and control/Tsuneo Yoshikawa.
p. cm.
Revised translation of: Robotto seigyo kisoron.
Includes bibliographical references.
ISBN: 978-0-262-51458-3
1. Robotics. I. Title.
TJ211.Y6713 1990
629.8′92—dc20 89-29363
CIP

Contents

Preface

Robots are now widely used in factories, and applications of robots in space, the oceans, nuclear industries, and other fields are being actively developed. Also, for the future, the use of robots in every facet of society, including the home, is being seriously considered. To support the development of these broad applications, robotics has evolved into a systematic approach to the engineering of robots.

This book has been written with the objective of presenting some fundamental concepts and methodologies for the analysis, design, and control of robot manipulators in an easily understandable way. I believe that this knowledge is useful not only in robotics but also in the analysis and control of other types of mechanical systems.

The book is based on class notes used at Kyoto University. It is intended as a text or reference book on robotics, mainly for graduate students in engineering. Junior and senior undergraduate students, however, should also be able to understand the material without much difficulty. The physical meanings of the concepts and equations used in the book are explained as fully as possible, and the required background in kinetics, linear algebra, and control theory is presented in an intuitively clear way to spare the reader from having to refer to texts in those other fields.

The book is organized as follows. After an overview in chapter 1, chapters 2 through 4 cover the analysis of robot manipulator mechanisms. Based on this analysis, chapters 5 through 7 discuss the control of robot manipulators.

Chapter 1 introduces several typical robot manipulator mechanisms and their controllers, in order to acquaint the reader with the kind of hardware that will be dealt with. Chapter 2 covers the kinematics of robot manipulators, studying geometrically the motion of manipulator links and objects related to the manipulation task in terms of position, velocity, and acceleration. Chapter 3 deals with the dynamics of robot manipulators, looking at how the manipulator's motion is affected by its mass distribution and applied forces. This chapter includes the derivation of the dynamic equations of motion, their use for control and simulation, and the identification of inertial parameters. Chapter 4 develops the concept of manipulability to analyze and evaluate quantitatively the manipulation ability of manipulators. This concept is examined first from the viewpoint of kinematics and then from the viewpoint of dynamics.

Chapter 5 covers various position-control algorithms that make the end effector of a manipulator follow a desired position trajectory. Chapter 6 discusses two typical force-control methods. These make the contact force between the end effector and its environment follow a desired force trajectory. Chapter 7 discusses, for manipulators with redundant degrees of freedom, a way to develop control algorithms for active utilization of the redundancy. The appendixes give compact reviews of the function atan2, pseudo-inverses, singular-value decomposition, and Lyapunov stability theory.

When writing a textbook in a changing field like robotics in which many new achievements are being unveiled day by day, one usually has a difficult time deciding what to include. I have attempted to include as many important results as possible. At the same time, I have tried to present them plainly with the help of many illustrative examples.

It is my pleasure to thank several people who have contributed in various ways to the completion of this book. The content and the form of this book are much influenced by Richard P. Paul's pioneering book *Robot Manipulators* (MIT Press, 1981), which I translated into Japanese in 1984. I wish to thank Yoshihiko Nakamura and Toshiharu Sugie, with whom I have worked on research projects that some parts of this book are based on. Yasuyoshi Yokokohji read the manuscript and provided many useful comments. Discussions with Junichi Imura and Kiyoshi Maekawa proved valuable in the writing of the section on adaptive control (section 5.6). Mike Lipsett, who happened to be with me at Kyoto University at a critical stage in the writing of the English version, contributed many improvements. Takashi Hosoda, Jun Koreishi, Junichi Imura, and Osamu Suzuki helped me with revisions and corrections. Masako Awakura performed the magic of turning all my vague scribbling into a finely typed manuscript.

This book is mostly a translation of my Japanese book *Robotto Seigyo Kisoron* (*Foundations of Robot Control*), published in Tokyo by Corona Publishing Co. Ltd. in 1988. I am grateful to Corona for its cooperation and support in publishing this English version. I also wish to thank Frank P. Satlow and Teresa Ehling of The MIT Press for patiently awaiting my manuscript. My wife, Sanae, supported and encouraged me at home during the writing of this book.

Foundations of Robotics

1 Overview of Robotic Mechanisms and Controller

A robot system generally consists of three subsystems: a motion subsystem, a recognition subsystem, and a control subsystem (figure 1.1). The motion subsystem is the physical structure that carries out desired motions, corresponding to human arms or legs. The recognition subsystem uses various sensors to gather information about any objects being acted upon, about the robot itself, and about the environment; it recognizes the robot's state, the objects, and the environment from the gathered information. The control subsystem influences the motion subsystem to achieve a given task using the information from the recognition subsystem.

This book covers mainly the theoretical fundamentals of mechanism analysis and control of robot manipulators which are necessary for designing their mechanisms and their controller. For the motion subsystem described above, manipulator mechanisms that function like human arms will be the subject of this book. Their kinematics, dynamics, and performance evaluation are discussed. For the control subsystem, position control of an end effector, control of the force applied by the end effector on an object, and the control of redundant manipulators are discussed. The recognition subsystem plays a key role in using robots outside of factories and in making robots intelligent. However, this subsystem will not be examined closely, since in this book a recognition subsystem need only provide information about position, velocity, and force.

This chapter discusses several typical mechanisms and controllers of robot manipulators in order to acquaint the reader with the hardware that will be dealt with in the following chapters.

1.1 Mechanisms

Most robot manipulators can be regarded as open-loop link mechanisms consisting of several links connected together by joints. Typical joints are *revolute joints* and *prismatic joints*, which are represented by the symbols shown in figure 1.2. Joint c in this figure is sometimes called the *pivot joint* to distinguish it from joint b. The endpoint of the mechanism is moved by driving these joints with appropriate actuators. A manipulator can usually be divided into an arm portion, a wrist portion, and a hand portion. Several typical mechanisms of the arm and wrist portions will be shown. The hand is not addressed here, since its mechanism depends on the task to be performed.

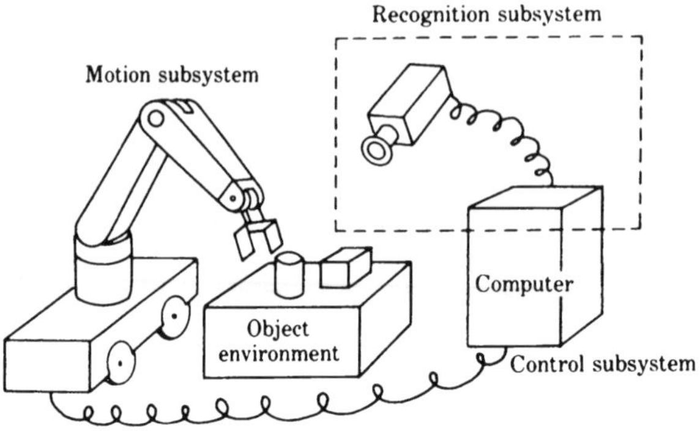

Figure 1.1
Robot system.

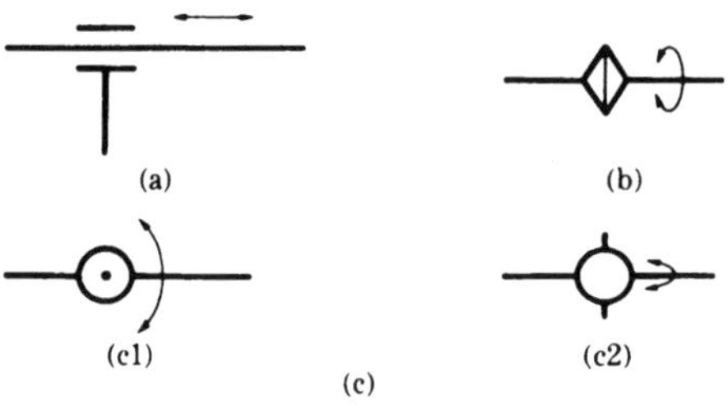

Figure 1.2
Symbols of joints (arrows show direction of motion). (a) Prismatic joint. (b) Revolute joint 1. (c) Revolute joint 2. (c1) Up-and-down rotation. (c2) Back-and-forth rotation.

Figure 1.3 shows several types of arm mechanisms: (a) the orthogonal-coordinate type, (b) the cylindrical-coordinate type, (c) the polar-coordinate type, (d) the vertical multi-joint type, and (e) the horizontal multi-joint type. Type a is structurally simple and rigid, and so its positioning accuracy is high. Types b–e are inferior to type a in positioning accuracy; however, they need less floor area for a base, and they have broader reach. Every mechanism in figure 1.3 has three degrees of freedom, which is the minimum number of degrees of freedom needed for placing the endpoint of the arm at an arbitrary point in three-dimensional space. Here the degree of freedom is defined as the minimal number of position variables necessary for completely specifying the configuration of a mechanism.

The wrist is connected to the end of the arm portion. The main role of the wrist is to change the orientation of the hand. Examples of wrist mechanisms are shown in figure 1.4. Type a is similar to the human wrist;

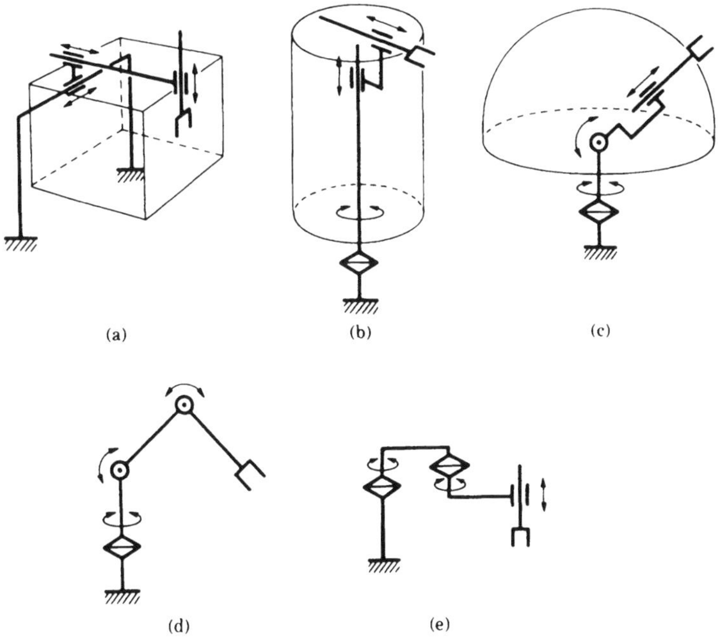

Figure 1.3
Arm mechanisms. (a) Orthogonal-coordinate type. (b) Cylindrical-coordinate type. (c) Polar-coordinate type. (d) Vertical multijoint type. (e) Horizontal multijoint type.

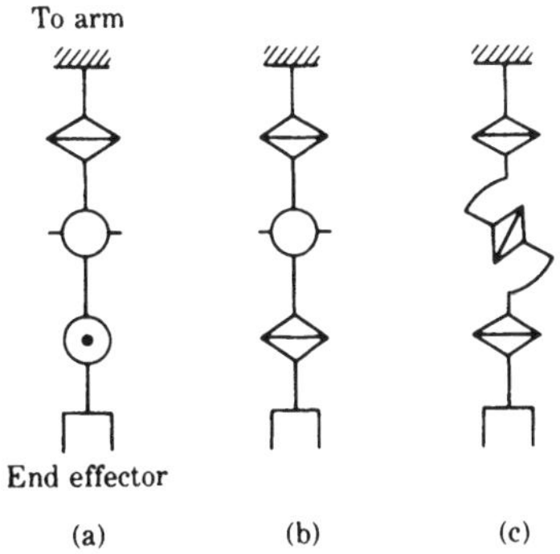

Figure 1.4
Wrist mechanisms.

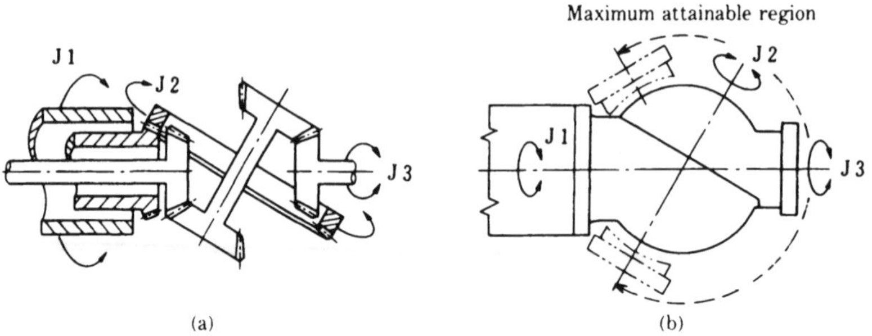

Figure 1.5
Three Roll Wrist. (a) Drive mechanism. (b) Profile.

type b is often used in industrial manipulators. Type c is equivalent to the Three Roll Wrist.[1] This can also be regarded as a variation of type b in which the axis of the middle joint is tilted a little. The Three Roll Wrist elegantly uses bevel gears as shown in figure 1.5a to make the attainable region of orientations as large as in figure 1.5b. These are all three-degrees-of-freedom mechanisms; thus, they have enough degrees of freedom to let the hand portion pose in an arbitrary orientation. However, each of these wrists has some configurations in which it can no longer change the hand orientation in a certain direction. Such a configuration is called a *singular configuration.* For instance, the configurations shown in figures 1.4b and 1.4c are singular ones because it is impossible to rotate the hand from side to side on the page.

The wrist mechanisms shown in figures 1.6 and 1.7 have been developed with the purpose of overcoming the degeneracy problem of singular configurations. Figure 1.6 shows the ET (Elephant Trunk) wrist,[2] a three-degrees-of-freedom wrist with a special mechanism that relocates the singular configurations out of the main working domain. More specifically, as figure 1.6a shows, it consists of five revolute joints, J1, J2, J3, J3′, and J2′, with each element of the pairs {J2,J2′} and {J3,J3′} rotating through the same angles. For instance, joints J2 and J2′ rotate as in figure 1.6b. Figure 1.6c shows a hardware implementation of the mechanism using two universal joints connected by gears. The only singular configurations of the ET wrist are those in which the approach direction Z_H of the hand portion and the outward direction Z_W of the wrist base are in completely opposite directions (for example, $\theta_2 = 90°$ in figure 1.6b). Figure 1.7 shows a four-degrees-of-freedom wrist,[3] which can get away from the singular configurations by actively using the mechanical redundancy.

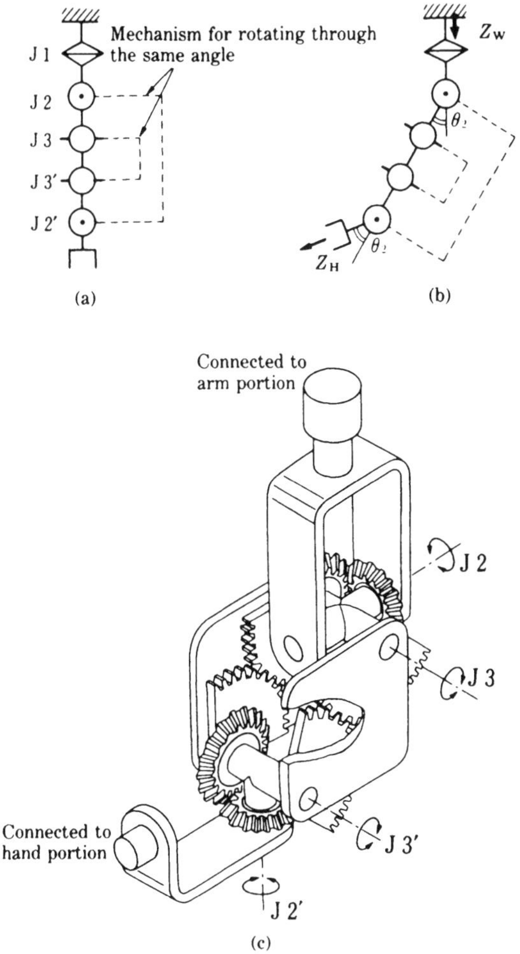

Figure 1.6
ET wrist. (a) Basic structure. (b) Example of motion. (c) Mechanism.

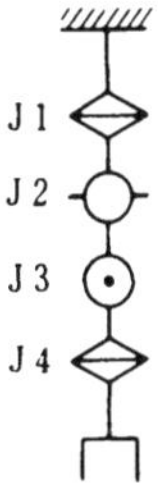

Figure 1.7
Four-degrees-of-freedom wrist.

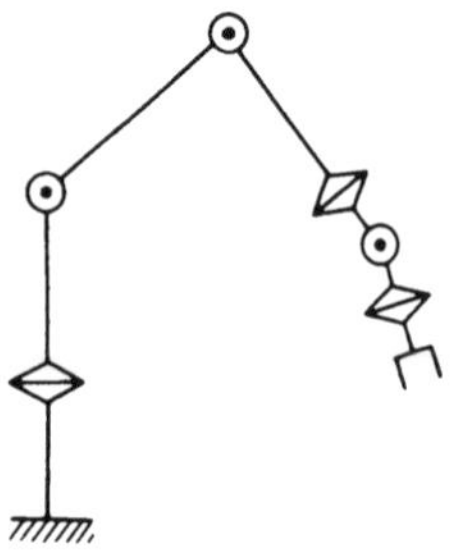

Figure 1.8
Combination of arm portion and wrist portion.

Figure 1.9
PUMA 260 (courtesy of Westinghouse Automation Division/Unimation Inc.).

Combining an arm and a wrist mechanism generally gives a manipulator with six degrees of freedom, excluding the degree of freedom in the hand. For example, figure 1.8 is the combination of figures 1.3d and 1.4b, and the design of the robot in figure 1.9 is based on this combination. Figure 1.10 is the combination of figures 1.3d and 1.4c, and figure 1.11 shows an example of this combination. Figure 1.12 is the combination of figures 1.3c and 1.4b; figure 1.13 shows an example of this kind of robot. Figure 1.14 is the combination of figures 1.3a and 1.4b, and figure 1.15 shows an example of this combination.

Depending on the purpose, there are often cases where six degrees of freedom are not required, and there are many industrial manipulators on the market that have only five degrees of freedom or fewer. One representative example is shown in figure 1.16, which is the combination of figure

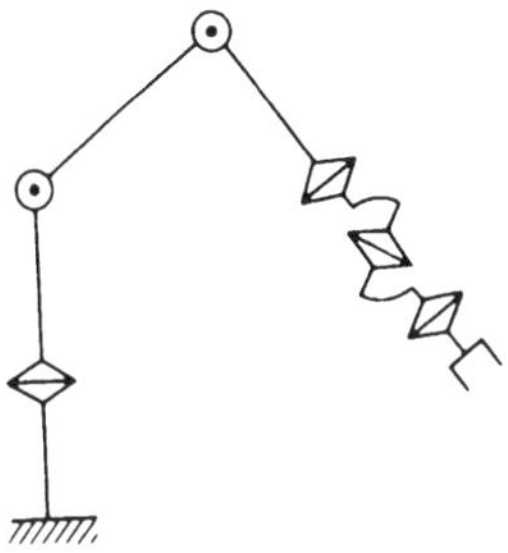

Figure 1.10
Combination of arm portion and wrist portion.

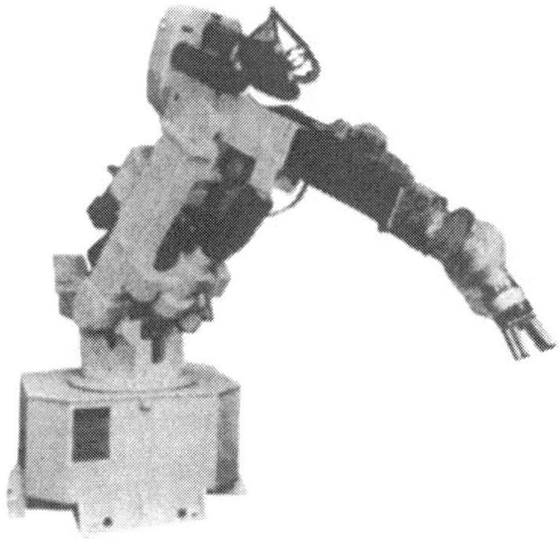

Figure 1.11
T3-786 Robot (courtesy of Cincinnati Milacron, Japan Branch).

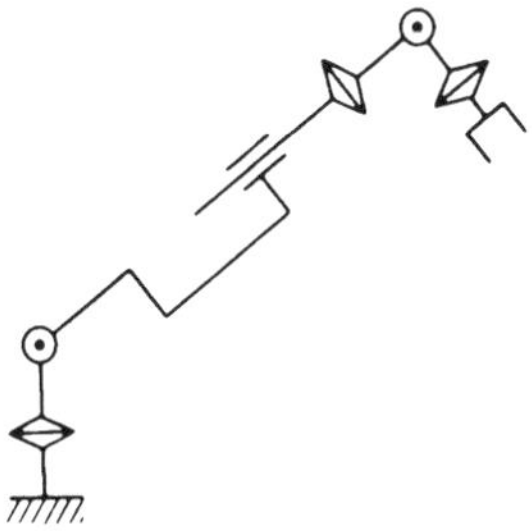

Figure 1.12
Combination of arm portion and wrist portion.

Figure 1.13
Kawasaki Unimate (courtesy of Kawasaki Heavy Industries, Ltd.).

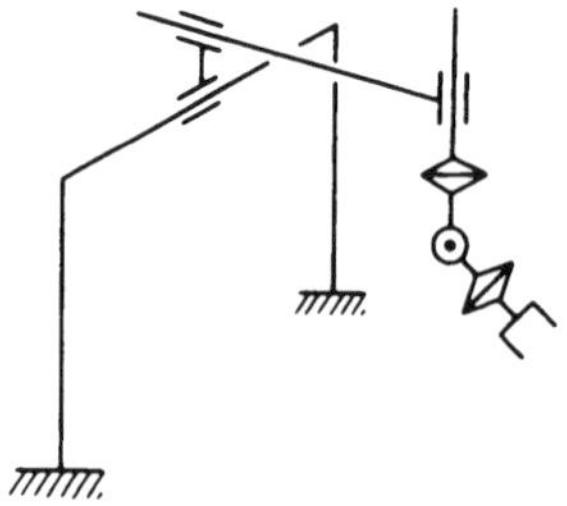

Figure 1.14
Combination of arm portion and wrist portion.

Figure 1.15
IBM 7565 Robotic System (1984) (courtesy of IBM Corp.).

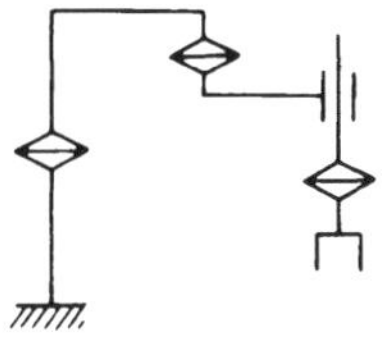

Figure 1.16
SCARA-type robot.

1.3e and a wrist portion with just one joint rotating about a vertical axis. This four-degrees-of-freedom manipulator is called a SCARA (Selective Compliance Assembly Robot Arm).[4] Manipulators with seven degrees of freedom or more have also been developed.

1.2 Controller

The fundamental elements of tasks performed by robot manipulators are (1) to move the end effector, with or without a load, along a desired trajectory and (2) to exert a desired force on an object when the end effector is in contact with it. The former is called *position control* (or *trajectory control*) and the latter *force control.*

Figure 1.17 is a rough sketch of a typical controller for position control. Joint positions and velocities are generally measured by joint sensors, such as potentiometers, tachometer-generators, and/or encoders. Using these data, the controller determines the inputs to the joint actuators so that the end effector follows the desired trajectory as closely as possible.

The detailed structure of a position controller is shown in figure 1.18. The outputs on the right of the figure are the joint positions of the manipulator. The joint-trajectory generator determines the desired joint trajectories from the desired trajectory for the end effector. The desired joint trajectories are then given to the joint controllers. Each joint controller is a servomechanism for a single joint position. Figure 1.19 shows a simple servomechanism that uses the position and velocity feedback with constant feedback gains. This kind of controller has often been used for general industrial manipulators. Generally, changes in dynamics are due to changes in the manipulator configuration; there is also interaction among the joints. The above controller design implicitly assumes the possibility of coping with changes in manipulator dynamics and joint interactions by regarding

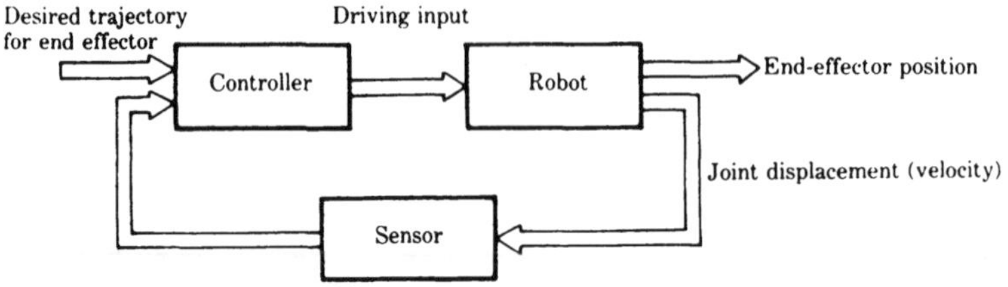

Figure 1.17
Rough sketch of position-control system.

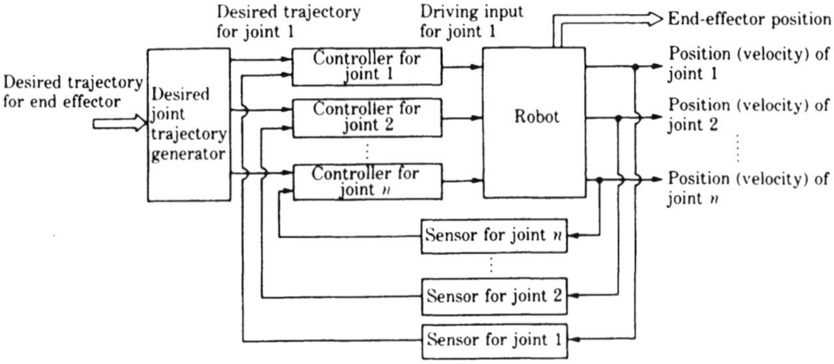

Figure 1.18
Example of controller.

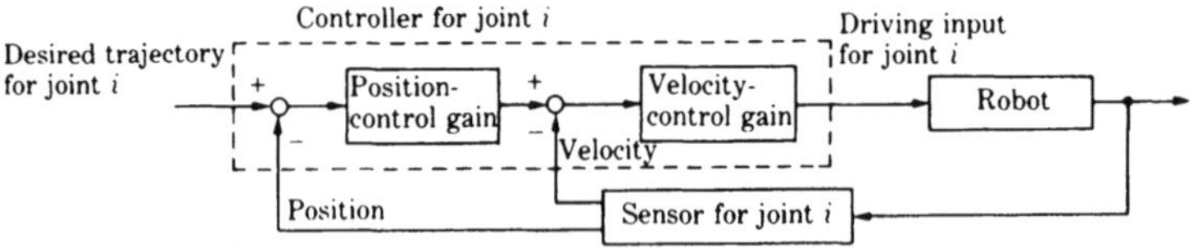

Figure 1.19
Position-velocity feedback servosystem.

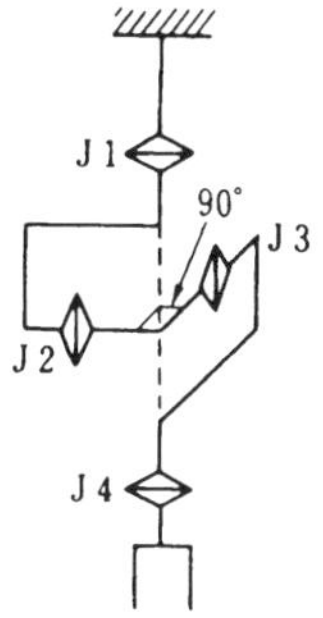

Figure 1.20
Four-joint wrist with distance between axes of joints J2 and J3 set to zero. (J2 and J3 are in the horizontal plane and orthogonal to each other.)

them as disturbances. However, when there are severe demands for fast and accurate positioning, the tracking performance of this type of controller is no longer adequate. Eventually it would be necessary to return to figure 1.17 and to design the controller taking into consideration the interaction among joints and the change of dynamics.

In force control, it is generally necessary to measure the forces driving the joints or the contact force between the end effector and the object by force sensors, and to feed these signals back to the controller.

In the following chapters, we will study the fundamentals of the analysis and control of robot systems such as those described above.

Exercises

1.1 How many degrees of freedom do you think the human arm has (except for the hand portion)? Draw a structural model of a manipulator equivalent to the human arm using the symbols in figure 1.2.

1.2 Figure 1.20 shows a wrist mechanism obtained from the four-degrees-of-freedom wrist shown in figure 1.7 by setting the distance between the axes of joints J2 and J3 to zero. Find the singular configurations of this wrist. Is it possible to avoid these singular configurations without changing the orientation of the end effector?

1.3 Consider the task of inserting a peg with a circular cross-section into a cylindrical hole in a plate with arbitrary position and inclination. How many degrees of freedom should a manipulator have in order to perform this task?

References

1. T. Stackhouse, "A New Concept in Robot Wrist Flexibility," in Proceedings of the Ninth International Symposium on Industrial Robots (1979), pp. 589–599.

2. J. P. Trevelyan et al., "ET—A Wrist Mechanism without Singular Positions," *International Journal of Robotics Research* 4, no. 4 (1986): 71–85.

3. T. Yoshikawa and S. Kiriyama, "Four-Joint Redundant Wrist Mechanism and Its Control," *ASME Journal of Dynamic Systems, Measurement, and Control* 111, no. 2 (1989): 200–204.

4. H. Makino and N. Furuya, "SCARA Robot and Its Family," in Proceedings of the International Conference on Assembly Automation (1982), pp. 433–444.

The following are well-written textbooks on robotics. They affected the style of this book in many ways.

R. P. Paul, *Robot Manipulators: Mathematics, Programming, and Control* (MIT Press, 1981).

H. Asada and J.-J. E. Slotine, *Robot Analysis and Control* (Wiley, 1986).

J. J. Craig, *Introduction to Robotics* (Addison-Wesley, 1986).

2 Kinematics

This chapter will be devoted to the kinematics of robot manipulators, which means studying geometrically the motion of the manipulator links and/or objects related to the manipulation task in terms of position, velocity, and acceleration.

First, to express the position and orientation of a rigid object, the method of assigning a coordinate frame to the object will be explained. Homogeneous transforms, which are convenient for describing the relations among many objects, will be introduced. Then an expression for finding the end effector's position in space from the description of the manipulator mechanism and its joint displacements will be derived. Methods for obtaining the joint displacements that realize a given end-effector position will also be discussed.

Next, the Jacobian matrix describing the relation between the joint's velocity and the end effector's velocity will be introduced. We will consider the problem of finding a joint velocity that achieves a given end effector velocity and discuss singular configurations and an application of the Jacobian matrix to some problems of statics.

2.1 Position and Orientation of Objects

2.1.1 Object Coordinate Frame

The first thing we have to do to analyze a manipulator is represent mathematically the position and orientation of the manipulator itself, the tool it holds, and the objects on which the robot works in three-dimensional space. For this purpose we adopt a method generally used in mechanics[1]: we attach an orthogonal coordinate frame to each object and express its position and orientation by the position of the origin and the directions of the three axes of the attached frame relative to a given reference orthogonal coordinate frame. The former is called the *object frame* and the latter the *reference frame*.

Consider the object shown in figure 2.1. The reference frame is denoted by Σ_A, its origin by O_A, and the three coordinate axes by X_A, Y_A, and Z_A. Similarly, the object frame is denoted by Σ_B, its origin by O_B, and the three axes by X_B, Y_B, and Z_B. The vector from O_A to O_B (i.e., the position vector of O_B relative to O_A), expressed in Σ_A, is denoted as ${}^A\boldsymbol{p}_B$.* The unit vectors

* Vectors and matrices are denoted by boldface italic letters, the only exception being identity matrices and zero matrices; those will be denoted by I and O, respectively.

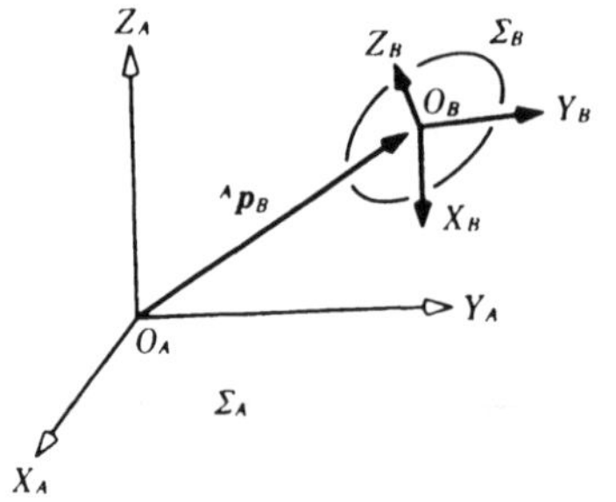

Figure 2.1
Reference frame and object frame.

in the directions of X_B, Y_B, and Z_B, expressed in Σ_A, are denoted ${}^A\boldsymbol{x}_B$, ${}^A\boldsymbol{y}_B$, and ${}^A\boldsymbol{z}_B$. Then the position of the object is represented by ${}^A\boldsymbol{p}_B$, and its orientation is represented by $\{{}^A\boldsymbol{x}_B, {}^A\boldsymbol{y}_B, {}^A\boldsymbol{z}_B\}$. The superscript A on the left means that the vector is expressed in the frame Σ_A. Hereafter, all frames denoted by Σ are right-hand orthogonal coordinate frames.

2.1.2 Rotation Matrix

It was established in subsection 2.1.1 that the orientation of an object can be specified by the three vectors $\{{}^A\boldsymbol{x}_B, {}^A\boldsymbol{y}_B, {}^A\boldsymbol{z}_B\}$. It is often convenient, however, to use a matrix defined by

$$ {}^A\boldsymbol{R}_B = [{}^A\boldsymbol{x}_B \; {}^A\boldsymbol{y}_B \; {}^A\boldsymbol{z}_B] \tag{2.1} $$

instead of the three vectors. This matrix ${}^A\boldsymbol{R}_B$, which can be regarded as describing the rotational part of the relative displacement of frame Σ_B from frame Σ_A, is called the *rotation matrix*.

Example 2.1 Consider the problem of expressing the position and orientation of a two-fingered hand. The hand frame Σ_H is attached to the hand as shown in figure 2.2a. In words, the origin O_H is taken to be at the midpoint of the two fingers. The Z_H axis is in the approach direction of the hand. The Y_H axis is in one of the two directions in the plane including the two fingers and normal to Z_H. The X_H axis is assigned so as to be normal to Z_H and Y_H, making Σ_H a right-hand coordinate system. We assume that, starting from the state (shown in figure 2.2b) where the hand frame Σ_H agrees with the reference frame Σ_A, the hand is rotated 90° around the axis that goes through $[0,0,2]^T$ of Σ_A and parallel to X_A. The hand's position

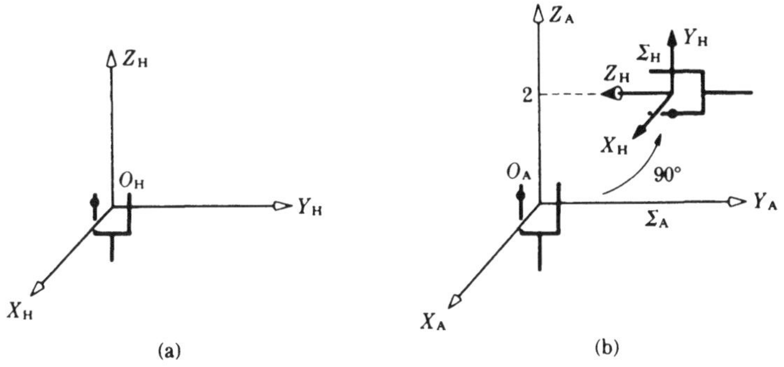

Figure 2.2
Representation of position and orientation of a hand. (The black dot on one finger distinguishes it from the other finger.) (a) Hand frame Σ_H. (b) Relation between Σ_A and Σ_H.

and orientation after rotation are given by

$$^{A}p_{H} = [0,2,2]^T$$

and

$$^{A}\boldsymbol{R}_{H} = \begin{bmatrix} 1 & 0 & 0 \\ 0 & 0 & -1 \\ 0 & 1 & 0 \end{bmatrix}. \ \square*$$

Some properties of the rotation matrix will now be given. Since $^{A}\boldsymbol{x}_B$, $^{A}\boldsymbol{y}_B$, and $^{A}\boldsymbol{z}_B$ are unit vectors orthogonal to one another, they satisfy

$$\begin{aligned} (^{A}\boldsymbol{x}_B)^T\, {}^{A}\boldsymbol{x}_B &= 1, \\ (^{A}\boldsymbol{y}_B)^T\, {}^{A}\boldsymbol{y}_B &= 1, \\ (^{A}\boldsymbol{z}_B)^T\, {}^{A}\boldsymbol{z}_B &= 1, \\ (^{A}\boldsymbol{x}_B)^T\, {}^{A}\boldsymbol{y}_B &= 0, \\ (^{A}\boldsymbol{y}_B)^T\, {}^{A}\boldsymbol{z}_B &= 0, \\ (^{A}\boldsymbol{z}_B)^T\, {}^{A}\boldsymbol{x}_B &= 0. \end{aligned} \tag{2.2}$$

Hence $^{A}\boldsymbol{R}_B$ satisfies

$$(^{A}\boldsymbol{R}_B)^T(^{A}\boldsymbol{R}_B) = \mathbf{I}_3, \tag{2.3}$$

* An open square (□) denotes the end of an example.

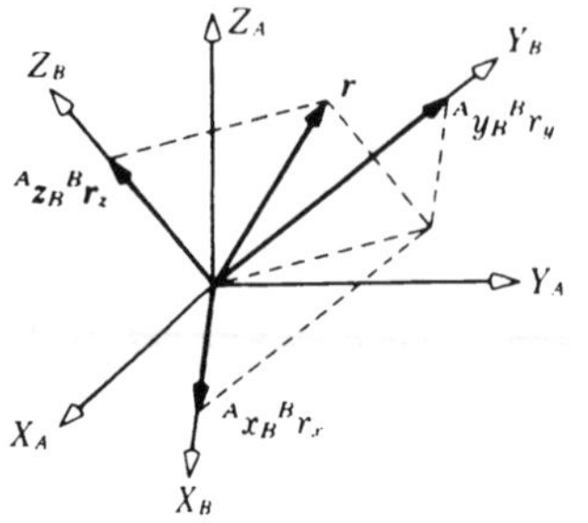

Figure 2.3
Interpretation of ${}^A\boldsymbol{r} = {}^A\boldsymbol{R}_B {}^B\boldsymbol{r}$.

where $\mathbf{I}_3$ is the 3×3 identity matrix. From equation 2.3, we have

$$ {}^A\boldsymbol{R}_B^{-1} = ({}^A\boldsymbol{R}_B)^T, \tag{2.4} $$

where $\boldsymbol{R}^{-1}$ denotes the inverse of a matrix $\boldsymbol{R}$. Therefore, the rotation matrix ${}^A\boldsymbol{R}_B$ is an orthogonal matrix.

Consider the case where the origins of Σ_A and Σ_B are at the same point, as shown in figure 2.3, and assume that a vector $\boldsymbol{r}$ is described by

$$ {}^A\boldsymbol{r} = [{}^A r_x, {}^A r_y, {}^A r_z]^T $$

when expressed in Σ_A, and by

$$ {}^B\boldsymbol{r} = [{}^B r_x, {}^B r_y, {}^B r_z]^T $$

when expressed in Σ_B. Then we have

$$ {}^A\boldsymbol{r} = {}^A\boldsymbol{x}_B {}^B r_x + {}^A\boldsymbol{y}_B {}^B r_y + {}^A\boldsymbol{z}_B {}^B r_z, $$

or

$$ {}^A\boldsymbol{r} = {}^A\boldsymbol{R}_B {}^B\boldsymbol{r}. \tag{2.5} $$

Replacing Σ_A and Σ_B yields

$$ {}^B\boldsymbol{r} = {}^B\boldsymbol{R}_A {}^A\boldsymbol{r}. \tag{2.6} $$

From equations 2.5 and 2.6 we have

$$ {}^A\boldsymbol{r} = {}^A\boldsymbol{R}_B {}^B\boldsymbol{R}_A {}^A\boldsymbol{r}. \tag{2.7} $$

Since equation 2.7 holds for any ${}^A\boldsymbol{r}$, we obtain

$$ {}^{A}\boldsymbol{R}_{B}\,{}^{B}\boldsymbol{R}_{A} = \mathrm{I}_3, \tag{2.8} $$

or

$$ {}^{B}\boldsymbol{R}_{A} = ({}^{A}\boldsymbol{R}_{B})^{-1} = ({}^{A}\boldsymbol{R}_{B})^{T}. \tag{2.9} $$

Further, consider the case where the origin of a third frame, Σ_C, coincides with the common origin of Σ_A and Σ_B, and assume that $\boldsymbol{r}$ is described by ${}^{C}\boldsymbol{r}$ when expressed by Σ_C. Then

$$ {}^{B}\boldsymbol{r} = {}^{B}\boldsymbol{R}_{C}\,{}^{C}\boldsymbol{r}, \tag{2.10} $$

$$ {}^{A}\boldsymbol{r} = {}^{A}\boldsymbol{R}_{C}\,{}^{C}\boldsymbol{r}. \tag{2.11} $$

Hence, from equations 2.5, 2.10, and 2.11, we have

$$ {}^{A}\boldsymbol{R}_{C}\,{}^{C}\boldsymbol{r} = {}^{A}\boldsymbol{R}_{B}\,{}^{B}\boldsymbol{R}_{C}\,{}^{C}\boldsymbol{r}. \tag{2.12} $$

Since equation 2.12 holds for any ${}^{C}\boldsymbol{r}$, we obtain the relation

$$ {}^{A}\boldsymbol{R}_{C} = {}^{A}\boldsymbol{R}_{B}\,{}^{B}\boldsymbol{R}_{C}. \tag{2.13} $$

An expression of ${}^{A}\boldsymbol{R}_{B}$ different from equation 2.1 can be obtained using equation 2.13. First, from equation 2.13 we have

$$ {}^{A}\boldsymbol{R}_{B} = ({}^{C}\boldsymbol{R}_{A})^{T}\,{}^{C}\boldsymbol{R}_{B}. \tag{2.14} $$

Let ${}^{C}\boldsymbol{x}_A$, ${}^{C}\boldsymbol{y}_A$, and ${}^{C}\boldsymbol{z}_A$ denote the unit vectors in the directions X_A, Y_A, and Z_A, and let ${}^{C}\boldsymbol{x}_B$, ${}^{C}\boldsymbol{y}_B$, and ${}^{C}\boldsymbol{z}_B$ denote those in the directions X_B, Y_B, and Z_B, both expressed in Σ_C. Then ${}^{A}\boldsymbol{R}_{B}$ can also be written as

$$ {}^{A}\boldsymbol{R}_{B} = \begin{bmatrix} ({}^{C}\boldsymbol{x}_A)^{T}\,{}^{C}\boldsymbol{x}_B & ({}^{C}\boldsymbol{x}_A)^{T}\,{}^{C}\boldsymbol{y}_B & ({}^{C}\boldsymbol{x}_A)^{T}\,{}^{C}\boldsymbol{z}_B \\ ({}^{C}\boldsymbol{y}_A)^{T}\,{}^{C}\boldsymbol{x}_B & ({}^{C}\boldsymbol{y}_A)^{T}\,{}^{C}\boldsymbol{y}_B & ({}^{C}\boldsymbol{y}_A)^{T}\,{}^{C}\boldsymbol{z}_B \\ ({}^{C}\boldsymbol{z}_A)^{T}\,{}^{C}\boldsymbol{x}_B & ({}^{C}\boldsymbol{z}_A)^{T}\,{}^{C}\boldsymbol{y}_B & ({}^{C}\boldsymbol{z}_A)^{T}\,{}^{C}\boldsymbol{z}_B \end{bmatrix}. \tag{2.15} $$

Note that, for example, the (1,1) element, $({}^{C}\boldsymbol{x}_A)^{T}\,{}^{C}\boldsymbol{x}_B$, is the cosine of the angle between the two vectors ${}^{C}\boldsymbol{x}_A$ and ${}^{C}\boldsymbol{x}_B$. The same holds for all other elements. For this reason, the rotation matrix ${}^{A}\boldsymbol{R}_{B}$ is also called the *directional cosine matrix*. The value of ${}^{A}\boldsymbol{R}_{B}$ is, of course, independent of the choice of Σ_C.

Although ${}^{A}\boldsymbol{R}_{B}$ has nine variables, they always satisfy equation 2.2. Hence, the representation by ${}^{A}\boldsymbol{R}_{B}$ is redundant. When any two of the three vectors ${}^{A}\boldsymbol{x}_B$, ${}^{A}\boldsymbol{y}_B$, and ${}^{A}\boldsymbol{z}_B$ are given, we can obtain the last vector using equation

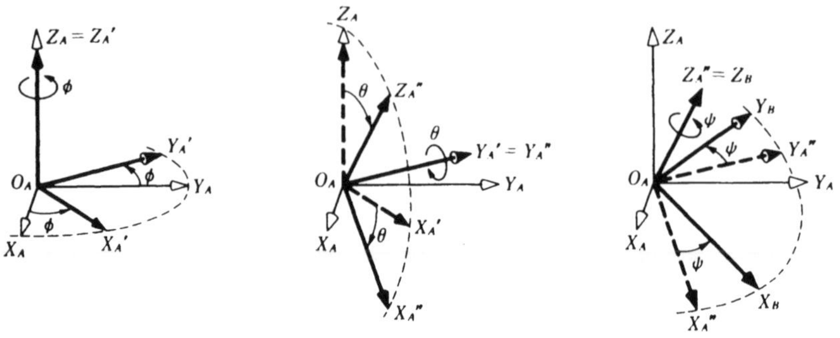

Figure 2.4
Euler angles (ϕ, θ, ψ).

2.2.* For instance, the pair $\{{}^A\boldsymbol{z}_B, {}^A\boldsymbol{x}_B\}$, which has six variables, can represent the orientation. So long as the elements of the rotation matrix themselves are used, there seems to be no way of representing the orientation by five or fewer variables. On the other hand, intuitively speaking, since equation 2.2 provides six relations to nine variables, the orientation should be describable by three variables, just as the position is. In fact, Euler angles and roll-pitch-yaw angles are convenient established representations. Both of them regard the object frame Σ_B as a result of three sequential rotations about some fixed axes from the reference frame Σ_A, and represent the orientation of Σ_B by the set of three rotational angles.

2.1.3 Euler Angles

There are several definitions of Euler angles. A rather common definition, illustrated in figure 2.4, is adopted here:

(i) The coordinate frame obtained from a rotation about the Z_A axis by an angle ϕ of a frame initially coincident with Σ_A is named $\Sigma_{A'}(O_A - X_{A'}Y_{A'}Z_{A'})$.
(ii) The frame obtained from $\Sigma_{A'}$ by a rotation about $Y_{A'}$ by an angle θ is named $\Sigma_{A''}(O_A - X_{A''}Y_{A''}Z_{A''})$.
(iii) The frame obtained from $\Sigma_{A''}$ by a rotation about $Z_{A''}$ by an angle ψ is named Σ_B.

Thus, the orientation of Σ_B with respect to Σ_A can be represented by the

* Strictly speaking, determining the last vector requires, besides equation 2.2, the condition that ${}^A\boldsymbol{x}_B$, ${}^A\boldsymbol{y}_B$, and ${}^A\boldsymbol{z}_B$ form a right-hand system. See exercise 2.17.

set of three angles (ϕ,θ,ψ), which are called te *Euler angles*. The relation between the Euler angles and the rotation matrix ${}^{A}\boldsymbol{R}_{B}$ is as follows.

First, from figure 2.4a, the relation between Σ_A and $\Sigma_{A'}$ is given by

$$ {}^{A}\boldsymbol{R}_{A'} = \begin{bmatrix} \cos\phi & -\sin\phi & 0 \\ \sin\phi & \cos\phi & 0 \\ 0 & 0 & 1 \end{bmatrix}. \tag{2.16} $$

Similarly, the rotation matrix ${}^{A'}\boldsymbol{R}_{A''}$ between $\Sigma_{A'}$ and $\Sigma_{A''}$, and the rotation matrix ${}^{A''}\boldsymbol{R}_{B}$ between $\Sigma_{A''}$ and Σ_B, are given by

$$ {}^{A'}\boldsymbol{R}_{A''} = \begin{bmatrix} \cos\theta & 0 & \sin\theta \\ 0 & 1 & 0 \\ -\sin\theta & 0 & \cos\theta \end{bmatrix} \tag{2.17} $$

and

$$ {}^{A''}\boldsymbol{R}_{B} = \begin{bmatrix} \cos\psi & -\sin\psi & 0 \\ \sin\psi & \cos\psi & 0 \\ 0 & 0 & 1 \end{bmatrix}. \tag{2.18} $$

From equation 2.13, the final rotation matrix ${}^{A}\boldsymbol{R}_{B}$ resulting from the three rotations is obtained from

$$ {}^{A}\boldsymbol{R}_{B} = {}^{A}\boldsymbol{R}_{A'}\,{}^{A'}\boldsymbol{R}_{A''}\,{}^{A''}\boldsymbol{R}_{B}, \tag{2.19} $$

which is

$$ {}^{A}\boldsymbol{R}_{B} = \begin{bmatrix} \cos\phi\cos\theta\cos\psi - \sin\phi\sin\psi & -\cos\phi\cos\theta\sin\psi - \sin\phi\cos\psi & \cos\phi\sin\theta \\ \sin\phi\cos\theta\cos\psi + \cos\phi\sin\psi & -\sin\phi\cos\theta\sin\psi + \cos\phi\cos\psi & \sin\phi\sin\theta \\ -\sin\theta\cos\psi & \sin\theta\sin\psi & \cos\theta \end{bmatrix}. \tag{2.20} $$

Let $\boldsymbol{R}(\hat{W},\alpha)$ denote the rotation matrix between a coordinate frame and the frame obtained by its rotation about an axis $\hat{W}$ by an angle α. Then equation 2.20 can also be written as

$$ {}^{A}\boldsymbol{R}_{B} = \boldsymbol{R}(Z_A,\phi)\boldsymbol{R}(Y_{A'},\theta)\boldsymbol{R}(Z_{A''},\psi). \tag{2.21} $$

Hence we have shown that the rotation matrix equivalent to any Euler angles (ϕ,θ,ψ) is given uniquely by equation 2.20.

Now consider the problem of obtaining the Euler angles for a given ${}^{A}\boldsymbol{R}_{B}$. Assume that

$$ {}^A\boldsymbol{R}_B = \begin{bmatrix} R_{11} & R_{12} & R_{13} \\ R_{21} & R_{22} & R_{23} \\ R_{31} & R_{32} & R_{33} \end{bmatrix} \tag{2.22} $$

is given. Equating each element of equation 2.20 and equation 2.22, we have

$$ \cos\phi\cos\theta\cos\psi - \sin\phi\sin\psi = R_{11}, \tag{2.23a} $$

$$ -\cos\phi\cos\theta\sin\psi - \sin\phi\cos\psi = R_{12}, \tag{2.23b} $$

$$ \cos\phi\sin\theta = R_{13}, \tag{2.23c} $$

$$ \sin\phi\cos\theta\cos\psi + \cos\phi\sin\psi = R_{21}, \tag{2.23d} $$

$$ -\sin\phi\cos\theta\sin\psi + \cos\phi\cos\psi = R_{22}, \tag{2.23e} $$

$$ \sin\phi\sin\theta = R_{23}, \tag{2.23f} $$

$$ -\sin\theta\cos\psi = R_{31}, \tag{2.23g} $$

$$ \sin\theta\ \sin\psi = R_{32}, \tag{2.23h} $$

$$ \cos\theta = R_{33}. \tag{2.23i} $$

From equations 2.23c and 2.23f,

$$ \sin\theta = \pm\sqrt{R_{13}{}^2 + R_{23}{}^2}. \tag{2.24} $$

Hence, from equations 2.24 and 2.23i we obtain

$$ \theta = \operatorname{atan2}(\pm\sqrt{R_{13}{}^2 + R_{23}{}^2}, R_{33}). \tag{2.25} $$

Either the top or the bottom symbol of $\pm$ or $\mp$ should be used consistently throughout this section. In equation 2.25, atan2 is a scalar function defined by

$$ \operatorname{atan2}(a,b) = \arg(b + ja), \tag{2.26} $$

where j is the imaginary unit and $\arg(\cdot)$ is the argument of a complex number (see figure 2.5). The function atan2 is a kind of arc tangent function that satisfies

$$ \theta = \operatorname{atan2}(\sin\theta, \cos\theta) \tag{2.27} $$

and

$$ \theta = \operatorname{atan2}(k\sin\theta, k\cos\theta) \tag{2.28} $$

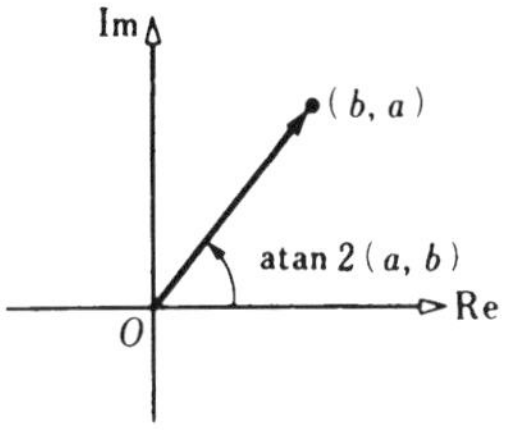

Figure 2.5
Function atan2.

for any positive real number k. Several properties of the function atan2 are also summarized in appendix 1.

Angles ϕ and ψ will be determined next. If $\sin\theta \neq 0$, we have

$$\phi = \text{atan2}(\pm R_{23}, \pm R_{13}) \tag{2.29}$$

from equations 2.23c and 2.23f, and

$$\psi = \text{atan2}(\pm R_{32}, \mp R_{31}) \tag{2.30}$$

from equations 2.23g and 2.23h. Hence, if $R_{13}^2 + R_{23}^2 \neq 0$, the Euler angles are obtained from equations 2.25, 2.29, and 2.30:

$$\phi = \text{atan2}(\pm R_{23}, \pm R_{13}), \tag{2.31a}$$

$$\theta = \text{atan2}(\pm\sqrt{R_{13}^2 + R_{23}^2}, R_{33}), \tag{2.31b}$$

$$\psi = \text{atan2}(\pm R_{32}, \mp R_{31}). \tag{2.31c}$$

It is also straightforward to show that these solutions satisfy the other equations in 2.23. Although there are two sets of Euler angles for a given ${}^A\boldsymbol{R}_B$, if we put the constraint $0 < \theta < \pi$ on θ we have the following unique Euler angles:

$$\phi = \text{atan2}(R_{23}, R_{13}), \tag{2.32a}$$

$$\theta = \text{atan2}(\sqrt{R_{13}^2 + R_{23}^2}, R_{33}), \tag{2.32b}$$

$$\psi = \text{atan2}(R_{32}, -R_{31}). \tag{2.32c}$$

On the other hand, if $R_{13}^2 + R_{23}^2 = 0$, we have

$$\phi = \text{arbitrary}, \tag{2.33a}$$

$$\theta = 90^\circ - R_{33} \times 90^\circ, \tag{2.33b}$$

$$\psi = \text{atan2}(R_{21}, R_{22}) - R_{33}\phi. \tag{2.33c}$$

In other words, in the case of $\theta = 0$ or $\theta = \pi$, there is an infinite number of combinations of ϕ and ψ for just one orientation. So special care should be taken in treating this case. If we wish to keep uniqueness even in this case, one way is to set $\phi = 0$ and $\psi = \text{atan2}(R_{21}, R_{22})$.

We can also find a general expression of the Euler angles for a given rotation matrix which needs no distinction between the cases $\sin\theta = 0$ and $\sin\theta \neq 0$; see exercise 2.2.

Example 2.2 The representation by Euler angles of the orientation in example 2.1 is

$$(\phi, \theta, \psi) = (-90°, 90°, 90°),$$

or

$$(\phi, \theta, \psi) = (90°, -90°, -90°). \square$$

2.1.4 Roll, Pitch, and Yaw Angles

The concept of roll, pitch, and yaw angles is basically the same as that of Euler angles except for a difference in the way we select the third rotational axis. In the case of roll, pitch, and yaw angles (figure 2.6),

(i) the frame obtained from Σ_A by a rotation about Z_A by ϕ is named $\Sigma_{A'}$, as with Euler angles,

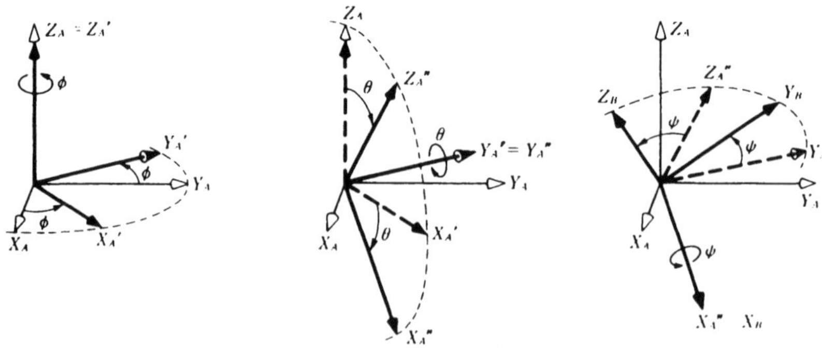

Figure 2.6
Roll, pitch, and yaw angles (ϕ, θ, ψ).

(ii) the frame obtained from $\Sigma_{A'}$ by a rotation about $Y_{A'}$ by θ is named $\Sigma_{A''}$, again as with Euler angles, and
(iii) the frame obtained from $\Sigma_{A''}$ by a rotation about $X_{A''}$ by ψ is named Σ_B.

Then ϕ, θ and ψ are called the roll, pitch, and yaw angles, respectively. The triple (ϕ,θ,ψ) is said to be the representation by the *roll, pitch, and yaw angles* of the orientation of Σ_B with respect to Σ_A.

Example 2.3 The representation by roll, pitch, and yaw angles of the orientation in example 2.1 is given by

$$(\phi,\theta,\psi) = (0°,0°,90°),$$

or

$$(\phi,\theta,\psi) = (180°,180°,-90°). \ \square$$

2.2 Coordinate Transformation

2.2.1 Homogeneous Transform

In figure 2.7 we assume that the relation between two coordinate frames Σ_A and Σ_B is given by the position vector ${}^A\boldsymbol{p}_B$ and the rotation matrix ${}^A\boldsymbol{R}_B$ of Σ_B with respect to Σ_A. Then the relation between the expressions ${}^A\boldsymbol{r}$ and ${}^B\boldsymbol{r}$ of a point in space by (respectively) Σ_A and Σ_B is

$$ {}^A\boldsymbol{r} = {}^A\boldsymbol{R}_B\, {}^B\boldsymbol{r} + {}^A\boldsymbol{p}_B. \tag{2.34}$$

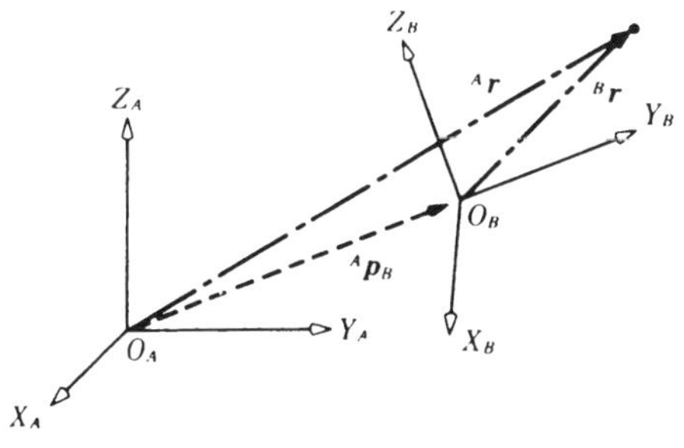

Figure 2.7
Frames Σ_A and Σ_B.

This equation can also be expressed as

$$\begin{bmatrix} {}^{A}\boldsymbol{r} \\ \hline 1 \end{bmatrix} = \left[\begin{array}{ccc|c} & {}^{A}\boldsymbol{R}_{B} & & {}^{A}\boldsymbol{p}_{B} \\ \hline 0 & 0 & 0 & 1 \end{array}\right] \begin{bmatrix} {}^{B}\boldsymbol{r} \\ \hline 1 \end{bmatrix} \triangleq {}^{A}\boldsymbol{T}_{B} \begin{bmatrix} {}^{B}\boldsymbol{r} \\ \hline 1 \end{bmatrix}. \tag{2.35}$$

In this new expression, the three-dimensional vectors ${}^{A}\boldsymbol{r}$ and ${}^{B}\boldsymbol{r}$ must be represented by the four-dimensional vectors obtained by adding the element 1 at the bottom of the original vectors. In return for this, the expression obtained is simpler in the sense that the transformation from the expression of a vector with respect to Σ_A to that with respect to Σ_B is done by the multiplication of just one matrix: ${}^{A}\boldsymbol{T}_{B}$. The transformation represented by the 4×4 matrix ${}^{A}\boldsymbol{T}_{B}$ is called the *homogeneous transform*. The vector $[{}^{A}\boldsymbol{r}^{T}, 1]^{T}$ may also be written as ${}^{A}\boldsymbol{r}$ when there is no confusion; for example, equation 2.35 may also be written as

$${}^{A}\boldsymbol{r} = {}^{A}\boldsymbol{T}_{B}\,{}^{B}\boldsymbol{r}. \tag{2.36}$$

Homogeneous transforms can be used for the following purposes:

(i) *Changing the coordinate frame with respect to which a point in space is expressed.* This is what we did in equations 2.35 and 2.36 when we wished to obtain the expression ${}^{A}\boldsymbol{r}$ with respect to Σ_A of a point expressed as ${}^{B}\boldsymbol{r}$ with respect to Σ_B.
(ii) *Describing the relation between two coordinate frames.* Since ${}^{A}\boldsymbol{T}_{B}$ contains both of the parameters (${}^{A}\boldsymbol{p}_{B}$ and ${}^{A}\boldsymbol{R}_{B}$) that represent the relation of Σ_B to Σ_A, ${}^{A}\boldsymbol{T}_{B}$ can be regarded as describing this relation. Although ${}^{A}\boldsymbol{T}_{B}$ has no merit over the pair $\{{}^{A}\boldsymbol{p}_{B}, {}^{A}\boldsymbol{R}_{B}\}$ in real numerical calculation, it allows for greater simplicity of expression.

Example 2.4 As is shown in figure 2.8, when Σ_B is obtained from Σ_A by a rotation about Z_A for α, their relation is described by

$${}^{A}\boldsymbol{T}_{B} = \begin{bmatrix} \cos\alpha & -\sin\alpha & 0 & 0 \\ \sin\alpha & \cos\alpha & 0 & 0 \\ 0 & 0 & 1 & 0 \\ 0 & 0 & 0 & 1 \end{bmatrix}. \square$$

Example 2.5 When Σ_B is obtained from Σ_A by a translation of 2 units in Y_A and then by a translation of 1 unit in Z_A, their relation is given by

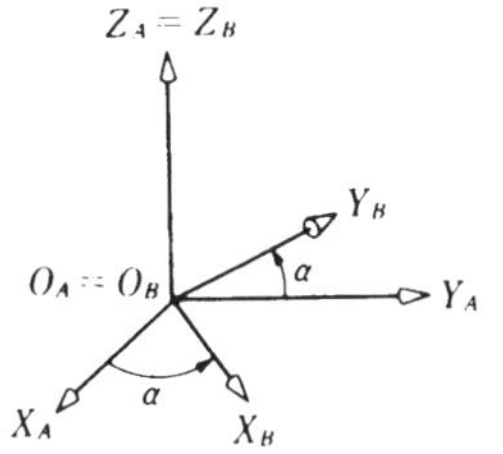

Figure 2.8
Frames Σ_A and Σ_B.

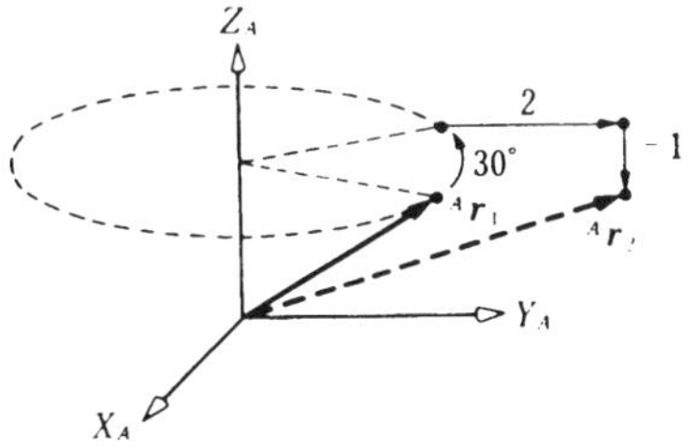

Figure 2.9
Transfer of a point.

$$ {}^A T_B = \begin{bmatrix} 1 & 0 & 0 & 0 \\ 0 & 1 & 0 & 2 \\ 0 & 0 & 1 & 1 \\ 0 & 0 & 0 & 1 \end{bmatrix}. \square $$

(iii) *Description of transfer of a point in space.* We assume that a point in space with a fixed coordinate frame is transferred in a given way. The homogeneous transform can be used to describe the relation between the original point location and the location after the transfer.

Example 2.6 As shown in figure 2.9, we consider a point ${}^A\boldsymbol{r}_1$ expressed in Σ_A. Let ${}^A\boldsymbol{r}_2$ denote the new location of this point after rotating 30° about Z_A and then translating 2 units along Y_A and -1 units along Z_A. The relation between ${}^A\boldsymbol{r}_1$ and ${}^A\boldsymbol{r}_2$ is described by

$$ {}^A\boldsymbol{r}_2 = \begin{bmatrix} \cos 30^\circ & -\sin 30^\circ & 0 & 0 \\ \sin 30^\circ & \cos 30^\circ & 0 & 2 \\ 0 & 0 & 1 & -1 \\ 0 & 0 & 0 & 1 \end{bmatrix} {}^A\boldsymbol{r}_1. \square $$

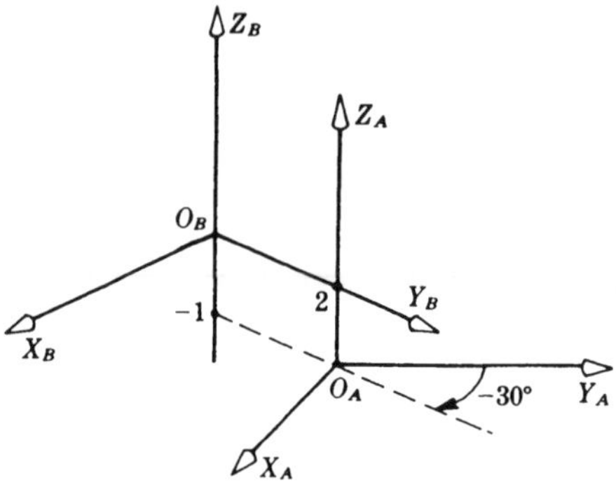

Figure 2.10
Frames Σ_A and Σ_B.

These three uses of homogeneous transformation are of course closely related, as example 2.7 will show.

Example 2.7 When the transform given in example 2.6 is regarded as ${}^{B}\boldsymbol{T}_A$ describing the relation between two frames Σ_A and Σ_B, we have the change in frame shown in figure 2.10. Note that Σ_B is obtained from a frame originally at the same place as Σ_A, first by translating it -2 units along Y_A and 1 unit along Z_A and then by rotating it $-30°$ about Z_A. Also note that the point whose representation in Σ_A is ${}^{A}\boldsymbol{r}_1$ is represented as ${}^{A}\boldsymbol{r}_2$ in Σ_B. □

2.2.2 Product and Inverse of Homogeneous Transform

Consider three frames, Σ_A, Σ_B, and Σ_C, and assume that the relations between Σ_A and Σ_B and between Σ_B and Σ_C are given by ${}^{A}\boldsymbol{T}_B$ and ${}^{B}\boldsymbol{T}_C$ respectively. Then the relation ${}^{A}\boldsymbol{T}_C$ between Σ_A and Σ_C is given by the product of ${}^{A}\boldsymbol{T}_B$ and ${}^{B}\boldsymbol{T}_C$:

$$ {}^{A}\boldsymbol{T}_C = {}^{A}\boldsymbol{T}_B\,{}^{B}\boldsymbol{T}_C. \tag{2.37} $$

This is an extension of equation 2.13.

The following two interpretations in terms of coordinate-frame transformations are possible for equation 2.37:

(i) The frame Σ_B is obtained from Σ_A by translating Σ_A by ${}^{A}\boldsymbol{p}_B$ with respect to Σ_A and then rotating the translated frame (using ${}^{A}\boldsymbol{R}_B$) about the origin of the translated frame itself. The frame Σ_C is obtained from Σ_B by translating by ${}^{B}\boldsymbol{p}_C$ and then rotating the translated frame (using ${}^{B}\boldsymbol{R}_C$) about the origin of the translated frame.

(ii) We denote as $\Sigma_{B'}$ the frame obtained by first rotating a frame initially coincident with Σ_A using ${}^B\boldsymbol{R}_C$ and then translating it by ${}^B\boldsymbol{p}_C$, both with respect to Σ_A. Further, we rotate $\Sigma_{B'}$ using ${}^A\boldsymbol{R}_B$ and translate it by ${}^A\boldsymbol{p}_B$, both with respect to Σ_A. Thus we obtain the frame Σ_C.

In interpretation i, the product of two transforms is interpreted from the left one (${}^A\boldsymbol{T}_B$), and the second transformation (${}^B\boldsymbol{T}_C$) is done with respect to the new frame obtained from the left transformation. In contrast, in interpretation ii the product is interpreted from the right transform (${}^B\boldsymbol{T}_C$), and both transformations are done with respect to the original frame. The difference of order between the translation and the rotation in interpretations i and ii could be understood by substituting into equation 2.37 the relation

$$ {}^A\boldsymbol{T}_B = \left[\begin{array}{c|c} {}^A\boldsymbol{R}_B & {}^A\boldsymbol{p}_B \\ \hline \boldsymbol{0} & 1 \end{array}\right] = \left[\begin{array}{c|c} \mathbf{I}_3 & {}^A\boldsymbol{p}_B \\ \hline \boldsymbol{0} & 1 \end{array}\right] \left[\begin{array}{c|c} {}^A\boldsymbol{R}_B & \boldsymbol{0} \\ \hline \boldsymbol{0} & 1 \end{array}\right], \tag{2.38} $$

and a similar relation for ${}^B\boldsymbol{T}_C$, where $\boldsymbol{0}$ denotes a vector or a matrix whose elements are all zeros.

Example 2.8 Assume that ${}^A\boldsymbol{T}_B$ and ${}^B\boldsymbol{T}_C$ are given by

$$ {}^A\boldsymbol{T}_B = \begin{bmatrix} \sqrt{3}/2 & -1/2 & 0 & 2 \\ 1/2 & \sqrt{3}/2 & 0 & 1 \\ 0 & 0 & 1 & 0 \\ 0 & 0 & 0 & 1 \end{bmatrix} $$

and

$$ {}^B\boldsymbol{T}_C = \begin{bmatrix} 1/\sqrt{2} & 1/\sqrt{2} & 0 & 1 \\ -1/\sqrt{2} & 1/\sqrt{2} & 0 & 1 \\ 0 & 0 & 1 & 0 \\ 0 & 0 & 0 & 1 \end{bmatrix}. $$

The two interpretations of ${}^A\boldsymbol{T}_C$ are illustrated schematically in figure 2.11. In this example the Z axis is always normal to the page and thus it is omitted from the figure. The final location of Σ_C is, of course, the same in both cases.
□

The inverse of ${}^A\boldsymbol{T}_B$ is, from equation 2.4,

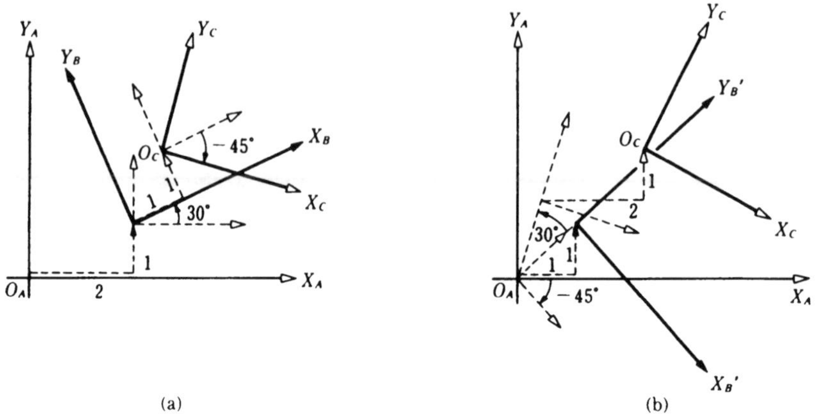

Figure 2.11
Interpretation of ${}^AT_C$. (a) Interpretation by (i). (b) Interpretation by (ii).

$$
{}^BT_A = {}^AT_B^{-1} = \left[\begin{array}{c|c} {}^A\boldsymbol{R}_B^T & -{}^A\boldsymbol{R}_B^T\, {}^A\boldsymbol{p}_B \\ \hline \boldsymbol{0} & 1 \end{array}\right]. \tag{2.39}
$$

2.3 Joint Variables and Position of End Effector

2.3.1 General Relation

In this subsection an overview is given of the relation between joint displacements (rotational displacements for revolute joints and linear displacements for prismatic joints) and end-effector position for a manipulator with n degrees of freedom.

In figure 2.12 the joints are numbered 1, 2, ..., n, starting from the base of the manipulator. The displacement of joint i is denoted q_i and is called the *joint variable*. The collection of joint variables

$$
\boldsymbol{q} = [q_1, q_2, \ldots, q_n]^T \tag{2.40}
$$

is called the *joint vector*. The position of the end effector is denoted by the m-dimensional vector

$$
\boldsymbol{r} = [r_1, r_2, \ldots, r_m]^T, \tag{2.41}
$$

where $m \leqq n$. For a general case where the end effector can take an arbitrary position and orientation in three-dimensional Euclidean space, we have

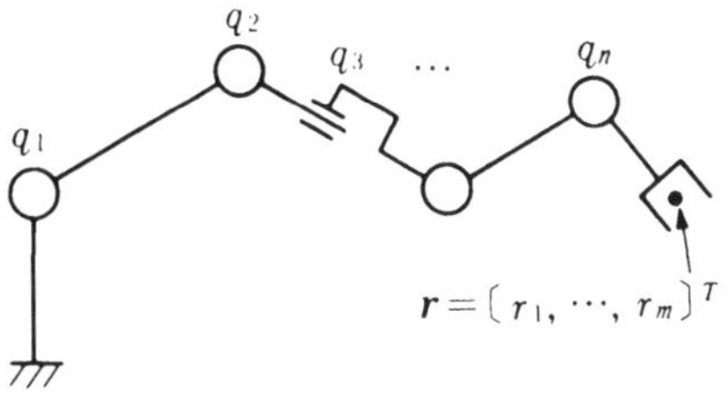

Figure 2.12
n-link manipulator.

$m = 6$. However, when the manipulator moves in a two-dimensional plane and we are concerned only with its endpoint position in the plane, we can set $m = 2$. If we are further concerned with the orientation of the endpoint in the plane, we have to set $m = 3$.

The relation between $\boldsymbol{r}$ and $\boldsymbol{q}$, determined by the manipulator mechanism, generally is nonlinear. We assume that this relation is given by

$$\boldsymbol{r} = \boldsymbol{f}_r(\boldsymbol{q}). \tag{2.42}$$

This equation is called the *kinematic equation* of the manipulator. When the joint vector $\boldsymbol{q}$ is given, the corresponding $\boldsymbol{r}$ is determined uniquely and the calculation is rather simple. However, when some task is assigned to the manipulator, what is given first is usually its end-effector position $\boldsymbol{r}$ or a trajectory of $\boldsymbol{r}$. Thus we have to calculate a joint vector $\boldsymbol{q}$ which will realize the required end-effector position $\boldsymbol{r}$—that is, we have to obtain $\boldsymbol{q}$ satisfying equation 2.42. This solution can be written formally as

$$\boldsymbol{q} = \boldsymbol{f}_r^{-1}(\boldsymbol{r}). \tag{2.43}$$

Note, however, that $\boldsymbol{q}$ does not necessarily exist, and even when it does exist it may not be unique. The problem of obtaining $\boldsymbol{r}$ for a given $\boldsymbol{q}$ is called the *direct kinematics problem*, and that of obtaining $\boldsymbol{q}$ corresponding to a given $\boldsymbol{r}$ is called the *inverse kinematics problem*. As we can see from the above argument, the inverse kinematics problem is usually the more difficult of the two.

Example 2.9 The relations 2.42 and 2.43 will be obtained for the two-degrees-of-freedom manipulator moving in the $X-Y$ plane as shown in figure 2.13. The joint vector in this case is $\boldsymbol{q} = [\theta_1, \theta_2]^T$, the end-effector position is given by $\boldsymbol{r} = [x, y]^T$, and the lengths of the links are l_1 and l_2. The relation 2.42 is easily obtained:

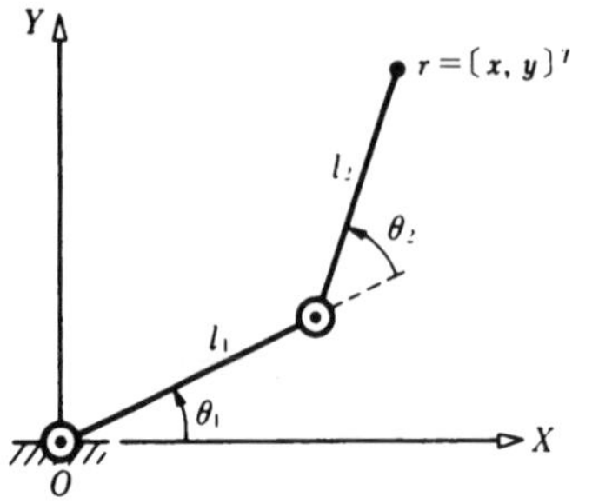

Figure 2.13
Two-link manipulator.

$$x = l_1\cos\theta_1 + l_2\cos(\theta_1 + \theta_2),$$

$$y = l_1\sin\theta_1 + l_2\sin(\theta_1 + \theta_2).$$

As for the relation 2.43, if $\boldsymbol{r}$ satisfies

$$(l_1 - l_2)^2 \leqq x^2 + y^2 \leqq (l_1 + l_2)^2$$

then there exists at least one $\boldsymbol{q}$ corresponding to $\boldsymbol{r}$. Further, if $x^2 + y^2 \neq 0$, using the function atan2, from equations A1.11, A1.4, and A1.6 of appendix 1, we obtain

$$\theta_1 = \operatorname{atan2}(y,x) \mp \operatorname{atan2}(\kappa, x^2 + y^2 + l_1{}^2 - l_2{}^2)$$

and

$$\theta_2 = \pm\operatorname{atan2}(\kappa, x^2 + y^2 - l_1{}^2 - l_2{}^2),$$

where

$$\kappa = \sqrt{(x^2 + y^2 + l_1{}^2 + l_2{}^2)^2 - 2[(x^2 + y^2)^2 + l_1{}^4 + l_2{}^4]}.$$

The two solutions given above correspond to the two arm configurations in figure 2.14. If, on the other hand, $x^2 + y^2 = (l_1 - l_2)^2 = 0$, then

$$\theta_1 = \text{arbitrary}$$

and

$$\theta_2 = \pm 180°;$$

that is, there are infinitely many solutions. □

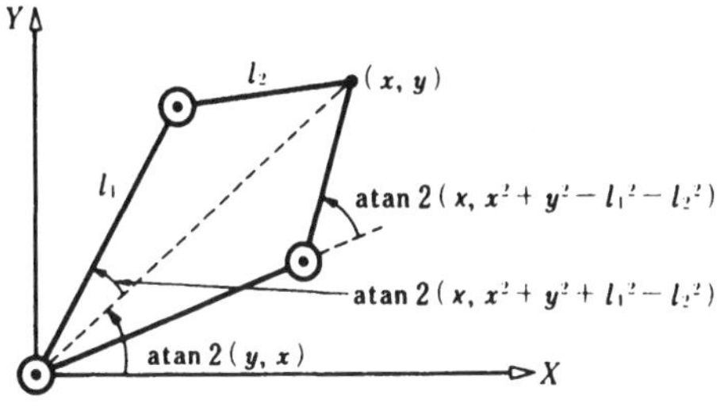

Figure 2.14
Solutions of inverse kinematics problem for two-link manipulator.

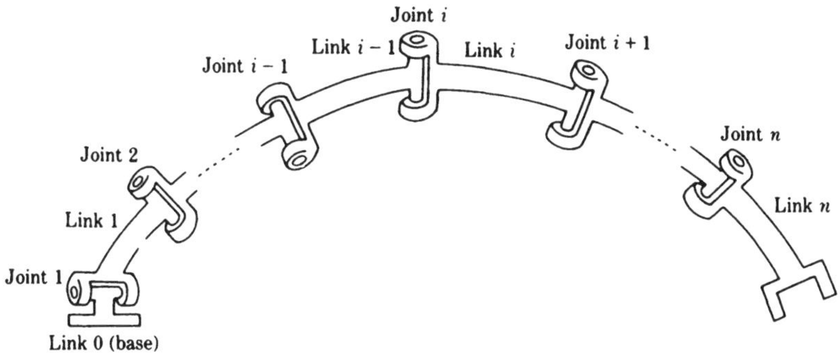

Figure 2.15
Link and joint numbers for n-link manipulator.

As example 2.9 shows, it is rather easy to solve the direct kinematics problem and the inverse kinematics problem for manipulators with around two degrees of freedom. However, both problems become increasingly difficult as the number of degrees of freedom increases. One way to cope with this difficulty is to assign an appropriate coordinate frame to each link and to describe the relation among the links by the relation among these frames. In this way, deriving the function $f_r(q)$ becomes systematic and obtaining $f_r^{-1}(r)$ analytically or numerically becomes much easier. This approach is developed in the following subsections.

2.3.2 Link Parameters

Consider a manipulator consisting of n links connected serially by n joints, with one degree of freedom each, which may be either revolute or prismatic. As is shown in figure 2.15, the links and the joints are numbered $1, \ldots, n$,

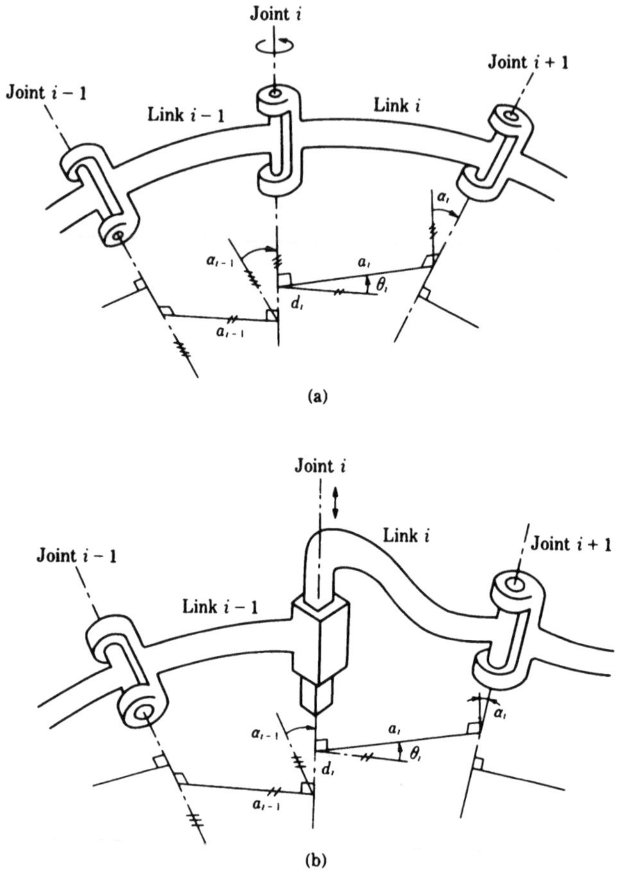

Figure 2.16
Joint axes, joint variables, and link parameters: (a) when joint i is revolute; (b) when joint i is prismatic.

starting from the base side. The base itself is called link 0; hence, link 0 is connected to link 1 by joint 1. For each joint i, the joint axis i is defined as the rotational axis in the case of a revolute joint or as an arbitrary straight line parallel to the direction of translation in the case of a prismatic joint. In figure 2.16, dashed lines show the joint axes in these two cases. The common normal between joint axes i and $i + 1$ is considered to be the mathematical model of link i. The common normals are shown as solid lines in the figure. When the joint axes i and $i + 1$ are parallel, the common normal is not unique, so we select one common normal arbitrarily as the mathematical model of link i.

With these preparations, we can now describe the size and shape of link i by two variables: the length a_i of the common normal, and the angle α_i between the orthogonal projections of joint axes i and $i + 1$ onto a plane normal to the common normal. The variable a_i is called the *link length*, and α_i is the *twist angle*.

The relative positional relation between links $i - 1$ and i at joint i can be described by the distance d_i between the feet of two common normals on the joint axis i, and the angle θ_i between the orthogonal projections of these common normals to a plane normal to the joint axis i. The variable d_i is called the *joint length*, and θ_i is called the *joint angle*. If joint i is revolute, d_i is constant and θ_i expresses the rotational angle of the joint; if joint i is prismatic, θ_i is constant and d_i expresses the translational distance of the joint. Hence, when joint i is revolute we adopt θ_i as the joint variable q_i, and when joint i is prismatic we adopt d_i. The other three variables are constant and are called *link parameters*. This way of describing link mechanisms using a_i, α_i, d_i, and θ_i is usually called the Denavit-Hartenberg notation.[2]

2.3.3 Link Frames

Now we will define coordinate frames, one fixed to each link. As is shown in figure 2.17, the origin of coordinate frame Σ_i of link i is set at the endpoint of the mathematical model of link i on joint axis i. The Z axis of Σ_i, denoted Z_i, is selected in such a way that it aligns with joint axis i in the direction pointing toward the distal end of the manipulator. When the direction toward the distal end is not clear, the direction of Z_i is arbitrary. The X axis of Σ_i, X_i, is selected so that it is on the common normal and points from joint i to joint $i + 1$. The Y axis, Y_i, is selected in such a way that Σ_i is a right-hand coordinate frame.

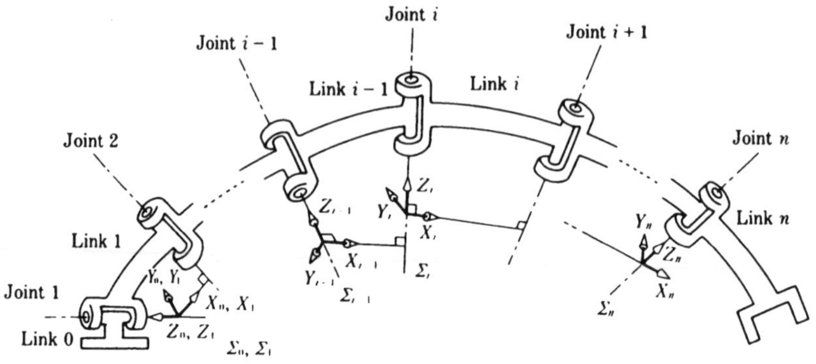

Figure 2.17
Link frame Σ_i. (Σ_0 and Σ_n are shown for the case when the joint variables are zero.)

By the above procedure, the link frames for links 1 through $n - 1$ are determined. For link 0, the link frame Σ_0 is defined to be equal to Σ_1 for an arbitrarily selected reference configuration of joint 1. For link n, the joint n is fixed at an arbitrarily selected configuration and the origin of Σ_n is set to be at the endpoint of the mathematical model of link $n - 1$ on joint axis n. The axis Z_n is aligned with the joint axis n with its direction pointed toward the distal end of the manipulator when the direction toward the distal end is clear. The axis X_n is aligned with X_{n-1}, and Y_n is determined in such a way that Σ_n is a right-hand frame.

Now that we have defined the frame Σ_i, provided that the positive sense of each variable is determined so that it harmonizes with Σ_i, the four variables introduced in the previous subsection can be expressed as follows:

a_i = the distance measured along the X_i axis from Z_i to Z_{i+1},

α_i = the angle measured clockwise about the X_i axis from Z_i to Z_{i+1},

d_i = the distance measured along the Z_i axis from X_{i-1} to X_i,

and

θ_i = the angle measured clockwise about the Z_i axis from X_{i-1} to X_i.

In other words, the frame Σ_i can be obtained from Σ_{i-1} by the following four transformations:

(i) translation along X_{i-1} for a distance a_{i-1},
(ii) rotation about X_{i-1} by an angle α_{i-1},

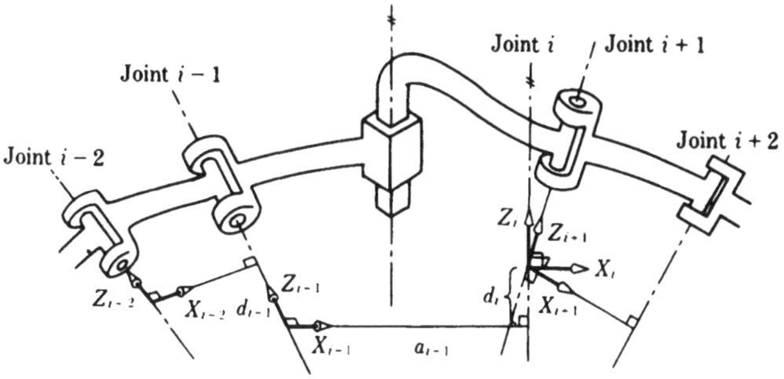

Figure 2.18
An assignment of link frame i when joint i is prismatic ($a_i = 0$, $d_{i+1} = 0$).

(iii) translation along Z_{i-1} after the rotation ii (which is Z_i) for a distance d_i, and
(iv) rotation about Z_{i-1} after the rotation ii (which is Z_i) by an angle θ_i.

Note that the above relation holds also between Σ_0 and Σ_1, and between Σ_{n-1} and Σ_n, with Σ_0 and Σ_n defined earlier by selecting the link parameters as follows:

$a_0 = \alpha_0 = 0$,
$d_1 = 0$ when joint 1 is revolute,
$\theta_1 = 0$ when joint 1 is prismatic,
$d_n = 0$ when joint n is revolute,
$\theta_n = 0$ when joint n is prismatic.

It is desirable to make as many link parameters zero as we can, since this will make the later analysis easier and will decrease the amount of computation necessary to solve the direct and inverse kinematics problems. Reviewing the procedure of determining the joint axes and the common normals from this viewpoint makes it clear that when they are not unique the following scheme is a desirable one.

When determining the joint axis i for a prismatic joint, we use the fact that its location is arbitrary while its direction is fixed. We can set a_{i-1} or a_i to zero, and d_{i-1} or d_{i+1} can also be set to zero. Hereafter we set $a_i = 0$ and $d_{i+1} = 0$ by having the joint axis i pass through the endpoint of the mathematical model of link $i+1$ on the joint axis $i+1$, as is shown in figure 2.18. When the joint axes i and $i+1$ are parallel, d_i or d_{i+1} can be

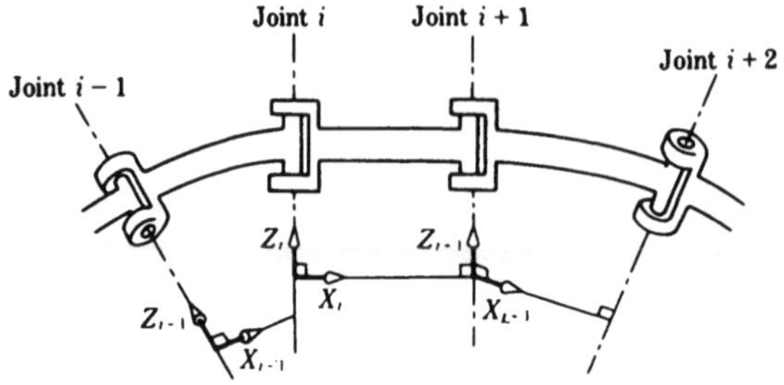

Figure 2.19
An assignment of link frame i when joint axes i and $i+1$ are parallel ($d_{i+1}=0$).

set to zero. Hereafter, as is shown in figure 2.19, we set $d_{i+1}=0$ by having the common normal pass through the endpoint of the mathematical model of link $i+1$ on the joint axis $i+1$. In these two cases, if there exists any arbitrariness in the location of the mathematical model of link $i+1$, we can further determine the link frames so as to set a_{i-1}, d_{i-1}, etc. to zero. Also note that in figures 2.18 and 2.19 the Y axes of the link frames are not shown because they are uniquely determined by the X and Z axes. This convention will be used hereafter.

In summary, the link frames are determined as follows:

(i) Determine the joint axes.

(ii) Determine the common normals.

(iii) Determine the link frames.

(iv) For joint axes and common normals that have arbitrariness in their location, return to step i or ii and modify their location to set as many parameters to zero as possible.

There are still cases where the above procedure does not yield a unique set of link frames. In those cases, we can just select one set of link frames arbitrarily.

Example 2.10 The Stanford manipulator,[3] developed mainly for research purposes, has the mechanism shown in figure 2.20. The link frames determined by the above procedure for this manipulator are shown in figure 2.21; the link parameters are given in table 2.1. Note that figure 2.21 shows a reference configuration for which $\theta_i=0\,(i=1,2,4,5,6)$ and all the X_i axes are in the same direction. Also note that d_3 is not taken to be zero in the figure, because a configuration with $d_3=0$ is unattainable. □

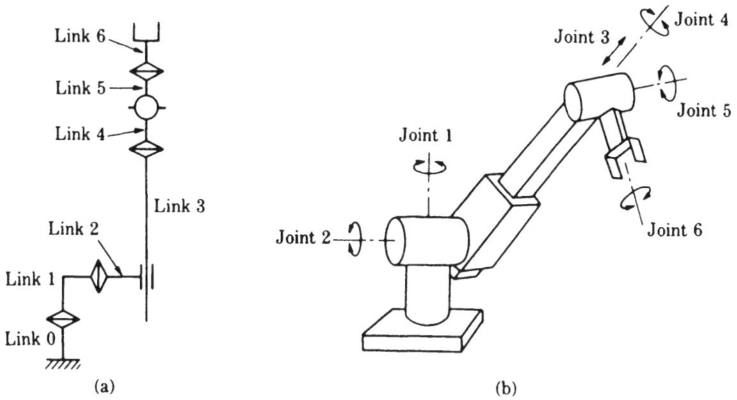

Figure 2.20
Stanford manipulator. (a) Link structure. (b) Appearance.

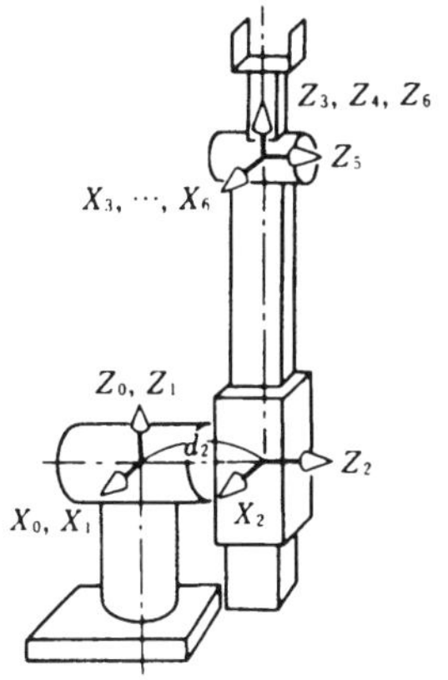

Figure 2.21
Link frames for Stanford manipulator.

Table 2.1
Link parameters for Stanford manipulator. (Parentheses indicate joint variables.)

i	a_{i-1}	α_{i-1}	d_i	θ_i
1	0	0°	0	(θ_1)
2	0	−90°	d_2	(θ_2)
3	0	90°	(d_3)	0°
4	0	0°	0	(θ_4)
5	0	−90°	0	(θ_5)
6	0	90°	0	(θ_6)

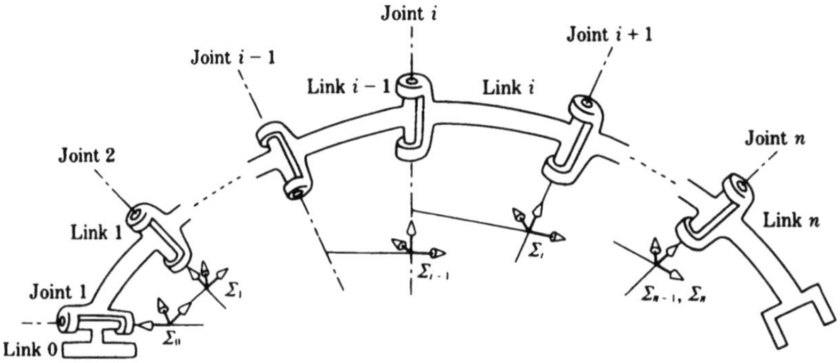

Figure 2.22
Another assignment of link frames.

The merit of the assignment scheme of link frames given above is that the frame of each link has its origin on the joint axis closer to the base of the link. Also, the Z axis of the frame agrees with the joint axis whose displacement directly causes the motion of that link. This assignment scheme appeared in Craig's *Introduction to Robotics.*[4] Another scheme of assigning link frames is shown in figure 2.22, where the origin of the frame is on the distal joint axis of the corresponding link. Its Z axis is the joint axis for the motion of the next link at the distal end. A more detailed description on this scheme can be found in Paul's *Robot Manipulators.*[5]

In principle, any set of n coordinate frames are feasible as link frames as long as each link has a frame fixed to it. Any assignment that sets the origin of Σ_i on joint axis i (when joint i is revolute) and aligns the Z_i axis with joint axis i has most of the merits of the Denavit-Hartenberg notation. The assignment scheme described in this subsection has been selected simply because it is intuitively easier to understand and because it gives a unique set of link frames for most manipulators.

2.3.4 Solution to Direct Kinematics Problem

The homogeneous transform that describes the relation between Σ_i and Σ_{i-1} is

$$ {}^{i-1}\boldsymbol{T}_i = \boldsymbol{T}_T(X_{i-1}, a_{i-1})\boldsymbol{T}_R(X_{i-1}, \alpha_{i-1})\boldsymbol{T}_T(Z_i, d_i)\boldsymbol{T}_R(Z_i, \theta_i), \tag{2.44} $$

where $\boldsymbol{T}_T(X, a)$ denotes a translation along the X axis for a distance a, and $\boldsymbol{T}_R(X, \alpha)$ denotes a rotation about the X axis by an angle α. From equation 2.44 we obtain

$$ {}^{i-1}\boldsymbol{T}_i = \begin{bmatrix} 1 & 0 & 0 & a_{i-1} \\ 0 & 1 & 0 & 0 \\ 0 & 0 & 1 & 0 \\ 0 & 0 & 0 & 1 \end{bmatrix} \begin{bmatrix} 1 & 0 & 0 & 0 \\ 0 & \cos\alpha_{i-1} & -\sin\alpha_{i-1} & 0 \\ 0 & \sin\alpha_{i-1} & \cos\alpha_{i-1} & 0 \\ 0 & 0 & 0 & 1 \end{bmatrix} $$

$$ \times \begin{bmatrix} 1 & 0 & 0 & 0 \\ 0 & 1 & 0 & 0 \\ 0 & 0 & 1 & d_i \\ 0 & 0 & 0 & 1 \end{bmatrix} \begin{bmatrix} \cos\theta_i & -\sin\theta_i & 0 & 0 \\ \sin\theta_i & \cos\theta_i & 0 & 0 \\ 0 & 0 & 1 & 0 \\ 0 & 0 & 0 & 1 \end{bmatrix} $$

$$ = \begin{bmatrix} \cos\theta_i & -\sin\theta_i & 0 & a_{i-1} \\ \cos\alpha_{i-1}\sin\theta_i & \cos\alpha_{i-1}\cos\theta_i & -\sin\alpha_{i-1} & -\sin\alpha_{i-1}d_i \\ \sin\alpha_{i-1}\sin\theta_i & \sin\alpha_{i-1}\cos\theta_i & \cos\alpha_{i-1} & \cos\alpha_{i-1}d_i \\ 0 & 0 & 0 & 1 \end{bmatrix}. \tag{2.45} $$

Let the homogeneous transform relating Σ_n to Σ_0 be ${}^0\boldsymbol{T}_n$. Then we have

$$ {}^0\boldsymbol{T}_n = {}^0\boldsymbol{T}_1\, {}^1\boldsymbol{T}_2 \cdots {}^{n-1}\boldsymbol{T}_n. \tag{2.46} $$

When the values of all link parameters are given, ${}^{i-1}\boldsymbol{T}_i$ is a function of q_i only. Hence, ${}^0\boldsymbol{T}_n$ is a function of the joint vector $\boldsymbol{q}$.

Let Σ_E be the coordinate frame fixed to the end effector that is attached to link n, and let ${}^n\boldsymbol{T}_E$ be the homogeneous transform describing the relation between Σ_E and Σ_n. Let Σ_R be the reference frame, and let ${}^R\boldsymbol{T}_0$ describe the relation between Σ_R and the base frame Σ_0. The transforms ${}^n\boldsymbol{T}_E$ and ${}^R\boldsymbol{T}_0$ are constant ones determined by the way the end effector is attached to link n and by the location of the base with respect to the reference frame. The relation between the end effector and the reference frame is then

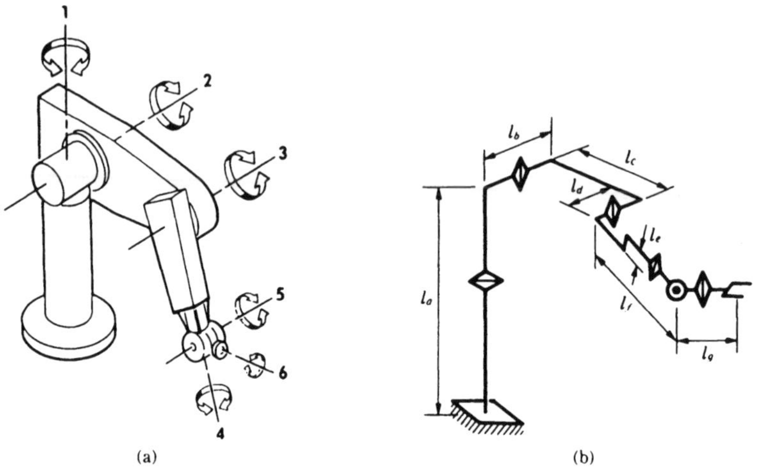

Figure 2.23
PUMA-type manipulator. (a) PUMA robot (courtesy of Westinghouse Automation Division/Unimation Inc.). (b) Link structure.

$$^{\mathrm{R}}\boldsymbol{T}_{\mathrm{E}} = {}^{\mathrm{R}}\boldsymbol{T}_{0}\,{}^{0}\boldsymbol{T}_{n}\,{}^{n}\boldsymbol{T}_{\mathrm{E}}. \tag{2.47}$$

Since the position vector $\boldsymbol{r}$ of the end effector is determined uniquely from $^{\mathrm{R}}\boldsymbol{T}_{\mathrm{E}}$ and since $^{0}\boldsymbol{T}_{n}$ is a function of $\boldsymbol{q}$, we can obtain the function $\boldsymbol{f}_r(\boldsymbol{q})$ of equation 2.42 from equation 2.47. Thus, if each element of $^{0}\boldsymbol{T}_{n}$ is obtained as a function of $\boldsymbol{q}$, the direct kinematics problem is basically solved.

Example 2.11 Let us assign the link frames to the PUMA-type manipulator shown in figure 2.23 and obtain $^{0}\boldsymbol{T}_{6}$. Following the scheme of the previous subsection, we obtain the link frames shown in figure 2.24 and the link parameters in table 2.2. Hence, from equation 2.45,

$$^{0}\boldsymbol{T}_{1} = \begin{bmatrix} \cos\theta_1 & -\sin\theta_1 & 0 & 0 \\ \sin\theta_1 & \cos\theta_1 & 0 & 0 \\ 0 & 0 & 1 & 0 \\ 0 & 0 & 0 & 1 \end{bmatrix}, \quad {}^{1}\boldsymbol{T}_{2} = \begin{bmatrix} \cos\theta_2 & -\sin\theta_2 & 0 & 0 \\ 0 & 0 & 1 & l_b - l_d \\ -\sin\theta_2 & -\cos\theta_2 & 0 & 0 \\ 0 & 0 & 0 & 1 \end{bmatrix},$$

$$^{2}\boldsymbol{T}_{3} = \begin{bmatrix} \cos\theta_3 & -\sin\theta_3 & 0 & l_c \\ \sin\theta_3 & \cos\theta_3 & 0 & 0 \\ 0 & 0 & 1 & 0 \\ 0 & 0 & 0 & 1 \end{bmatrix}, \quad {}^{3}\boldsymbol{T}_{4} = \begin{bmatrix} \cos\theta_4 & -\sin\theta_4 & 0 & l_e \\ 0 & 0 & 1 & l_f \\ -\sin\theta_4 & -\cos\theta_4 & 0 & 0 \\ 0 & 0 & 0 & 1 \end{bmatrix},$$

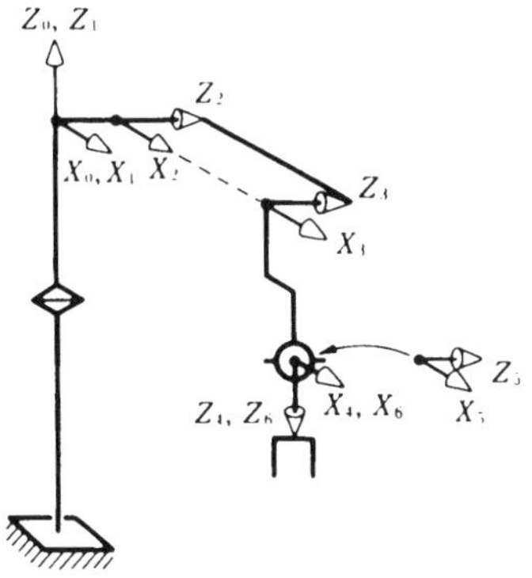

Figure 2.24
Link frames for PUMA robot.

Table 2.2
Link parameters.

i	a_{i-1}	α_{i-1}	d_i	θ_i
1	0	0°	0	(θ_1)
2	0	−90°	$l_b - l_d$	(θ_2)
3	l_c	0°	0	(θ_3)
4	l_e	−90°	l_f	(θ_4)
5	0	90°	0	(θ_5)
6	0	−90°	0	(θ_6)

$$
{}^4\boldsymbol{T}_5 = \begin{bmatrix} \cos\theta_5 & -\sin\theta_5 & 0 & 0 \\ 0 & 0 & -1 & 0 \\ \sin\theta_5 & \cos\theta_5 & 0 & 0 \\ 0 & 0 & 0 & 1 \end{bmatrix}, \quad {}^5\boldsymbol{T}_6 = \begin{bmatrix} \cos\theta_6 & -\sin\theta_6 & 0 & 0 \\ 0 & 0 & 1 & 0 \\ -\sin\theta_6 & -\cos\theta_6 & 0 & 0 \\ 0 & 0 & 0 & 1 \end{bmatrix}. \tag{2.48}
$$

Now we calculate ${}^0\boldsymbol{T}_6$. We first find ${}^0\boldsymbol{T}_3$ for the arm portion and ${}^3\boldsymbol{T}_6$ for the wrist portion; then we multiply them. Finding these two transforms is just a convenience for later use. The transform ${}^0\boldsymbol{T}_3$ is given by*

$$
{}^0\boldsymbol{T}_3 = \begin{bmatrix} C_1 C_{23} & -C_1 S_{23} & -S_1 & l_c C_1 C_2 - (l_b - l_d) S_1 \\ S_1 C_{23} & -S_1 S_{23} & C_1 & l_c S_1 C_2 + (l_b - l_d) C_1 \\ -S_{23} & -C_{23} & 0 & -l_c S_2 \\ 0 & 0 & 0 & 1 \end{bmatrix}.
$$

The transform ${}^3\boldsymbol{T}_6$ is given by

$$
{}^3\boldsymbol{T}_6 = \begin{bmatrix} C_4 C_5 C_6 - S_4 S_6 & -C_4 C_5 S_6 - S_4 C_6 & -C_4 S_5 & l_e \\ S_5 C_6 & -S_5 S_6 & C_5 & l_f \\ -S_4 C_5 C_6 - C_4 S_6 & S_4 C_5 S_6 - C_4 C_6 & S_4 S_5 & 0 \\ 0 & 0 & 0 & 1 \end{bmatrix}. \tag{2.49}
$$

Thus, we finally obtain

$$
{}^0\boldsymbol{T}_6 = \begin{bmatrix} R_{11} & R_{12} & R_{13} & p_x \\ R_{21} & R_{22} & R_{23} & p_y \\ R_{31} & R_{32} & R_{33} & p_z \\ 0 & 0 & 0 & 1 \end{bmatrix}, \tag{2.50}
$$

where

$$
R_{11} = C_1[C_{23}(C_4 C_5 C_6 - S_4 S_6) - S_{23} S_5 C_6] + S_1(S_4 C_5 C_6 + C_4 S_6),
$$

$$
R_{12} = C_1[-C_{23}(C_4 C_5 S_6 + S_4 C_6) + S_{23} S_5 S_6] - S_1(S_4 C_5 S_6 - C_4 C_6),
$$

* Here we use the following notations: $C_1 = \cos\theta_1$, $S_1 = \sin\theta_1$, $C_{23} = \cos(\theta_2 + \theta_3)$, and $S_{23} = \sin(\theta_2 + \theta_3)$. This kind of notation will be used throughout the book. For example, $S_{123} = \sin(\theta_1 + \theta_2 + \theta_3)$, and $C_{234} = \cos(\theta_2 + \theta_3 + \theta_4)$.

$$R_{13} = -C_1(C_{23}C_4S_5 + S_{23}C_5) - S_1S_4S_5,$$

$$R_{21} = S_1[C_{23}(C_4C_5C_6 - S_4S_6) - S_{23}S_5C_6] - C_1(S_4C_5C_6 + C_4S_6), \tag{2.51}$$

$$R_{22} = S_1[-C_{23}(C_4C_5S_6 + S_4C_6) + S_{23}S_5S_6] + C_1(S_4C_5S_6 - C_4C_6),$$

$$R_{23} = -S_1(C_{23}C_4S_5 + S_{23}C_5) + C_1S_4S_5,$$

$$R_{31} = -S_{23}(C_4C_5C_6 - S_4S_6) - C_{23}S_5C_6,$$

$$R_{32} = S_{23}(C_4C_5S_6 + S_4C_6) + C_{23}S_5S_6,$$

$$R_{33} = S_{23}C_4S_5 - C_{23}C_5,$$

$$p_x = C_1(l_cC_2 + l_eC_{23} - l_fS_{23}) - (l_b - l_d)S_1, \tag{2.52a}$$

$$p_y = S_1(l_cC_2 + l_eC_{23} - l_fS_{23}) + (l_b - l_d)C_1, \tag{2.52b}$$

$$p_z = -l_cS_2 - l_eS_{23} - l_fC_{23}. \square \tag{2.52c}$$

Example 2.12 For the PUMA-type manipulator in example 2.11, assume that the reference frame Σ_R and the end-effector frame Σ_E are as illustrated in figure 2.25. Assume also that the end-effector position vector $\boldsymbol{r}$ is

$$\boldsymbol{r} = [r_1, r_2, \ldots, r_6]^T,$$

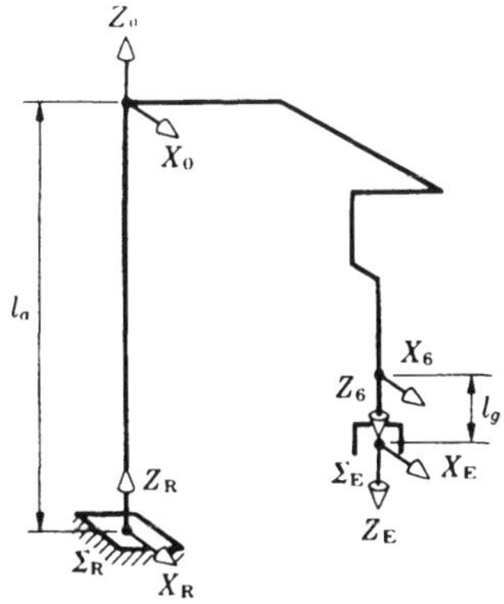

Figure 2.25
Reference frame Σ_R and end-effector frame Σ_E.

where r_1, r_2, and r_3 are the X, Y, and Z coordinates of the origin of Σ_E and where r_4, r_5, and r_6 are the Euler angles of Σ_E with respect to Σ_R. We first solve the direct kinematics problem; then we find the value $\boldsymbol{r}$ for the case where the joint vector is

$$\boldsymbol{q}^* = [0°, -45°, 0°, 0°, -45°, 90°]^T.$$

First,

$$^R\boldsymbol{T}_0 = \begin{bmatrix} 1 & 0 & 0 & 0 \\ 0 & 1 & 0 & 0 \\ 0 & 0 & 1 & l_a \\ 0 & 0 & 0 & 1 \end{bmatrix}$$

and

$$^n\boldsymbol{T}_E = \begin{bmatrix} 1 & 0 & 0 & 0 \\ 0 & 1 & 0 & 0 \\ 0 & 0 & 1 & l_g \\ 0 & 0 & 0 & 1 \end{bmatrix}.$$

Hence, from equations 2.47 and 2.50,

$$^R\boldsymbol{T}_E = \begin{bmatrix} R_{11} & R_{12} & R_{13} & p_x + R_{13}l_g \\ R_{21} & R_{22} & R_{23} & p_y + R_{23}l_g \\ R_{31} & R_{32} & R_{33} & p_z + l_a + R_{33}l_g \\ 0 & 0 & 0 & 1 \end{bmatrix}.$$

From equations 2.32 and 2.33, the corresponding position vector $\boldsymbol{r}$ is given by

$$r_1 = p_x + R_{13}l_g,$$

$$r_2 = p_y + R_{23}l_g,$$

$$r_3 = p_z + l_a + R_{33}l_g,$$

$$r_4 = \text{atan2}(R_{23}, R_{13}),$$

$$r_5 = \text{atan2}(\sqrt{R_{13}^2 + R_{23}^2}, R_{33}),$$

$$r_6 = \begin{cases} \text{atan2}(R_{32}, -R_{31}) & \text{if } R_{13}^2 + R_{23}^2 \neq 0 \\ \text{atan2}(R_{21}, R_{22}) - R_{33}r_4 & \text{if } R_{13}^2 + R_{23}^2 = 0. \end{cases}$$

Second, when $\boldsymbol{q} = \boldsymbol{q}^*$ we have

$$R_{11} = 0, \quad R_{12} = 0, \quad R_{13} = 1,$$
$$R_{21} = -1, \quad R_{22} = 0, \quad R_{23} = 0,$$
$$R_{31} = 0, \quad R_{32} = -1, \quad R_{33} = 0,$$
$$p_x = (l_c + l_e + l_f)/\sqrt{2},$$
$$p_y = l_b - l_d,$$
$$p_z = (l_c + l_e - l_f)/\sqrt{2}.$$

Thus we obtain

$$r = [(l_c + l_e + l_f)/\sqrt{2} + l_g, l_b - l_d, (l_c + l_e - l_f)/\sqrt{2} + l_a, 0°, 90°, -90°]^T. \square$$

2.4 Inverse Kinematics Problem

We will now consider the inverse kinematics problem—that is, the problem of finding the joint vector q that realizes a given value of the end-effector position vector r (in other words, the value of all or part of the elements of ${}^0T_n$).

One approach to this problem is to find a closed-form solution by using algebra or geometry. Another approach is to find a numerical solution by some successive-approximation algorithm.[6] Although the former approach is generally more desirable in applying the solution to real-time control of robots, it is not always possible to obtain closed-form solutions for manipulators with an arbitrary mechanism. Rather, the class of manipulator mechanisms for which the closed-form solutions are guaranteed is very limited. Notice, however, that most of the manipulators in industrial use today belong to this class. The algebraic approach to closed-form solutions means finding q through various algebraic transformations of equation 2.42 or equation 2.47; the geometric approach means finding q by using geometrical heuristics to take advantage of the special structure of the manipulator.

It is sometimes advantageous to use both approaches together to solve a problem. First we will solve a simple example using each of the two approaches.

Example 2.13 Consider the three-degrees-of-freedom manipulator shown in figure 2.26a. Assume that the end position of the manipulator is expressed by ${}^0r = [r_x, r_y, r_z]^T$, the position vector with respect to Σ_0. The problem is

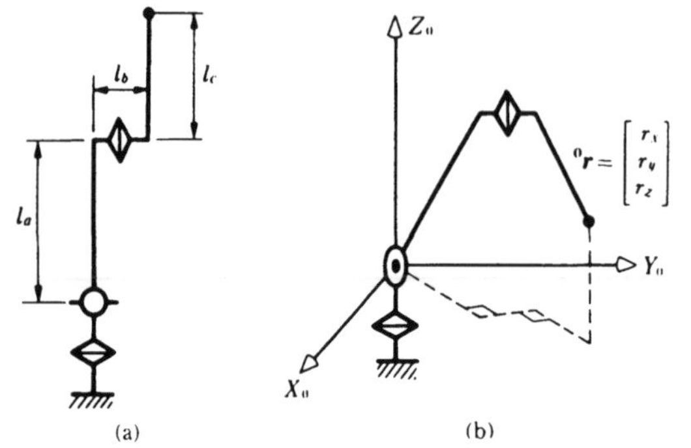

Figure 2.26
Three-link manipulator. (a) Size. (b) Endpoint position.

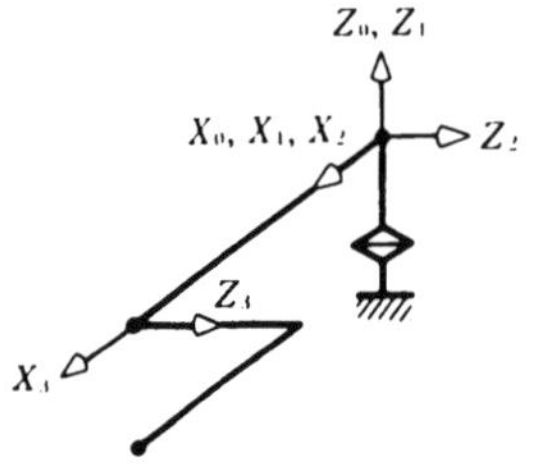

Figure 2.27
Link frames.

to find the three joint angles that realize any desired end position $\boldsymbol{r}$. First, in order to derive the kinematic equation, we determine the link frames as shown in figure 2.27. The link parameters are then given as in table 2.3. The transforms ${}^{i-1}\boldsymbol{T}_i$ are given by

$$ {}^0\boldsymbol{T}_1 = \begin{bmatrix} C_1 & -S_1 & 0 & 0 \\ S_1 & C_1 & 0 & 0 \\ 0 & 0 & 1 & 0 \\ 0 & 0 & 0 & 1 \end{bmatrix}, \tag{2.53a} $$

$$ {}^1\boldsymbol{T}_2 = \begin{bmatrix} C_2 & -S_2 & 0 & 0 \\ 0 & 0 & 1 & 0 \\ -S_2 & -C_2 & 0 & 0 \\ 0 & 0 & 0 & 1 \end{bmatrix}, \tag{2.53b} $$

Table 2.3
Link parameters.

i	a_{i-1}	α_{i-1}	d_i	θ_i
1	0	0	0	(θ_1)
2	0	$-90°$	0	(θ_2)
3	l_a	0	0	(θ_3)

and

$$ {}^2\boldsymbol{T}_3 = \begin{bmatrix} C_3 & -S_3 & 0 & l_a \\ S_3 & C_3 & 0 & 0 \\ 0 & 0 & 1 & 0 \\ 0 & 0 & 0 & 1 \end{bmatrix}. \tag{2.53c} $$

Therefore,

$$ \begin{aligned} {}^0\boldsymbol{T}_3 &= \begin{bmatrix} C_1C_2 & -C_1S_2 & -S_1 & 0 \\ S_1C_2 & -S_1S_2 & C_1 & 0 \\ -S_2 & -C_2 & 0 & 0 \\ 0 & 0 & 0 & 1 \end{bmatrix} {}^2\boldsymbol{T}_3 \\ &= \left[\begin{array}{c|c|c|c} C_1C_2C_3 - C_1S_2S_3 & -C_1C_2S_3 - C_1S_2C_3 & -S_1 & l_aC_1C_2 \\ S_1C_2C_3 - S_1S_2S_3 & -S_1C_2S_3 - S_1S_2C_3 & C_1 & l_aS_1C_2 \\ -S_2C_3 - C_2S_3 & S_2S_3 - C_2C_3 & 0 & -l_aS_2 \\ 0 & 0 & 0 & 1 \end{array}\right]. \end{aligned} \tag{2.54} $$

From figures 2.26a and 2.27 we can easily show that the end position relative to Σ_3 is given by ${}^3\boldsymbol{r} = [l_c, 0, l_b]^T$. Hence,

$$ {}^0\boldsymbol{r} = {}^0\boldsymbol{T}_3\,{}^3\boldsymbol{r}. \tag{2.55} $$

The kinematic equation is obtained from equations 2.54 and 2.55 as

$$ \begin{aligned} r_x &= l_c(C_1C_2C_3 - C_1S_2S_3) - l_bS_1 + l_aC_1C_2, \\ r_y &= l_c(S_1C_2C_3 - S_1S_2S_3) + l_bC_1 + l_aS_1C_2, \\ r_z &= l_c(-S_2C_3 - C_2S_3) - l_aS_2. \end{aligned} \tag{2.56} $$

Now we find the joint angles θ_i $(i = 1, 2, 3)$ from equation 2.56 using an algebraic approach. Since equation 2.56 itself is not very suitable for this purpose, let us consider the following equation instead:

$$({}^0\boldsymbol{T}_2)^{-1}\,{}^0\boldsymbol{r} = {}^2\boldsymbol{T}_3\,{}^3\boldsymbol{r}. \tag{2.57}$$

Substituting equation 2.53 into equation 2.57, we have

$$\begin{bmatrix} C_1C_2 & S_1C_2 & -S_2 & 0 \\ -C_1S_2 & -S_1S_2 & -C_2 & 0 \\ -S_1 & C_1 & 0 & 0 \\ 0 & 0 & 0 & 1 \end{bmatrix} {}^0\boldsymbol{r} = \begin{bmatrix} C_3 & -S_3 & 0 & l_a \\ S_3 & C_3 & 0 & 0 \\ 0 & 0 & 1 & 0 \\ 0 & 0 & 0 & 1 \end{bmatrix} {}^3\boldsymbol{r},$$

or

$$C_1C_2r_x + S_1C_2r_y - S_2r_z = l_cC_3 + l_a, \tag{2.58a}$$

$$-C_1S_2r_x - S_1S_2r_y - C_2r_z = l_cS_3, \tag{2.58b}$$

$$-S_1r_x + C_1r_y = l_b. \tag{2.58c}$$

If we further consider

$$({}^0\boldsymbol{T}_1)^{-1}\,{}^0\boldsymbol{r} = {}^1\boldsymbol{T}_3\,{}^3\boldsymbol{r}, \tag{2.59}$$

we obtain

$$C_1r_x + S_1r_y = l_cC_{23} + l_aC_2, \tag{2.60a}$$

$$-S_1r_x + C_1r_y = l_b, \tag{2.60b}$$

$$r_z = -l_cS_{23} - l_aS_2. \tag{2.60c}$$

Since the variables θ_i are fairly well separated in equations 2.58 and 2.60, it is rather easy to find a way to solve these equations for θ_i. For example, we can obtain θ_1 from equation 2.58c or 2.60b as follows:

$$\theta_1 = \operatorname{atan2}(-r_x, r_y) \pm \operatorname{atan2}(\sqrt{r_x^2 + r_y^2 - l_b^2}, l_b), \tag{2.61}$$

where we have used equation A1.17 of appendix 1. Summing the squares of equations 2.60a, 2.60b, and 2.60c, we have

$$r_x^2 + r_y^2 + r_z^2 = l_a^2 + l_b^2 + l_c^2 + 2l_al_cC_3. \tag{2.62}$$

Hence, θ_3 is given by

$$\theta_3 = \pm\operatorname{atan2}(\kappa, r_x^2 + r_y^2 + r_z^2 - l_b^2 - l_a^2 - l_c^2), \tag{2.63}$$

where

$$\kappa = \{(r_x^2 + r_y^2 + r_z^2 - l_b^2 + l_a^2 + l_c^2)^2$$
$$- 2[(r_x^2 + r_y^2 + r_z^2 - l_b^2)^2 + l_a^4 + l_c^4]\}^{1/2}. \quad (2.64)$$

As for the last variable θ_2, from equations 2.58a and 2.58b we have

$$[r_z^2 + (C_1 r_x + S_1 r_y)^2]S_2 = -r_z(l_c C_3 + l_a) - (C_1 r_x + S_1 r_y)l_c S_3,$$
$$[r_z^2 + (C_1 r_x + S_1 r_y)^2]C_2 = (C_1 r_x + S_1 r_y)(l_c C_3 + l_a) - r_z l_c S_3. \quad (2.65)$$

Thus we obtain

$$\theta_2 = \text{atan2}[-r_z(l_c C_3 + l_a) - (C_1 r_x + S_1 r_y)l_c S_3,$$
$$(C_1 r_x + S_1 r_y)(l_c C_3 + l_a) - r_z l_c S_3]. \quad (2.66)$$

One value of θ_2 is determined for each combination of two values of θ_1 and two values of θ_3 (given by equations 2.61 and 2.63, respectively). As is shown above, the solution can be more easily found when a transformation such as 2.57 and 2.59 is used rather than just 2.55. Next we will solve the same inverse kinematics problem using a geometric approach. By projecting the arm onto the X_0–Y_0 plane of Σ_0, we obtain figure 2.28. Thus we have

$$l_b = C_1 r_y - S_1 r_x,$$

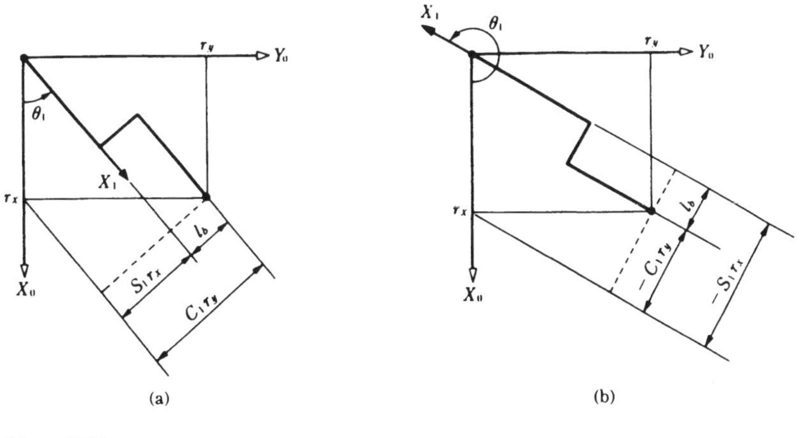

Figure 2.28
Projection of manipulator on X_0–Y_0 plane (a) when the X_1 axis and $[r_x, r_y]^T$ are in the same direction; (b) when the X_1 axis and $[r_x, r_y]^T$ are in opposite directions.

and θ_1 is given by equation 2.61. The "plus or minus" sign in equation 2.61 is "plus" when the arm is posed as in figure 2.28a; it is "minus" when the arm is posed as in figure 2.28b. Figure 2.29 is another projection of the arm shown in figure 2.26, this time onto the X_1-Y_1 plane of Σ_1. From this figure, as in example 2.9, we obtain θ_2 and θ_3. That is, θ_3 is given by equation 2.63 and θ_2 is given by

$$\theta_2 = \text{atan2}(-r_z, \sqrt{r_x{}^2 + r_y{}^2 - l_b{}^2}) \mp \text{atan2}(\kappa, r_x{}^2 + r_y{}^2 + r_z{}^2 - l_b{}^2 + l_a{}^2 - l_c{}^2)$$

(in the case of figure 2.29a; the sign "±" is in the same order as in equation 2.63) or

$$\theta_2 = \text{atan2}(-r_z, -\sqrt{r_x{}^2 + r_y{}^2 - l_b{}^2}) \mp \text{atan2}(\kappa, r_x{}^2 + r_y{}^2 + r_z{}^2 - l_b{}^2 - l_a{}^2 - l_c{}^2)$$

(in the case of figure 2.29b). The above expression for θ_2 is different from equation 2.66, which was found by an algebraic approach, but they can be shown to be equivalent. Note that when we adopt a geometric approach, we should be careful to examine every possible solution. □

In the above example we considered the case where only the three-dimensional position of the end effector is of concern. For a general manipulator with six degrees of freedom, however, the position and orienta-

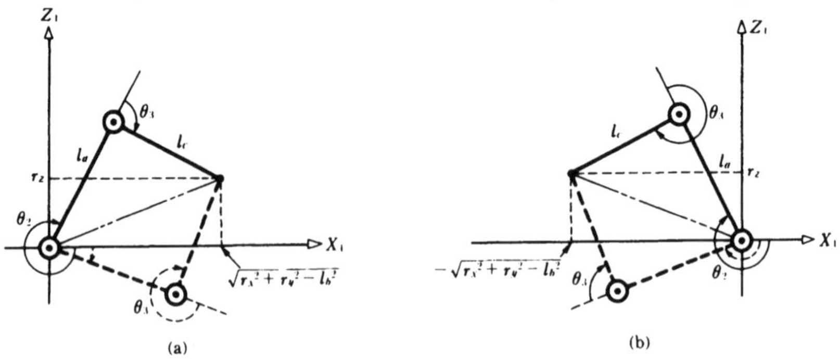

Figure 2.29
Projection of manipulator on X_1-Z_1 plane (solid and broken lines are two possible arm configurations). (a) Case of figure 2.28a. (b) Case of figure 2.28b.

tion of the end effector should be considered in the inverse kinematics problem. We will now look at two approaches that are often effective in solving this problem. The first approach is algebraic, the second geometric.

(1) Modification of Kinematic Equation (ref. 5) As example 2.13 showed, transformation of the kinematic equation was effective in reaching the solution. Here we will consider an extension of this approach. The original kinematic equation, given by

$$^{0}T_6 = {}^{0}T_1(q_1)\,{}^{1}T_2(q_2)\ldots{}^{5}T_6(q_6), \tag{2.67}$$

is equivalent to twelve simultaneous algebraic equations with six unknown variables $(q_1, q_2, \ldots, q_6)$. By transforming equation 2.67 into

$$[{}^{0}T_1(q_1)\ldots{}^{i-1}T_i(q_i)]^{-1}\,{}^{0}T_6[{}^{j}T_{j+1}(q_{j+1})\ldots{}^{5}T_6(q_6)]^{-1}$$
$$= {}^{i}T_{i+1}(q_{i+1})\ldots{}^{j-1}T_j(q_j), \quad i<j \tag{2.68}$$

we obtain another equivalent set of twelve simultaneous algebraic equations for every (i, j) pair such that $i<j$. By selecting simpler ones among these equations, we can very often obtain a solution rather easily.

(2) Pieper's Approach[7] Many industrial manipulators have a wrist with three revolute joints whose axes intersect at one common point, as shown in figure 2.30. In such cases, the origins of Σ_4, Σ_5, and Σ_6 are all located at

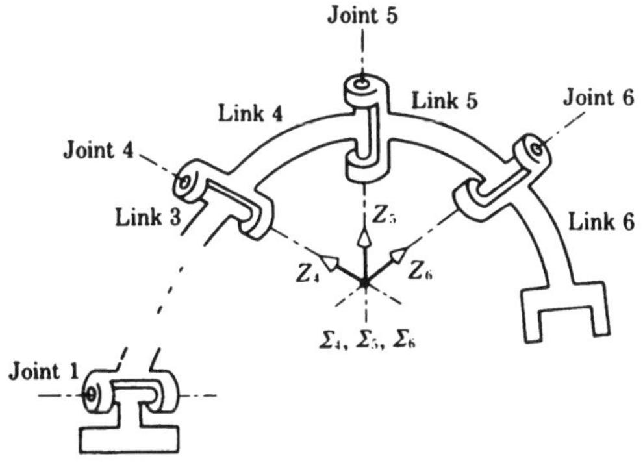

Figure 2.30
Pieper's method.

this point. Specifying the position and orientation of the end effector determines the position of the origin of Σ_6, and therefore that of Σ_4. The position of the origin of Σ_4, which is represented by three variables (i.e., X, Y, Z coordinate variables), is a function of three joint variables: q_1, q_2, and q_3. This means that we can generally determine the values of q_1, q_2, and q_3 from the given position and orientation of the end effector. We can then find the position and orientation of Σ_3, and hence the orientation of Σ_6 with respect to Σ_3. Finally, from this orientation of Σ_6 we can determine the joint variables q_4, q_5, and q_6. Pieper showed a more general result: that a closed-form solution can be obtained for a manipulator which has three consecutive revolute joints whose joint axes intersect at a point.

For manipulators with no fewer than seven degrees of freedom, there is generally an infinite number of joint solutions for a given realizable position and orientation of the end effector, implying that the manipulator has redundancy.

Example 2.14 Consider the inverse kinematics problem for the PUMA-type arm shown in figure 2.23. The problem can be reduced to that of finding a $\boldsymbol{q}$ that satisfies equations 2.51 and 2.52 for given values of elements R_{ij}, p_x, p_y, and p_z of ${}^0\boldsymbol{T}_6$. Since the three distal joints satisfy Pieper's condition, p_x, p_y, and p_z that represent the origin of Σ_4 are functions of only θ_1, θ_2, and θ_3, as is shown by equation 2.52. First we determine θ_1, θ_2, and θ_3 from equation 2.52. By using a procedure similar to that in example 2.13, we get

$$\theta_1 = \text{atan2}(-p_x, p_y) \pm \text{atan2}(\sqrt{p_x^2 + p_y^2 - (l_b - l_d)^2}, l_b - l_d), \tag{2.69}$$

$$\theta_3 = \text{atan2}(-l_f, l_e) \pm \text{atan2}(\sqrt{l_c^2(l_e^2 + l_f^2) - \kappa_a^2}, \kappa_a), \tag{2.70}$$

$$\kappa_a = [p_x^2 + p_y^2 + p_z^2 - l_e^2 - l_f^2 - l_c^2 - (l_b - l_d)^2]/2, \tag{2.71}$$

$$\theta_2 = \text{atan2}[-(l_e S_3 + l_f C_3)(C_1 p_x + S_1 p_y) - (l_e C_3 - l_f S_3 + l_c) p_z,$$
$$(l_e C_3 - l_f S_3 + l_c)(C_1 p_x + S_1 p_y) - (l_e S_3 + l_f C_3) p_z]. \tag{2.72}$$

We next find θ_4, θ_5, and θ_6 from

$$[{}^0\boldsymbol{T}_3]^{-1}\,{}^0\boldsymbol{T}_6 = {}^3\boldsymbol{T}_4(\theta_4)\,{}^4\boldsymbol{T}_5(\theta_5)\,{}^5\boldsymbol{T}_6(\theta_6). \tag{2.73}$$

Denoting the upper left 3×3 submatrix of the left-hand side of equation 2.73 as $[\hat{R}_{ij}]$, where $i, j = 1, 2, 3$, we have

$$\begin{bmatrix} \hat{R}_{11} & \hat{R}_{12} & \hat{R}_{13} \\ \hat{R}_{21} & \hat{R}_{22} & \hat{R}_{23} \\ \hat{R}_{31} & \hat{R}_{32} & \hat{R}_{33} \end{bmatrix} = \begin{bmatrix} C_4C_5C_6 - S_4S_6 & -C_4C_5S_6 - S_4C_6 & -C_4S_5 \\ S_5C_6 & -S_5S_6 & C_5 \\ -S_4C_5C_6 - C_4S_6 & S_4C_5S_6 - C_4C_6 & S_4S_5 \end{bmatrix} \tag{2.74}$$

Similarly to equations 2.31 and 2.33, the values of θ_4, θ_5, and θ_6 that satisfy equation 2.74 are given by

$$\theta_4 = \mathrm{atan2}(\pm\hat{R}_{33}, \mp\hat{R}_{13}), \tag{2.75a}$$

$$\theta_5 = \mathrm{atan2}(\pm\sqrt{\hat{R}_{13}{}^2 + \hat{R}_{33}{}^2}, \hat{R}_{23}), \tag{2.75b}$$

$$\theta_6 = \mathrm{atan2}(\mp\hat{R}_{22}, \pm\hat{R}_{21}) \tag{2.75c}$$

when $\hat{R}_{13}{}^2 + \hat{R}_{33}{}^2 \neq 0$, and by

$$\theta_4 = \text{arbitrary}, \tag{2.76a}$$

$$\theta_5 = 90^\circ - \hat{R}_{23} \times 90^\circ, \tag{2.76b}$$

$$\theta_6 = \mathrm{atan2}(-\hat{R}_{31}, -\hat{R}_{32}) - \theta_4\hat{R}_{23} \tag{2.76c}$$

when $\hat{R}_{13} = \hat{R}_{33} = 0$. Therefore, there exist two values for θ_1, two values for θ_3, and two sets of values for $\{\theta_4, \theta_5, \theta_6\}$ for each combination of θ_1 and θ_2, resulting in eight solutions $\{\theta_1, \theta_2, \ldots, \theta_6\}$ of the inverse kinematics problem. □

2.5 Jacobian Matrix

2.5.1 Translational and Rotational Velocity of Objects

In this section we will develop methods for expressing the velocity of an object moving in space. In section 2.1 we expressed the position and orientation of an object in terms of the relation of the object frame Σ_B (attached to the object) to the reference frame Σ_A. Extending this idea, we can express the velocity of an object in terms of the velocity of the object frame with respect to the reference frame (that is, the translational velocity and the rotational velocity of the object frame).

The translational velocity of the object frame can naturally be expressed by the time derivative of the position vector ${}^A\boldsymbol{p}_B$ representing the origin of Σ_B with respect to Σ_A. This is denoted ${}^A\dot{\boldsymbol{p}}_B$; that is, ${}^A\dot{\boldsymbol{p}}_B = d\,{}^A\boldsymbol{p}_B/dt$, where t is the time variable. For expressing the rotational velocity of the object frame, we can consider the following two methods:

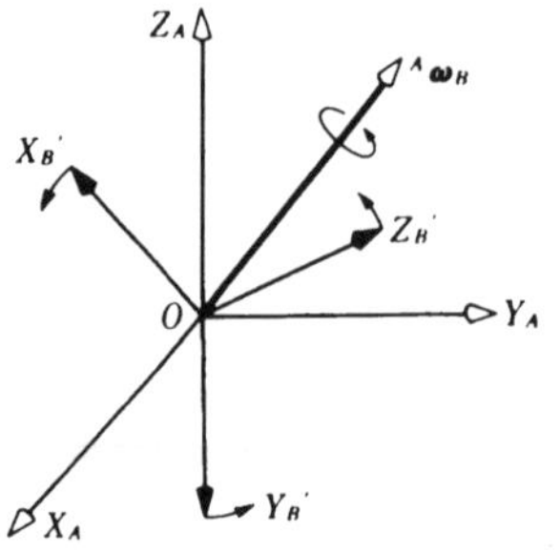

Figure 2.31
Angular velocity vector $^A\omega_B$.

Method I Select a vector $^A\boldsymbol{\phi}_B$ consisting of three variables for expressing the orientation (e.g., Euler angles, or roll, pitch, and yaw angles), and use its time derivative $^A\dot{\boldsymbol{\phi}}_B = d^A\boldsymbol{\phi}_B/dt$ to express the rotational velocity of the object frame. (The superscript A and the subscript B of $^A\boldsymbol{\phi}_B$ indicate that $\boldsymbol{\phi}$ describes the orientation of Σ_B with respect to Σ_A.)

Method II Consider (figure 2.31) the third frame, $\Sigma_{B'}$, which always has the same origin as the reference frame Σ_A and which has the same orientation as the object frame Σ_B. Then the motion of $\Sigma_{B'}$ with respect to Σ_A at each instant of time is a rotation about an axis passing through the origin. This means that the rotational velocity of $\Sigma_{B'}$ can be described by the vector $^A\omega_B$, which has the same direction as the instantaneous axis of rotation and a magnitude proportional to the rotational speed about this axis. The vector $^A\omega_B$ is called the *angular velocity vector.*

Since both of these methods will be used in this book, depending on the situation, a brief description of the merits and demerits of each method follows.

The integral of $^A\dot{\boldsymbol{\phi}}_B$ in method I obviously corresponds to $^A\boldsymbol{\phi}_B$, which has a clear physical meaning, whereas the integral of $^A\omega_B$ in method II does not have any clear meaning, as can be seen from the following example.

Example 2.15 Consider the following two cases. Case 1 has a time history $^A\omega_B$ given by

$$^A\omega_B = \begin{bmatrix} \pi/2 \\ 0 \\ 0 \end{bmatrix}, \quad 0 \leqq t \leqq 1$$

$$^A\omega_B = \begin{bmatrix} 0 \\ \pi/2 \\ 0 \end{bmatrix}, \quad 1 < t \leqq 2$$

and case 2 has $^A\omega_B$ given by

$$^A\omega_B = \begin{bmatrix} 0 \\ \pi/2 \\ 0 \end{bmatrix}, \quad 0 \leqq t \leqq 1$$

$$^A\omega_B = \begin{bmatrix} \pi/2 \\ 0 \\ 0 \end{bmatrix}, \quad 1 < t \leqq 2.$$

Assume that Σ_A and Σ_B are coincident at $t = 0$. The integral of $^A\omega_B$ for both cases is calculated to be

$$\int_0^2 {}^A\omega_B \, dt = \begin{bmatrix} \pi/2 \\ \pi/2 \\ 0 \end{bmatrix}.$$

However, the value of rotation matrix $^A\boldsymbol{R}_B$ at time $t = 2$, which is denoted as $^A\hat{\boldsymbol{R}}_B$, is

$$^A\hat{\boldsymbol{R}}_B = \begin{bmatrix} 0 & 1 & 0 \\ 0 & 0 & -1 \\ -1 & 0 & 0 \end{bmatrix}$$

for case 1 and

$$^A\hat{\boldsymbol{R}}_B = \begin{bmatrix} 0 & 0 & 1 \\ 1 & 0 & 0 \\ 0 & 1 & 0 \end{bmatrix}$$

for case 2. Thus, although the integrals of $^A\omega_B$ are the same, the orientations of Σ_B at time $t = 2$ are quite different. Figure 2.32 illustrates the two different orientations of an object at time $t = 2$ corresponding to our cases 1 and 2, which started from the same orientation at time $t = 0$. □

From the viewpoint of the physical meaning of the vector expressing the velocity, $^A\omega_B$ is superior to $^A\dot{\boldsymbol{\phi}}_B$. The three elements of $^A\omega_B$ represent the orthogonal angular velocity components about the X, Y, and Z axes of Σ_A

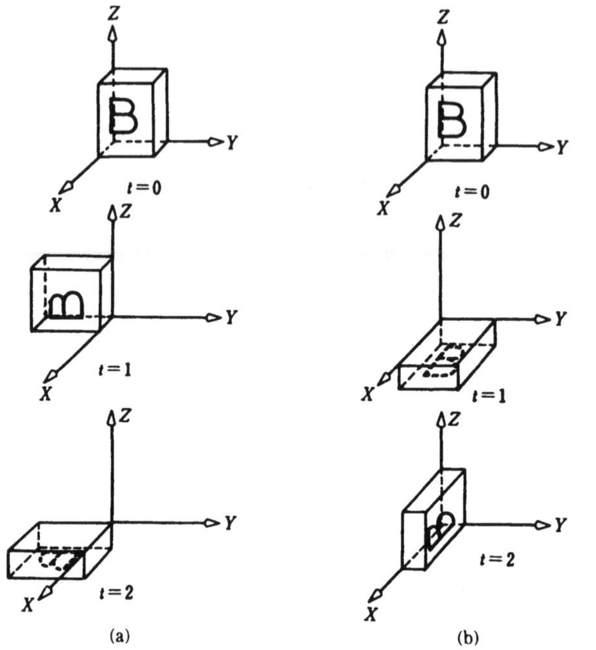

Figure 2.32
Two motions with the same integral of ${}^A\omega_B$. (a) Case 1. (b) Case 2.

as shown in figure 2.33a. In contrast, those of ${}^A\dot{\boldsymbol{\phi}}_B$ generally represent non-orthogonal components about the three axes of a skew coordinate system whose coordinate axes vary depending on the present value of ${}^A\boldsymbol{\phi}_B$.

For example, when the Euler angles are used as ${}^A\boldsymbol{\phi}_B$, the relation between ${}^A\dot{\boldsymbol{\phi}}_B$ and ${}^A\omega_B$ is given by

$$ {}^A\omega_B = \begin{bmatrix} 0 & -\sin\phi & \cos\phi\sin\theta \\ 0 & \cos\phi & \sin\phi\sin\theta \\ 1 & 0 & \cos\theta \end{bmatrix} {}^A\dot{\boldsymbol{\phi}}_B, \tag{2.77} $$

and we have the skew coordinate system shown in figure 2.33b.

The coefficient matrix on the right-hand side of equation 2.77 becomes singular when $\sin\theta = 0$. This means that although any rotational velocity can be described by ${}^A\omega_B$, there are rotational velocities that cannot be described by ${}^A\dot{\boldsymbol{\phi}}_B$ when the orientation of Σ_B satisfies $\sin\theta = 0$. For example, ${}^A\omega_B = [\cos\phi, \sin\phi, 0]^T$ cannot be expressed by ${}^A\dot{\boldsymbol{\phi}}_B$. Orientations of this kind are called *representational singularities* of ${}^A\boldsymbol{\phi}_B$.

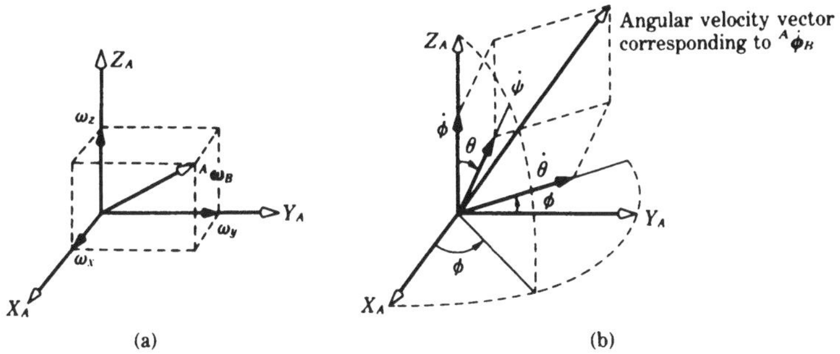

Figure 2.33
Two representations of angular velocity: (a) $^A\omega_B$; (b) $^A\dot{\phi}_B$ (case of Euler angles).

2.5.2 Definition of the Jacobian Matrix

Suppose that the following relation holds between a k-dimensional vector $\xi = [\xi_1, \xi_2, \ldots, \xi_k]^T$ and an l-dimensional vector $\boldsymbol{\eta} = [\eta_1, \eta_2, \ldots, \eta_l]^T$:

$$\eta_j = f_j(\xi_1, \xi_2, \ldots, \xi_k), \quad j = 1, 2, \ldots, l. \tag{2.78}$$

Then the $l \times k$ matrix

$$\boldsymbol{J}_\eta(\xi) = \begin{bmatrix} \frac{\partial \eta_1}{\partial \xi_1} & \frac{\partial \eta_1}{\partial \xi_2} & \cdots & \frac{\partial \eta_1}{\partial \xi_k} \\ \frac{\partial \eta_2}{\partial \xi_1} & \frac{\partial \eta_2}{\partial \xi_2} & \cdots & \frac{\partial \eta_2}{\partial \xi_k} \\ \vdots & \vdots & & \vdots \\ \frac{\partial \eta_l}{\partial \xi_1} & \frac{\partial \eta_l}{\partial \xi_2} & \cdots & \frac{\partial \eta_l}{\partial \xi_k} \end{bmatrix} \triangleq \frac{\partial \boldsymbol{\eta}}{\partial \xi^T} \tag{2.79}$$

is called the *Jacobian matrix*[8] of $\boldsymbol{\eta}$ with respect to ξ. Further, suppose that ξ and $\boldsymbol{\eta}$ are functions of time. Then differentiating equation 2.78 with respect to time and substituting equation 2.79 yields

$$\dot{\boldsymbol{\eta}} = \boldsymbol{J}_\eta(\xi)\dot{\xi}. \tag{2.80}$$

As is seen from equation 2.80, the Jacobian matrix is an extension of the derivative for a scalar function of a scalar variable to the case of vectors.

Using the Jacobian matrix, we can express the relation between the end-effector velocity and the joint velocity of a manipulator in a compact form. Differentiating equation 2.42 with respect to time yields

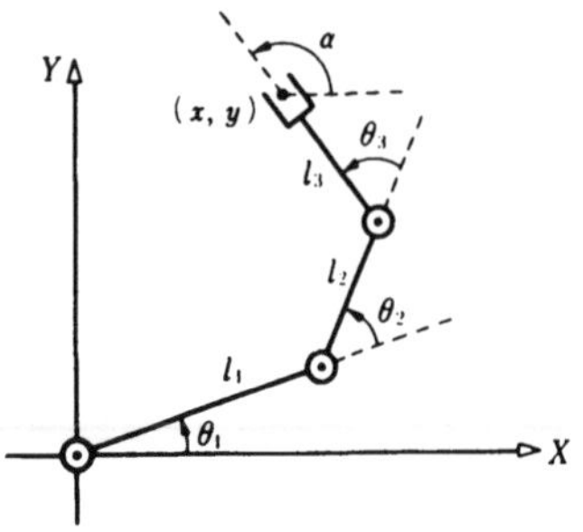

Figure 2.34
Three-link planar manipulator.

$$\dot{\boldsymbol{r}} = \boldsymbol{J}_r(\boldsymbol{q})\dot{\boldsymbol{q}}, \tag{2.81}$$

where $\boldsymbol{J}_r(\boldsymbol{q})$, the Jacobian matrix of $\boldsymbol{r}$ with respect to $\boldsymbol{q}$, is given by

$$\boldsymbol{J}_r(\boldsymbol{q}) = \frac{\partial \boldsymbol{r}}{\partial \boldsymbol{q}^T}. \tag{2.82}$$

The matrix $\boldsymbol{J}_r(\boldsymbol{q})$ will henceforth be written as $\boldsymbol{J}_r$, for simplicity.

Example 2.16 Let us find the Jacobian matrix for the three-link planar manipulator shown in figure 2.34. We let $\boldsymbol{r} = [x,y,\alpha]^T$, where x and y determine the position and α determines the orientation of the endpoint. Then

$$x = l_1 C_1 + l_2 C_{12} + l_3 C_{123},$$

$$y = l_1 S_1 + l_2 S_{12} + l_3 S_{123},$$

$$\alpha = \theta_1 + \theta_2 + \theta_3.$$

Differentiating these equations yields

$$\dot{x} = -(l_1 S_1 + l_2 S_{12} + l_3 S_{123})\dot{\theta}_1 - (l_2 S_{12} + l_3 S_{123})\dot{\theta}_2 - l_3 S_{123}\dot{\theta}_3,$$

$$\dot{y} = (l_1 C_1 + l_2 C_{12} + l_3 C_{123})\dot{\theta}_1 + (l_2 C_{12} + l_3 C_{123})\dot{\theta}_2 + l_3 C_{123}\dot{\theta}_3,$$

$$\dot{\alpha} = \dot{\theta}_1 + \dot{\theta}_2 + \dot{\theta}_3.$$

Hence we obtain

$$\boldsymbol{J}_r = \begin{bmatrix} -(l_1 S_1 + l_2 S_{12} + l_3 S_{123}) & -(l_2 S_{12} + l_3 S_{123}) & -l_3 S_{123} \\ (l_1 C_1 + l_2 C_{12} + l_3 C_{123}) & (l_2 C_{12} + l_3 C_{123}) & l_3 C_{123} \\ 1 & 1 & 1 \end{bmatrix}. \quad \square$$

When method I is used for expressing the rotational velocity of the end effector, and when the vector $\boldsymbol{r}$ in equation 2.41 is defined by

$$\boldsymbol{r} = \begin{bmatrix} {}^{\mathrm{R}}\boldsymbol{p}_{\mathrm{E}} \\ {}^{\mathrm{R}}\boldsymbol{\phi}_{\mathrm{E}} \end{bmatrix}, \tag{2.83}$$

then the relation between the end-effector velocity and the joint velocity is given by equation 2.81. (Here ${}^{\mathrm{R}}\boldsymbol{p}_{\mathrm{E}}$ and ${}^{\mathrm{R}}\boldsymbol{\phi}_{\mathrm{E}}$ are, respectively, the three-dimensional vectors expressing the position and orientation of the end-effector frame Σ_{E} with respect to the reference frame Σ_{R}.)

When method II is used to express the rotational velocity of the end effector, the vector

$$\boldsymbol{v} = \begin{bmatrix} {}^{\mathrm{R}}\dot{\boldsymbol{p}}_{\mathrm{E}} \\ {}^{\mathrm{R}}\boldsymbol{\omega}_{\mathrm{E}} \end{bmatrix} \tag{2.84}$$

expresses the total end-effector velocity. (Here ${}^{\mathrm{R}}\boldsymbol{\omega}_{\mathrm{E}}$ is the angular velocity vector of Σ_{E} with respect to Σ_{R}.) By defining a proper matrix $\boldsymbol{J}_v(\boldsymbol{q})$ which is a function of $\boldsymbol{q}$, we can obtain the following relation between $\boldsymbol{v}$ and $\dot{\boldsymbol{q}}$:

$$\boldsymbol{v} = \boldsymbol{J}_v(\boldsymbol{q})\dot{\boldsymbol{q}}. \tag{2.85}$$

Since the integral of ${}^{\mathrm{R}}\boldsymbol{\omega}_{\mathrm{E}}$ does not have any clear physical meaning, the coefficient matrix $\boldsymbol{J}_v(\boldsymbol{q})$ of equation 2.85 does not have any corresponding function f_j in equation 2.78. Because of the similarity of equations 2.85 and 2.81, however, $\boldsymbol{J}_v(\boldsymbol{q})$ is also called the Jacobian matrix. The matrix $\boldsymbol{J}_v(\boldsymbol{q})$ will also be written as $\boldsymbol{J}_v$ hereafter.

When Euler angles are used as ${}^{\mathrm{R}}\boldsymbol{\phi}_{\mathrm{E}}$ (see equation 2.77), the relation between $\boldsymbol{J}_r$ and $\boldsymbol{J}_v$ is given by

$$\boldsymbol{J}_v = \boldsymbol{T}_r\boldsymbol{J}_r \tag{2.86a}$$

and

$$\boldsymbol{T}_r = \left[\begin{array}{ccc|ccc} 1 & 0 & 0 & 0 & 0 & 0 \\ 0 & 1 & 0 & 0 & 0 & 0 \\ 0 & 0 & 1 & 0 & 0 & 0 \\ \hline 0 & 0 & 0 & 0 & -\sin\phi & \cos\phi\sin\theta \\ 0 & 0 & 0 & 0 & \cos\phi & \sin\phi\sin\theta \\ 0 & 0 & 0 & 1 & 0 & \cos\theta \end{array}\right] \tag{2.86b}$$

under the assumption that $\sin\theta \neq 0$.

When a manipulator's end effector can make a rotational motion with two or three degrees of freedom even after fixing its position, $\boldsymbol{J}_r$ and $\boldsymbol{J}_v$ are generally different. However, for a manipulator with fewer degrees of freedom whose end effector, after fixing its position, cannot move at all or can only rotate about a fixed axis, $\boldsymbol{J}_r$ and $\boldsymbol{J}_v$ are essentially the same. For example, in the case of the three-link manipulator in example 2.16, if we consider a Z axis such that a right-hand coordinate frame is formed, and if we let

$\boldsymbol{r} = [x,y,0,0,0,\alpha]^T$,

then we have

$\dot{\boldsymbol{r}} = [\dot{x},\dot{y},0,0,0,\dot{\alpha}]^T$.

Hence, $\boldsymbol{J}_v$ is a 6×3 matrix obtained from $\boldsymbol{J}_r$ by just adding nine zero elements to it.

Using $\boldsymbol{T}_r$ from equation 2.86b, we can write the relation between $\boldsymbol{v}$ and $\dot{\boldsymbol{r}}$ as $\boldsymbol{v} = \boldsymbol{T}_r \dot{\boldsymbol{r}}$.

2.5.3 Link Velocities of a Manipulator

First of all, an important equation will be derived here for later use. Consider two orthogonal coordinate frames Σ_A and Σ_B, and let ${}^A\omega_B$ denote the angular velocity of Σ_B with respect to Σ_A. Then, for an arbitrary vector ${}^B\boldsymbol{p}$ expressed in Σ_B, the time derivative of $({}^A\boldsymbol{R}_B{}^B\boldsymbol{p})$ is given by

$$\frac{d}{dt}({}^A\boldsymbol{R}_B{}^B\boldsymbol{p}) = {}^A\boldsymbol{R}_B\frac{d}{dt}({}^B\boldsymbol{p}) + \frac{d}{dt}({}^A\boldsymbol{R}_B){}^B\boldsymbol{p}. \tag{2.87}$$

By using the notations ${}^A\boldsymbol{R}_B = [{}^A\boldsymbol{x}_B\,{}^A\boldsymbol{y}_B\,{}^A\boldsymbol{z}_B]$ and ${}^B\boldsymbol{p} = [{}^Bp_x, {}^Bp_y, {}^Bp_z]^T$, we can rewrite the second term in equation 2.87 as

$$\begin{aligned}\frac{d}{dt}({}^A\boldsymbol{R}_B){}^B\boldsymbol{p} &= \frac{d}{dt}({}^A\boldsymbol{x}_B){}^Bp_x + \frac{d}{dt}({}^A\boldsymbol{y}_B){}^Bp_y + \frac{d}{dt}({}^A\boldsymbol{z}_B){}^Bp_z \\ &= {}^A\omega_B \times {}^A\boldsymbol{x}_B{}^Bp_x + {}^A\omega_B \times {}^A\boldsymbol{y}_B{}^Bp_y + {}^A\omega_B \times {}^A\boldsymbol{z}_B{}^Bp_z \\ &= {}^A\omega_B \times ({}^A\boldsymbol{x}_B{}^Bp_x + {}^A\boldsymbol{y}_B{}^Bp_y + {}^A\boldsymbol{z}_B{}^Bp_z) \\ &= {}^A\omega_B \times ({}^A\boldsymbol{R}_B{}^B\boldsymbol{p}).\end{aligned} \tag{2.88}$$

Here $\times$ denotes the vector product which is defined for any two vectors ${}^A\boldsymbol{a} = [a_x,a_y,a_z]^T$ and ${}^A\boldsymbol{b} = [b_x,b_y,b_z]^T$ by

$$^A\boldsymbol{a} \times {}^A\boldsymbol{b} = {}^A\boldsymbol{c}, \tag{2.89}$$

where

$$^A\boldsymbol{c} = \begin{bmatrix} a_y b_z - a_z b_y \\ a_z b_x - a_x b_z \\ a_x b_y - a_y b_x \end{bmatrix}. \tag{2.90}$$

Consequently, from equations 2.87 and 2.88 we obtain

$$\frac{d}{dt}({}^A\boldsymbol{R}_B {}^B\boldsymbol{p}) = {}^A\boldsymbol{R}_B \frac{d}{dt}({}^B\boldsymbol{p}) + {}^A\omega_B \times ({}^A\boldsymbol{R}_B {}^B\boldsymbol{p}). \tag{2.91}$$

This equation is often used to derive relations among the link velocities and the link accelerations of a manipulator.

Next we will establish a relation among relative velocities of three moving frames, Σ_A, Σ_B, and Σ_C. Take Σ_A as the reference frame. As in figure 2.35, denote the vector from O_A to O_B expressed in Σ_A as ${}^A\boldsymbol{p}_B$, the vector from O_A to O_C expressed in Σ_A as ${}^A\boldsymbol{p}_C$, and the vector from O_B to O_C expressed in Σ_B as ${}^B\boldsymbol{p}_{CB}$. Similarly, the angular velocities of Σ_B and Σ_C with respect to Σ_A are ${}^A\omega_B$ and ${}^A\omega_C$, respectively, and the angular velocity of Σ_C with respect to Σ_B is ${}^B\omega_{CB}$. Then the following relations hold:

$${}^A\boldsymbol{p}_C = {}^A\boldsymbol{p}_B + {}^A\boldsymbol{R}_B {}^B\boldsymbol{p}_{CB}, \tag{2.92}$$

$${}^A\omega_C = {}^A\omega_B + {}^A\boldsymbol{R}_B {}^B\omega_{CB}. \tag{2.93}$$

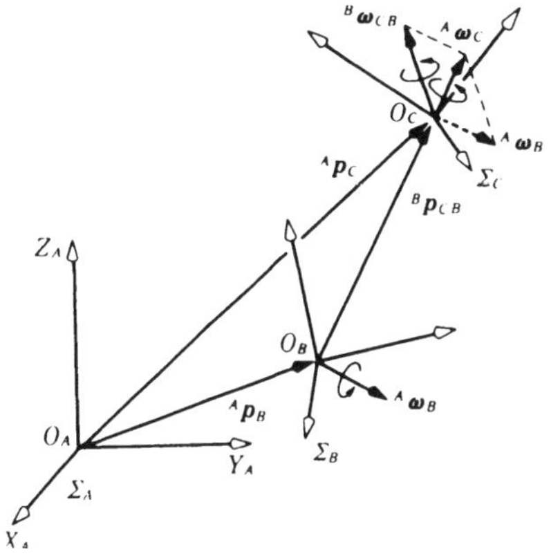

Figure 2.35
Relative velocities among frames.

Differentiating equation 2.92 with respect to time and substituting equation 2.91 yields

$$
\begin{aligned}
{}^A\dot{p}_C &= {}^A\dot{p}_B + \frac{d}{dt}({}^A R_B\, {}^B p_{CB}) \\
&= {}^A\dot{p}_B + {}^A R_B \frac{d}{dt}({}^B p_{CB}) + {}^A\omega_B \times ({}^A R_B\, {}^B p_{CB}),
\end{aligned} \tag{2.94}
$$

where ${}^A\dot{p}_B = d\,{}^A p_B/dt$. Thus, equation 2.93 is the relation between the rotational velocities of Σ_B and Σ_C with respect to Σ_A, and equation 2.94 is that between the translational velocities.

Now we will use the equations obtained above to derive the relations among the link velocities of a serial-link manipulator. We define the numbers of links and joints as in subsection 2.3.2, and attach link frame Σ_i to each link as in subsection 2.3.3. As is shown in figure 2.36, ${}^0p_i$ denotes the vector from the origin of Σ_0, O_0, to the origin of Σ_i, O_i, expressed in Σ_0, and ${}^{i-1}\hat{p}_i$ denotes the vector from O_{i-1} to O_i, expressed in Σ_{i-1}. Note that ${}^{i-1}\hat{p}_i$ is given by

$$[a_{i-1}, -\sin\alpha_{i-1} d_i, \cos\alpha_{i-1} d_i]^T$$

from equation 2.45. Regarding velocities, we denote the rotational and translational velocities of link i with respect to the base as ${}^0\omega_i$ and ${}^0\dot{p}_i = d({}^0p_i)/dt$, respectively. We further denote the upper left 3×3 submatrix of

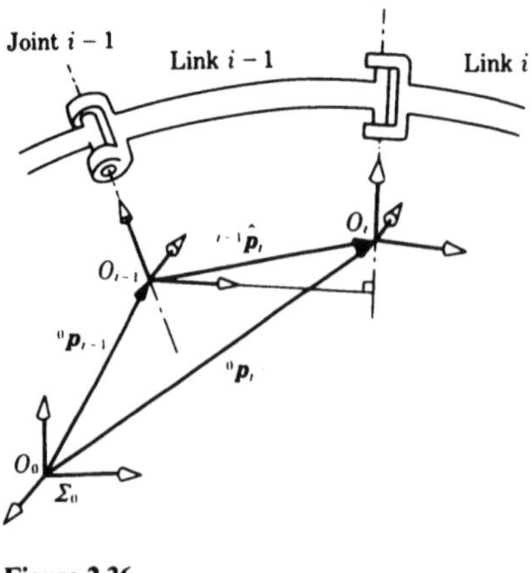

Figure 2.36
Vectors ${}^0p_i$ and ${}^{i-1}\hat{p}_i$.

${}^{j}T_i$ as ${}^{j}R_i$ because it is a rotation matrix. Then, by a correspondence of $\Sigma_A \leftrightarrow \Sigma_0$, $\Sigma_B \leftrightarrow \Sigma_{i-1}$, and $\Sigma_C \leftrightarrow \Sigma_i$ between two sets of frames $\{\Sigma_A, \Sigma_B, \Sigma_C\}$ and $\{\Sigma_0, \Sigma_{i-1}, \Sigma_i\}$, we obtain the following results:

Revolute Joint If joint i is revolute, the angle θ_i is the joint variable q_i, and ${}^{i-1}\hat{p}_i$ is a constant vector. Since ${}^{i-1}\omega_{i,i-1}$, the rotational velocity of Σ_i with respect to Σ_{i-1}, is a vector in the direction of the Z_i axis with magnitude $\dot{q}_i$:

$$ {}^{i-1}\omega_{i,i-1} = {}^{i-1}R_i[0,0,1]^T\dot{q}_i. $$

Hence, from equations 2.93 and 2.94 we obtain

$$ {}^{0}\omega_i = {}^{0}\omega_{i-1} + {}^{0}R_i e_z \dot{q}_i, \tag{2.95} $$

$$ {}^{0}\dot{p}_i = {}^{0}\dot{p}_{i-1} + {}^{0}\omega_{i-1} \times ({}^{0}R_{i-1}\,{}^{i-1}\hat{p}_i), \tag{2.96} $$

where

$$ e_z = [0,0,1]^T. \tag{2.97} $$

Prismatic Joint If joint i is prismatic, then the distance d_i is the joint variable q_i,

$$ d({}^{i-1}\hat{p}_i) = {}^{i-1}R_i e_z \dot{q}_i, $$

and

$$ {}^{i-1}\omega_{i,i-1} = \mathbf{0}. $$

Thus we obtain

$$ {}^{0}\omega_i = {}^{0}\omega_{i-1}, \tag{2.98} $$

$$ {}^{0}\dot{p}_i = {}^{0}\dot{p}_{i-1} + {}^{0}R_i e_z \dot{q}_i + {}^{0}\omega_{i-1} \times ({}^{0}R_{i-1}\,{}^{i-1}\hat{p}_i). \tag{2.99} $$

2.5.4 General Expression of the Jacobian Matrix J_v

Here we will derive a general expression of the Jacobian matrix J_v in equation 2.85 based on the result of the previous subsection. Since the end-effector frame Σ_E and the link frame Σ_n are both fixed to link n, we obtain the following expression of the end-effector velocity from equations 2.93 and 2.94 by considering the correspondence of $\Sigma_A \leftrightarrow \Sigma_0$, $\Sigma_B \leftrightarrow \Sigma_n$, and $\Sigma_C \leftrightarrow \Sigma_E$:

$$ {}^{0}\omega_E = {}^{0}\omega_n, \tag{2.100} $$

$$ {}^{0}\dot{p}_E = {}^{0}\dot{p}_n + {}^{0}\omega_n \times ({}^{0}R_n\,{}^{n}\hat{p}_E). \tag{2.101} $$

From equations 2.95–2.101 and ${}^0\omega_0 = {}^0\dot{p}_0 = \mathbf{0}$, we can express ${}^0\omega_E$ and ${}^0\dot{\boldsymbol{p}}_E$ as linear functions of $\dot{q}_1, \dot{q}_2, \ldots, \dot{q}_n$. From these linear functions we can obtain an expression for $\boldsymbol{J}_v$. For example, if all n joints are revolute, we have from equations 2.100, 2.101, 2.95, and 2.96

$$
{}^0\omega_E = \sum_{i=1}^{n} {}^0\boldsymbol{R}_i \boldsymbol{e}_z \dot{q}_i, \tag{2.102}
$$

$$
{}^0\dot{\boldsymbol{p}}_E = \sum_{j=1}^{n} \left[({}^0\boldsymbol{R}_j \boldsymbol{e}_z \dot{q}_j) \times \left(\sum_{i=j}^{n} {}^0\boldsymbol{R}_i {}^i\hat{\boldsymbol{p}}_{i+1} \right) \right], \tag{2.103}
$$

where ${}^n\hat{\boldsymbol{p}}_{n+1} = {}^n\hat{\boldsymbol{p}}_E$ for notational convenience. Defining ${}^0\boldsymbol{z}_i$ and ${}^0\boldsymbol{p}_{E,j}$ by

$$
{}^0\boldsymbol{z}_i \mathrel{\hat{=}} {}^0\boldsymbol{R}_i \boldsymbol{e}_z \tag{2.104}
$$

and

$$
{}^0\boldsymbol{p}_{E,i} \mathrel{\hat{=}} \sum_{j=i}^{n} {}^0\boldsymbol{R}_j {}^j\hat{\boldsymbol{p}}_{j+1} = {}^0\boldsymbol{p}_{E,i+1} + {}^0\boldsymbol{R}_i {}^i\hat{\boldsymbol{p}}_{i+1}, \tag{2.105}
$$

we obtain

$$
\boldsymbol{J}_v = \begin{bmatrix} {}^0\boldsymbol{z}_1 \times {}^0\boldsymbol{p}_{E,1} & {}^0\boldsymbol{z}_2 \times {}^0\boldsymbol{p}_{E,2} & \cdots & {}^0\boldsymbol{z}_n \times {}^0\boldsymbol{p}_{E,n} \\ {}^0\boldsymbol{z}_1 & {}^0\boldsymbol{z}_2 & \cdots & {}^0\boldsymbol{z}_n \end{bmatrix}. \tag{2.106}
$$

As illustrated in figure 2.37, ${}^0\boldsymbol{z}_i$ represents joint axis i, and ${}^0\boldsymbol{p}_{E,i}$ represents the vector from a point on joint axis i to the end effector. Thus, the ith row vector of matrix $\boldsymbol{J}_v$ implies a very natural result: that the translational velocity of the end effector is given by $({}^0\boldsymbol{z}_i \times {}^0\boldsymbol{p}_{E,i})\dot{q}_i$ and the rotational

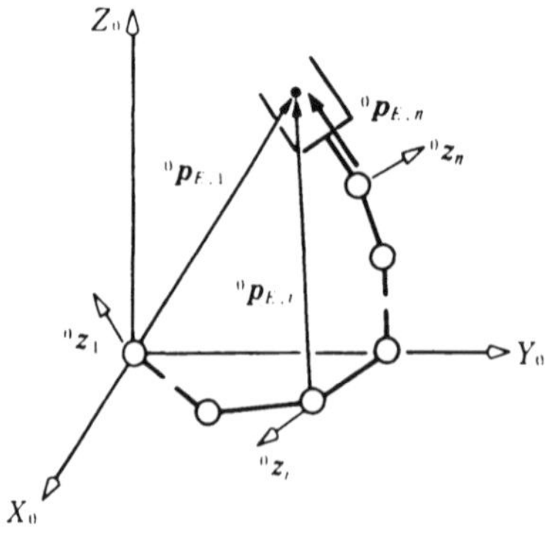

Figure 2.37
Vectors ${}^0\boldsymbol{z}_i$ and ${}^0\boldsymbol{p}_{E,i}$.

velocity is given by ${}^0z_i\dot{q}_i$. For more general manipulators with both revolute and prismatic joints, a similar argument leads to

$$J_v = [J_{v1}, J_{v2}, \dots, J_{vn}], \tag{2.107}$$

where

$$J_{vi} = \begin{cases} \begin{bmatrix} {}^0z_i \times {}^0p_{E,i} \\ {}^0z_i \end{bmatrix} & \text{if joint } i \text{ is revolute,} \\ \begin{bmatrix} {}^0z_i \\ \mathbf{0} \end{bmatrix} & \text{if joint } i \text{ is prismatic.} \end{cases} \tag{2.108}$$

Hence, we can calculate J_v from ${}^0T_i$ $(i = 1, 2, \dots, n+1)$ by using the following relations:

$${}^0T_i = \left[\begin{array}{ccc|c} {}^0x_i & {}^0y_i & {}^0z_i & {}^0p_i \\ \hline 0 & 0 & 0 & 1 \end{array}\right], \quad i = 1, 2, \dots, n+1, \tag{2.109}$$

$${}^0p_{E,i} = {}^0p_E - {}^0p_i. \tag{2.110}$$

The first three elements of J_{vi} can also be calculated from $\partial({}^0p_E)/\partial q_i$.

Example 2.17 Let us find the Jacobian matrix for the PUMA-type manipulator in figure 2.23, assuming that the end-effector frame is assigned as shown in figure 2.25. Using ${}^0T_i$ obtained in example 2.11 and ${}^nT_E$ given in example 2.12, we can calculate the first three rows of J_v by $\partial({}^0p_E)/\partial q^T$ and the remaining three rows by ${}^0z_i$ $(i = 1, 2, \dots, n)$. The result is as follows:

$$J_{v1} = \begin{bmatrix} -p_y - R_{23}l_g \\ p_x + R_{13}l_g \\ 0 \\ 0 \\ 0 \\ 1 \end{bmatrix},$$

$$J_{v2} = \begin{bmatrix} C_1 p_z + C_1 R_{33} l_g \\ S_1 p_z + S_1 R_{33} l_g \\ -l_c C_2 - l_e C_{23} + l_f S_{23} + (C_{23} C_2 S_5 + S_{23} C_5) l_g \\ -S_1 \\ C_1 \\ 0 \end{bmatrix},$$

$$J_{v3} = \begin{bmatrix} -C_1(l_e S_{23} + l_f C_{23}) + C_1 R_{33} l_g \\ -S_1(l_e S_{23} + l_f C_{23}) + S_1 R_{33} l_g \\ -l_e C_{23} + l_f S_{23} + (C_{23} C_4 S_5 + S_{23} C_5) l_g \\ -S_1 \\ C_1 \\ 0 \end{bmatrix},$$

$$J_{v4} = \begin{bmatrix} (C_1 C_{23} S_4 S_5 - S_1 C_4 S_5) l_g \\ (S_1 C_{23} S_4 S_5 - C_1 C_4 S_5) l_g \\ -S_{23} S_4 S_5 l_g \\ -C_1 S_{23} \\ -S_1 S_{23} \\ -C_{23} \end{bmatrix},$$

$$J_{v5} = \begin{bmatrix} -[C_1(C_{23} C_4 C_5 - S_{23} S_5) + S_1 S_4 C_5] l_g \\ -[S_1(C_{23} C_4 C_5 - S_{23} S_5) + C_1 S_4 C_5] l_g \\ (S_{23} C_4 C_5 + C_{23} S_5) l_g \\ C_1 C_{23} S_4 - S_1 C_4 \\ S_1 C_{23} S_4 + C_1 C_4 \\ -S_{23} S_4 \end{bmatrix},$$

$$J_{v6} = \begin{bmatrix} 0 \\ 0 \\ 0 \\ R_{13} \\ R_{23} \\ R_{33} \end{bmatrix}. \square$$

2.5.5 Joint Velocity for Achieving Desired End-Effector Velocity

We now know how to calculate the position of the end effector, $\boldsymbol{r}$, for a given joint position $\boldsymbol{q}$, and how to find the $\boldsymbol{q}$ that achieves a given $\boldsymbol{r}$. We also know that the end-effector velocity $\boldsymbol{v}$ for a given joint velocity $\dot{\boldsymbol{q}}$ can be calculated by equation 2.85. In this subsection we will consider the problem of finding the joint velocity, $\dot{\boldsymbol{q}}$, that results in a given end-effector velocity $\boldsymbol{v}$ (or $\dot{\boldsymbol{r}}$). This can be regarded as a problem of inverse kinematics in a broader sense.

First, consider the case where $n = 6$ and $\boldsymbol{J}_v$ is nonsingular. Then from equation 2.85 we have

$$\dot{q} = J_v^{-1} v. \tag{2.111}$$

Hence, in principle we can obtain $\dot{q}$ by calculating the inverse of J_v and multiplying it by v. In practice, however, it requires less computation to solve the algebraic equation 2.85 directly by some numerical algorithm such as Gauss' elimination method. When an analytical solution to the inverse kinematics problem is available, as in example 2.14, it is also possible to reduce the amount of computation by using the equation derived from the differentiation of the analytical solution (ref. 5).

We next consider the case when $n \geqq 7$ and the rank of $J_v = 6$. Then, using equation A2.22 in appendix 2, the general solution of equation 2.85 is given by

$$\dot{q} = J_v^{+} v + (\mathbf{I} - J_v^{+} J_v)k, \tag{2.112}$$

where J_v^{+} is the pseudo-inverse of J_v and where k is an arbitrary n-dimensional constant vector. This k implies that there are an infinite number of solutions to equation 2.85. It also implies that the manipulator has some redundancy in its configuration if the task is only to position and orient its end effector. However, once the value of k is given somehow, we can calculate $\dot{q}$ from equation 2.112. Exploiting redundancy will be discussed in detail in chapter 7.

We can also obtain the joint velocity $\dot{q}$ that realizes the given end-effector velocity $\dot{r}$ by using J_r instead of J_v. For example, if J_r is nonsingular, we obtain instead of equation 2.111

$$\dot{q} = J_r^{-1} \dot{r}. \tag{2.113}$$

We should be careful, however, about the fact that when the manipulator is at the representational singularity described in subsection 2.5.1, we cannot use equation 2.113 because J_r is singular.

2.5.6 Singular Configurations

In section 1.1 it was pointed out that even for wrist mechanisms with three degrees of freedom, there are configurations for which the end effector cannot be rotated about a certain axis. Those configurations were called *singular configurations*. Such situations are not limited to the end-effector orientations; they also exist for end-effector positions. For example, consider the two-link manipulator shown in figure 2.38. If its configuration is given by A in the figure, which is different from B ($\theta_2 = 0°$) and C ($\theta_2 =$

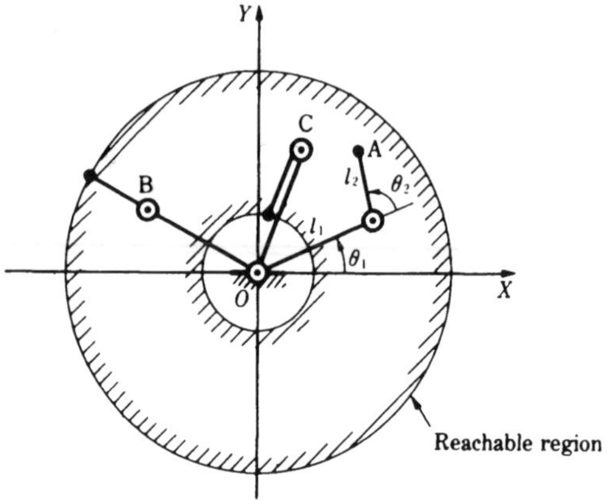

Figure 2.38
Singular configurations of two-link manipulator.

180°), then any desired velocity of the endpoint in the $X-Y$ plane is realizable by a finite joint velocity. However, at configurations B and C a velocity that has a nonzero component in the direction from the origin O to the endpoint cannot be realized by any finite joint velocity. Generalizing this situation, we define the singular configurations of a general n-link manipulator as those for which end-effector velocities (translational velocities, rotational velocities, or their combinations) in a certain direction cannot be realized by any finite joint velocity.

We will now define the above concept of singular configurations more mathematically, using the Jacobian matrix. Let us consider an n-link manipulator and denote its Jacobian matrix as $\boldsymbol{J}_v$. Let an integer n' be given by

$$n' = \max_{\boldsymbol{q}} \operatorname{rank} \boldsymbol{J}_v(\boldsymbol{q}). \tag{2.114}$$

If a configuration $\boldsymbol{q} = \boldsymbol{q}_s$ satisfies

$$\operatorname{rank} \boldsymbol{J}_v(\boldsymbol{q}) < n', \tag{2.115}$$

then we define this $\boldsymbol{q}_s$ as the *singular configuration.* Equation 2.114 means that the manipulator under consideration has the ability to produce any end-effector velocity vector in some n'-dimensional space at any configuration other than an exceptional configuration. Equation 2.115 implies that we call these exceptional configurations singular. Note that if $n > 6$ we have $n' = 6$, and that if $n \leq 6$ we have $n' = n$, unless the mechanism is very special. Also note that if $n' = n = 6$, from equation 2.115 a necessary and sufficient condition for $\boldsymbol{q}$ to be a singular configuration is

$$\det \boldsymbol{J}_v(\boldsymbol{q}) = 0, \tag{2.116}$$

where $\det \boldsymbol{J}$ denotes the determinant of a matrix $\boldsymbol{J}$. Therefore, $\dot{\boldsymbol{q}}$ cannot be calculated by equation 2.111 or 2.112 at a singular configuration. Moreover, even when the configuration is not right at a singular configuration, if it is close to one, $\dot{\boldsymbol{q}}$ calculated from equation 2.111 or 2.112 may become so excessively large that this $\dot{\boldsymbol{q}}$ cannot be achieved.

We can determine the singular configurations from $\boldsymbol{J}_r$ instead of $\boldsymbol{J}_v$. Let n' be given by

$$n' = \max_{\boldsymbol{q}} \operatorname{rank} \boldsymbol{J}_r(\boldsymbol{q}). \tag{2.117}$$

Then the singular configurations always satisfy

$$\operatorname{rank} \boldsymbol{J}_r(\boldsymbol{q}) < n'. \tag{2.118}$$

However, since the set of $\boldsymbol{q}$ satisfying inequality 2.118 includes not only the real singular configurations but also representational ones, we need to check whether a singular configuration is a real one or not. When $n = n' \leqq 6$ and $\boldsymbol{J}_r$ is square, a necessary condition for a $\boldsymbol{q}$ to be singular is given by

$$\det \boldsymbol{J}_r(\boldsymbol{q}) = 0. \tag{2.119}$$

Example 2.18 We will now check that the singular configurations of the two-link manipulator in figure 2.38 are given by B and C in the figure. Let $\boldsymbol{r} = [x,y]^T$ and $\boldsymbol{q} = [\theta_1,\theta_2]^T$; then the Jacobian $\boldsymbol{J}_r$ is

$$\boldsymbol{J}_r = \begin{bmatrix} -l_1 S_1 - l_2 S_{12} & -l_2 S_{12} \\ l_1 C_1 + l_2 C_{12} & l_2 C_{12} \end{bmatrix}.$$

Thus we have

$$\det \boldsymbol{J}_r = l_1 l_2 S_2.$$

Since there is obviously no representational singularity, we can conclude from equation 2.119 that the singular configurations are given by $\theta_2 = 0°$ or $\theta_2 = 180°$. □

For the two-link manipulator in example 2.18, the hatched region in figure 2.38 represents the zone of points which the manipulator end effector can reach in the $X-Y$ plane. This is called the *reachable region*. In the case of a general manipulator with an m-dimensional end-effector vector, the reachable region is also of dimension m. Although the singular configurations in the above example are all on the boundary of the reachable region, this is not always true. Singular configurations can also exist inside the reachable region, as example 2.19 shows.

Example 2.19 For PUMA-type manipulators with no offsets (i.e., for manipulators in figure 2.23 with $l_b = l_d = l_e = 0$), there are three kinds of singular configurations, shown in figure 2.39. Those shown in diagram a are called *shoulder singularities* (the wrist position is right above the shoulder); those in diagram b are called *elbow singularities* (the elbow is stretched straight); those in diagram c are called *wrist singularities* (the wrist is stretched straight).[9] The singularities of diagram b are on the boundary of the reachable region, but those of diagrams a and c can be inside the reachable region. □

There are two approaches for coping with the performance deterioration due to singular configurations. One is simply to avoid using the singular configurations and their neighboring region by planning the given task carefully. Another is to change the mechanism design. We can, for example, move the singular configurations to an unimportant area of the reachable region by some sophisticated mechanism, or we can add some extra degrees of freedom to the manipulator so that the singular configurations can be avoided by means of the added redundancy.[10]

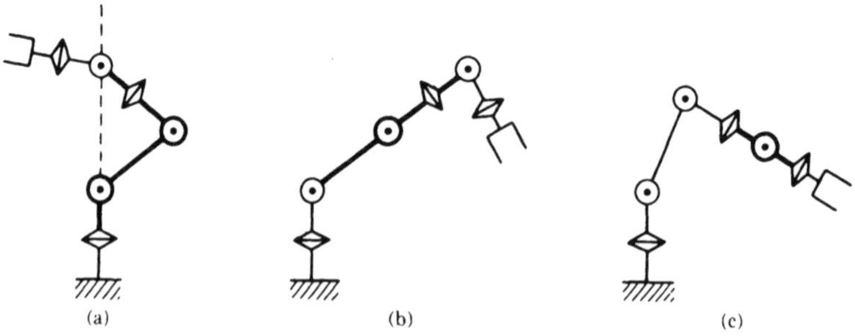

Figure 2.39
Singular configurations. (a) Shoulder singularities. (b) Elbow singularities. (c) Wrist singularities.

2.6 Statics and Jacobian Matrices

2.6.1 Equivalent Forces Represented in Different Frames

Suppose that two coordinate frames, Σ_B and Σ_C, are fixed to an object as shown in figure 2.40, and that the object is moving relative to a reference frame, Σ_A. From equations 2.93 and 2.94, the relation between the velocities of Σ_B and Σ_C, relative to Σ_A and expressed in Σ_A, is given by

$$ {}^{A}\omega_C = {}^{A}\omega_B, \tag{2.120}$$

$$ {}^{A}\dot{p}_C = {}^{A}\dot{p}_B + {}^{A}\omega_B \times ({}^{A}R_B\,{}^{B}p_{CB}). \tag{2.121}$$

Putting the above equations together, we have

$$\begin{bmatrix} {}^{A}\dot{p}_C \\ {}^{A}\omega_C \end{bmatrix} = \begin{bmatrix} \mathbf{I} & -[{}^{A}p_{CB}\times] \\ \mathbf{0} & \mathbf{I} \end{bmatrix} \begin{bmatrix} {}^{A}\dot{p}_B \\ {}^{A}\omega_B \end{bmatrix}, \tag{2.122}$$

where the notation $[\cdot\times]$ denotes, for an arbitrary three-dimensional vector $a = [a_x, a_y, a_z]^T$,

$$[a\times] = \begin{bmatrix} 0 & -a_z & a_y \\ a_z & 0 & -a_x \\ -a_y & a_x & 0 \end{bmatrix}. \tag{2.123}$$

Note that, from the above definition, the following two equalities hold for

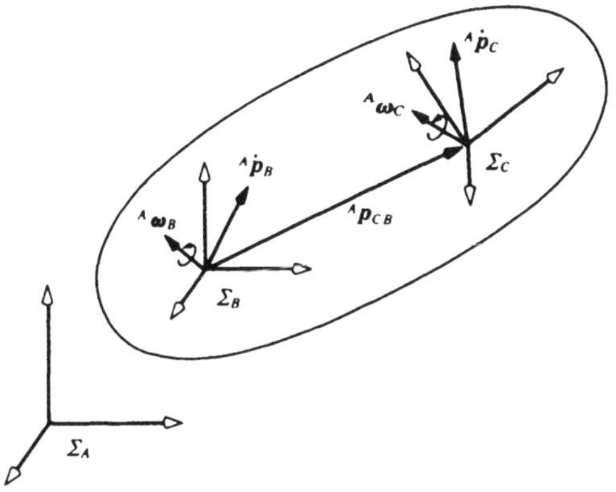

Figure 2.40
Frames Σ_B and Σ_C fixed to an object.

two arbitrary three-dimensional vectors, $\boldsymbol{a}$ and $\boldsymbol{b}$:

$$[\boldsymbol{a} \times]\boldsymbol{b} = \boldsymbol{a} \times \boldsymbol{b}, \tag{2.124}$$

$$[\boldsymbol{a} \times]^T = -[\boldsymbol{a} \times]. \tag{2.125}$$

Also note that, when we denote the vectors $\boldsymbol{a}$ and $\boldsymbol{b}$ expressed in Σ_B as ${}^B\boldsymbol{a}$ and ${}^B\boldsymbol{b}$, respectively, we have from equation 2.90

$$({}^A\boldsymbol{R}_B{}^B\boldsymbol{a}) \times ({}^A\boldsymbol{R}_B{}^B\boldsymbol{b}) = {}^A\boldsymbol{R}_B({}^B\boldsymbol{a} \times {}^B\boldsymbol{b}).$$

Now we denote the vectors ${}^A\dot{\boldsymbol{p}}_C$ and ${}^A\boldsymbol{\omega}_C$ expressed in Σ_B as ${}^C\dot{\boldsymbol{p}}_{CA}$ and ${}^C\boldsymbol{\omega}_{CA}$, respectively, and define ${}^B\dot{\boldsymbol{p}}_{BA}$ and ${}^B\boldsymbol{\omega}_{BA}$ similarly. Then, using the rotation matrices ${}^A\boldsymbol{R}_B$ and ${}^A\boldsymbol{R}_C$, we find

$${}^A\dot{\boldsymbol{p}}_C = {}^A\boldsymbol{R}_C{}^C\dot{\boldsymbol{p}}_{CA}, \quad {}^A\boldsymbol{\omega}_C = {}^A\boldsymbol{R}_C{}^C\boldsymbol{\omega}_{CA},$$

$${}^A\dot{\boldsymbol{p}}_B = {}^A\boldsymbol{R}_B{}^B\dot{\boldsymbol{p}}_{BA}, \quad {}^A\boldsymbol{\omega}_B = {}^A\boldsymbol{R}_B{}^B\boldsymbol{\omega}_{BA}.$$

Thus we have

$$\begin{bmatrix} {}^C\dot{\boldsymbol{p}}_{CA} \\ {}^C\boldsymbol{\omega}_{CA} \end{bmatrix} = \boldsymbol{J}_{CB}\begin{bmatrix} {}^B\dot{\boldsymbol{p}}_{BA} \\ {}^B\boldsymbol{\omega}_{BA} \end{bmatrix}, \tag{2.126}$$

where

$$\boldsymbol{J}_{CB} = \begin{bmatrix} {}^C\boldsymbol{R}_B & -{}^C\boldsymbol{R}_B[{}^B\boldsymbol{p}_{CB} \times] \\ \boldsymbol{0} & {}^C\boldsymbol{R}_B \end{bmatrix}. \tag{2.127}$$

The matrix $\boldsymbol{J}_{CB}$ is the Jacobian matrix relating the velocities of Σ_B and Σ_C with respect to Σ_A. This $\boldsymbol{J}_{CB}$ is determined from the homogeneous transform ${}^B\boldsymbol{T}_C$ (that is, ${}^B\boldsymbol{R}_C$ and ${}^B\boldsymbol{p}_{CB}$) relating Σ_B and Σ_C, and it is independent of Σ_A.

On the other hand, let ${}^A\boldsymbol{f}_C$ and ${}^A\boldsymbol{n}_C$ denote the force and moment acting on the origin of Σ_C, which are equivalent to the force ${}^A\boldsymbol{f}_B$ and moment ${}^A\boldsymbol{n}_B$ acting on the origin of Σ_B. Then

$${}^A\boldsymbol{f}_B = {}^A\boldsymbol{f}_C, \tag{2.128}$$

$${}^A\boldsymbol{n}_B = {}^A\boldsymbol{n}_C + {}^A\boldsymbol{p}_{CB} \times {}^A\boldsymbol{f}_C. \tag{2.129}$$

From these equations we obtain the following equations in a way similar to the way we obtained equation 2.126:

$$\begin{bmatrix} {}^B\boldsymbol{f}_B \\ {}^B\boldsymbol{n}_B \end{bmatrix} = \begin{bmatrix} {}^B\boldsymbol{R}_C & \boldsymbol{0} \\ [{}^B\boldsymbol{p}_{CB} \times]{}^B\boldsymbol{R}_C & {}^B\boldsymbol{R}_C \end{bmatrix}\begin{bmatrix} {}^C\boldsymbol{f}_C \\ {}^C\boldsymbol{n}_C \end{bmatrix}. \tag{2.130}$$

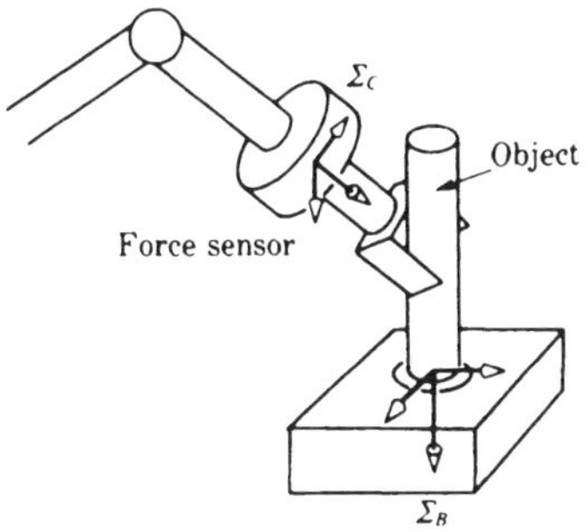

Figure 2.41
Object frame Σ_B and force sensor frame Σ_C.

From equations 2.130 and 2.127, we finally obtain

$$\begin{bmatrix} {}^B\boldsymbol{f}_B \\ {}^B\boldsymbol{n}_B \end{bmatrix} = \boldsymbol{J}_{CB}{}^T \begin{bmatrix} {}^C\boldsymbol{f}_C \\ {}^C\boldsymbol{n}_C \end{bmatrix}. \tag{2.131}$$

Note the fact (observed from equations 2.126 and 2.131) that the Jacobian matrix $\boldsymbol{J}_{CB}$ relates the velocities of Σ_B and Σ_C, whereas the transpose of $\boldsymbol{J}_{CB}$ relates the forces and moments of Σ_C and Σ_B.

Example 2.20 Suppose that a hand is grasping an object as shown in figure 2.41, and that we can use the wrist force sensor to measure the force and moment occurring at the wrist expressed in the sensor frame Σ_C. We want to know the force and moment exerted on the tip of the object expressed in the object frame Σ_B fixed to the tip from the sensor output. We assume that the hand is not moving, and that the relative position of Σ_C with respect to Σ_B is known. We also neglect the gravity force. This problem can be solved by the following procedure: We first obtain ${}^B\boldsymbol{T}_C$ and calculate $\boldsymbol{J}_{CB}{}^T$ by using the relation

$${}^B\boldsymbol{T}_C = \left[\begin{array}{ccc|c} & {}^B\boldsymbol{R}_C & & {}^B\boldsymbol{p}_{CB} \\ \hline 0 & 0 & 0 & 1 \end{array}\right].$$

Next we determine the force (${}^B\boldsymbol{f}_B$) and the moment (${}^B\boldsymbol{n}_B$) exerted on the tip of the object by substituting the sensor output (${}^C\boldsymbol{f}_C$ and ${}^C\boldsymbol{n}_C$) into equation 2.131. For example, when the sensor output is given by ${}^C\boldsymbol{f}_C = [30, -10, -50]^T$ (in newtons) and ${}^C\boldsymbol{n}_C = [0.5, 0.2, 0]^T$ (in newton-meters), then ${}^B\boldsymbol{T}_C$ is given by

$$
{}^{B}T_C = \begin{bmatrix} 1/\sqrt{2} & 0 & 1/\sqrt{2} & -0.025\sqrt{2} \\ 0 & 1 & 0 & 0 \\ -1/\sqrt{2} & 0 & 1/\sqrt{2} & -0.025\sqrt{2}-0.06 \\ 0 & 0 & 0 & 1 \end{bmatrix}.
$$

Hence,

$$
J_{CB}{}^T = \begin{bmatrix} 1/\sqrt{2} & 0 & 1/\sqrt{2} & 0 & 0 & 0 \\ 0 & 1 & 0 & 0 & 0 & 0 \\ -1/\sqrt{2} & 0 & 1/\sqrt{2} & 0 & 0 & 0 \\ 0 & 0.025\sqrt{2}+0.06 & 0 & 1/\sqrt{2} & 0 & 1/\sqrt{2} \\ -0.05-0.03\sqrt{2} & 0 & -0.03\sqrt{2} & 0 & 1 & 0 \\ 0 & -0.025\sqrt{2} & 0 & -1/\sqrt{2} & 0 & 1/\sqrt{2} \end{bmatrix}.
$$

Therefore, we find

$${}^{B}\boldsymbol{f}_B = [-10/\sqrt{2},\ -10,\ -40\sqrt{2}]^T \text{ (N)},$$

$${}^{B}\boldsymbol{n}_B = [-0.6,\ -1.3+0.6\sqrt{2}, 0]^T \text{ (Nm)}. \quad \square$$

2.6.2 Joint Driving Force Equivalent to Force Applied to Tip of Manipulator

For an n-link manipulator, let us consider the problem of finding the joint driving force, $\boldsymbol{\tau} = [\tau_1, \tau_2, \ldots, \tau_n]^T$, which is equivalent to the force ${}^{0}\boldsymbol{f}_{\mathrm{E}}$ and moment ${}^{0}\boldsymbol{n}_{\mathrm{E}}$ applied to the origin of the end-effector frame Σ_{E}. Here τ_i is the joint driving force exerted at joint i between links $i-1$ and i. When joint i is revolute, τ_i is a torque about the Z_i axis; when joint i is prismatic, τ_i is a force along the Z_i axis.

By the correspondences $\Sigma_A \leftrightarrow \Sigma_0$, $\Sigma_B \leftrightarrow \Sigma_i$, and $\Sigma_C \leftrightarrow \Sigma_{\mathrm{E}}$, we obtain from equations 2.128 and 2.129

$${}^{0}\boldsymbol{f}_i = {}^{0}\boldsymbol{f}_{\mathrm{E}}, \tag{2.132}$$

$${}^{0}\boldsymbol{n}_i = {}^{0}\boldsymbol{n}_{\mathrm{E}} + {}^{0}\boldsymbol{p}_{\mathrm{E},i} \times {}^{0}\boldsymbol{f}_{\mathrm{E}}. \tag{2.133}$$

The relation between τ_i and the pair $\{{}^{0}\boldsymbol{f}_i, {}^{0}\boldsymbol{n}_i\}$ is

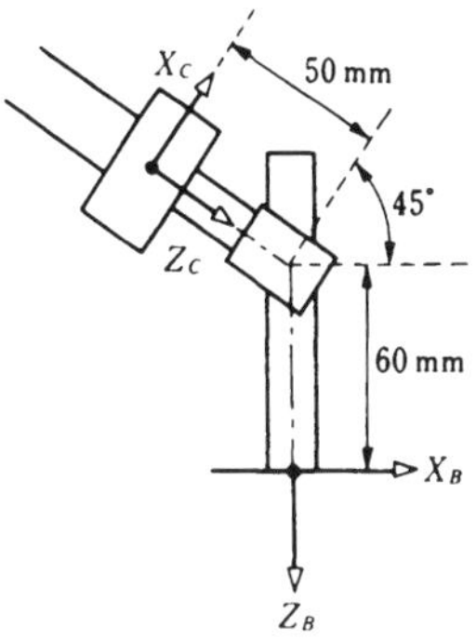

Figure 2.42
Relation between Σ_B and Σ_C.

$$\begin{aligned}\tau_i &= {}^0z_i^{\,T}\,{}^0\boldsymbol{n}_i \\ &= {}^0z_i^{\,T}\,{}^0\boldsymbol{n}_E + {}^0z_i^{\,T}({}^0\boldsymbol{p}_{E,i} \times {}^0\boldsymbol{f}_E) \\ &= {}^0z_i^{\,T}\,{}^0\boldsymbol{n}_E + ({}^0z_i \times {}^0\boldsymbol{p}_{E,i})^T\,{}^0\boldsymbol{f}_E \end{aligned} \tag{2.134}$$

for revolute joints and

$$\tau_i = {}^0z_i^{\,T}\,{}^0\boldsymbol{f}_i = {}^0z_i^{\,T}\,{}^0\boldsymbol{f}_E \tag{2.135}$$

for prismatic joints. Hence, using $\boldsymbol{J}_v$ given by equation 2.107, we have

$$\boldsymbol{\tau} = \boldsymbol{J}_v^{\,T}\begin{bmatrix} {}^0\boldsymbol{f}_E \\ {}^0\boldsymbol{n}_E \end{bmatrix}. \tag{2.136}$$

The main results in this section, described by equations 2.131 and 2.136, can also be derived using the principle of virtual work (see reference 1). For example, equation 2.136 can be derived as follows: From equation 2.85, the virtual displacement of the end effector, $\delta\boldsymbol{d}$, expressed by Σ_0 corresponding to $\boldsymbol{v}$ and the virtual displacement of the joints, $\delta\boldsymbol{q}$, satisfies

$$\delta\boldsymbol{d} = \boldsymbol{J}_v\delta\boldsymbol{q}. \tag{2.137}$$

On the other hand, from the principle of virtual work we have

$$(\delta\boldsymbol{q})^T\boldsymbol{\tau} = (\delta\boldsymbol{d})^T\begin{bmatrix} {}^0\boldsymbol{f}_E \\ {}^0\boldsymbol{n}_E \end{bmatrix}. \tag{2.138}$$

Hence, from equations 2.137 and 2.138 we obtain

$$\tau = J_v{}^T \begin{bmatrix} {}^0f_E \\ {}^0n_E \end{bmatrix}. \tag{2.139}$$

Although we have discussed only positions and velocities in this chapter, a similar argument can also be developed for accelerations of objects and manipulator links. For example, by differentiating equation 2.81 we get the following relation between the acceleration of the manipulator joint, $\ddot{q}$, and the acceleration of the end effector, $\ddot{r}$:

$$\ddot{r} = J_r(q)\ddot{q} + \dot{J}_r(q)\dot{q}. \tag{2.140}$$

When the end-effector velocity is expressed by v, by differentiating equation 2.85 we obtain

$$\dot{v} = J_v(q)\ddot{q} + \dot{J}_v(q)\dot{q}. \tag{2.141}$$

Relations among the accelerations of manipulator links can also be derived by arguments similar to those in subsection 2.5.3. This will be done in subsection 3.4.2.

Exercises

2.1 Derive the roll, pitch, and yaw angles equivalent to a given rotation matrix (equation 2.22) in a form similar to equations 2.32 and 2.33.

2.2 Show that the Euler angles for a given rotation matrix (equation 2.22) can be expressed as

$$\phi = \text{atan2}(\pm R_{23}, \pm R_{13}),$$

$$\theta = \text{atan2}(\cos\phi R_{13} + \sin\phi R_{23}, R_{33}),$$

$$\psi = \text{atan2}(-\sin\phi R_{11} + \cos\phi R_{21}, -\sin\phi R_{12} + \cos\phi R_{22}).$$

2.3 The tetrahedron in figure 2.43 has an object frame Σ_B attached to its square corner. Give the position and orientation of the tetrahedron with respect to the reference frame Σ_A shown in figure 2.44. Use the rotation matrix to describe the orientation.

2.4 Solve exercise 2.3 using both the Euler-angles method and the method of roll, pitch, and yaw angles to describe the orientation.

2.5 Give the position and orientation of the tetrahedron in figure 2.43 when it is placed in Σ_A as shown in figure 2.45. Use Euler angles to describe

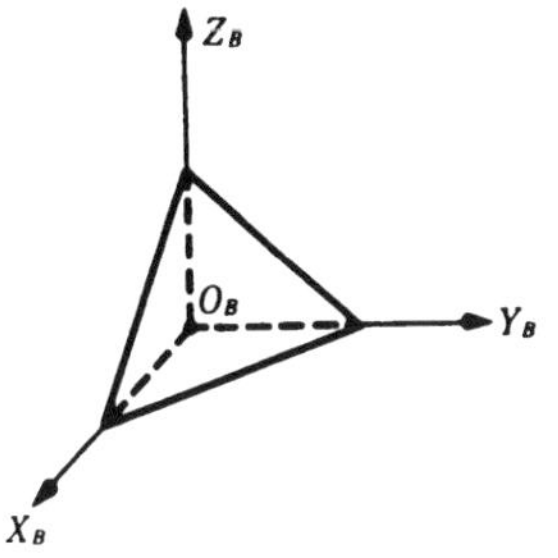

Figure 2.43
Object frame Σ_B.

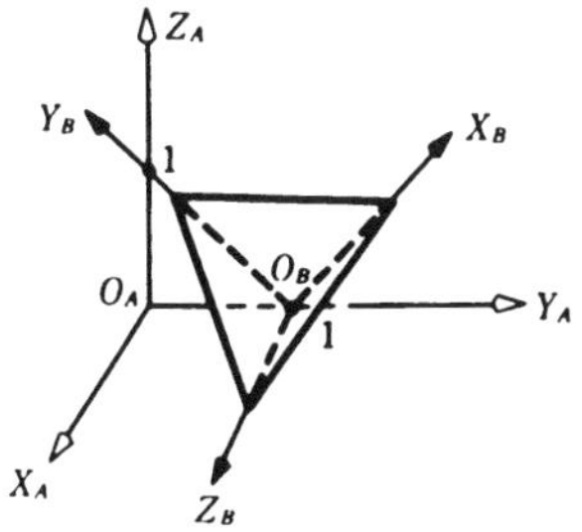

Figure 2.44
Object frame Σ_B and reference frame Σ_A.

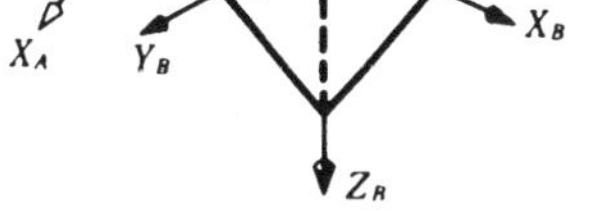

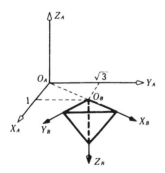

Figure 2.45
Expression of position and orientation of object. (Z_B and Z_A are parallel.)

the orientation. Explain the cases when there are infinitely many Euler-angle expressions of orientation.

2.6 A frame Σ_B, which was initially coincident with another frame Σ_A, is rotated about the Y_A axis by 30° and then translated 3 units along the X_A axis and 2 units along the Z_A axis. Give the relation between the description ${}^A\boldsymbol{r}$ of an arbitrary point in Σ_A and the description ${}^B\boldsymbol{r}$ of the same point in Σ_B by a homogeneous transform.

2.7 Generalizing the idea of describing a three-dimensional position vector ${}^A\boldsymbol{r}$ by a four-dimensional vector $[{}^A\boldsymbol{r}^T, 1]^T$, introduced in subsection 2.2.1, let us regard the four-dimensional vector $[x,y,z,k]^T$ as representing the three-dimensional position $[x/k, y/k, z/k]^T$. Under this convention, study the physical meanings of the following two homogeneous transforms:

$$\boldsymbol{T}_s = \begin{bmatrix} a & 0 & 0 & 0 \\ 0 & b & 0 & 0 \\ 0 & 0 & c & 0 \\ 0 & 0 & 0 & 1 \end{bmatrix},$$

where a, b, and c are positive constants, and

$$\boldsymbol{T}_p = \begin{bmatrix} 1 & 0 & 0 & 0 \\ 0 & 1 & 0 & 0 \\ 0 & 0 & 1 & 0 \\ 0 & -1/f & 0 & 1 \end{bmatrix}.$$

($\boldsymbol{T}_s$ is called the *stretching transform*, and $\boldsymbol{T}_p$ is called the *perspective transform*—see reference 5.)

2.8 Suppose

$${}^A\boldsymbol{T}_B = \begin{bmatrix} 0 & -1 & 0 & 1 \\ 1 & 0 & 0 & 2 \\ 0 & 0 & 1 & 3 \\ 0 & 0 & 0 & 1 \end{bmatrix}$$

and

$${}^B\boldsymbol{T}_C = \begin{bmatrix} 1 & 0 & 0 & 4 \\ 0 & 1 & 0 & 2 \\ 0 & 0 & 1 & 2 \\ 0 & 0 & 0 & 1 \end{bmatrix}.$$

Give two different interpretations of the product ${}^AT_B\,{}^BT_C$, using a figure like figure 2.11.

2.9 Assign link frames to the SCARA-type manipulator in figure 1.16 and obtain ${}^0T_4$.

2.10 Assign link frames to the manipulator in figure 1.12 and obtain ${}^0T_6$.

2.11 Solve the inverse kinematics problem for the SCARA-type manipulator in figure 1.16 on the basis of the result of exercise 2.9. Assume that the end-effector position vector $\boldsymbol{r}$ is given by the four-dimensional vector consisting of the three-dimensional position and the angle about the vertical axis of the wrist joint.

2.12 Solve the inverse kinematics problem for the manipulator in figure 1.12 on the basis of the result of exercise 2.10.

2.13 Sketch figures of the eight solutions obtained in example 2.14 for the end-effector position shown in figure 2.23b.

2.14 Derive the Jacobian matrix $\boldsymbol{J}_v$ of the Stanford manipulator in figure 2.20 for the case when the end-effector frame is assigned as in figure 2.46.

2.15 Prove that the arm configurations given in figure 2.39 are singular ones.

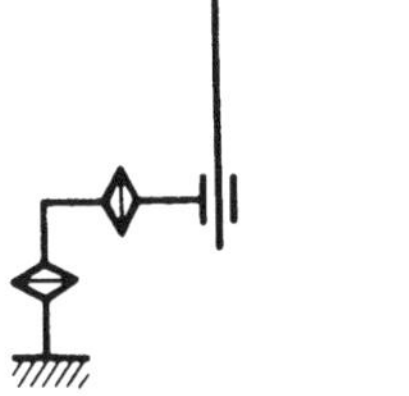

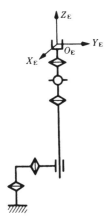

Figure 2.46
End-effector frame Σ_E.

2.16 Assume that the PUMA-type manipulator is in the configuration of figure 2.24. Calculate the joint driving force equivalent to the following force and moment in the end-effector frame Σ_E shown in figure 2.25.

$${}^0\boldsymbol{f}_E = [0,0,100]^T \text{ (N)},$$

$${}^0\boldsymbol{n}_E = [10,0,0]^T \text{ (Nm)}.$$

2.17 For any rotation matrix ${}^A\boldsymbol{R}_B = [{}^A\boldsymbol{x}_B, {}^A\boldsymbol{y}_B, {}^A\boldsymbol{z}_B]$ we have

$$({}^A\boldsymbol{x}_B)^T\,{}^A\boldsymbol{x}_B = 1, \quad ({}^A\boldsymbol{y}_B)^T\,{}^A\boldsymbol{y}_B = 1, \quad ({}^A\boldsymbol{z}_B)^T\,{}^A\boldsymbol{z}_B = 1, \quad {}^A\boldsymbol{x}_B{}^T \times {}^A\boldsymbol{y}_B = {}^A\boldsymbol{z}_B.$$

Conversely, for any three vectors ${}^A\boldsymbol{x}_B$, ${}^A\boldsymbol{y}_B$, and ${}^A\boldsymbol{z}_B$ satisfying the above equations, the matrix $[{}^A\boldsymbol{x}_B, {}^A\boldsymbol{y}_B, {}^A\boldsymbol{z}_B]$ is a rotation matrix. Show that equation 2.2 can be derived from the above equations. Explain why the above equations cannot be derived from equation 2.2. Hint: For any vectors ${}^A\boldsymbol{a}$, ${}^A\boldsymbol{b}$, and ${}^A\boldsymbol{c}$, we have the following equalities:

$${}^A\boldsymbol{c}^T({}^A\boldsymbol{a} \times {}^A\boldsymbol{b}) = {}^A\boldsymbol{a}^T({}^A\boldsymbol{b} \times {}^A\boldsymbol{c}),$$

$${}^A\boldsymbol{c} \times ({}^A\boldsymbol{a} \times {}^A\boldsymbol{b}) = ({}^A\boldsymbol{c}^T\,{}^A\boldsymbol{b})\,{}^A\boldsymbol{a} - ({}^A\boldsymbol{c}^T\,{}^A\boldsymbol{a})\,{}^A\boldsymbol{b}.$$

References

1. H. Goldstein, *Classical Mechanics* (Addison-Wesley, 1950).

2. J. Denavit and R. S. Hartenberg, "A Kinematic Notation for Lower-Pair Mechanisms Based on Matrices," *ASME Journal of Applied Mechanics* 77 (1955): 215–221.

3. V. D. Scheinman, Design of a Computer Controlled Manipulator, memo AIM 92, Stanford Artificial Intelligence Laboratory, 1969.

4. J. J. Craig, *Introduction to Robotics* (Addison-Wesley, 1986).

5. R. P. Paul, *Robot Manipulators* (MIT Press, 1981).

6. L. W. Tsai and A. P. Morgan, "Solving the Kinematics of the Most General Six- and Five-Degree-of-Freedom Manipulators by Continuation Methods," *ASME Journal of Mechanisms, Transmission, and Automation in Design* 107 (1985): 189–200.

7. D. L. Pieper, The Kinematics of Manipulators Under Computer Control, memo AIM 72, Stanford Artificial Intelligence Laboratory, 1968.

8. K. Itô (ed.), *Encyclopedic Dictionary of Mathematics* (MIT Press, 1986).

9. M. Uchiyama, "A Study of Computer Control of a Mechanical Arm (1st Report: Calculation of Coordinative Motion Considering Singular Points)," *Bulletin of the Japan Society of Mechanical Engineers* 22 (1979): 1640–1647.

10. J. M. Hollerbach, "Optimum Kinematic Design for a Seven Degree of Freedom Manipulator," in *Robotics Research: The Second International Symposium*, ed. H. Hanafusa and H. Inoue (MIT Press, 1985), pp. 215–222.

3 Dynamics

This chapter presents the fundamentals for analyzing the dynamic characteristics of manipulators. First, we will briefly outline the difference between the Lagrangian formulation and the Newton-Euler formulation for deriving the dynamics equations of robot manipulators. We then will describe in detail the derivation procedures of the dynamics equations using both formulations, and discuss the use of these equations and the required amount of computation. Finally, we will develop an identification method for the inertial parameters of manipulators.

3.1 Lagrangian and Newton-Euler Formulations

It is necessary to analyze the dynamic characteristics of a manipulator in order to control it, to simulate it, and to evaluate its performance. A manipulator is most often an open-loop link mechanism, which may not be a good structure from the viewpoint of dynamics (it is usually not very rigid, its positioning accuracy is poor, and there is dynamic coupling among its joint motions). This structure, however, allows us to derive a set of simple, easily understandable equations of motion.

Two methods for obtaining the equations of motion are well known: the Lagrangian and the Newton-Euler formulations. At first the Lagrangian formulation was adopted.[1,2] This approach has a drawback in that the derivation procedure is not easy to understand physically; it uses the concept of the Lagrangian, which is related to kinetic energy. However, the resulting equation of motion is in a simple, easily understandable form and is suitable for examining the effects of various parameters on the motion of the manipulator. For this reason, this approach has been the standard one since the 1970s.

Recently, as the need for more rapid and accurate operation of manipulators has increased, the need for real-time computation of the dynamics equations has been felt more strongly.[3] As will be shown later in this chapter, the Newton-Euler formulation has been found to be superior to the Lagrangian formulation for the purpose of fast calculation.[4–6] Also, the Newton-Euler formulation is valid for computer simulation of manipulators.[7]

3.2 Some Basics of Kinetics

3.2.1 Newton's Equation and Euler's Equation

A rigid body with no constraints has six degrees of positional freedom. Thus, a set of six independent equations can describe its motion. It is well known that these equations are given by Newton's and Euler's equations of motion.

Let us consider a rigid body in an inertial coordinate frame $\Sigma_U(O_U - X_U Y_U Z_U)$, as shown in figure 3.1. We assume that the rigid body has linear momentum $\boldsymbol{D}$ and angular momentum $\boldsymbol{E}$ about its center of mass G. The total external force acting on it is $\boldsymbol{F}$, and the external moment about G is $\boldsymbol{N}$. We also assume that all these vectors are expressed in Σ_U, but we will omit the leading superscript U when no confusion occurs. From Newton's second law of motion, we have

$$\boldsymbol{F} = \frac{d\boldsymbol{D}}{dt}, \tag{3.1}$$

$$\boldsymbol{N} = \frac{d\boldsymbol{E}}{dt}. \tag{3.2}$$

If we further assume that the mass of the body is constant, $\bar{m}$, and the position vector of G is given by $\boldsymbol{s}$, we have $\boldsymbol{D} = \bar{m}\dot{\boldsymbol{s}}$. Hence, equation 3.1 reduces to the following form, known as Newton's equation:

$$\boldsymbol{F} = \bar{m}\ddot{\boldsymbol{s}}. \tag{3.3}$$

Note that Newton's equation is valid only when an inertial reference frame is used.

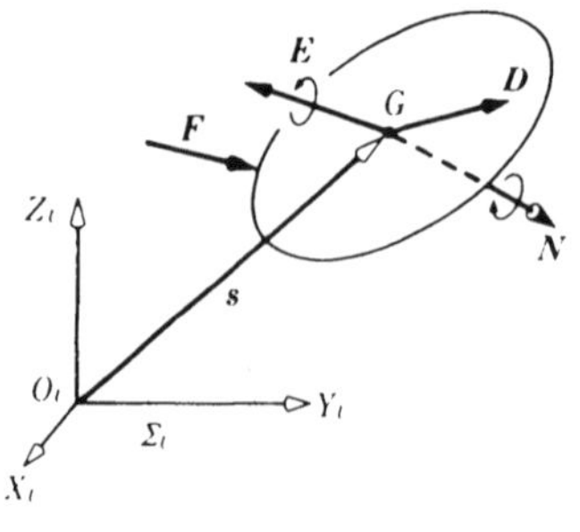

Figure 3.1
Rigid body and inertial coordinate frame.

On the other hand, to find the angular momentum $\boldsymbol{E}$, let ω denote the angular velocity vector, dv the volume of an infinitesimal particle of the rigid body, ρ its density, $\boldsymbol{r}$ its position vector from G, and $\dot{\boldsymbol{r}} = d\boldsymbol{r}/dt$ its velocity vector. Since the angular momentum of dv is $\boldsymbol{r} \times (\dot{\boldsymbol{r}}\rho\, dv)$ and the relation $\dot{\boldsymbol{r}} = \omega \times \boldsymbol{r}$ holds, we have

$$\begin{aligned} \boldsymbol{E} &= \int_V \boldsymbol{r} \times (\omega \times \boldsymbol{r})\rho\, dv \\ &= \int_V [(\boldsymbol{r}^T\boldsymbol{r})\omega - (\boldsymbol{r}^T\omega)\boldsymbol{r}]\rho\, dv \\ &= \int_V [\boldsymbol{r}^T\boldsymbol{r}\mathbf{I}_3 - \boldsymbol{r}\boldsymbol{r}^T]\rho\, dv\omega, \end{aligned} \tag{3.4}$$

where $\int_V$ denotes the integral over the whole rigid body and $\mathbf{I}_3$ denotes the 3×3 identity matrix. If we define

$$\boldsymbol{I} = \int_V [\boldsymbol{r}^T\boldsymbol{r}\mathbf{I}_3 - \boldsymbol{r}\boldsymbol{r}^T]\rho\, dv, \tag{3.5}$$

then $\boldsymbol{E} = \boldsymbol{I}\omega$ and equation 3.2 can be rewritten as

$$\boldsymbol{N} = \frac{d}{dt}(\boldsymbol{I}\omega). \tag{3.6}$$

This $\boldsymbol{I}$ is called the *inertia tensor*.

For any given orthogonal frame $\Sigma_A(O_A - X_A Y_A Z_A)$, let the X_A, Y_A, and Z_A components of ${}^A\boldsymbol{r}$ be ${}^Ar_x$, ${}^Ar_y$, and ${}^Ar_z$, respectively. Then the inertia tensor ${}^A\boldsymbol{I}$ with respect to Σ_A is given by

$${}^A\boldsymbol{I} = \begin{bmatrix} {}^AI_{xx} & {}^AI_{xy} & {}^AI_{xz} \\ {}^AI_{xy} & {}^AI_{yy} & {}^AI_{yz} \\ {}^AI_{xz} & {}^AI_{yz} & {}^AI_{zz} \end{bmatrix}, \tag{3.7}$$

where

$$\begin{aligned} {}^AI_{xx} &= \int_V ({}^Ar_y{}^2 + {}^Ar_z{}^2)\rho\, dv, \\ {}^AI_{yy} &= \int_V ({}^Ar_z{}^2 + {}^Ar_x{}^2)\rho\, dv, \end{aligned} \tag{3.8a}$$

$$^{A}I_{zz} = \int_V ({}^{A}r_x{}^2 + {}^{A}r_y{}^2)\rho\, dv,$$

$$^{A}I_{xy} = -{}^{A}H_{xy} = -\int_V {}^{A}r_x\, {}^{A}r_y \rho\, dv,$$

$$^{A}I_{yz} = -{}^{A}H_{yz} = -\int_V {}^{A}r_y\, {}^{A}r_z \rho\, dv, \tag{3.8b}$$

$$^{A}I_{xz} = -{}^{A}H_{xz} = -\int_V {}^{A}r_x\, {}^{A}r_z \rho\, dv.$$

Here ${}^{A}I_{xx}$, ${}^{A}I_{yy}$, and ${}^{A}I_{zz}$ are called the *moments of inertia* and ${}^{A}H_{xy}$, ${}^{A}H_{yz}$, and ${}^{A}H_{xz}$ are called the *products of inertia*. Hence, $\boldsymbol{I}$ given by equation 3.5 is the inertia tensor with respect to frame $\Sigma_{UG}(G - X_{UG} Y_{UG} Z_{UG})$ with its origin at the center of mass G and with its coordinate axes parallel to those of Σ_U.

When we consider the rotational motion of a rigid body on the basis of equation 3.6, the analysis and the computation are not very transparent. This is because the elements of $\boldsymbol{I}$ change with time as the orientation of the rigid body relative to Σ_{UG} changes with time. To avoid this difficulty, we express equation 3.6 with respect to the object frame $\Sigma_B(G - X_B Y_B Z_B)$ fixed to the rigid body as shown in figure 3.2. Denoting $\boldsymbol{E}$, $\boldsymbol{N}$, $\boldsymbol{I}$, and $\boldsymbol{\omega}$ expressed with respect to Σ_B as ${}^{B}\boldsymbol{E}$, ${}^{B}\boldsymbol{N}$, ${}^{B}\boldsymbol{I}$, and ${}^{B}\boldsymbol{\omega}$, respectively, we have

$$\boldsymbol{E} = {}^{U}\boldsymbol{R}_B\, {}^{B}\boldsymbol{E}, \tag{3.9}$$

$$\boldsymbol{N} = {}^{U}\boldsymbol{R}_B\, {}^{B}\boldsymbol{N}, \tag{3.10}$$

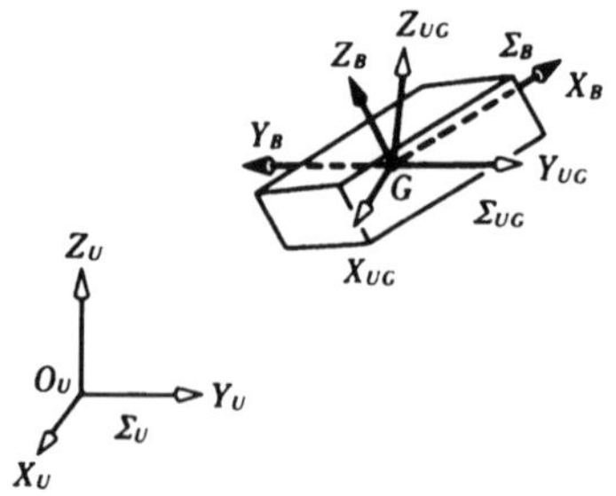

Figure 3.2
Frames Σ_B and Σ_{UG}.

$$\boldsymbol{I} = {}^U\boldsymbol{R}_B\,{}^B\boldsymbol{I}({}^U\boldsymbol{R}_B)^T, \tag{3.11}$$

$$\omega = {}^U\boldsymbol{R}_B\,{}^B\omega. \tag{3.12}$$

Hence we obtain

$$^B\boldsymbol{E} = {}^B\boldsymbol{I}\,{}^B\omega. \tag{3.13}$$

In this case $^B\boldsymbol{I}$ is a constant determined solely by the rigid body. Now we note that, from equation 2.90, the following relation generally holds for any $^B\boldsymbol{a}$ and $^B\boldsymbol{b}$:

$$({}^U\boldsymbol{R}_B\,{}^B\boldsymbol{a}) \times ({}^U\boldsymbol{R}_B\,{}^B\boldsymbol{b}) = {}^U\boldsymbol{R}_B({}^B\boldsymbol{a} \times {}^B\boldsymbol{b}). \tag{3.14}$$

Using this and equations 3.9, 3.13, and 2.91, we get

$$\begin{aligned}\frac{d\boldsymbol{E}}{dt} &= {}^U\boldsymbol{R}_B\frac{d}{dt}({}^B\boldsymbol{E}) + \omega \times ({}^U\boldsymbol{R}_B\,{}^B\boldsymbol{E})\\ &= {}^U\boldsymbol{R}_B\,{}^B\boldsymbol{I}\frac{d}{dt}({}^B\omega) + \omega \times ({}^U\boldsymbol{R}_B\,{}^B\boldsymbol{I}\,{}^B\omega).\end{aligned} \tag{3.15}$$

Hence, from equations 3.6, 3.10, 3.14, and 3.15, we obtain

$$^B\boldsymbol{N} = {}^B\boldsymbol{I}\frac{d}{dt}({}^B\omega) + {}^B\omega \times ({}^B\boldsymbol{I}\,{}^B\omega). \tag{3.16}$$

This is Euler's equation of motion expressed in Σ_B. This equation can also be rewritten in Σ_U. From equations 2.91 and 3.12, the time derivative of ω is

$$\begin{aligned}\frac{d}{dt}(\omega) &= \frac{d}{dt}({}^U\boldsymbol{R}_B\,{}^B\omega)\\ &= {}^U\boldsymbol{R}_B\frac{d}{dt}({}^B\omega) + \omega \times \omega\\ &= {}^U\boldsymbol{R}_B\frac{d}{dt}({}^B\omega).\end{aligned} \tag{3.17}$$

Applying equation 3.17 to equation 3.16, we obtain

$$\boldsymbol{N} = \boldsymbol{I}\frac{d}{dt}(\omega) + \omega \times (\boldsymbol{I}\omega). \tag{3.18}$$

This is Euler's equation of motion expressed in Σ_U.

If we take Σ_B such that the coordinate axes coincide with the principal axes of the moment of inertia of the rigid body, then ${}^B\boldsymbol{I}$ becomes a diagonal matrix diag$[I_x,I_y,I_z]$. Introducing the notations ${}^B\boldsymbol{N} = [{}^BN_x, {}^BN_y, {}^BN_z]^T$ and ${}^B\boldsymbol{\omega} = [{}^B\omega_x, {}^B\omega_y, {}^B\omega_z]^T$, we obtain from equation 3.16 the following well-known expression for the motion of a top:

$$\begin{aligned} {}^BN_x &= I_x {}^B\dot{\omega}_x - (I_y - I_z) {}^B\omega_y {}^B\omega_z, \\ {}^BN_y &= I_y {}^B\dot{\omega}_y - (I_z - I_x) {}^B\omega_z {}^B\omega_x, \\ {}^BN_z &= I_z {}^B\dot{\omega}_z - (I_x - I_y) {}^B\omega_x {}^B\omega_y. \end{aligned} \tag{3.19}$$

3.2.2 Lagrange's Equation

We have used orthogonal coordinate variables so far to describe the position of objects. One of the merits of Lagrange's equation of motion is that any variables can be used instead of orthogonal coordinates as long as they can uniquely specify the positions of objects. These variables are called *generalized coordinates.* Although Lagrange's equation of motion is usually derived from Hamilton's principle, we will derive it from Newton's equation of motion because that is intuitively easier.

Suppose that a system of particles with n degrees of freedom can be described by the generalized coordinates $q_1,q_2,\ldots,q_n$. The three-dimensional position vector $\boldsymbol{x}_\mu$ for an arbitrary particle P_μ of the system in an inertial frame Σ_U is

$$\boldsymbol{x}_\mu = \boldsymbol{x}_\mu(q_1,q_2,\ldots,q_n,t). \tag{3.20}$$

With the mass of particle P_μ denoted as m_μ and the force working on P_μ as $\boldsymbol{F}_\mu$, Newton's equation of motion yields

$$\boldsymbol{F}_\mu = m_\mu \ddot{\boldsymbol{x}}_\mu. \tag{3.21}$$

Taking the inner product of $\partial \boldsymbol{x}_\mu/\partial q_i$ with equation 3.21 and summing for all of the particles in the system, we have

$$\sum_\mu \boldsymbol{F}_\mu{}^T \frac{\partial \boldsymbol{x}_\mu}{\partial q_i} = \sum_\mu m_\mu \ddot{\boldsymbol{x}}_\mu{}^T \frac{\partial \boldsymbol{x}_\mu}{\partial q_i}, \quad i = 1, 2, \ldots, n. \tag{3.22}$$

From equation 3.20 we have

$$\dot{\boldsymbol{x}}_\mu = \sum_{i=1}^{n} \frac{\partial \boldsymbol{x}_\mu}{\partial q_i} \dot{q}_i + \frac{\partial \boldsymbol{x}_\mu}{\partial t}, \tag{3.23}$$

$$\frac{\partial \dot{\boldsymbol{x}}_\mu}{\partial \dot{q}_i} = \frac{\partial \boldsymbol{x}_\mu}{\partial q_i}. \tag{3.24}$$

Hence, equation 3.22 can be rewritten as

$$Q_i = \frac{d}{dt}\left(\frac{\partial K}{\partial \dot{q}_i}\right) - \frac{\partial K}{\partial q_i}, \tag{3.25}$$

where

$$K = \sum_\mu \frac{m_\mu}{2} \dot{\boldsymbol{x}}_\mu{}^T \dot{\boldsymbol{x}}_\mu \tag{3.26}$$

and

$$Q_i = \sum_\mu \boldsymbol{F}_\mu{}^T \frac{\partial \boldsymbol{x}_\mu}{\partial q_i}, \tag{3.27}$$

K is called the kinetic energy of the system, and Q_i is called the generalized force corresponding to q_i.

We further divide the force $\boldsymbol{F}_\mu$ into two parts: $\boldsymbol{F}_{\mu a}$ (the force due to gravity) and $\boldsymbol{F}_{\mu b}$ (the remainder). The gravity force, $\boldsymbol{F}_{\mu a}$, can be expressed by a suitable potential energy P as

$$\boldsymbol{F}_{\mu a} = -\frac{\partial P}{\partial \boldsymbol{x}_\mu}. \tag{3.28}$$

Introducing the Lagrangian function $L = K - P$ and using equations 3.25, 3.27, and 3.28, we finally obtain

$$Q_{ib} = \frac{d}{dt}\left(\frac{\partial L}{\partial \dot{q}_i}\right) - \frac{\partial L}{\partial q_i}, \tag{3.29}$$

where

$$Q_{ib} = \sum_\mu \boldsymbol{F}_{\mu b}{}^T \frac{\partial \boldsymbol{x}_\mu}{\partial q_i}. \tag{3.30}$$

Equation 3.29 is called *Lagrange's equation of motion.*

We usually write a kinetic-energy expression K and a potential-energy expression P when determining an explicit equation of motion. Thus, the following alternative form is more convenient than equation 3.29:

$$Q_{ib} = \frac{d}{dt}\left(\frac{\partial K}{\partial \dot{q}_i}\right) - \frac{\partial K}{\partial q_i} + \frac{\partial P}{\partial q_i}. \tag{3.29'}$$

Note that we can derive equations 3.29 and 3.29′ also for a system of rigid bodies with n degrees of freedom just by regarding the rigid bodies as a collection of many small particles with infinitesimal mass. In this case, the kinetic energy K of a rigid body can be expressed as

$$K = \frac{1}{2}\bar{m}\dot{s}^T\dot{s} + \frac{1}{2}\omega^T I\omega, \tag{3.31}$$

where $\dot{s}$ is the translational velocity of the center of mass G, ω is the angular velocity, $\bar{m}$ is the mass, and I is the inertia tensor of the rigid body.

Readers who wish to know more about the foundations of kinetics should see references 8–10.

3.3 Derivation of Dynamics Equations Based on Lagrangian Formulation

3.3.1 Two-Link Manipulator

Before treating general manipulators, we will derive the dynamics equation of a simple two-link manipulator moving in the $X-Y$ plane. Let us consider the manipulator in figure 3.3. The following notations are used in the figure:

θ_i the joint angle of joint i,

m_i the mass of link i,

$\tilde{I}_i$ the moment of inertia of link i about the axis that passes through the center of mass and is parallel to the Z axis,

l_i the length of link i,

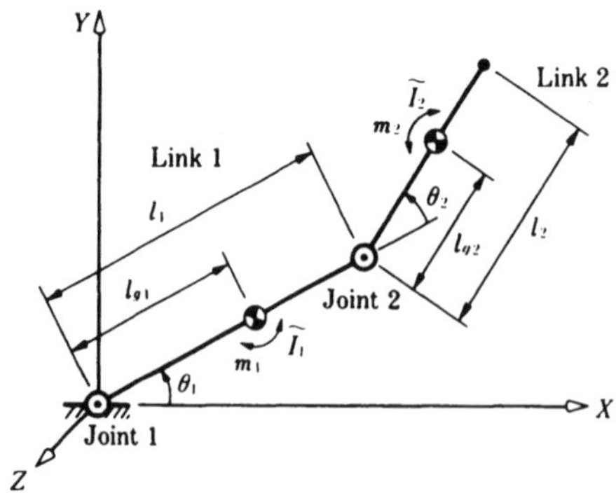

Figure 3.3
Two-link manipulator.

l_{gi} the distance between joint i and the center of mass of link i (the center of mass is assumed to be on the straight line connecting the two joints).

We assume that the first joint driving torque τ_1 acts between the base and link 1, and the second joint driving torque τ_2 acts between links 1 and 2. We will also assume that the gravitational force acts in the negative Y direction.

Choosing $q_1 = \theta_1$ and $q_2 = \theta_2$ as generalized coordinates, we will find the Lagrangian function. Let the kinetic energy and the potential energy for link i be K_i and P_i, respectively. For link 1, we have

$$K_1 = \tfrac{1}{2} m_1 l_{g1}^2 \dot{\theta}_1^2 + \tfrac{1}{2} \tilde{I}_1 \dot{\theta}_1^2, \tag{3.32}$$

$$P_1 = m_1 \hat{g} l_{g1} S_1, \tag{3.33}$$

where $\hat{g}$ is the magnitude of gravitational acceleration. For link 2, since the position of its center of mass $s_2 = [s_{2x}, s_{2y}]^T$ is given by

$$s_{2x} = l_1 C_1 + l_{g2} C_{12}, \tag{3.34a}$$

$$s_{2y} = l_1 S_1 + l_{g2} S_{12}, \tag{3.34b}$$

we have the relation

$$\begin{aligned} \dot{s}_2^T \dot{s}_2 = {} & l_1^2 \dot{\theta}_1^2 + l_{g2}^2 (\dot{\theta}_1 + \dot{\theta}_2)^2 \\ & + 2 l_1 l_{g2} C_2 (\dot{\theta}_1^2 + \dot{\theta}_1 \dot{\theta}_2). \end{aligned} \tag{3.35}$$

Hence,

$$K_2 = \tfrac{1}{2} m_2 \dot{s}_2^T \dot{s}_2 + \tfrac{1}{2} \tilde{I}_2 (\dot{\theta}_1 + \dot{\theta}_2)^2 \tag{3.36}$$

and

$$P_2 = m_2 \hat{g} (l_1 S_1 + l_{g2} S_{12}). \tag{3.37}$$

Calculating $L = K_1 + K_2 - P_1 - P_2$ and substituting this into equation 3.29 yields the equations of motion for the two-link manipulator:

$$\begin{aligned} \tau_1 = {} & [m_1 l_{g1}^2 + \tilde{I}_1 + m_2 (l_1^2 + l_{g2}^2 + 2 l_1 l_{g2} C_2) + \tilde{I}_2] \ddot{\theta}_1 \\ & + [m_2 (l_{g2}^2 + l_1 l_{g2} C_2) + \tilde{I}_2] \ddot{\theta}_2 - m_2 l_1 l_{g2} S_2 (2 \dot{\theta}_1 \dot{\theta}_2 + \dot{\theta}_2^2) \\ & + m_1 \hat{g} l_{g1} C_1 + m_2 \hat{g} (l_1 C_1 + l_{g2} C_{12}), \end{aligned} \tag{3.38a}$$

$$\begin{aligned} \tau_2 = {} & [m_2 (l_{g2}^2 + l_1 l_{g2} C_2) + \tilde{I}_2] \ddot{\theta}_1 + (m_2 l_{g2}^2 + \tilde{I}_2) \ddot{\theta}_2 \\ & + m_2 l_1 l_{g2} S_2 \dot{\theta}_1^2 + m_2 \hat{g} l_{g2} C_{12}. \end{aligned} \tag{3.38b}$$

This can also be rewritten as

$$\tau_1 = M_{11}\ddot{\theta}_1 + M_{12}\ddot{\theta}_2 + h_{122}\dot{\theta}_2^{\,2} + 2h_{112}\dot{\theta}_1\dot{\theta}_2 + g_1, \tag{3.39a}$$

$$\tau_2 = M_{21}\ddot{\theta}_1 + M_{22}\ddot{\theta}_2 + h_{211}\dot{\theta}_1^{\,2} + g_2, \tag{3.39b}$$

where

$$M_{11} = m_1 l_{g1}^{\,2} + \bar{I}_1 + m_2(l_1^{\,2} + l_{g2}^{\,2} + 2l_1 l_{g2} C_2) + \bar{I}_2, \tag{3.40a}$$

$$M_{12} = M_{21} = m_2(l_{g2}^{\,2} + l_1 l_{g2} C_2) + \bar{I}_2, \tag{3.40b}$$

$$M_{22} = m_2 l_{g2}^{\,2} + \bar{I}_2, \tag{3.40c}$$

$$h_{122} = h_{112} = -h_{211} = -m_2 l_1 l_{g2} S_2, \tag{3.41}$$

$$g_1 = m_1 \hat{g} l_{g1} C_1 + m_2 \hat{g}(l_1 C_1 + l_{g2} C_{12}), \tag{3.42a}$$

$$g_2 = m_2 \hat{g} l_{g2} C_{12}. \tag{3.42b}$$

We call M_{ii} the *effective inertia*, M_{ij} the *coupling inertia*, h_{ijj} the *centrifugal acceleration coefficient*, and h_{ijk} $(j \neq k)$ the *Coriolis acceleration coefficient*. The term g_i represents the gravity force.

We can further rewrite equation 3.39 in a more compact form by noting that the kinetic energy $K = K_1 + K_2$ may be expressed in a quadratic form as

$$K = \tfrac{1}{2}\dot{\boldsymbol{\theta}}^T \boldsymbol{M}(\boldsymbol{\theta})\dot{\boldsymbol{\theta}}, \tag{3.43}$$

where $\dot{\boldsymbol{\theta}} = [\dot{\theta}_1, \dot{\theta}_2]^T$ and $\boldsymbol{M}(\boldsymbol{\theta})$ is the following positive-definite matrix:

$$\boldsymbol{M}(\boldsymbol{\theta}) = \begin{bmatrix} M_{11} & M_{12} \\ M_{12} & M_{22} \end{bmatrix}. \tag{3.44}$$

Using equations 3.43, 3.44, and 3.29, the equations of motion 3.39 are also given by

$$\boldsymbol{\tau} = \boldsymbol{M}(\boldsymbol{\theta})\ddot{\boldsymbol{\theta}} + \boldsymbol{h}(\boldsymbol{\theta},\dot{\boldsymbol{\theta}}) + \boldsymbol{g}(\boldsymbol{\theta}), \tag{3.45}$$

where, with col[·] denoting a column vector,

$$\boldsymbol{h}(\boldsymbol{\theta},\dot{\boldsymbol{\theta}}) = \text{col}\left[\sum_{j=1}^{2}\sum_{k=1}^{2}\left(\frac{\partial M_{ij}}{\partial \theta_k} - \frac{1}{2}\frac{\partial M_{jk}}{\partial \theta_i}\right)\dot{\theta}_j\dot{\theta}_k\right], \tag{3.46}$$

$$\boldsymbol{g}(\boldsymbol{\theta}) = \text{col}[g_i], \tag{3.47}$$

and where $\boldsymbol{M}(\boldsymbol{\theta})\ddot{\boldsymbol{\theta}}$ is the inertial force term, $\boldsymbol{h}(\boldsymbol{\theta},\dot{\boldsymbol{\theta}})$ is the centrifugal and

Coriolis force term, and $\boldsymbol{g}(\boldsymbol{\theta})$ is the gravity force term. $\boldsymbol{M}(\boldsymbol{\theta})$ is called the *inertia matrix in joint coordinates.*

3.3.2 *n*-Link Manipulator

We will now find the equations of motion of a general n-link manipulator, using the homogeneous transforms among the link frames fixed to each link (see reference 3). For simplicity, we assume that the base of the manipulator is fixed to an inertial frame Σ_U, and we regard Σ_0 as the reference frame. We also assume that the joint driving force τ_i at joint i works between links $i-1$ and i, and that its value is positive when it works in the direction that makes the joint variable larger. This kind of driving mechanism is called a *serial drive.*

In subsection 2.3.3 we introduced the frame $\Sigma_i(O_i - X_i Y_i Z_i)$ fixed to link i (see figure 2.17). One characteristic of Σ_i is that its origin is on an axis of joint i, which is closer to the base than the other joint (joint $i+1$) of link i. When joint i is revolute, the axis of rotation coincides with the Z_i axis; when joint i is prismatic, the direction of translation coincides with that of the Z_i axis. We also introduced the homogeneous transform ${}^{i-1}\boldsymbol{T}_i$ relating Σ_i to Σ_{i-1}. Hence, the homogeneous transform ${}^{0}\boldsymbol{T}_i$ given by

$$ {}^{0}\boldsymbol{T}_i = {}^{0}\boldsymbol{T}_1 {}^{1}\boldsymbol{T}_2 \cdots {}^{i-1}\boldsymbol{T}_i \tag{3.48} $$

is the one relating Σ_i to the reference frame Σ_0. Note that ${}^{i-1}\boldsymbol{T}_i$ is a function of q_i, the joint variable at joint i.

Suppose that we are given an arbitrary point on link i which is expressed as ${}^{i}\boldsymbol{r}$ with respect to Σ_i (see figure 3.4). The position of the same point with respect to the reference frame Σ_0 is given by

$$ {}^{0}\boldsymbol{r} = {}^{0}\boldsymbol{T}_i {}^{i}\boldsymbol{r}. \tag{3.49} $$

Since ${}^{i}\boldsymbol{r}$ relative to Σ_i is constant, $d\,{}^{i}\boldsymbol{r}/dt = \boldsymbol{0}$. Thus,

$$ \frac{d\,{}^{0}\boldsymbol{r}}{dt} = {}^{0}\dot{\boldsymbol{r}} = \left(\sum_{j=1}^{i} \frac{\partial\,{}^{0}\boldsymbol{T}_i}{\partial q_j} \dot{q}_j \right) {}^{i}\boldsymbol{r}. \tag{3.50} $$

Using equation 3.50 and the relation ${}^{0}\dot{\boldsymbol{r}}^T\,{}^{0}\dot{\boldsymbol{r}} = \mathrm{tr}[{}^{0}\dot{\boldsymbol{r}}\,{}^{0}\dot{\boldsymbol{r}}^T]$, we have

$$ {}^{0}\dot{\boldsymbol{r}}^T\,{}^{0}\dot{\boldsymbol{r}} = \sum_{j=1}^{i} \sum_{k=1}^{i} \mathrm{tr}\left(\frac{\partial\,{}^{0}\boldsymbol{T}_i}{\partial q_j} {}^{i}\boldsymbol{r}\,{}^{i}\boldsymbol{r}^T \frac{\partial\,{}^{0}\boldsymbol{T}_i^T}{\partial q_k} \right) \dot{q}_j \dot{q}_k, \tag{3.51} $$

where $\mathrm{tr}(\cdot)$ denotes the trace of a matrix.

With these preparations, we can now calculate the kinetic energy K_i and the potential energy P_i of link i. The kinetic energy of link i is found by

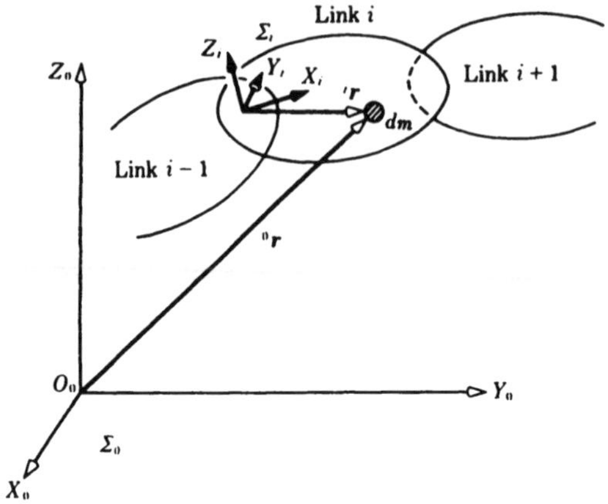

Figure 3.4
Point $^i\boldsymbol{r}$ on link i.

integrating the kinetic energy of the differential element over the whole body of link i. Denoting the kinetic energy of the differential element as dK_i, its volume as dm, its density as ρ, and its position as $^i\boldsymbol{r}$, we have

$$K_i = \int_{\text{link}\, i} dK_i = \int_{\text{link}\, i} \tfrac{1}{2}\, {}^0\dot{\boldsymbol{r}}^T\, {}^0\dot{\boldsymbol{r}} \rho\, dv$$

$$= \tfrac{1}{2} \sum_{j=1}^{i} \sum_{k=1}^{i} \operatorname{tr}\left(\frac{\partial\, {}^0\boldsymbol{T}_i}{\partial q_j} \hat{\boldsymbol{H}}_i \frac{\partial\, {}^0\boldsymbol{T}_i^T}{\partial q_k} \right) \dot{q}_j \dot{q}_k, \tag{3.52}$$

where $\int_{\text{link}\, i}$ denotes the integral over the whole body of link i and where $\hat{\boldsymbol{H}}_i$ is the pseudo inertia matrix defined by

$$\hat{\boldsymbol{H}}_i = \int_{\text{link}\, i} {}^i\boldsymbol{r}\, {}^i\boldsymbol{r}^T \rho\, dv$$

$$= \begin{bmatrix} \dfrac{-\hat{I}_{ixx} + \hat{I}_{iyy} + \hat{I}_{izz}}{2} & \hat{H}_{ixy} & \hat{H}_{ixz} & m_i \hat{s}_{ix} \\ \hat{H}_{ixy} & \dfrac{\hat{I}_{ixx} - \hat{I}_{iyy} + \hat{I}_{izz}}{2} & \hat{H}_{iyz} & m_i \hat{s}_{iy} \\ \hat{H}_{ixz} & \hat{H}_{iyz} & \dfrac{\hat{I}_{ixx} + \hat{I}_{iyy} - \hat{I}_{izz}}{2} & m_i \hat{s}_{iz} \\ m_i \hat{s}_{ix} & m_i \hat{s}_{iy} & m_i \hat{s}_{iz} & m_i \end{bmatrix}. \tag{3.53}$$

With ${}^i\boldsymbol{r} = [{}^ir_x, {}^ir_y, {}^ir_z]^T$, the elements of $\hat{\boldsymbol{H}}_i$ are given by

$$\hat{I}_{ixx} = \int_{\text{link } i} ({}^ir_y{}^2 + {}^ir_z{}^2)\rho\, dv \quad \text{(moment of inertia)}, \tag{3.54a}$$

$$\hat{H}_{ixy} = \int_{\text{link } i} {}^ir_x\, {}^ir_y \rho\, dv \quad \text{(product of inertia)}, \tag{3.54b}$$

$$m_i = \int_{\text{link } i} \rho\, dv \quad \text{(mass of link i)}, \tag{3.54c}$$

$$\hat{s}_{ix} = \int_{\text{link } i} {}^ir_x \rho\, dv/m_i \quad \text{(center of mass)}, \tag{3.54d}$$

and by similar equations for $\hat{I}_{iyy}$, $\hat{I}_{izz}$, $\hat{H}_{ixz}$, $\hat{H}_{iyz}$, $\hat{s}_{iy}$, and $\hat{s}_{iz}$. Since $\hat{\boldsymbol{H}}_i$ is defined with respect to Σ_i fixed to link i, the value of $\hat{\boldsymbol{H}}_i$ is a constant independent of $\boldsymbol{q}$. Note that we can regard $\hat{\boldsymbol{H}}_i$ as consisting of the zeroth (m_i), first ($m_i\hat{s}_{ix}$, $m_i\hat{s}_{iy}$, $m_i\hat{s}_{iz}$), and second moments (top left 3×3 submatrix of $\hat{\boldsymbol{H}}_i$) of link i.

Before proceeding further, let us clarify the relation between $\hat{\boldsymbol{H}}_i$ and the inertia tensor of link i. From equations 3.7 and 3.54, the inertia tensor of link i with respect to Σ_i is given by

$${}^i\hat{\boldsymbol{I}}_i = \begin{bmatrix} \hat{I}_{ixx} & -\hat{H}_{ixy} & -\hat{H}_{ixz} \\ -\hat{H}_{ixy} & \hat{I}_{iyy} & -\hat{H}_{iyz} \\ -\hat{H}_{ixz} & -\hat{H}_{iyz} & \hat{I}_{izz} \end{bmatrix}. \tag{3.55}$$

Another expression (which will be used later, in subsection 3.4.3) is the inertia tensor with respect to the frame with its origin at the center of mass (which is generally different from the origin of Σ_i) and with its coordinate axes parallel to those of Σ_i. Let us denote this tensor by

$${}^i\boldsymbol{I}_i = \begin{bmatrix} I_{ixx} & -H_{ixy} & -H_{ixz} \\ -H_{ixy} & I_{iyy} & -H_{iyz} \\ -H_{ixz} & -H_{iyz} & I_{izz} \end{bmatrix}. \tag{3.56}$$

The following relations hold between elements of ${}^i\hat{\boldsymbol{I}}_i$ and ${}^i\boldsymbol{I}_i$:

$$\hat{I}_{ixx} = I_{ixx} + m_i(\hat{s}_{iy}{}^2 + \hat{s}_{iz}{}^2), \tag{3.57a}$$

$$\hat{H}_{ixy} = H_{ixy} + m_i\hat{s}_{ix}\hat{s}_{iy}. \tag{3.57b}$$

Similar relations also hold for $\hat{I}_{iyy}$, $\hat{I}_{izz}$, $\hat{H}_{iyz}$, and $\hat{H}_{ixz}$. Putting these relations together, we get

$$ {}^i\hat{I}_i = {}^iI_i + m_i[{}^i\hat{s}_i \times]^T[{}^i\hat{s}_i \times] $$
$$ = {}^iI_i - m_i[{}^i\hat{s}_i \times]^2, \quad (3.58) $$

where ${}^i\hat{s}_i$ is the vector from O_i to the center of mass of link i expressed in Σ_i; it is expressed as

$$ {}^i\hat{s}_i = [\hat{s}_{ix}, \hat{s}_{iy}, \hat{s}_{iz}]^T. $$

(Recall that the notation $[\cdot \times]$ was defined by equation 2.123). Equation 3.58 is known as the *parallel-axis theorem* (reference 8).

Next we calculate the potential energy P_i of link i. Let $\tilde{g} = [\tilde{g}_x, \tilde{g}_y, \tilde{g}_z, 0]^T$ be the gravitational acceleration vector in Σ_0, and let the reference plane be the one normal to $\tilde{g}$ which includes the origin of Σ_0. Then we obtain

$$ P_i = -m_i \tilde{g}^T\, {}^0T_i\, {}^i\hat{s}_i. \quad (3.59) $$

The Lagrangian in this case is

$$ L = \sum_{i=1}^{n} (K_i - P_i). \quad (3.60) $$

Substituting this into equation 3.29 and changing the order of the trace and differentiation operations yields

$$ \tau_i = \sum_{k=i}^{n} \sum_{j=1}^{k} \mathrm{tr}\left(\frac{\partial\, {}^0T_k}{\partial q_j} \hat{H}_k \frac{\partial\, {}^0T_k^T}{\partial q_i} \right) \ddot{q}_j $$
$$ + \sum_{k=i}^{n} \sum_{j=1}^{k} \sum_{m=1}^{k} \mathrm{tr}\left(\frac{\partial^2\, {}^0T_k}{\partial q_j \partial q_m} \hat{H}_k \frac{\partial\, {}^0T_k^T}{\partial q_i} \right) \dot{q}_j \dot{q}_m - \sum_{j=i}^{n} m_j \tilde{g}^T \frac{\partial\, {}^0T_j}{\partial q_i} {}^j\hat{s}_j. \quad (3.61) $$

Rewriting this equation, we finally have the general equation of motion:

$$ \tau = M(q)\ddot{q} + h(q,\dot{q}) + g(q), \quad (3.62) $$

where $M(q)$ is the $n \times n$ symmetric inertia matrix whose (i,j) element is

$$ M_{ij} = \sum_{k=\max(i,j)}^{n} \mathrm{tr}\left(\frac{\partial\, {}^0T_k}{\partial q_j} \hat{H}_k \frac{\partial\, {}^0T_k^T}{\partial q_i} \right), \quad (3.63) $$

$h(q,\dot{q})$ is the n-dimensional vector respresenting the centrifugal and Coriolis forces whose ith element is given by

$$h_i = \sum_{j=1}^{n} \sum_{m=1}^{n} \sum_{k=\max(i,j,m)}^{n} \operatorname{tr}\left(\frac{\partial^2\, {}^0\boldsymbol{T}_k}{\partial q_j \partial q_m} \hat{\boldsymbol{H}}_k \frac{\partial\, {}^0\boldsymbol{T}_k{}^T}{\partial q_i} \right) \dot{q}_j \dot{q}_m, \tag{3.64}$$

and $\boldsymbol{g}(\boldsymbol{q})$ is the n-dimensional vector representing the gravity load whose ith element is given by

$$g_i = -\sum_{j=1}^{n} m_j \tilde{\boldsymbol{g}}^T \frac{\partial\, {}^0\boldsymbol{T}_j}{\partial q_i} {}^j\hat{\boldsymbol{s}}_j. \tag{3.65}$$

Note that the total kinetic energy, $K = \sum_{i=1}^{n} K_i$, may be written as

$$K = \tfrac{1}{2} \dot{\boldsymbol{q}}^T \boldsymbol{M}(\boldsymbol{q}) \dot{\boldsymbol{q}}. \tag{3.66}$$

Since generally $K > 0$ for any nonzero $\dot{q}$, $\boldsymbol{M}(\boldsymbol{q})$ is a positive-definite matrix. Also, from equations 3.29′, 3.62, and 3.66, we have

$$\boldsymbol{h}(\boldsymbol{q},\dot{\boldsymbol{q}}) = \dot{\boldsymbol{M}}\dot{\boldsymbol{q}} - \operatorname{col}\left[\frac{1}{2} \dot{\boldsymbol{q}}^T \frac{\partial \boldsymbol{M}}{\partial q_i} \dot{\boldsymbol{q}} \right]. \tag{3.67}$$

Further, $\boldsymbol{h}(\boldsymbol{q},\dot{\boldsymbol{q}})$ and h_{ijm} can be expressed in terms of M_{ij} as

$$\boldsymbol{h}(\boldsymbol{q},\dot{\boldsymbol{q}}) = \operatorname{col}\left[\sum_{j=1}^{n} \sum_{k=1}^{n} \left(\frac{\partial M_{ij}}{\partial q_k} - \frac{1}{2} \frac{\partial M_{jk}}{\partial q_i} \right) \dot{q}_j \dot{q}_k \right], \tag{3.68}$$

$$h_{ijk} = \frac{\partial M_{ij}}{\partial q_k} - \frac{1}{2} \frac{\partial M_{jk}}{\partial q_i}. \tag{3.69}$$

The matrices

$$\frac{\partial\, {}^0\boldsymbol{T}_i}{\partial q_j}$$

and

$$\frac{\partial^2\, {}^0\boldsymbol{T}_i}{(\partial q_j \partial q_k)} = \frac{\partial^2\, {}^0\boldsymbol{T}_i}{(\partial q_k \partial q_j)}$$

appearing in the above equations can be calculated using the following relations. First we note that, from equation 2.45,

$$\frac{\partial\, {}^{i-1}\boldsymbol{T}_i}{\partial q_i} = {}^{i-1}\boldsymbol{T}_i \boldsymbol{\Delta}_i, \tag{3.70}$$

where

$$\boldsymbol{\Delta}_i = \begin{cases} \begin{bmatrix} 0 & -1 & 0 & 0 \\ 1 & 0 & 0 & 0 \\ 0 & 0 & 0 & 0 \\ 0 & 0 & 0 & 0 \end{bmatrix} & \text{if R} \\ \begin{bmatrix} 0 & 0 & 0 & 0 \\ 0 & 0 & 0 & 0 \\ 0 & 0 & 0 & 1 \\ 0 & 0 & 0 & 0 \end{bmatrix} & \text{if P.} \end{cases} \tag{3.71}$$

Here "if R" means that joint i is revolute, and "if P" means that joint i is prismatic. Hence,

$$\frac{\partial\,{}^0\boldsymbol{T}_i}{\partial q_j} = {}^0\boldsymbol{T}_1\,{}^1\boldsymbol{T}_2 \cdots {}^{j-1}\boldsymbol{T}_j\,\boldsymbol{\Delta}_j\,{}^j\boldsymbol{T}_{j+1} \cdots {}^{i-1}\boldsymbol{T}_i, \tag{3.72}$$

$$\frac{\partial^2\,{}^0\boldsymbol{T}_i}{\partial q_j \partial q_k} = \begin{cases} {}^0\boldsymbol{T}_1 \cdots {}^{j-1}\boldsymbol{T}_j\,\boldsymbol{\Delta}_j\,{}^j\boldsymbol{T}_{j+1} \cdots {}^{k-1}\boldsymbol{T}_k\,\boldsymbol{\Delta}_k\,{}^k\boldsymbol{T}_{k+1} \cdots {}^{i-1}\boldsymbol{T}_i, & i \geqq k \geqq j \\ \boldsymbol{0}, & \max(j,k) > i. \end{cases} \tag{3.73}$$

The case when the dynamics of the actuators at joints cannot be neglected will be treated in subsection 5.2.1.

Example 3.1 Let us check that the equations of motion 3.39 for the two-link manipulator can also be derived from equation 3.61. We define the link frames Σ_i as in figure 3.5. Then

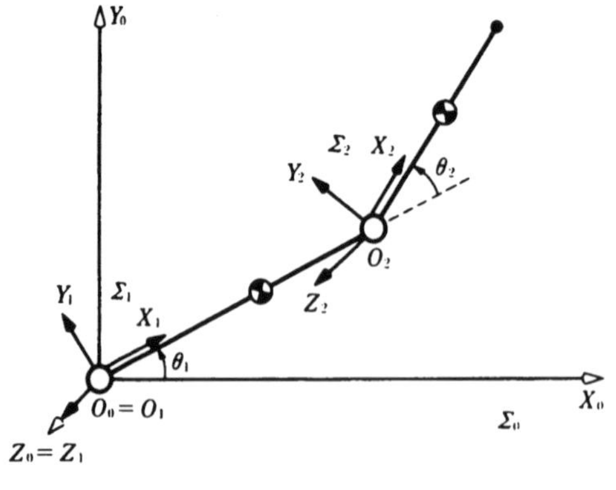

Figure 3.5
Link frames for two-link manipulator.

$$
{}^0\boldsymbol{T}_1 = \begin{bmatrix} C_1 & -S_1 & 0 & 0 \\ S_1 & C_1 & 0 & 0 \\ 0 & 0 & 1 & 0 \\ 0 & 0 & 0 & 1 \end{bmatrix},
$$

$$
{}^1\boldsymbol{T}_2 = \begin{bmatrix} C_2 & -S_2 & 0 & l_1 \\ S_2 & C_2 & 0 & 0 \\ 0 & 0 & 1 & 0 \\ 0 & 0 & 0 & 1 \end{bmatrix},
$$

and

$$
\frac{\partial\, {}^0\boldsymbol{T}_1}{\partial q_1} = \begin{bmatrix} -S_1 & -C_1 & 0 & 0 \\ C_1 & -S_1 & 0 & 0 \\ 0 & 0 & 0 & 0 \\ 0 & 0 & 0 & 0 \end{bmatrix},
$$

$$
\frac{\partial\, {}^0\boldsymbol{T}_2}{\partial q_1} = \frac{\partial\, {}^0\boldsymbol{T}_1}{\partial q_1}\, {}^1\boldsymbol{T}_2
$$

$$
= \begin{bmatrix} -S_{12} & -C_{12} & 0 & -l_1 S_1 \\ C_{12} & -S_{12} & 0 & l_1 C_1 \\ 0 & 0 & 0 & 0 \\ 0 & 0 & 0 & 0 \end{bmatrix},
$$

$$
\frac{\partial\, {}^0\boldsymbol{T}_2}{\partial q_2} = \begin{bmatrix} -S_{12} & -C_{12} & 0 & 0 \\ C_{12} & -S_{12} & 0 & 0 \\ 0 & 0 & 0 & 0 \\ 0 & 0 & 0 & 0 \end{bmatrix}.
$$

Thus, from equation 3.63 we obtain

$$
M_{22} = \mathrm{tr}\left(\frac{\partial\, {}^0\boldsymbol{T}_2}{\partial q_2} \hat{\boldsymbol{H}}_2 \frac{\partial\, {}^0\boldsymbol{T}_2{}^T}{\partial q_2}\right) = I_{2zz} = \bar{I}_2 + m_2 l_{g2}{}^2
$$

and the other equations in 3.40. Also, by calculating the coefficients of $\dot{q}_j \dot{q}_m$ on the right-hand side of equation 3.69, we find

$$
h_{211} = \frac{\partial M_{21}}{\partial q_1} - \frac{1}{2}\frac{\partial M_{11}}{\partial q_2}
$$

$$
= m_2 l_1 l_{g2} S_2
$$

and the other equations in 3.41. Finally, noting that $\tilde{g} = [0, -\mathcal{g}, 0, 0]^T$ and ${}^j\hat{s}_j = [l_{gj}, 0, 0, 1]^T$, we obtain from equation 3.65

$$g_2 = -m_2 \tilde{g}^T \frac{\partial\, {}^0\boldsymbol{T}_2}{\partial q_2} {}^2\hat{s}_2$$

$$= m_2 \mathcal{g} l_{g2} C_{12}$$

and the other equation in 3.42. Thus, we have derived equation 3.39 from equation 3.61. □

3.3.3 Parallel-Drive Two-Link Manipulator

The manipulators discussed in subsections 3.3.1 and 3.3.2 are of the serial-drive type, in the sense that the joint driving force τ_i works between links $i-1$ and i for all i. A parallel drive is another type often used. An example of this type is the two-link manipulator shown in figure 3.6. Actuator 1 provides the driving torque τ_1 between the base and link 1; actuator 2 provides the driving torque τ_2 between the base and link 2 through a belt. This is called a *parallel-drive manipulator* because τ_1 and τ_2 can be regarded as working in parallel.

Instead of the belt, a chain, a set of gears, or a parallelogram linkage could also be used to transmit the torque τ_2. Figure 3.7 shows a mechanism consisting of the above parallel-drive mechanism and one revolute joint. This mechanism is often used for the arm portion of a manipulator because the actuators can be located near the base, to reduce the mass and the moments of inertia.

The equations of motion for the manipulator in figure 3.6 will be derived using the Lagrangian formulation. The only difference between this manipulator and the serial-drive two-link manipulator treated in subsection 3.3.1 is that in this case τ_2 works between the base and link 2 instead of between

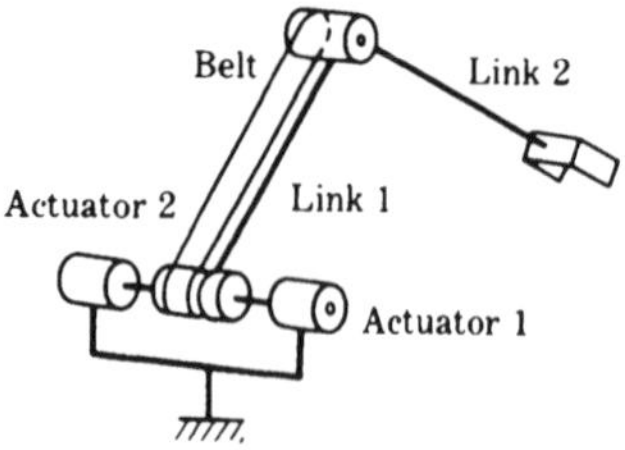

Figure 3.6
Parallel-drive two-link manipulator.

links 1 and 2. We can take care of this difference by taking as θ_2 the angle between the base and link 2 instead of that between links 1 and 2. Kinetically speaking, we make this change because τ_2 is the generalized force corresponding to the generalized coordinate θ_2. Figure 3.8 shows the joint variables thus taken.

With all other parameters of the manipulator defined as in figure 3.3, the kinetic energy K_1 and the potential energy P_1 of link 1 are given by equations 3.32 and 3.33. As for link 2, the position $s_2 = [s_{2x}, s_{2y}]^T$ of the center of mass is

$$s_{2x} = l_1 C_1 + l_{g2} C_2, \tag{3.74a}$$

$$s_{2y} = l_1 S_1 + l_{g2} S_2, \tag{3.74b}$$

and $\dot{s}_2{}^T \dot{s}_2$ is given by

$$\dot{s}_2{}^T \dot{s}_2 = l_1{}^2 \dot{\theta}_1{}^2 + l_{g2}{}^2 \dot{\theta}_2{}^2 + 2 l_1 l_{g2} \cos(\theta_2 - \theta_1) \dot{\theta}_1 \dot{\theta}_2. \tag{3.75}$$

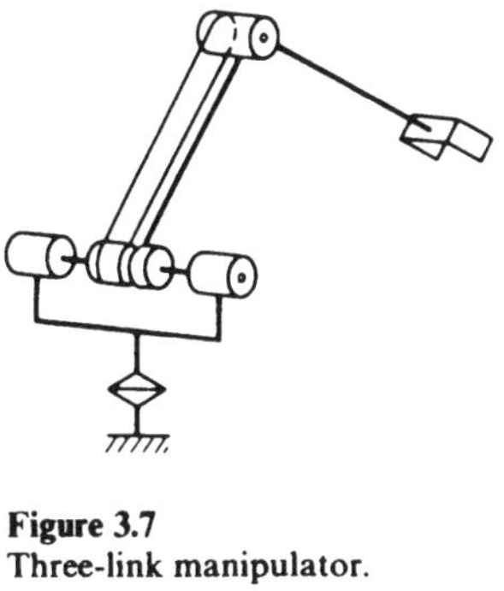

Figure 3.7
Three-link manipulator.

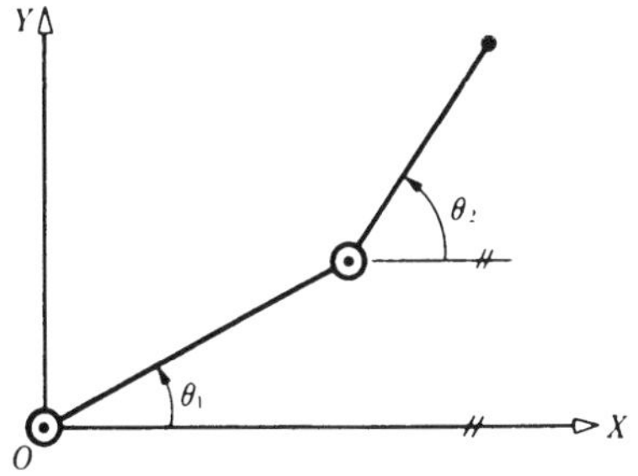

Figure 3.8
Joint variables for parallel-drive manipulator.

Hence, the kinetic energy is

$$K_2 = \tfrac{1}{2}m_2\dot{s}_2{}^T\dot{s}_2 + \tfrac{1}{2}\tilde{I}_2\dot{\theta}_2{}^2 \tag{3.76}$$

and the potential energy is

$$P_2 = m_2\hat{g}[l_1S_1 + l_{g2}S_2]. \tag{3.77}$$

Substituting $L = K_1 + K_2 - P_1 - P_2$ into equation 3.29, we obtain

$$\tau_1 = [m_1l_{g1}{}^2 + \tilde{I}_1 + m_2l_1{}^2]\ddot{\theta}_1 + [m_2l_1l_{g2}\cos(\theta_2 - \theta_1)]\ddot{\theta}_2 - m_2l_1l_{g2}\sin(\theta_2 - \theta_1)\dot{\theta}_2{}^2 + (m_1l_{g1} + m_2l_1)\hat{g}C_1, \tag{3.78a}$$

$$\tau_2 = [m_2l_1l_{g2}\cos(\theta_2 - \theta_1)]\ddot{\theta}_1 + [m_2l_{g2}{}^2 + \tilde{I}_2]\ddot{\theta}_2 + m_2l_1l_{g2}\sin(\theta_2 - \theta_1)\dot{\theta}_1{}^2 + m_2l_{g2}\hat{g}C_2. \tag{3.78b}$$

Comparing equations 3.38 and 3.78, we can see that there is a fairly big difference in dynamics between the serial-drive type and the parallel-drive type even for otherwise identical two-link manipulators. For instance, the off-diagonal elements of the inertia matrix for equation 3.78 (i.e., the coefficients of the second term on the right-hand side of equation 3.78a and of the first term on the right-hand side of equation 3.78b) are always smaller than those of equation 3.38. In particular, these elements vanish when $l_{g2} = 0$. This occurs when the center of mass of link 2 is right on the axis of joint 2. Hence, we can conclude that the parallel-drive type has less coupling between links 1 and 2 than the serial-drive type. Note, however, that the mechanism of the serial-drive type is generally simpler than that of the parallel-drive type.

3.4 Derivation of Dynamics Equations Based on Newton-Euler Formulation

3.4.1 Basic Procedure of Newton-Euler Formulation

The basic procedure for deriving the equations of motion based on the Newton-Euler formulation will be outlined here, with the serial-drive three-link planar manipulator in figure 3.9a used as an example. This procedure can be easily understood if we consider it as a way to calculate the joint driving force for realizing a given trajectory of joint vector $\boldsymbol{q}$.

Suppose that the present values of joint displacements q_i and joint velocities $\dot{q}_i$ and the desired values of joint accelerations $\ddot{q}_i$ are given for all

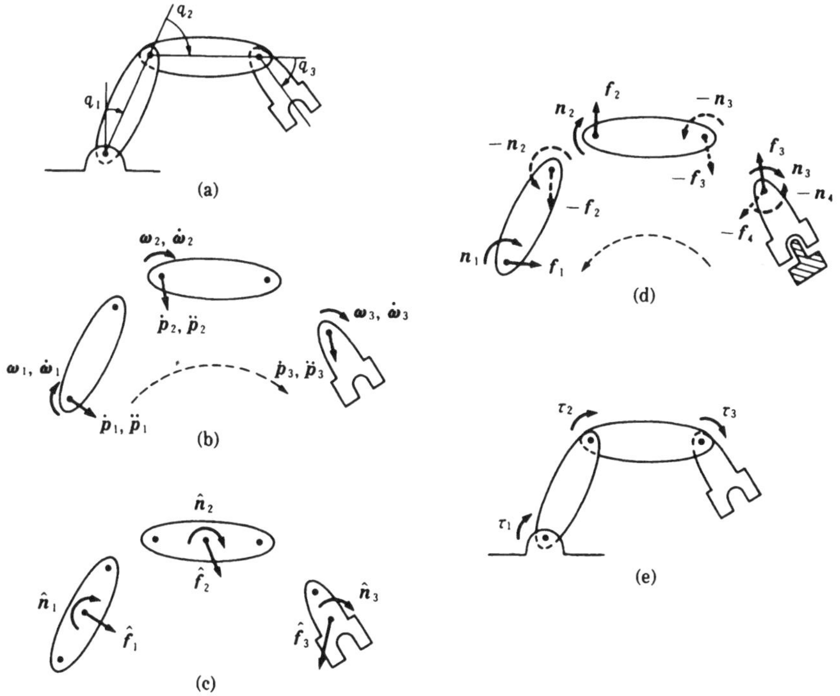

Figure 3.9
Newton-Euler formulation.

links. Also suppose that the force f_4 and moment n_4 exerted on the end link by the environment or a grasped object are given. First, we calculate the angular velocity ω_i, the angular acceleration $\dot{\omega}_i$, the linear velocity $\dot{p}_i$, and the linear acceleration $\ddot{p}_i$ of link i with respect to the reference frame, starting from the base and moving outward to the end link (figure 3.9b). Second, using Newton's and Euler's equations, we calculate the force $\hat{f}_i$ and the moment $\hat{n}_i$ that must be applied to the center of mass of link i to realize such motion (figure 3.9c). Third, we calculate the force f_i and the moment n_i that must be applied at joint i to produce $\hat{f}_i$ and $\hat{n}_i$, starting from the end link and moving inward to the base, with the given values of f_4 and n_4 as the boundary condition (figure 3.9d). Finally, we calculate the joint driving force τ_i (figure 3.9e).

The set of equations necessary for the above calculations corresponds to the equations of motion based on the Newton-Euler formulation.

3.4.2 Link Accelerations of a Manipulator

The relation among the link velocities of a manipulator was derived in subsection 2.5.3. The next step is to derive the relation among the link accelerations. As in subsection 2.5.3, we first consider a relative motion among three frames Σ_A, Σ_B, and Σ_C, shown in figure 2.35. Their velocities satisfy equations 2.93 and 2.94; that is,

$$^{A}\boldsymbol{\omega}_C = {}^{A}\boldsymbol{\omega}_B + {}^{A}\boldsymbol{R}_B{}^{B}\boldsymbol{\omega}_{CB}, \tag{3.79}$$

$$^{A}\dot{\boldsymbol{p}}_C = {}^{A}\dot{\boldsymbol{p}}_B + {}^{A}\boldsymbol{R}_B\frac{d}{dt}({}^{B}\boldsymbol{p}_{CB}) + {}^{A}\boldsymbol{\omega}_B \times ({}^{A}\boldsymbol{R}_B{}^{B}\boldsymbol{p}_{CB}). \tag{3.80}$$

Differentiating equation 3.79 and applying the relation 2.91 yields

$$^{A}\dot{\boldsymbol{\omega}}_C = {}^{A}\dot{\boldsymbol{\omega}}_B + {}^{A}\boldsymbol{R}_B{}^{B}\dot{\boldsymbol{\omega}}_{CB} + {}^{A}\boldsymbol{\omega}_B \times ({}^{A}\boldsymbol{R}_B{}^{B}\boldsymbol{\omega}_{CB}). \tag{3.81}$$

Likewise, differentiating equation 3.80 and applying the relation 2.91, we have

$$\begin{aligned} {}^{A}\ddot{\boldsymbol{p}}_C = {}^{A}\ddot{\boldsymbol{p}}_B &+ {}^{A}\boldsymbol{R}_B\frac{d^2}{dt^2}({}^{B}\boldsymbol{p}_{CB}) + 2\,{}^{A}\boldsymbol{\omega}_B \times \left[{}^{A}\boldsymbol{R}_B\frac{d}{dt}({}^{B}\boldsymbol{p}_{CB})\right] \\ &+ {}^{A}\dot{\boldsymbol{\omega}}_B \times ({}^{A}\boldsymbol{R}_B{}^{B}\boldsymbol{p}_{CB}) + {}^{A}\boldsymbol{\omega}_B \times [{}^{A}\boldsymbol{\omega}_B \times ({}^{A}\boldsymbol{R}_B{}^{B}\boldsymbol{p}_{CB})]. \end{aligned} \tag{3.82}$$

The relation among accelerations of the link frames defined in subsection 2.3.3 can be derived on the basis of equations 3.81 and 3.82. As in the case of link velocities, we define vectors ${}^{0}\boldsymbol{p}_i$ and ${}^{i-1}\hat{\boldsymbol{p}}_i$ as shown in figure 3.10. We then consider the correspondences $\Sigma_A \leftrightarrow \Sigma_0$, $\Sigma_B \leftrightarrow \Sigma_{i-1}$, and $\Sigma_C \leftrightarrow \Sigma_i$ to obtain the following equations:

Revolute joint If joint i is revolute, by an argument similar to that used to find equations 2.95 and 2.96 we obtain

$${}^{0}\dot{\boldsymbol{\omega}}_i = {}^{0}\dot{\boldsymbol{\omega}}_{i-1} + {}^{0}\boldsymbol{R}_i\boldsymbol{e}_z\ddot{q}_i + {}^{0}\boldsymbol{\omega}_{i-1} \times ({}^{0}\boldsymbol{R}_i\boldsymbol{e}_z\dot{q}_i) \tag{3.83}$$

and

$$\begin{aligned} {}^{0}\ddot{\boldsymbol{p}}_i = {}^{0}\ddot{\boldsymbol{p}}_{i-1} &+ {}^{0}\dot{\boldsymbol{\omega}}_{i-1} \times ({}^{0}\boldsymbol{R}_{i-1}{}^{i-1}\hat{\boldsymbol{p}}_i) \\ &+ {}^{0}\boldsymbol{\omega}_{i-1} \times [{}^{0}\boldsymbol{\omega}_{i-1} \times ({}^{0}\boldsymbol{R}_{i-1}{}^{i-1}\hat{\boldsymbol{p}}_i)], \end{aligned} \tag{3.84}$$

where $\boldsymbol{e}_z = [0,0,1]^T$.

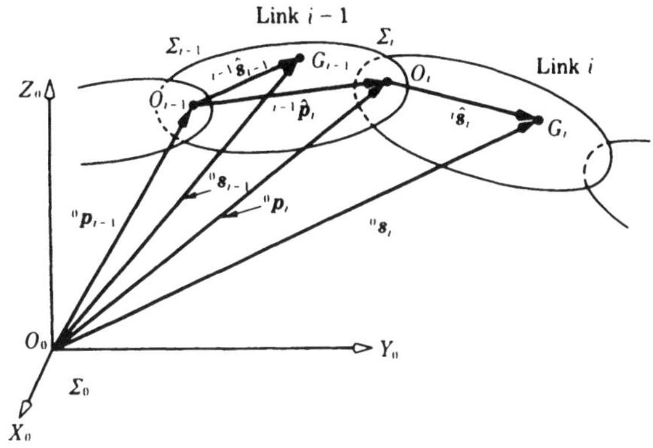

Figure 3.10
Vectors ^0p_i, $^{i-1}\hat{p}_i$, and $^i\hat{s}_i$.

Prismatic joint If joint i is prismatic, by an argument similar to that used to find equations 2.98 and 2.99 we obtain

$$^0\dot{\omega}_i = {}^0\dot{\omega}_{i-1} \tag{3.85}$$

and

$$\begin{aligned} ^0\ddot{p}_i = {}^0\ddot{p}_{i-1} + {}^0R_i e_z \ddot{q}_i + 2\,{}^0\omega_{i-1} \times ({}^0R_i e_z \dot{q}_i) \\ + {}^0\dot{\omega}_{i-1} \times ({}^0R_{i-1}{}^{i-1}\hat{p}_i) + {}^0\omega_{i-1} \times [{}^0\omega_{i-1} \times ({}^0R_{i-1}{}^{i-1}\hat{p}_i)]. \end{aligned} \tag{3.86}$$

3.4.3 *n*-Link Manipulator

In this subsection we will derive the equations of motion for a general n-link manipulator based on the Newton-Euler formulation (refs. 4, 11).

First, from equations 2.95 and 2.98, the angular velocities satisfy

$$^0\omega_i = \begin{cases} ^0\omega_{i-1} + {}^0R_i e_z \dot{q}_i & \text{if R,} \\ ^0\omega_{i-1} & \text{if P.} \end{cases} \tag{3.87}$$

Second, from equations 3.83–3.86, the accelerations satisfy

$$^0\dot{\omega}_i = \begin{cases} ^0\dot{\omega}_{i-1} + {}^0R_i e_z \ddot{q}_i + {}^0\omega_{i-1} \times ({}^0R_i e_z \dot{q}_i) & \text{if R,} \\ ^0\dot{\omega}_{i-1} & \text{if P,} \end{cases} \tag{3.88}$$

and

$$
{}^0\ddot{\boldsymbol{p}}_i = \begin{cases} {}^0\ddot{\boldsymbol{p}}_{i-1} + {}^0\dot{\omega}_{i-1} \times ({}^0\boldsymbol{R}_{i-1}{}^{i-1}\hat{\boldsymbol{p}}_i) \\ \quad + {}^0\omega_{i-1} \times [{}^0\omega_{i-1} \times ({}^0\boldsymbol{R}_{i-1}{}^{i-1}\hat{\boldsymbol{p}}_i)] \quad \text{if R,} \\ {}^0\ddot{\boldsymbol{p}}_{i-1} + {}^0\boldsymbol{R}_i\boldsymbol{e}_z\ddot{q}_i + 2\,{}^0\omega_{i-1} \times ({}^0\boldsymbol{R}_i\boldsymbol{e}_z\dot{q}_i) \\ \quad + {}^0\dot{\omega}_{i-1} \times ({}^0\boldsymbol{R}_{i-1}{}^{i-1}\hat{\boldsymbol{p}}_i) \\ \quad + {}^0\omega_{i-1} \times [{}^0\omega_{i-1} \times ({}^0\boldsymbol{R}_{i-1}{}^{i-1}\hat{\boldsymbol{p}}_i)] \quad \text{if P.} \end{cases} \tag{3.89}
$$

The linear acceleration of the center of mass of each link becomes necessary later. To find this acceleration we define ${}^0\boldsymbol{s}_i$ as the vector from O_0 to the center of mass G_i of link i, expressed in Σ_0. The vector ${}^0\boldsymbol{s}_i$ is shown in figure 3.10. We recall that ${}^i\hat{\boldsymbol{s}}_i$ is, as defined in relation to equation 3.58, the vector from the origin O_i of Σ_i to G_i expressed in Σ_i. We also denote an arbitrary coordinate frame with its origin located at G_i as Σ_{Gi}. Then, by considering the correspondences $\Sigma_A \leftrightarrow \Sigma_0$, $\Sigma_B \leftrightarrow \Sigma_i$, and $\Sigma_C \leftrightarrow \Sigma_{Gi}$, and using equation 3.82, we obtain

$$
{}^0\ddot{\boldsymbol{s}}_i = {}^0\ddot{\boldsymbol{p}}_i + {}^0\dot{\omega}_i \times ({}^0\boldsymbol{R}_i{}^i\hat{\boldsymbol{s}}_i) + {}^0\omega_i \times [{}^0\omega_i \times ({}^0\boldsymbol{R}_i{}^i\hat{\boldsymbol{s}}_i)]. \tag{3.90}
$$

Second, we let m_i be the mass of link i and let ${}^0\boldsymbol{I}_i$ be the inertia tensor with respect to the frame with its origin located at the center of mass and with the same orientation as Σ_0. Then the total external force ${}^0\hat{\boldsymbol{f}}_i$ and the total external moment ${}^0\hat{\boldsymbol{n}}_i$ are given by Newton's equation (3.3) and Euler's equation (3.18) as

$$
{}^0\hat{\boldsymbol{f}}_i = m_i\,{}^0\ddot{\boldsymbol{s}}_i \tag{3.91}
$$

and

$$
{}^0\hat{\boldsymbol{n}}_i = {}^0\boldsymbol{I}_i\,{}^0\dot{\omega}_i + {}^0\omega_i \times ({}^0\boldsymbol{I}_i\,{}^0\omega_i). \tag{3.92}
$$

Let ${}^0\boldsymbol{f}_i$ and ${}^0\boldsymbol{n}_i$ be the force and the moment exerted by link $i-1$ on link i. Also let ${}^0\hat{\boldsymbol{s}}_i = {}^0\boldsymbol{R}_i{}^i\hat{\boldsymbol{s}}_i$ and ${}^0\hat{\boldsymbol{p}}_{i+1} = {}^0\boldsymbol{R}_i{}^i\hat{\boldsymbol{p}}_{i+1}$. Then

$$
{}^0\boldsymbol{f}_i - {}^0\boldsymbol{f}_{i+1} = {}^0\hat{\boldsymbol{f}}_i \tag{3.93}
$$

and

$$
{}^0\boldsymbol{n}_i - {}^0\boldsymbol{n}_{i+1} = {}^0\hat{\boldsymbol{p}}_{i+1} \times {}^0\boldsymbol{f}_{i+1} + {}^0\hat{\boldsymbol{n}}_i + {}^0\hat{\boldsymbol{s}}_i \times {}^0\hat{\boldsymbol{f}}_i. \tag{3.94}
$$

Finally, the relation between the joint driving force τ_i and $\{{}^0\boldsymbol{f}_i, {}^0\boldsymbol{n}_i\}$ is given by

$$\tau_i = \begin{cases} {}^0z_i{}^{T\,0}n_i & \text{if R,} \\ {}^0z_i{}^{T\,0}f_i & \text{if P.} \end{cases} \tag{3.95}$$

Equations 3.87–3.95 are the equations of motion by the Newton-Euler formulation.

In the above formulation, all vectors were expressed with respect to the base frame Σ_0. If we express the vectors related to link i with respect to link frame Σ_i, a constant inertia tensor ${}^iI_i$ appears instead of ${}^0I_i$ and constant vectors ${}^iz_i$, ${}^{i-1}\hat{p}_i$, ${}^i\hat{s}_i$ appear instead of ${}^0z_i$, ${}^0\hat{p}_i$, ${}^0\hat{s}_i$, making the numerical computation easier (references 4, 6). This change of frames in which the vectors are expressed results in the following equations:

$$ {}^i\omega_i = \begin{cases} {}^{i-1}R_i{}^{T\,i-1}\omega_{i-1} + e_z\dot{q}_i & \text{if R,} \\ {}^{i-1}R_i{}^{T\,i-1}\omega_{i-1} & \text{if P,} \end{cases} \tag{3.87'}$$

$$ {}^i\dot{\omega}_i = \begin{cases} {}^{i-1}R_i{}^{T\,i-1}\dot{\omega}_{i-1} + e_z\ddot{q}_i + ({}^{i-1}R_i{}^{T\,i-1}\omega_{i-1}) \times e_z\dot{q}_i & \text{if R,} \\ {}^{i-1}R_i{}^{T\,i-1}\dot{\omega}_{i-1} & \text{if P,} \end{cases} \tag{3.88'}$$

$$ {}^i\ddot{p}_i = \begin{cases} {}^{i-1}R_i{}^T[{}^{i-1}\ddot{p}_{i-1} + {}^{i-1}\dot{\omega}_{i-1} \times {}^{i-1}\hat{p}_i \\ \quad + {}^{i-1}\omega_{i-1} \times ({}^{i-1}\omega_{i-1} \times {}^{i-1}\hat{p}_i)] & \text{if R,} \\ {}^{i-1}R_i{}^T[{}^{i-1}\ddot{p}_{i-1} + {}^{i-1}\dot{\omega}_{i-1} \times {}^{i-1}\hat{p}_i \\ \quad + {}^{i-1}\omega_{i-1} \times ({}^{i-1}\omega_{i-1} \times {}^{i-1}\hat{p}_i)] \\ \quad + 2({}^{i-1}R_i{}^{T\,i-1}\omega_{i-1}) \times (e_z\dot{q}_i) + e_z\ddot{q}_i & \text{if P,} \end{cases} \tag{3.89'}$$

$$ {}^i\ddot{s}_i = {}^i\ddot{p}_i + {}^i\dot{\omega}_i \times {}^i\hat{s}_i + {}^i\omega_i \times ({}^i\omega_i \times {}^i\hat{s}_i), \tag{3.90'}$$

$$ {}^i\hat{f}_i = m_i\,{}^i\ddot{s}_i, \tag{3.91'}$$

$$ {}^i\hat{n}_i = {}^iI_i\,{}^i\dot{\omega}_i + {}^i\omega_i \times ({}^iI_i\,{}^i\omega_i), \tag{3.92'}$$

$$ {}^if_i = {}^iR_{i+1}\,{}^{i+1}f_{i+1} + {}^i\hat{f}_i, \tag{3.93'}$$

$$ {}^in_i = {}^iR_{i+1}\,{}^{i+1}n_{i+1} + {}^i\hat{n}_i + {}^i\hat{s}_i \times {}^i\hat{f}_i + {}^i\hat{p}_{i+1} \times ({}^iR_{i+1}\,{}^{i+1}f_{i+1}), \tag{3.94'}$$

$$ \tau_i = \begin{cases} e_z{}^{T\,i}n_i & \text{if R,} \\ e_z{}^{T\,i}f_i & \text{if P.} \end{cases} \tag{3.95'}$$

Note that we have made use of the property 3.14 of the vector product in deriving the above equations.

If it is necessary to consider gravity, we only have to set

$$ {}^0\ddot{p}_0 = -\tilde{g} = -[\tilde{g}_x, \tilde{g}_y, \tilde{g}_z]^T. $$

If it is necessary to consider friction at joints, we may include a friction term γ_{Fi} to equation 3.95:

$$\tau_i = \begin{cases} {}^0z_i^{T}\,{}^0\boldsymbol{n}_i + \gamma_{Fi} & \text{if R,} \\ {}^0z_i^{T}\,{}^0\boldsymbol{f}_i + \gamma_{Fi} & \text{if P.} \end{cases} \tag{3.96}$$

Various mathematical models of friction can be used for γ_{Fi}. For a simple model consisting of viscous friction and Coulomb friction, equation 3.96 becomes

$$\tau_i = \begin{cases} {}^0z_i^{T}\,{}^0\boldsymbol{n}_i + \gamma_{FVi}\dot{q}_i + \gamma_{FCi}\,\mathrm{sgn}(\dot{q}_i) & \text{if R,} \\ {}^0z_i^{T}\,{}^0\boldsymbol{f}_i + \gamma_{FVi}\dot{q}_i + \gamma_{FCi}\,\mathrm{sgn}(\dot{q}_i) & \text{if P,} \end{cases} \tag{3.97}$$

where γ_{FVi} is the viscous friction coefficient, γ_{FCi} is the Coulomb friction coefficient, and

$$\mathrm{sgn}(\dot{q}) = \begin{cases} 1 & \text{if } \dot{q} > 0, \\ 0 & \text{if } \dot{q} = 0, \\ -1 & \text{if } \dot{q} < 0. \end{cases} \tag{3.98}$$

If there is significant static friction when $\dot{q} = 0$, the model of equation 3.97 may not be appropriate.

Example 3.2 Let us again derive the equations of motion for the two-link manipulator in figure 3.3, this time on the basis of the Newton-Euler formulation. In the following equations, $*$ denotes the elements which we will not explicitly calculate because they are not related to τ_1 or τ_2. From the mechanism of the manipulator we have

$${}^{i-1}\boldsymbol{R}_i = \begin{bmatrix} C_i & -S_i & 0 \\ S_i & C_i & 0 \\ 0 & 0 & 1 \end{bmatrix}, \quad i = 1, 2$$

$$\bar{\boldsymbol{g}} = \begin{bmatrix} 0 \\ -\hat{g} \\ 0 \end{bmatrix}, \quad {}^0\hat{\boldsymbol{p}}_1 = \begin{bmatrix} 0 \\ 0 \\ 0 \end{bmatrix}, \quad {}^1\hat{\boldsymbol{p}}_2 = \begin{bmatrix} l_1 \\ 0 \\ 0 \end{bmatrix},$$

$${}^i\boldsymbol{I}_i = \begin{bmatrix} * & * & * \\ * & * & * \\ * & * & \tilde{I}_i \end{bmatrix}, \quad {}^1\hat{\boldsymbol{s}}_1 = \begin{bmatrix} l_{g1} \\ 0 \\ 0 \end{bmatrix}, \quad {}^2\hat{\boldsymbol{s}}_2 = \begin{bmatrix} l_{g2} \\ 0 \\ 0 \end{bmatrix}.$$

If we consider the case where no external force or moment is applied to the end effector, the terminal conditions are

$$^3\boldsymbol{f}_3 = \mathbf{0}, \quad ^3\boldsymbol{n}_3 = \mathbf{0}$$

and the initial conditions are

$$^0\ddot{\boldsymbol{p}}_0 = -\bar{\boldsymbol{g}}, \quad ^0\boldsymbol{\omega}_0 = \mathbf{0}, \quad ^0\dot{\boldsymbol{\omega}}_0 = \mathbf{0}.$$

The "if R" portions of equations 3.87′–3.95′ with $i = 1, 2$, and with the above boundary conditions, are the equations of motion for the manipulator under consideration based on the Newton-Euler formulation. We can of course show that these simultaneous equations are equivalent to equations 3.38 by eliminating several intermediate variables. This is shown below: From equation 3.87′,

$$^1\boldsymbol{\omega}_1 = \begin{bmatrix} 0 \\ 0 \\ \dot{\theta}_1 \end{bmatrix}, \quad ^2\boldsymbol{\omega}_2 = \begin{bmatrix} 0 \\ 0 \\ \dot{\theta}_1 + \dot{\theta}_2 \end{bmatrix}.$$

From equation 3.88′,

$$^1\dot{\boldsymbol{\omega}}_1 = \begin{bmatrix} 0 \\ 0 \\ \ddot{\theta}_i \end{bmatrix}, \quad ^2\dot{\boldsymbol{\omega}}_2 = \begin{bmatrix} 0 \\ 0 \\ \ddot{\theta}_1 + \ddot{\theta}_2 \end{bmatrix}.$$

From equation 3.89′,

$$^1\ddot{\boldsymbol{p}}_1 = \begin{bmatrix} S_1\hat{g} \\ C_1\hat{g} \\ 0 \end{bmatrix},$$

$$^2\ddot{\boldsymbol{p}}_2 = \begin{bmatrix} S_{12}\hat{g} - l_1(C_2\dot{\theta}_1{}^2 - S_2\ddot{\theta}_1) \\ C_{12}\hat{g} + l_1(S_2\dot{\theta}_1{}^2 + C_2\ddot{\theta}_1) \\ 0 \end{bmatrix}.$$

From equation 3.90′,

$$^1\ddot{\boldsymbol{s}}_1 = \begin{bmatrix} S_1\hat{g} - l_{g1}\dot{\theta}_1{}^2 \\ C_1\hat{g} + l_{g1}\ddot{\theta}_1 \\ 0 \end{bmatrix}, \tag{3.99}$$

$$^2\ddot{\boldsymbol{s}}_2 = \begin{bmatrix} S_{12}\hat{g} - l_1(C_2\dot{\theta}_1{}^2 - S_2\ddot{\theta}_1) - l_{g2}(\dot{\theta}_1 + \dot{\theta}_2)^2 \\ C_{12}\hat{g} + l_1(S_2\dot{\theta}_1{}^2 + C_2\ddot{\theta}_1) + l_{g2}(\ddot{\theta}_1 + \ddot{\theta}_2) \\ 0 \end{bmatrix}. \tag{3.100}$$

From equations 3.91′ and 3.92′,

$$^1\hat{f}_1 = m_1\,^1\ddot{s}_1, \quad ^2\hat{f}_2 = m_2\,^2\ddot{s}_2, \tag{3.101}$$

$$^1\hat{n}_1 = \begin{bmatrix} * \\ * \\ \bar{I}_1\ddot{\theta}_1 \end{bmatrix}, \quad ^2\hat{n}_2 = \begin{bmatrix} * \\ * \\ \bar{I}_2(\ddot{\theta}_1 + \ddot{\theta}_2) \end{bmatrix}. \tag{3.102}$$

From equations 3.93′ and 3.94′,

$$^2f_2 = m_2\,^2\ddot{s}_2, \tag{3.103}$$

$$^1f_1 = \begin{bmatrix} C_2 & -S_2 & 0 \\ S_2 & C_2 & 0 \\ 0 & 0 & 1 \end{bmatrix} m_2\,^2\ddot{s}_2 + m_1\,^1\ddot{s}_1, \tag{3.104}$$

$$^2n_2 = \begin{bmatrix} * \\ * \\ \bar{I}_2(\ddot{\theta}_1 + \ddot{\theta}_2) + l_{g2}[C_{12}\hat{g} + l_1(S_2\dot{\theta}_1{}^2 + C_2\ddot{\theta}_1) + l_{g2}(\ddot{\theta}_1 + \ddot{\theta}_2)]m_2 \end{bmatrix}, \tag{3.105}$$

$$^1n_1 = \begin{bmatrix} * \\ * \\ \{\bar{I}_2(\ddot{\theta}_1 + \ddot{\theta}_2) + l_{g2}[C_{12}\hat{g} + l_1(S_2\dot{\theta}_1{}^2 + C_2\ddot{\theta}_1) \\ \quad + l_{g2}(\ddot{\theta}_1 + \ddot{\theta}_2)]m_2 \\ + \bar{I}_1\ddot{\theta}_1 + m_1 l_{g1}(C_1\hat{g} + l_{g1}\ddot{\theta}_1) \\ + m_2[l_1{}^2\ddot{\theta}_1 + l_1 l_{g2}C_2(\ddot{\theta}_1 + \ddot{\theta}_2) \\ \quad - l_1 l_{g2}S_2(\dot{\theta}_1 + \dot{\theta}_2)^2 + \hat{g}l_1C_1]\} \end{bmatrix}. \tag{3.106}$$

From equation 3.95′,

$$\tau_1 = [0,0,1]\,^1n_1, \quad \tau_2 = [0,0,1]\,^2n_2. \tag{3.107}$$

We can easily see from equations 3.105, 3.106, and 3.107 that the equations of motion given by the Newton-Euler formulation agree with equations 3.38 given by the Lagrangian formulation. □

3.5 Use of Dynamics Equations and Computational Load

3.5.1 Real-Time Control—Inverse Dynamics Problem

The conventional way of solving differential equations (in our case, the equations of motion) is to obtain the motion trajectory of the object when the applied force is known. In some control algorithms of manipulators, however, it is necessary to compute in real time the joint driving force $\boldsymbol{\tau}(t)$ to realize a desired joint trajectory $\boldsymbol{q}(t)$ given as a time function. This is often called the *inverse dynamics problem*, because this problem is the inverse of the conventional one (which is called the *direct dynamics problem* to distinguish it from the former).

One approach to the inverse dynamics problem is first to calculate $\dot{\boldsymbol{q}}(t)$ and $\ddot{\boldsymbol{q}}(t)$ from the given $\boldsymbol{q}(t)$ and then to calculate $\boldsymbol{\tau}(t)$ from these values using equation 3.62 obtained by the Lagrangian formulation. Another approach is to use equations 3.87′–3.95′ obtained by the Newton-Euler formulation instead of equation 3.62. Although the two approaches give the same solution in principle, it is known that the Newton-Euler formulation requires less computation than the Lagrangian formulation (reference 4). The following example in linear algebra will help us understand by analogy the difference in computational loads of the two approaches.

Suppose we wish to calculate the value of an n-dimensional vector $\boldsymbol{x}$ satisfying

$$\boldsymbol{x} = \boldsymbol{C}\boldsymbol{y}, \quad \boldsymbol{C} = \boldsymbol{A}\boldsymbol{B}, \tag{3.108}$$

where $\boldsymbol{A}$ and $\boldsymbol{B}$ are known $n \times n$ matrices and $\boldsymbol{y}$ is a known n-dimensional vector. There are two typical methods of computation. One is to compute $\boldsymbol{C}$ from $\boldsymbol{A}$ and $\boldsymbol{B}$ and then to find $\boldsymbol{x}$ from $\boldsymbol{C}$ and $\boldsymbol{y}$. The other is to obtain $\boldsymbol{z} = \boldsymbol{B}\boldsymbol{y}$ and then to compute $\boldsymbol{A}\boldsymbol{z}$. The former requires $(n^3 + n^2)$ multiplications and $(n^3 - n)$ additions, the latter only $2n^2$ multiplications and $(2n^2 - 2n)$ additions. We could consider that the former corresponds to the Lagrangian formulation and the latter the Newton-Euler formulation. In fact, it is known (ref. 4), as is shown in table 3.1, that the computa-

Table 3.1
Comparison of computational load.

Method	Multiplication	Addition
Lagrangian	$32\frac{1}{2}n^4 + 86\frac{5}{12}n^3 + 171\frac{1}{4}n^2 + 53\frac{1}{3}n - 128$ (66,271)	$25n^4 + 66\frac{1}{3}n^3 + 129\frac{1}{2}n^2 + 42\frac{1}{3}n - 96$ (51,548)
Newton-Euler	$150n - 48$ (852)	$131n - 48$ (738)

This table is quoted from reference 11. The integer n is the number of joints of manipulators and the number in parentheses for the case of $n = 6$. The assignment of link frames in reference 11 follows that in figure 2.22. When the assignment described in this section is used, the numbers are a little different from those in the table.

tional load of the Lagrangian formulation for a general n-link manipulator is of order n^4 and that of the Newton-Euler formulation is of order n.

We can easily understand this difference in computational loads by the following rough evaluation. In the Newton-Euler formulation, we can perform the calculation of equations 3.87′–3.95′ for any joint i by N_m multiplications and N_a additions for some integers N_m and N_a which are independent of i. Thus, for an n-link manipulator the calculation is done by $N_m n$ multiplications and $N_a n$ additions. On the other hand, in the Lagrangian formulation we have to calculate equation 3.62. The second term on the right-hand side, $\boldsymbol{h}(\boldsymbol{q},\dot{\boldsymbol{q}})$, has a computational requirement of order n^4, since the computational requirement of its ith element, h_i, by equation 3.64 is of order n^3.

More details of various usages of dynamic equations for real-time control and of the structure of their control system will be discussed in chapters 5 and 6.

3.5.2 Simulation—Direct Dynamics Problem

To do dynamic computer simulations of a manipulator, we need to determine its motion for a given joint driving force. This means that we have to solve the differential equations which are the equations of motion. For this direct dynamics problem, the Newton-Euler formulation is again advantageous in view of its relative speed of computation (reference 7). A basic procedure for solving the inverse dynamics problem with a digital computer is described using the equations of motion 3.62 for conceptual ease.

Suppose that we are given the initial state of the manipulator at time $t = 0$, i.e., the joint displacement $\boldsymbol{q}(0)$ and velocity $\dot{\boldsymbol{q}}(0)$, and the joint driving force $\boldsymbol{\tau}(t)$ for the period from the initial time to a terminal time. We first specify a small time step, Δt. Then we calculate the state of the manipulator, $\boldsymbol{q}(t)$ and $\dot{\boldsymbol{q}}(t)$, at times $t = 0, \Delta t, 2\Delta t, 3\Delta t, \ldots$, step by step until the terminal time. In this procedure, the equations of motion are used to calculate $\boldsymbol{q}(t + \Delta t)$ and $\dot{\boldsymbol{q}}(t + \Delta t)$ at time $t + \Delta t$ when $\boldsymbol{q}(t)$ and $\dot{\boldsymbol{q}}(t)$ at time t are available from the previous step.

One of the simplest ways to do this is as follows: Solving equation 3.62 for $\ddot{\boldsymbol{q}}$, we obtain

$$\ddot{\boldsymbol{q}} = \boldsymbol{M}^{-1}(\boldsymbol{q})[\boldsymbol{\tau} - \boldsymbol{h}(\boldsymbol{q},\dot{\boldsymbol{q}}) - \boldsymbol{g}(\boldsymbol{q})]. \tag{3.109}$$

We can calculate $\ddot{\boldsymbol{q}}(t)$ by substituting the known values of $\boldsymbol{q}(t)$ and $\dot{\boldsymbol{q}}(t)$ into equation 3.109. Assuming that the value of $\ddot{q}(t)$ remains constant during the interval $[t, t + \Delta t]$, we have

$$\dot{q}(t + \Delta t) = \dot{q}(t) + \ddot{q}(t)\Delta t, \tag{3.110a}$$

$$q(t + \Delta t) = q(t) + \dot{q}(t)\Delta t + \ddot{q}(t)(\Delta t)^2/2. \tag{3.110b}$$

Neglecting the term with $(\Delta t)^2$ in equation 3.110b, we obtain

$$q(t + \Delta t) \cong q(t) + \dot{q}(t)\Delta t. \tag{3.110c}$$

Thus, we can calculate $q(t + \Delta t)$ and $\dot{q}(t + \Delta t)$ using equations 3.110a and 3.110c.

The above method corresponds to the so-called Euler method for obtaining a numerical solution of ordinary differential equations, and can be considered as a method based on the Taylor-series expansion in Δt up to the first-order term. A large step size reduces the total number of steps, so it is faster to compute. However, a large change in $\ddot{q}$ may occur between t and $t + \Delta t$, which violates the assumption of $\ddot{q}(t)$ being constant in the interval. The Runge-Kutta method and many other methods use estimates of $\dot{q}$ and $\ddot{q}$ at several time instants in the interval $[t, t + \Delta t]$ for a more accurate solution.[12]

In any of the above numerical methods, it is necessary to obtain $\ddot{q}$ satisfying equation 3.109 for given q, $\dot{q}$, and τ. To do this, rather than usng equation 3.109 directly, it is more efficient to adopt the following procedure (ref. 7): First, rewrite equation 3.62 as

$$M(q)\ddot{q} = \tau - \tau_N, \tag{3.111a}$$

$$\tau_N = h(q, \dot{q}) + g(q). \tag{3.111b}$$

Then τ_N can be found by using the fact that τ_N coincides with τ calculated from the Newton-Euler formulation (equations 3.87′–3.95′) with $\ddot{q} = 0$. The matrix $M(q)$ can also be determined by using the fact that its jth column vector M_j coincides with τ calculated from the Newton-Euler formulation with $\ddot{q} = e_j$ (the unit vector with the jth element equal to $1, j = 1, 2, \ldots, n$) and with all the other terms that are unaffected by $\ddot{q}$ set equal to zero. Having calculated τ_N and $M(q)$, and given τ, we know that 3.111a is an algebraic equation with unknown vector $\ddot{q}$. As is well known, this equation can be effectively solved by the Gauss elimination method.

The amount of computation needed for the above procedure is

$$\tfrac{1}{6}n^3 + (75 + \tfrac{1}{2})n^2 + (114 + \tfrac{1}{3})n - 22$$

multiplications and

$$\tfrac{1}{6}n^3 + 55n^2 + (82 + \tfrac{5}{6})n - 11$$

additions (ref. 7). Hence, when $n = 6$, there are 3,418 multiplications and 2,502 additions. This is, of course, less than the amount needed for the procedure in which τ_N and $M(q)$ are calculated directly by the Lagrangian formulation (that is, by means of equations 3.63, 3.64, and 3.65).

3.6 Identification of Manipulator Dynamics

3.6.1 Identification Problem of Manipulators

When we wish to use the dynamic equations of motion for a manipulator, the values of various parameters in the equations must be known. These parameters can be divided into two groups: kinematic parameters and dynamic parameters. Kinematic parameters are those that appear in the kinematic equations as well as in the dynamic equations; and dynamic parameters are those that appear only in the dynamic equations. Kinematic parameters are typically given by the set of link parameters, which can be obtained from the drawings or by static measurements of sizes from a manipulator itself. Dynamic parameters usually consist of inertial parameters (i.e., zeroth-, first-, and second-order moments of inertia of the links), and friction constants. The inertial parameters could be calculated by measuring the size and weight of each part of a manipulator, either before assembling it or by dismantling an already assembled manipulator. Not only are these practices time consuming; they usually do not produce very accurate results. It would be more practical to estimate the dynamic parameters by some identification method based on data taken during certain test motions of the manipulator.[13,14]

Various identification schemes have been developed for general dynamic systems.[15] Roughly speaking, the identification problem of manipulators is also one of these problems. However, it has the following special features:

(i) Since the structures of manipulators are not very complex, a black-box approach (identification of the structure and its order) is not necessary. It is usually enough to consider the problem as that of identifying the parameters of a system with a known structure.
(ii) Since the dynamics change when a manipulator grasps an object or

performs some task, it is desirable to identify this change and to use the result for control. This process requires an on-line identification method.

An identification scheme taking these points into consideration is the subject of the next subsection.

3.6.2 Identification Scheme Based on Lagrangian Formulation

As can be seen from equation 3.61, which is based on the Lagrangian formulation, all the dynamic parameters are contained in the pseudo inertia matrix $\boldsymbol{\hat{H}}_i$ given by equation 3.53. Note that, since

$$m_i\,{}^i\hat{s}_i = \boldsymbol{\hat{H}}_i[0,0,0,1]^T, \tag{3.112}$$

the third term on the right-hand side of equation 3.61, which represents the gravity force, can also be expressed using $\boldsymbol{\hat{H}}_i$. Note also that, for any pair of $n \times m$ matrix $\boldsymbol{A} = [a_{ij}]$ and $m \times n$ matrix $\boldsymbol{B} = [b_{ij}]$, we have

$$\operatorname{tr}(\boldsymbol{AB}) = \sum_{i=1}^{n} \sum_{j=1}^{m} a_{ij} b_{ji} = \operatorname{tr}(\boldsymbol{BA}). \tag{3.113}$$

Using equation 3.113, we can rewrite the dynamic equation 3.61 as

$$\begin{aligned}\tau_i = {} & \sum_{k=i}^{n} \sum_{j=1}^{k} \operatorname{tr}\left(\frac{\partial\, {}^0\boldsymbol{T}_k{}^T}{\partial q_i} \frac{\partial\, {}^0\boldsymbol{T}_k}{\partial q_j} \boldsymbol{\hat{H}}_k\right) \ddot{q}_j \\ & + \sum_{k=i}^{n} \sum_{j=1}^{k} \sum_{m=1}^{k} \operatorname{tr}\left(\frac{\partial\, {}^0\boldsymbol{T}_k{}^T}{\partial q_i} \frac{\partial^2\, {}^0\boldsymbol{T}_k}{\partial q_j \partial q_m} \boldsymbol{\hat{H}}_k\right) \dot{q}_j \dot{q}_m \\ & - \sum_{k=i}^{n} \boldsymbol{\bar{g}}^T \frac{\partial\, {}^0\boldsymbol{T}_k}{\partial q_i} \boldsymbol{\hat{H}}_k [0,0,0,1]^T.\end{aligned} \tag{3.114}$$

This can further be rewritten as

$$\tau_i = \sum_{k=i}^{n} \operatorname{tr}(\boldsymbol{D}_{ik} \boldsymbol{\hat{H}}_k), \tag{3.115}$$

where

$$\boldsymbol{D}_{ik} = \frac{\partial\, {}^0\boldsymbol{T}_k{}^T}{\partial q_i} \left\{ \sum_{j=1}^{k} \left[\ddot{q}_j \frac{\partial\, {}^0\boldsymbol{T}_k}{\partial q_j} + \dot{q}_j \left(\sum_{m=1}^{k} \dot{q}_m \frac{\partial^2\, {}^0\boldsymbol{T}_k}{\partial q_j \partial q_m} \right) \right] - \boldsymbol{\bar{g}}[0,0,0,1] \right\}. \tag{3.116}$$

Note that the kinematic parameters are all contained in the homogeneous transforms ${}^0\boldsymbol{T}_i$ $(i = 1, 2, \ldots, n)$, and the dynamic parameters are all contained in $\boldsymbol{\hat{H}}_i$ $(i = 1, 2, \ldots, n)$.

We assume that all the kinematic parameters are known, but the dynamic ones are unknown. The identification problem we consider is that of estimating the unknown parameters in $\hat{\boldsymbol{H}}_i$ from a set of data acquired during a test motion of the manipulator. We have two kinds of data: data about motion (i.e., the position q_i, velocity $\dot{q}_i$, and acceleration $\ddot{q}_i$ of each joint) and data about force (i.e., the joint driving force τ_i, and measurements from force sensors attached to the manipulator, if any).

We first consider the case where only the joint driving forces are available as data about force. From equation 3.113, it can be easily understood that the right-hand side of equation 3.115 is linear in all elements of $\hat{\boldsymbol{H}}_i$. In order to make this fact clearer, we define the parameter vector $\boldsymbol{\phi}_i$, which has a one-to-one correspondence with $\hat{\boldsymbol{H}}_i$:

$$\boldsymbol{\phi}_i = [\phi_{i1},\phi_{i2},\ldots,\phi_{i10}]^T$$
$$= [m_i, m_i\hat{s}_{ix}, m_i\hat{s}_{iy}, m_i\hat{s}_{iz}, \hat{I}_{ixx}, \hat{I}_{iyy}, \hat{I}_{izz}, \hat{I}_{ixy}, \hat{I}_{iyz}, \hat{I}_{ixz}]^T. \quad (3.117)$$

Then equation 3.115 can be expressed as

$$\tau_i = \boldsymbol{K}_i\boldsymbol{\phi}, \quad (3.118)$$

where $\boldsymbol{\phi}$ is a $10n$-dimensional unknown parameter vector given by

$$\boldsymbol{\phi} = [\boldsymbol{\phi}_1{}^T, \boldsymbol{\phi}_2{}^T, \ldots, \boldsymbol{\phi}_n{}^T]^T \quad (3.119)$$

and $\boldsymbol{K}_i$ is a $10n$-dimensional row vector determined by $\boldsymbol{D}_{ik}$ ($k = i, i+1, \ldots, n$). More specifically, $\boldsymbol{K}_i$ is given as follows: Write

$$\boldsymbol{K}_i = [\boldsymbol{K}_{i1}, \boldsymbol{K}_{i2}, \ldots, \boldsymbol{K}_{in}], \quad (3.120a)$$

$$\boldsymbol{K}_{ij} = [K_{ij1}, K_{ij2}, \ldots, K_{ij10}], \quad (3.120b)$$

and write the (j,h) element of $\boldsymbol{D}_{ik}$ as $(\boldsymbol{D}_{ik})_{jh}$. Then, for $j = 1, 2, \ldots, i-1$, we have

$$\boldsymbol{K}_{ij} = \boldsymbol{0}, \quad (3.120c)$$

and for $j = i, i+1, \ldots, n$, we have

$$K_{ij1} = (D_{ij})_{44},$$

$$K_{ij2} = (D_{ij})_{14} + (D_{ij})_{41},$$

$$K_{ij3} = (D_{ij})_{24} + (D_{ij})_{42},$$

$$K_{ij4} = (D_{ij})_{34} + (D_{ij})_{43},$$

$$K_{ij5} = [-(D_{ij})_{11} + (D_{ij})_{22} + (D_{ij})_{33}]/2,$$
$$K_{ij6} = [(D_{ij})_{11} - (D_{ij})_{22} + (D_{ij})_{33}]/2, \qquad (3.120d)$$
$$K_{ij7} = [(D_{ij})_{11} + (D_{ij})_{22} - (D_{ij})_{33}]/2,$$
$$K_{ij8} = (D_{ij})_{12} + (D_{ij})_{21},$$
$$K_{ij9} = (D_{ij})_{23} + (D_{ij})_{32}.$$
$$K_{ij10} = (D_{ij})_{31} + (D_{ij})_{13}.$$

Summing equation 3.118 up for $i = 1, 2, \ldots, n$, we obtain the linear equation[16]

$$\boldsymbol{\tau} = \boldsymbol{K}\boldsymbol{\phi}, \qquad (3.121)$$

where

$$\boldsymbol{K} = \begin{bmatrix} \boldsymbol{K}_1 \\ \boldsymbol{K}_2 \\ \vdots \\ \boldsymbol{K}_n \end{bmatrix}. \qquad (3.122)$$

Each element of $\boldsymbol{K}$ of equation 3.122 is a continuous function of $\boldsymbol{q}$, $\dot{\boldsymbol{q}}$, and $\ddot{\boldsymbol{q}}$. Therefore, it is possible to identify some elements of $\boldsymbol{\phi}$ from data $\boldsymbol{q}$, $\dot{\boldsymbol{q}}$, $\ddot{\boldsymbol{q}}$, and $\boldsymbol{\tau}$ taken from various motions of the manipulator. However, not all the elements are identifiable. Let us address the question of which part of $\boldsymbol{\phi}$ is identifiable.[17] For this purpose, we consider an expression of $\boldsymbol{K}$ as a product of two matrices,

$$\boldsymbol{K} = \boldsymbol{K}_d \boldsymbol{L}_d, \qquad (3.123)$$

where $\boldsymbol{K}_d$ is an $n \times n_d$ matrix whose elements are functions of $\boldsymbol{q}$, $\dot{\boldsymbol{q}}$, and $\ddot{\boldsymbol{q}}$; $\boldsymbol{L}_d$ is an $n_d \times 10n$ constant matrix; and n_d is a positive integer satisfying $n_d \leqq 10n$. The matrix $\boldsymbol{L}_d$ can be a function of the link parameters because we regard the link parameters as known constants. Further, we assume that the row vectors of $\boldsymbol{L}_d$ are linearly independent, which implies that the rank of $\boldsymbol{L}_d$ is n_d. There is an infinite number of pairs of $\boldsymbol{K}_d$ and $\boldsymbol{L}_d$ satisfying equation 3.123. We select one pair $\boldsymbol{K}_d^*$ and $\boldsymbol{L}_d^*$ such that n_d takes the smallest value, which we call n_d^*. Then, of the identifiable linear functions of the parameter $\boldsymbol{\phi}$, the one with the largest dimension is given by

$$\boldsymbol{\phi}_d^* = \boldsymbol{L}_d^* \boldsymbol{\phi}, \qquad (3.124)$$

and we write

$$\boldsymbol{\tau} = \boldsymbol{K}_d{}^*\boldsymbol{\phi}_d{}^*. \tag{3.125}$$

A collection of data $\boldsymbol{\tau}$, $\boldsymbol{q}$, $\dot{\boldsymbol{q}}$, and $\ddot{\boldsymbol{q}}$ gathered at an instant in time will be called a *data point*. We consider an arbitrary set of N data points and let $\boldsymbol{\tau}$, $\boldsymbol{K}_d$, and $\boldsymbol{K}_d{}^*$ for the ith data point be $\boldsymbol{\tau}(i)$, $\boldsymbol{K}_d(i)$, and $\boldsymbol{K}_d{}^*(i)$. We further define

$$\boldsymbol{\tau}_g = \begin{bmatrix} \boldsymbol{\tau}(1) \\ \boldsymbol{\tau}(2) \\ \vdots \\ \boldsymbol{\tau}(N) \end{bmatrix}, \quad \boldsymbol{K}_g{}^* = \begin{bmatrix} \boldsymbol{K}_d{}^*(1) \\ \boldsymbol{K}_d{}^*(2) \\ \vdots \\ \boldsymbol{K}_d{}^*(N) \end{bmatrix}. \tag{3.126}$$

Then we have

$$\boldsymbol{\tau}_g = \boldsymbol{K}_g{}^*\boldsymbol{\phi}_d{}^*. \tag{3.127}$$

If $N \geqq n_d{}^*$, then we can show that

$$\text{rank } \boldsymbol{K}_g{}^* = n_d{}^* \tag{3.128}$$

for almost all sets of data points. If it should accidentally happen that equation 3.128 were not satisfied by the given set of data points, we would only have to add more data points until that equation held. The minimum mean square error estimate of $\boldsymbol{\phi}_d{}^*$ (that is, the estimate minimizing $\|\boldsymbol{\tau}_g - \boldsymbol{K}_g{}^*\boldsymbol{\phi}_d{}^*\|$) is given by

$$\boldsymbol{\phi}_d{}^* = (\boldsymbol{K}_g{}^{*T}\boldsymbol{K}_g{}^*)^{-1}\boldsymbol{K}_g{}^{*T}\boldsymbol{\tau}_g. \tag{3.129}$$

(See equations A2.23 and A2.13 in appendix 2.)

Instead of giving an algorithm for finding an $\boldsymbol{L}_d{}^*$ for a given $\boldsymbol{K}$, we will consider a different approach to finding an $\boldsymbol{L}_d{}^*$. We assume that somehow a candidate $\boldsymbol{L}_d$ for $\boldsymbol{L}_d{}^*$ satisfying equation 3.123 is given, and that we are asked to confirm whether this $\boldsymbol{L}_d$ is really an $\boldsymbol{L}_d{}^*$. The answer is that $\boldsymbol{\phi}_d = \boldsymbol{L}_d\boldsymbol{\phi}$ is an identifiable linear function of $\boldsymbol{\phi}$ with the largest dimension if there exist an integer N and a set of data points such that the rank of

$$\boldsymbol{K}_g = [\boldsymbol{K}_d{}^T(1), \boldsymbol{K}_d{}^T(2), \ldots, \boldsymbol{K}_d{}^T(N)]^T$$

is n_d.

We can use a hypothetical set of data points in the above criterion, because we need data about motion but not data about force.

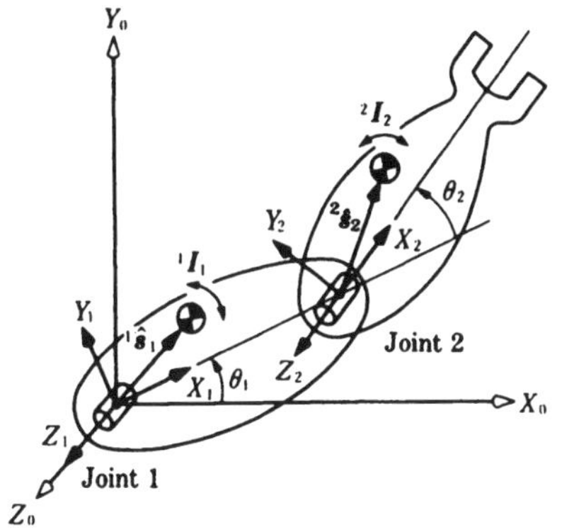

Figure 3.11
Two-link manipulator.

Example 3.3 Consider the serial-drive two-link manipulator shown in figure 3.11. The two axes are parallel to the axis Z_0 of the reference frame. The length of link 1 is denoted by l_1. Gravity acts in the negative Y_0 direction. We will consider the identification problem for this manipulator when the joint driving forces τ_1 and τ_2 are measurable. We first assign the link frames Σ_1 and Σ_2 so that each origin is in the X_0–Y_0 plane. We denote the mass of link i as m_i, the center of mass as ${}^i\hat{\boldsymbol{s}}_i$, and the inertial tensor as ${}^i\boldsymbol{I}_i$. The dynamic equations found by the Lagrangian formulation are

$$\tau_1 = M_{11}\ddot{\theta}_1 + M_{12}\ddot{\theta}_2 + h_{122}\dot{\theta}_2{}^2 + 2h_{112}\dot{\theta}_1\dot{\theta}_2 + g_1 \tag{3.130}$$

and

$$\tau_2 = M_{12}\ddot{\theta}_1 + M_{22}\ddot{\theta}_2 + h_{211}\dot{\theta}_1{}^2 + g_2, \tag{3.131}$$

where the coefficients are

$$M_{11} = m_1 l_{g1}{}^2 + {}^1I_{1zz} + m_2[l_1{}^2 + l_{g2}{}^2 + 2l_1(C_2\hat{s}_{2x} - S_2\hat{s}_{2y})] + {}^2I_{2zz}, \tag{3.132a}$$

$$M_{12} = m_2[l_{g2}{}^2 + l_1(C_2\hat{s}_{2x} - S_2\hat{s}_{2y})] + {}^2I_{2zz}, \tag{3.132b}$$

$$M_{22} = m_2 l_{g2}{}^2 + {}^2I_{2zz}, \tag{3.132c}$$

$$l_{g1}{}^2 = \hat{s}_{1x}{}^2 + \hat{s}_{1y}{}^2, \quad l_{g2}{}^2 = \hat{s}_{2x}{}^2 + \hat{s}_{2y}{}^2, \tag{3.133}$$

$$-h_{122} = -h_{112} = h_{211} = m_2 l_1(\hat{s}_{2x}S_2 + \hat{s}_{2y}C_2), \tag{3.134}$$

$$g_1 = m_1\hat{g}(\hat{s}_{1x}C_1 - \hat{s}_{1y}S_1) + m_2\hat{g}(l_1C_1 + \hat{s}_{2x}C_{12} - \hat{s}_{2y}S_{12}), \tag{3.135a}$$

$$g_2 = m_2\hat{g}(\hat{s}_{2x}C_{12} - \hat{s}_{2y}S_{12}). \tag{3.135b}$$

Next we find equation 3.121 and study the identifiability of $\boldsymbol{\phi}$. Noting that $\phi_{i1} = m_i$,

$$[\phi_{i2},\phi_{i3},\phi_{i4}] = [m_i\hat{s}_{ix},m_i\hat{s}_{iy},m_i\hat{s}_{iz}],$$

and

$$\phi_{i7} = \hat{I}_{izz} = {}^iI_{izz} + m_il_{gi}^2,$$

we have from equations 3.130 and 3.131

$$\begin{aligned}\tau_1 = {} & [\phi_{17} + \phi_{21}l_1^2 + \phi_{27} + 2l_1(C_2\phi_{22} - S_2\phi_{23})]\ddot{\theta}_1 \\ & + [\phi_{27} + l_1(C_2\phi_{22} - S_2\phi_{23})]\ddot{\theta}_2 \\ & - l_1(S_2\phi_{22} + C_2\phi_{23})(\dot{\theta}_2^2 + 2\dot{\theta}_1\dot{\theta}_2) \\ & + \hat{g}(C_1\phi_{12} - S_1\phi_{13} + l_1C_1\phi_{21} + C_{12}\phi_{22} - S_{12}\phi_{23}),\end{aligned} \tag{3.136}$$

and

$$\begin{aligned}\tau_2 = {} & [\phi_{27} + l_1(C_2\phi_{22} - S_2\phi_{23})]\ddot{\theta}_1 + \phi_{27}\ddot{\theta}_2 \\ & + l_1(S_2\phi_{22} + C_2\phi_{23})\dot{\theta}_1^2 + \hat{g}(C_{12}\phi_{22} - S_{12}\phi_{23}),\end{aligned} \tag{3.137}$$

or

$$\begin{bmatrix}\tau_1 \\ \tau_2\end{bmatrix} = \boldsymbol{K}\begin{bmatrix}\boldsymbol{\phi}_1 \\ \boldsymbol{\phi}_2\end{bmatrix}, \tag{3.138}$$

where

$$\boldsymbol{K} = \left[\begin{array}{c|ccc|cccccc|cccc|cccccc} 0 & \hat{g}C_1 & -\hat{g}S_1 & 0 & 0 & 0 & \ddot{\theta}_1 & 0 & 0 & 0 & l_1^2\ddot{\theta}_1 + \hat{g}l_1C_1 & k_{1,2,2} & k_{1,2,3} & 0 & 0 & 0 & \ddot{\theta}_1 + \ddot{\theta}_2 & 0 & 0 & 0 \\ 0 & 0 & 0 & 0 & 0 & 0 & 0 & 0 & 0 & 0 & 0 & k_{2,2,2} & k_{2,2,3} & 0 & 0 & 0 & \ddot{\theta}_1 + \ddot{\theta}_2 & 0 & 0 & 0 \end{array}\right], \tag{3.139}$$

$$k_{1,2,2} = l_1C_2(2\ddot{\theta}_1 + \ddot{\theta}_2) - l_1S_2(\dot{\theta}_2^2 + 2\dot{\theta}_1\dot{\theta}_2) + \hat{g}C_{12}, \tag{3.140a}$$

$$k_{2,2,2} = l_1C_2\ddot{\theta}_1 + l_1S_2\dot{\theta}_1^2 + \hat{g}C_{12}, \tag{3.140b}$$

$$k_{1,2,3} = -l_1S_2(2\ddot{\theta}_1 + \ddot{\theta}_2) - l_1C_2(\dot{\theta}_2^2 + 2\dot{\theta}_1\dot{\theta}_2) - \hat{g}S_{12}, \tag{3.140c}$$

$$k_{2,2,3} = -l_1S_2\ddot{\theta}_1 + l_1C_2\dot{\theta}_1^2 - \hat{g}S_{12}, \tag{3.140d}$$

One way of guessing the identifiable parameters is to consider equations 3.136 and 3.137 with several special data points. For example, from the case $\ddot{\theta}_i = \dot{\theta}_i = 0$ $(i = 1, 2)$ we can easily see that ϕ_{22}, ϕ_{23}, ϕ_{13}, and $\phi_{12} + l_1\phi_{21}$ are identifiable. Considering another case, when $\dot{\theta}_i = 0$ and $\ddot{\theta}_i \neq 0$, we see that ϕ_{27} and $\phi_{17} + l_1{}^2\phi_{21}$ are identifiable. A candidate for $\boldsymbol{\phi}_d = \boldsymbol{L}_d\boldsymbol{\phi}$ is, therefore, given by

$$\boldsymbol{\phi}_d = \begin{bmatrix} \phi_{12} + l_1\phi_{21} \\ \phi_{13} \\ \phi_{17} + l_1{}^2\phi_{21} \\ \phi_{22} \\ \phi_{23} \\ \phi_{27} \end{bmatrix}. \tag{3.141}$$

The corresponding $\boldsymbol{K}_d$ is

$$\boldsymbol{K}_d = \begin{bmatrix} \hat{g}C_1 & -\hat{g}S_1 & \ddot{\theta}_1 & k_{1,2,2} & k_{1,2,3} & \ddot{\theta}_1 + \ddot{\theta}_2 \\ 0 & 0 & 0 & k_{2,2,2} & k_{2,2,3} & \ddot{\theta}_1 + \ddot{\theta}_2 \end{bmatrix}, \tag{3.142}$$

and $n_d = 6$. Now we will check whether this n_d is actually $n_d{}^*$. Let us take, for example, the following data points:

Data point 1: $\theta_i = \dot{\theta}_i = \ddot{\theta}_i = 0$,

Data point 2: $\theta_1 = 90°$, $\theta_2 = 0$, $\dot{\theta}_i = \ddot{\theta}_i = 0$,

Data point 3: $\theta_i = 0$, $\dot{\theta}_i = 0$, $\ddot{\theta}_1 \neq 0$, $\ddot{\theta}_2 = 0$.

Then

$$\operatorname{rank}\begin{bmatrix} \boldsymbol{K}_d(1) \\ \boldsymbol{K}_d(2) \\ \boldsymbol{K}_d(3) \end{bmatrix} = 6.$$

Therefore we have $n_d{}^* = 6$, verifying that $\boldsymbol{\phi}_d$ given by equation 3.141 is really a $\boldsymbol{\phi}_d{}^*$ and that $\boldsymbol{K}_d$ given by equation 3.142 is the corresponding $\boldsymbol{K}_d{}^*$. (Equation 3.138 can also be determined from equations 3.120 and 3.116, but here we have derived it from a more common form of the dynamic equations 3.130 and 3.131.) □

Finally, let us consider the identification problem when some outputs from a force sensor are available. As a preparation, note that the force exerted on the sensor is expressed analytically using the Lagrangian formulation. A force sensor is a device that measures the torque about an axis, the force along an axis, or a set of several such forces and torques simultaneously. For simplicity, we will consider only the case of a one-axis force sensor attached to a link of a manipulator.

The link with the sensor is divided into two links with a virtual joint between them. When the sensor is a torque sensor, the virtual joint is assumed to be revolute. When the sensor is a force sensor, the virtual joint is assumed to be prismatic. The axis of the virtual joint is assigned to be the axis of the force sensor. We derive the dynamic equation for this virtual manipulator with the extra degree of freedom using the Lagrangian formulation. From this dynamic equation with the velocity and acceleration of the virtual joint set equal to zero, the force or torque exerted on the sensor can be found as the joint driving force for the virtual joint with its sign changed. We can also determine the force and torque exerted on a multi-axis force sensor by regarding it as a combination of one-axis force sensors and repeating the above procedure.

Example 3.4 Consider a one-link manipulator with a force sensor as shown in figure 3.12. The joint is revolute, with its axis Z_1 equal to Z_0. The sensor measures the torque about an axis Z_2 parallel to Z_0. We want to identify the dynamic parameters using the sensor output as well as the torque measurement at the joint.

We first determine the analytical expression for the output of the force sensor. The two-joint manipulator produced by adding a virtual joint at the force sensor is exactly the same as that in example 3.3. Its dynamic

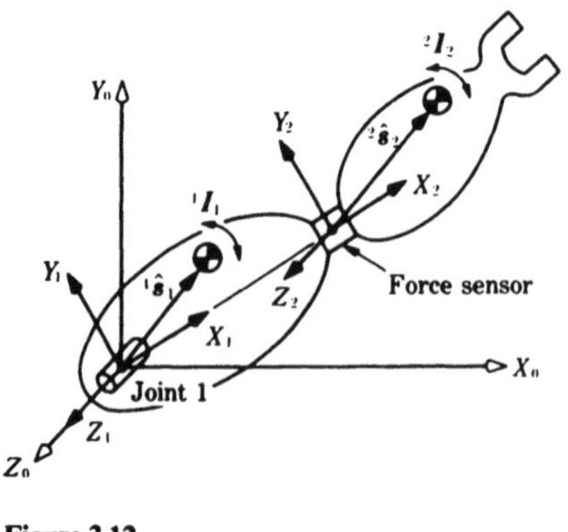

Figure 3.12
One-link manipulator with force sensor.

equation, therefore, is given by equations 3.130–3.135. Setting $\theta_2 = \dot{\theta}_2 = \ddot{\theta}_2 = 0$, we have

$$\begin{aligned} \tau_1 &= M_{11}\ddot{\theta}_1 + g_1, \\ \tau_2 &= M_{12}\ddot{\theta}_1 + h_{211}\dot{\theta}_1^2 + g_2, \end{aligned} \tag{3.143}$$

where

$$M_{11} = m_1 l_{g1}^2 + {}^1I_{1zz} + m_2(l_1^2 + l_{g2}^2 + 2l_1\hat{s}_{2x}) + {}^2I_{2zz},$$

$$M_{12} = m_2(l_{g2}^2 + l_1\hat{s}_{2x}) + {}^2I_{2zz},$$

$$h_{211} = m_2 l_1 \hat{s}_{2y},$$

$$g_1 = m_1\hat{g}(\hat{s}_{1x}C_1 - \hat{s}_{1y}S_1) + m_2\hat{g}(l_1C_1 + \hat{s}_{2x}C_1 - \hat{s}_{2y}S_1),$$

$$g_2 = m_2\hat{g}(\hat{s}_{2x}C_1 - \hat{s}_{2y}S_1).$$

From equation 3.143 we obtain

$$\begin{aligned} \tau_1 &= (\phi_{17} + \phi_{21}l_1^2 + \phi_{27} + 2l_1\phi_{22})\ddot{\theta}_1 \\ &\quad + \hat{g}(C_1\phi_{12} - S_1\phi_{13} + l_1C_1\phi_{21} + C_1\phi_{22} - S_1\phi_{23}), \\ \tau_2 &= (\phi_{27} + l_1\phi_{22})\ddot{\theta}_1 + l_1\phi_{23}\dot{\theta}_1^2 + \hat{g}(C_1\phi_{22} - S_1\phi_{23}). \end{aligned}$$

By an argument similar to that for example 3.3, we can conclude that $\boldsymbol{\phi}_d$ given by equation 3.141 is a $\boldsymbol{\phi}_d^*$. In this case we have

$$\boldsymbol{K}_d^* = \left[\begin{array}{c|c|c|c|c|c} \hat{g}C_1 & -\hat{g}S_1 & \ddot{\theta}_1 & 2l_1\ddot{\theta}_1 + \hat{g}C_1 & -\hat{g}S_1 & \ddot{\theta}_1 \\ 0 & 0 & 0 & l_1\ddot{\theta}_1 + \hat{g}C_1 & l_1\dot{\theta}_1^2 - \hat{g}S_1 & \ddot{\theta}_1 \end{array}\right]. \ \square$$

Even when the friction at joints cannot be neglected, if we can measure the joint driving torque on the actuator side we can identify the Coulomb-friction and viscous-friction coefficients, along with other dynamic parameters, using an approach similar to the one described above. For example, if the model of friction is given by equation 3.97, instead of equation 3.121 we have

$$\begin{aligned} \boldsymbol{\tau} &= \boldsymbol{K\phi} + \mathrm{diag}[\dot{q}_i]\boldsymbol{\phi}_V + \mathrm{diag}[\mathrm{sgn}(\dot{q}_i)]\boldsymbol{\phi}_C \\ &= [\boldsymbol{K} \mid \mathrm{diag}[\dot{q}_i] \mid \mathrm{diag}[\mathrm{sgn}(\dot{q}_i)]]\,[\boldsymbol{\phi}^T, \boldsymbol{\phi}_V^T, \boldsymbol{\phi}_C^T]^T, \end{aligned} \tag{3.144}$$

where

$$\boldsymbol{\phi}_V = [\gamma_{FV1}, \gamma_{FV2}, \ldots, \gamma_{FVn}]^T, \tag{3.145a}$$

$$\boldsymbol{\phi}_C = [\gamma_{FC1}, \gamma_{FC2}, \ldots, \gamma_{FCn}]^T. \tag{3.145b}$$

Hence, by regarding $[\boldsymbol{\phi}^T, \boldsymbol{\phi}_V{}^T, \boldsymbol{\phi}_C{}^T]^T$ as a new $\boldsymbol{\phi}$, and by regarding the coefficient matrix $[\boldsymbol{K} \mid \text{diag}[\dot{q}_i] \mid \text{diag}[\text{sgn}(\dot{q}_i)]]$ (which relates this new $\boldsymbol{\phi}$ to $\boldsymbol{\tau}$) as a new $\boldsymbol{K}$, we obtain an equation of the same form as equation 3.121. Therefore, using equation 3.129 we can identify $\boldsymbol{\phi}_V$ and $\boldsymbol{\phi}_C$ as well as $\boldsymbol{\phi}_d{}^*$.

3.6.3 Identification of Load

Since the load grasped by the end effector may be considered part of the last link, we can gain information about the dynamic parameters of the load through identification of $\boldsymbol{\phi}_n$.

Example 3.5 Suppose that the manipulator of example 3.3 is grasping a load as in figure 3.13. Also suppose that the true value of parameter $\boldsymbol{\phi}_d{}^*$ when the manipulator does not grasp the load is known to be $\boldsymbol{\phi}_d{}^{*a}$ and the identified value of the same parameter when it grasps the load turns out to be $\boldsymbol{\phi}_d{}^{*b}$. We will examine what information can be gained from these data about the mass m_l, the location of the center of mass, ${}^2\hat{\boldsymbol{s}}_l$, and the inertia tensor ${}^2\boldsymbol{I}_l$ of the load with respect to Σ_2. As we distinguished $\boldsymbol{\phi}_d{}^{*a}$ and $\boldsymbol{\phi}_d{}^{*b}$, let us distinguish other parameters without load from those with load by using the superscripts a and b, respectively. Then, by definition, $\phi_{21}{}^b$, $\phi_{22}{}^b$, $\phi_{23}{}^b$, and $\phi_{27}{}^b$ are

$$\phi_{21}{}^b = m_2 + m_l, \tag{3.146a}$$

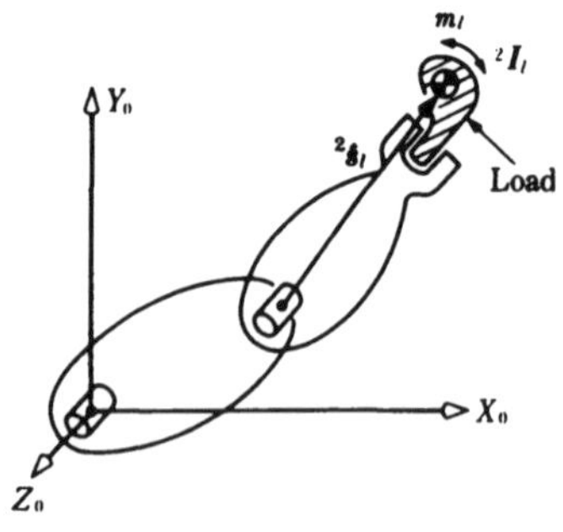

Figure 3.13
Two-link manipulator with load.

$$\phi_{22}{}^{b} = m_2 \hat{s}_{2x} + m_l \hat{s}_{lx}, \tag{3.146b}$$

$$\phi_{23}{}^{b} = m_2 \hat{s}_{2y} + m_l \hat{s}_{ly}, \tag{3.146c}$$

$$\phi_{27}{}^{b} = {}^2I_{2zz} + m_2 l_{g2}{}^2 + {}^2I_{lzz} + m_l l_{gl}{}^2, \tag{3.146d}$$

where ${}^2\hat{s}_l = [\hat{s}_{lx}, \hat{s}_{ly}, \hat{s}_{lz}]^T$ and

$$l_{gl} = \sqrt{\hat{s}_{lx}{}^2 + \hat{s}_{ly}{}^2}. \tag{3.147}$$

Hence, when we let $\boldsymbol{\phi}_d{}^* = [\phi_{d1}, \ldots, \phi_{d6}]^T$ we have

$$m_l = \phi_{21}{}^{b} - \phi_{21}{}^{a} = (\phi_{d1}{}^{b} - \phi_{d1}{}^{a})/l_1, \tag{3.148a}$$

$$m_l \hat{s}_{lx} = \phi_{22}{}^{b} - \phi_{22}{}^{a} = \phi_{d4}{}^{b} - \phi_{d4}{}^{a}, \tag{3.148b}$$

$$m_l \hat{s}_{ly} = \phi_{23}{}^{b} - \phi_{23}{}^{a} = \phi_{d5}{}^{b} - \phi_{d5}{}^{a}, \tag{3.148c}$$

$${}^2I_{lzz} + m_l l_{gl}{}^2 = \phi_{27}{}^{b} - \phi_{27}{}^{a} = \phi_{d6}{}^{b} - \phi_{d6}{}^{a}. \tag{3.148d}$$

From these equations we can obtain the values of m_l, $\hat{s}_{lx}$, $\hat{s}_{ly}$, and ${}^2\hat{I}_{lzz} = {}^2I_{lzz} + m_l l_{gl}{}^2$. Although we cannot know the mass m_2 of link 2, we can find the mass m_l of the load alone. □

Exercises

3.1 Prove equation 3.11 using equation 3.5.

3.2 Derive the equations of motion for the two-link manipulator in figure 3.14 using the Lagrangian formulation. Let l_{g1} be the distance between joint

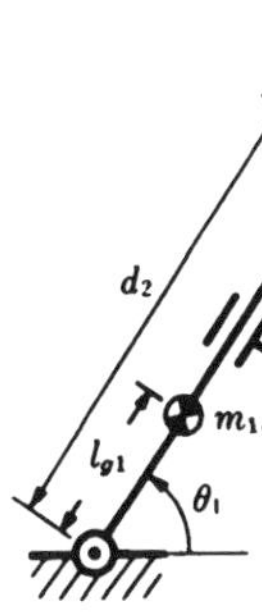

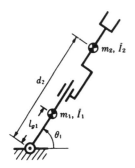

Figure 3.14
Two-link manipulator

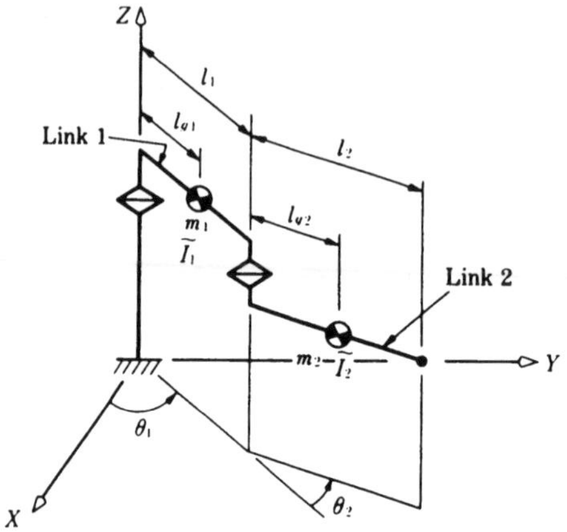

Figure 3.15
Two-link manipulator.

1 and the center of mass of link 1, let m_i be the mass of link i, and let $\bar{I}_i$ be the moment of inertia about the center of mass of link i. Assume that gravity acts vertically downward.

3.3 Derive the equations of motion for the two-link manipulator in figure 3.14 using the Newton-Euler formulation. Show that the result is equivalent to that of exercise 3.2.

3.4 Derive the equations of motion for the two-link manipulator in figure 3.15 using the Lagrangian formulation. In the figure, θ_i is the joint angle of link i, m_i is the mass of link i, $\bar{I}_i$ is the moment of inertia of link i about the axis that passes through the center of mass and is parallel to the Z axis, l_i is the length of link i, and l_{gi} is the distance between joint i and the center of mass of link i. Assume that the first joint driving torque, τ_1, acts between the base and link 1, that the second joint driving torque, τ_2, acts between links 1 and 2, and that gravity acts in the $-Z$ direction.

3.5 Suppose that $l_b = 0$ for the three-link manipulator of example 2.13, which is illustrated in figure 2.26. Derive the equations of motion for this manipulator, using the Lagrangian formulation. Assume that it has a serial drive, that the center of mass of link 1 is on the Z_1 axis, and that the centers of mass of links 2 and 3 are at ${}^2\hat{s}_2 = [l_{g2},0,0]^T$ on X_2 and ${}^3\hat{s}_3 = [l_{g3},0,0]^T$ on X_3, respectively. Also assume that the inertia tensor of link i about the

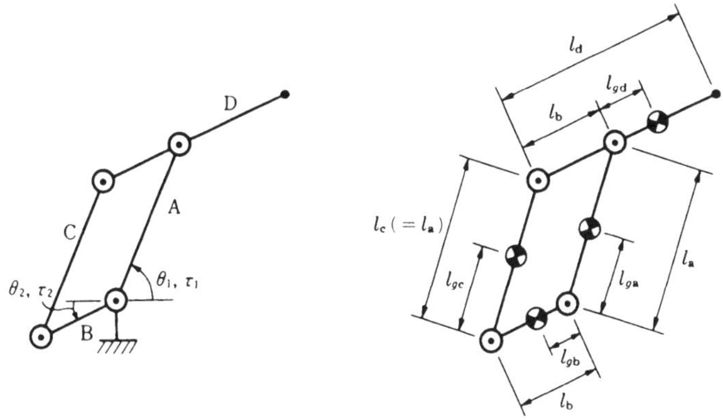

Figure 3.16
Parallel-drive two-degrees-of-freedom manipulator.

center of mass expressed in its own link frame is given by a diagonal matrix, $\mathrm{diag}[I_{ix}, I_{iy}, I_{iz}]$, and that gravity acts in the $-Z_0$ direction.

3.6 Solve exercise 3.5 using the Newton-Euler formulation.

3.7 Derive the equations of motion for a parallel-drive two-link manipulator using the parallelogram shown in figure 3.16. Assume that the lengths of links A, B, C, and D are l_a, l_b, $l_c (= l_a)$, and l_d; that their centers of mass are at l_{ga}, l_{gb}, l_{gc}, and l_{gd} as shown in the figure; that their masses are m_a, m_b, m_c, and m_d; and that their moments of inertia about the center of mass are $\tilde{I}_a$, $\tilde{I}_b$, $\tilde{I}_c$, and $\tilde{I}_d$. Also assume that torque τ_1 works between the base and link A, that torque τ_2 works between the base and link B, and that gravity is directed downward.

3.8 Give an identifiable parameter vector $\boldsymbol{\phi}_d^*$ for the manipulator in exercise 3.7 when the value of the joint driving force is available as the data about force.

References

1. J. J. Uicker, "Dynamic Force Analysis of Spatial Linkages," *ASME Journal of Applied Mechanics* 34 (1967): 418–424.

2. M. Kahn and B. Roth, "The Near-Minimum-Time Control of Open Loop Kinematic Chains," *ASME Journal of Dynamic Systems, Measurement, and Control* 93 (1971): 164–172.

3. R. Paul, *Robot Manipulators* (MIT Press, 1981).

4. J. Y. S. Luh, M. W. Walker, and R. P. C. Paul, "On-line Computational Scheme for Mechanical Manipulators," *ASME Journal of Dynamic Systems, Measurement, and Control* 102 (1980): 69–76.

5. Y. Stepanenko and M. Vukobratovic, "Dynamics of Articulated Open-Chain Active Mechanisms," *Mathematical Biosciences* 28 (1976): 137–170.

6. D. E. Orin et al., "Kinematic and Kinetic Analysis of Open-Chain Linkages Utilizing Newton-Euler Methods," *Mathematical Biosciences* 43, no. 1/2 (1979): 107–130.

7. M. W. Walker and D. E. Orin, "Efficient Dynamic Computer Simulation of Robot Mechanisms," *ASME Journal of Dynamic Systems, Measurement, and Control* 104 (1982): 205–211.

8. K. R. Symon, *Mechanics*, third edition (Addison-Wesley, 1971).

9. I. Shames, *Engineering Mechanics*, second edition (Prentice-Hall, 1967).

10. H. Goldstein, *Classical Mechanics*, second edition (Addison-Wesley, 1980).

11. J. M. Hollerbach, "A Recursive Lagrangian Formulation of Manipulator Dynamics and a Comparative Study of Dynamics Formulation Complexity," *IEEE Transactions on Systems, Man, and Cybernetics* 10 (1980): 730–736.

12. K. Itô (ed.), *Encyclopedic Dictionary of Mathematics* (MIT Press, 1986).

13. H. Mayeda, K. Osuka, and A. Kangawa, "A New Identification Method for Serial Manipulator Arms," in Proceedings of Ninth IFAC World Congress (1984), vol. VI, pp. 74–79.

14. C. G. Atkeson, C. H. An, and J. M. Hollerbach, "Estimation of Inertial Parameters of Manipulator Loads and Links," *International Journal of Robotics Research* 5, no. 3 (1986): 101–119.

15. P. Eykhoff, *System Identification: Parameter and State Estimation* (Wiley, 1974).

16. P. K. Khosla, Real-Time Control and Identification of Direct-Drive Manipulators, Ph. D. thesis, Robotics Institute, Carnegie-Mellon University, 1986.

17. T. Yoshikawa, "Evaluation of Identification Tests for Manipulators," in Proceedings of USA-Japan Symposium on Flexible Automation (1988), pp. 65–71.

4 Manipulability

Various factors should be taken into account when we choose the mechanism and the size of a robot manipulator at the design stage, or when we determine the posture of the manipulator in the workspace for performing a given task during operation. An important factor among these is the ease of arbitrarily changing the position and orientation of the end effector at the tip of the manipulator.

In this chapter we will develop an approach for evaluating quantitatively this ability of manipulators from the viewpoints of both kinematics and dynamics. First, from the kinematics aspect, the concepts of the manipulability ellipsoid and the manipulability measure will be introduced.[1,2] Various robotic mechanisms will be analyzed using the manipulability measure. Then, the dynamic-manipulability ellipsoid and the dynamic-manipulability measure, which are extensions to the dynamic case, will be discussed.[3]

For a total evaluation of manipulators, we should of course consider many other factors, including size of workspace,[4,5] positioning accuracy, load capacity, speed, reliability, safety, cost, ease of operation, and settling time.

4.1 Manipulability Ellipsoid and Manipulability Measure

Consider a manipulator with n degrees of freedom, as in subsection 2.3.1. The joint variables are denoted by an n-dimensional vector, $\boldsymbol{q}$. An m-dimensional vector $\boldsymbol{r} = [r_1, r_2, \ldots, r_m]^T$ ($m \leq n$) describes the position and/or orientation of the end effector. The kinematic relation between $\boldsymbol{q}$ and $\boldsymbol{r}$ is assumed to be

$$\boldsymbol{r} = \boldsymbol{f}_r(\boldsymbol{q}). \tag{4.1}$$

The relation between the velocity vector $\boldsymbol{v}$ corresponding to $\boldsymbol{r}$ and the joint velocity $\dot{\boldsymbol{q}}$ is

$$\boldsymbol{v} = \boldsymbol{J}(\boldsymbol{q})\dot{\boldsymbol{q}}, \tag{4.2}$$

where $\boldsymbol{J}(\boldsymbol{q})$ is the Jacobian matrix. $\boldsymbol{J}(\boldsymbol{q})$ may also be written as $\boldsymbol{J}$ hereafter. For the case where $n \geqq 6$ and both the position and the orientation of the end effector are considered ($m = 6$), the matrix $\boldsymbol{J}$ means $\boldsymbol{J}_v$ given by equation 2.85. On the other hand, for the case where only the position of the end effector is of concern or, as pointed out in subsection 2.5.2, the axis of rotation of the end effector is invariant with respect to the reference frame, we can use $\dot{\boldsymbol{r}} = \boldsymbol{J}_r(\boldsymbol{q})\dot{\boldsymbol{q}}$ in place of equation 4.2. All the arguments in this chapter are valid for the latter case if we simply replace $\boldsymbol{v}$ with $\dot{\boldsymbol{r}}$ and $\boldsymbol{J}$ with $\boldsymbol{J}_r$.

Now we consider the set of all end-effector velocities $\boldsymbol{v}$ which are realizable by joint velocities such that the Euclidean norm of $\dot{\boldsymbol{q}}$,

$$\|\dot{\boldsymbol{q}}\| = (\dot{q}_1{}^2 + \dot{q}_2{}^2 + \cdots + \dot{q}_n{}^2)^{1/2},$$

satisfies $\|\dot{\boldsymbol{q}}\| \leqq 1$. This set is an ellipsoid in the m-dimensional Euclidean space. In the direction of the major axis of the ellipsoid, the end effector can move at high speed. On the other hand, in the direction of the minor axis the end effector can move only at low speed. If the ellipsoid is almost a sphere, the end effector can move in all directions uniformly. Also, the larger the ellipsoid is, the faster the end effector can move. Since this ellipsoid represents an ability of manipulation, it is called the *manipulability ellipsoid*. (See the schematic representation in figure 4.1.)

We now prove that the manipulability ellipsoid is given by the set of all $\boldsymbol{v}$ satisfying

$$\boldsymbol{v}^T(\boldsymbol{J}^+)^T\boldsymbol{J}^+\boldsymbol{v} \leqq 1, \quad \boldsymbol{v} \in \mathrm{R}(\boldsymbol{J}), \tag{4.3a}$$

where $\boldsymbol{J}^+$ is the pseudo-inverse matrix of $\boldsymbol{J}$ and where $\mathrm{R}(\boldsymbol{J})$ denotes the range of $\boldsymbol{J}$. From equations 4.2 and A2.22 we obtain

$$\dot{\boldsymbol{q}} = \boldsymbol{J}^+\boldsymbol{v} + (\mathbf{I} - \boldsymbol{J}^+\boldsymbol{J})\boldsymbol{k},$$

where $\boldsymbol{k}$ is an arbitrary constant vector. From this equation, equations

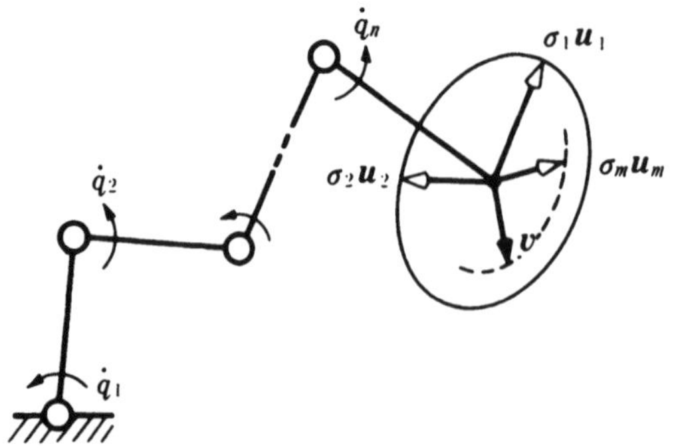

Figure 4.1
Manipulability ellipsoid.

A2.2 and A2.4, and the equality $(\mathbf{I} - J^+J)^T J^+ = \mathbf{0}$, we have

$$\begin{aligned}\|\dot{q}\|^2 &= \dot{q}^T\dot{q} \\ &= v^T(J^+)^T J^+ v + 2k^T(\mathbf{I} - J^+J)^T J^+ v \\ &\quad + k^T(\mathbf{I} - J^+J)^T(\mathbf{I} - J^+J)k \\ &= v^T(J^+)^T J^+ v + k^T(\mathbf{I} - J^+J)^T(\mathbf{I} - J^+J)k \\ &\geqq v^T(J^+)^T J^+ v.\end{aligned}$$

Hence, if $\|\dot{q}\| \leqq 1$, then $v^T(J^+)^T J^+ v \leqq 1$ holds. It is clear from equation 4.2 that any velocity v realizable by an appropriate $\dot{q}$ satisfies $v \in R(J)$. Conversely, if we let an arbitrarily selected v satisfying equation 4.3a be v^*, then since $v^* \in R(J)$ there exists a vector z such that $v^* = Jz$. Hence, by letting

$$\dot{q}^* = J^+ v^*,$$

we have

$$J\dot{q}^* = JJ^+ v^* = JJ^+ Jz = Jz = v^*$$

and

$$\|\dot{q}^*\| = v^{*T}(J^+)^T J^+ v^* \leqq 1.$$

This completes the proof of equation 4.3a.

If the manipulator is not in a singular configuration (that is, if rank $J = m$), then, since $v \in R(J)$ for any v, the manipulability ellipsoid is given by

$$v^T(J^+)^T J^+ v \leqq 1 \tag{4.3b}$$

rather than by equation 4.3a.

Now we find the principal axes of the manipulability ellipsoid by making use of the singular-value decomposition (see appendix 3) of J. We let the singular-value decomposition of J be

$$J = U\Sigma V^T, \tag{4.4a}$$

where U and V are, respectively, $m \times m$ and $n \times n$ orthogonal matrices, and where Σ is an $m \times n$ matrix defined by

$$\boldsymbol{\Sigma} = \left[\begin{array}{cccc|c} \sigma_1 & & & 0 & \\ & \cdot & & & \\ & & \cdot & & \mathbf{0} \\ & & & \cdot & \\ 0 & & & \sigma_m & \end{array}\right], \quad \sigma_1 \geqq \sigma_2 \geqq \cdots \geqq \sigma_m \geqq 0. \tag{4.4b}$$

The scalars $\sigma_1, \sigma_2, \ldots, \sigma_m$ are called *singular values* of $\boldsymbol{J}$, and they are equal to the m larger values of the n roots $\{\sqrt{\lambda_i},\, i = 1,2,\ldots,n\}$, where λ_i $(i = 1,2,\ldots,n)$ are eigenvalues of the matrix $\boldsymbol{J}^T\boldsymbol{J}$. Further, we let $\boldsymbol{u}_i$ be the ith column vector of $\boldsymbol{U}$. Then the principal axes of the manipulability ellipsoid are $\sigma_1\boldsymbol{u}_1, \sigma_2\boldsymbol{u}_2, \ldots, \sigma_m\boldsymbol{u}_m$ (see figure 4.1). This is now shown.

From equations 4.4 and A2.16,

$$\boldsymbol{J}^+ = \boldsymbol{V}\boldsymbol{\Sigma}^+\boldsymbol{U}^T, \tag{4.5a}$$

where $\boldsymbol{\Sigma}^+$ is the pseudo-inverse of $\boldsymbol{\Sigma}$, which is given by

$$\boldsymbol{\Sigma}^+ = \left[\begin{array}{cccc} {\sigma_1}^{-1} & & & 0 \\ & \cdot & & \\ & & \cdot & \\ & & & \cdot \\ 0 & & & {\sigma_m}^{-1} \\ \hline & \mathbf{0} & & \end{array}\right], \tag{4.5b}$$

where ${\sigma_i}^{-1} = 0$ if $\sigma_i = 0$ for notational convenience. We consider the following orthogonal transformation of $\boldsymbol{v}$:

$$\tilde{\boldsymbol{v}} = \boldsymbol{U}^T\boldsymbol{v} = \mathrm{col}[\tilde{v}_i].$$

Then, by equation 4.3a, we have

$$\sum_{\sigma_i \neq 0} \frac{1}{{\sigma_i}^2}{\tilde{v}_i}^2 \leqq 1.$$

This implies that the direction of the coordinate axis for $\tilde{v}_i$ (that is, the direction of $\boldsymbol{u}_i$) is that of a principal axis, and that the radius in that direction is given by σ_i. Therefore, the principal axes are $\sigma_1\boldsymbol{u}_1, \sigma_2\boldsymbol{u}_2, \ldots, \sigma_m\boldsymbol{u}_m$.

One of the representative measures for the ability of manipulation derived from the manipulability ellipsoid is the volume of the ellipsoid. This is given by $c_m w$, where

$$w = \sigma_1 \sigma_2 \cdots \sigma_m, \tag{4.6}$$

$$c_m = \begin{cases} (2\pi)^{m/2}/[2 \cdot 4 \cdot 6 \cdot \cdots \cdot (m-2) \cdot m] & \text{if } m \text{ is even} \\ 2(2\pi)^{(m-1)/2}/[1 \cdot 3 \cdot 5 \cdot \cdots \cdot (m-2) \cdot m] & \text{if } m \text{ is odd.} \end{cases} \tag{4.7}$$

Since the coefficient c_m is a constant when m is fixed, the volume is proportional to w. Hence, we can regard w as a representative measure. We call w the *manipulability measure* for manipulator configuration $\boldsymbol{q}$.

The manipulability measure w has the following properties:

(i) $w = \sqrt{\det \boldsymbol{J}(\boldsymbol{q})\boldsymbol{J}^T(\boldsymbol{q})}$. (4.8)

(ii) When $m = n$ (that is, when we consider non-redundant manipulators), the measure w reduces to

$$w = |\det \boldsymbol{J}(\boldsymbol{q})|. \tag{4.9}$$

(iii) Generally $w \geqq 0$ holds, and $w = 0$ if and only if

$$\operatorname{rank} \boldsymbol{J}(\boldsymbol{q}) < \mathrm{m} \tag{4.10}$$

(in other words, if and only if the manipulator is in a singular configuration). From this fact we can regard the manipulability measure as a kind of distance of the manipulator configuration from singular ones.

(iv) When $m = n$, the set of all $\boldsymbol{v}$ which is realizable by a joint velocity $\dot{\boldsymbol{q}}$ such that

$$|\dot{q}_i| \leqq 1, \quad i = 1, 2, \ldots, m \tag{4.11}$$

is a parallelpiped in m-dimensional space, with a volume of $2^m w$. In other words, the measure w is proportional to the volume of the parallel-piped. This gives another physical interpretation of w, different from the volume of the manipulability ellipsoid, although this is valid only for the case of $m = n$.

In the next section various robotic mechanisms will be evaluated from the viewpoint of manipulability. First, however, several general remarks are in order.

So far, we have implicitly assumed that the maximum velocities of all joints are the same and that the linear velocities and angular velocities can be regarded as having the same degree of importance. In order to satisfy this assumption, the following normalization of the variables in necessary: After fixing a set of units for distance, angle, and time (typically, meters, radians, and seconds), we denote the maximum (angular) velocity of joint i as $q_{i\max}$. We also select a desirable maximum (angular) velocity $v_{j\max}$ for each element of the end-effector velocity v_j, taking into consideration the class of tasks that the manipulator is supposed to perform. Then, letting

$$\hat{\dot{\boldsymbol{q}}} = [\hat{\dot{q}}_1, \hat{\dot{q}}_2, \ldots, \hat{\dot{q}}_n]^T, \quad \hat{\dot{q}}_i = \dot{q}_i / \dot{q}_{i\max}, \tag{4.12}$$

$$\hat{\boldsymbol{v}} = [\hat{v}_1, \hat{v}_2, \ldots, \hat{v}_m]^T, \quad \hat{v}_j = v_j / v_{j\max}, \tag{4.13}$$

we have

$$\hat{\boldsymbol{v}} = \hat{\boldsymbol{J}}(\boldsymbol{q}) \hat{\dot{\boldsymbol{q}}}, \tag{4.14}$$

where

$$\hat{\boldsymbol{J}}(\boldsymbol{q}) = \boldsymbol{T}_v \boldsymbol{J}(\boldsymbol{q}) \boldsymbol{T}_q^{-1}, \tag{4.15}$$

$$\boldsymbol{T}_v = \operatorname{diag}\left(\frac{1}{v_{1\max}}, \frac{1}{v_{2\max}}, \ldots, \frac{1}{v_{m\max}} \right), \tag{4.16}$$

$$\boldsymbol{T}_q = \operatorname{diag}\left(\frac{1}{\dot{q}_{1\max}}, \frac{1}{\dot{q}_{2\max}}, \ldots, \frac{1}{\dot{q}_{n\max}} \right), \tag{4.17}$$

and diag($\cdot$) denotes a diagonal matrix. Since the normalized variables $\hat{\boldsymbol{v}}$ and $\hat{\dot{\boldsymbol{q}}}$ satisfy the assumption that we have made implicitly for $\boldsymbol{v}$ and $\boldsymbol{q}$, we can define the manipulability ellipsoid and the manipulability measure using the normalized Jacobian $\hat{\boldsymbol{J}}(\boldsymbol{q})$. Especially when $n = m$, the relation between the measure w for $\boldsymbol{J}(\boldsymbol{q})$ and the manipulability measure $\hat{w}$ for the normalized Jacobian $\hat{\boldsymbol{J}}(\boldsymbol{q})$ is given by

$$\begin{aligned} \hat{w} &= \det \boldsymbol{T}_v \det \boldsymbol{J}(\boldsymbol{q}) \det \boldsymbol{T}_q^{-1} \\ &= \left[\prod_{i=1}^{m} (\dot{q}_{i\max} / v_{i\max}) \right] w. \end{aligned} \tag{4.18}$$

Thus, the transformations 4.12 and 4.13 have only the effect of multiplying w by a scalar constant

$$\prod_{i=1}^{m} (\dot{q}_{i\max} / v_{i\max}).$$

In other words, the relative shape of w as a function of the arm configuration $\boldsymbol{q}$ is independent of the normalization of $\boldsymbol{v}$ and $\dot{\boldsymbol{q}}$.

It is also easy to take into consideration the effects of actuators and transmission mechanisms. Let $\boldsymbol{q}_a$ be the position vector of the actuators, and let the relation between $\boldsymbol{q}_a$ and $\boldsymbol{q}$ be expressed by

$$\boldsymbol{q}_a = \boldsymbol{G}_r \boldsymbol{q}, \tag{4.19}$$

where $\boldsymbol{G}_r$ is an $m \times m$ constant matrix representing the transmission ratio. Then we have

$$\boldsymbol{v} = \boldsymbol{J}(\boldsymbol{q})\boldsymbol{G}_r^{-1}\dot{\boldsymbol{q}}_a. \tag{4.20}$$

Regarding $\boldsymbol{J}(\boldsymbol{q})\boldsymbol{G}_r^{-1}$ as a new Jacobian, we can develop a similar argument as above. Note that when differential gears are used, $\boldsymbol{G}_r$ is not diagonal.

Finally, let us consider the relation between the manipulability and the force (and moment) which can be exerted on an object by an end effector. We assume that a manipulator is not in a singular configuration, i.e., rank $\boldsymbol{J} = m$. We let the force exerted by the end effector of the manipulator at rest on the object be represented by an m-dimensional vector $\boldsymbol{f}$ corresponding to $\boldsymbol{v}$. From equation 2.139, the joint driving torque $\boldsymbol{\tau}$ which is equivalent to $\boldsymbol{f}$ satisfies

$$\boldsymbol{\tau} = \boldsymbol{J}^T(\boldsymbol{q})\boldsymbol{f}. \tag{4.21}$$

Hence, the set of all $\boldsymbol{f}$ realizable by some $\boldsymbol{\tau}$ such that $\|\boldsymbol{\tau}\| \leqq 1$ forms an ellipsoid in the m-dimensional Euclidean space described by

$$\boldsymbol{f}^T \boldsymbol{J}(\boldsymbol{q})\boldsymbol{J}^T(\boldsymbol{q})\boldsymbol{f} \leqq 1. \tag{4.22}$$

This ellipsoid is called the *manipulating-force ellipsoid*. Its volume, c_m/w, is inversely proportional to the manipulability measure. The principal axes of the manipulating-force ellipsoid are given by $\boldsymbol{u}_1/\sigma_1, \boldsymbol{u}_2/\sigma_2, \ldots, \boldsymbol{u}_m/\sigma_m$. This means that the direction in which a large manipulating force can be generated is the one in which the manipulability is poor, and vice versa.

4.2 Best Configurations of Robotic Mechanisms from Manipulability Viewpoint

4.2.1 Two-Link Mechanism

In this section, the manipulability measure is calculated for various robotic mechanisms, and the best configurations of these mechanisms from the viewpoint of manipulability are determined. These configurations will be called the *optimal configurations*. The end-effector position for the optimal

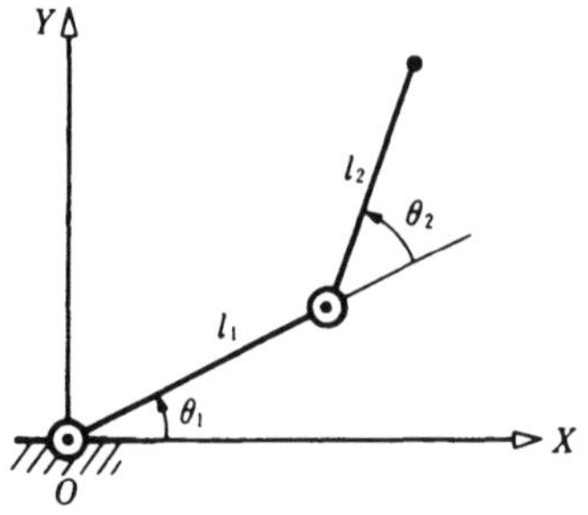

Figure 4.2
Two-link mechanism.

configuration in the workspace gives the most desirable position for manipulation tasks.

Let us consider a two-link mechanism shown in figure 4.2. When the hand position $[x,y]^T$ is used for $\boldsymbol{r}$, the Jacobian matrix is

$$\boldsymbol{J} = \begin{bmatrix} -l_1 S_1 - l_2 S_{12} & -l_2 S_{12} \\ l_1 C_1 + l_2 C_{12} & l_2 C_{12} \end{bmatrix} \tag{4.23}$$

and the manipulability measure w is

$$w = |\det \boldsymbol{J}| = l_1 l_2 |S_2|. \tag{4.24}$$

Thus, the manipulator takes its optimal configuration when $\theta_2 = \pm 90°$, for any given values of l_1, l_2, and θ_1. If the lengths l_1 and l_2 can be specified under the condition of constant total length (that is, $l_1 + l_2 =$ constant), then the manipulability measure attains its maximum when $l_1 = l_2$ for any given θ_1 and θ_2.

When the human arm is regarded as a two-link mechanism by neglecting the degree of freedom of sideward direction at the shoulder and the degree of freedom at the wrist, it approximately satisfies the relation $l_1 = l_2$. Moreover, when we use our hands to perform some task such as writing letters, the angle of the elbow is usually in the neighborhood of 90°. Thus, it could be said that humans unconsciously use the arm postures that are best from the viewpoint of manipulability.

We now find the two principal axes of the manipulability ellipsoid for the case of $l_1 = l_2 = 1$. They are specified by σ_1, σ_2, $\boldsymbol{u}_1$, and $\boldsymbol{u}_2$, which can be derived as follows using the method described in appendix 3.

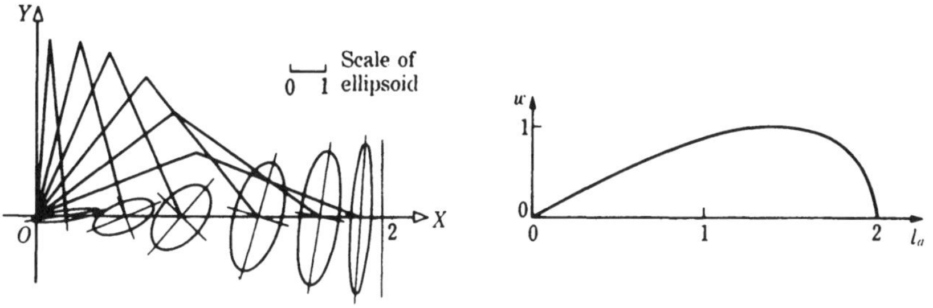

Figure 4.3
Manipulability ellipsoid and manipulability measure.

First, JJ^T is given by

$$JJ^T = \begin{bmatrix} (S_1+S_{12})^2+S_{12}{}^2 & -(S_1+S_{12})(C_1+C_{12})-S_{12}C_{12} \\ -(S_1+S_{12})(C_1+C_{12})-S_{12}C_{12} & (C_1+C_{12})^2+C_{12}{}^2 \end{bmatrix},$$

and its eigenvalues are

$$\lambda_1 = [3 + 2C_2 + \sqrt{5 + 12C_2 + 8C_2{}^2}]/2,$$

$$\lambda_2 = [3 + 2C_2 - \sqrt{5 + 12C_2 + 8C_2{}^2}]/2.$$

Thus, the singular values are given by $\sigma_i = \sqrt{\lambda_i}$, where $i = 1, 2$. Next, from equation A3.8′,

$$\boldsymbol{u}_i = [\{(S_1 + S_{12})(C_1 + C_{12}) + S_{12}C_{12}\}/\kappa_i, \{(S_1 + S_{12})^2 + S_{12} - \lambda_i\}/\kappa_i]^T,$$

where

$$\kappa_i = \{[(S_1 + S_{12})(C_1 + C_{12}) + S_{12}C_{12}]^2 + [(S_1 + S_{12})^2 + S_{12} - \lambda_i]^2\}^{1/2}.$$

Figure 4.3 shows the manipulability ellipsoid and the manipulability measure for $l_1 = l_2 = 1$ obtained by the use of the above expressions. Figure 4.4 shows the manipulating-force ellipsoid. From figure 4.3 we can clearly see the direction in which it is easy to manipulate the end effector; from figure 4.4 we can see the direction in which it is easy to exert a force on the object.

4.2.2 SCARA-Type Robot Manipulator

Let us consider the SCARA-type manipulator with four degrees of freedom shown in figure 4.5. Let $\boldsymbol{r} = [x,y,z,\alpha]^T$, where $[x,y,z]^T$ is the hand position

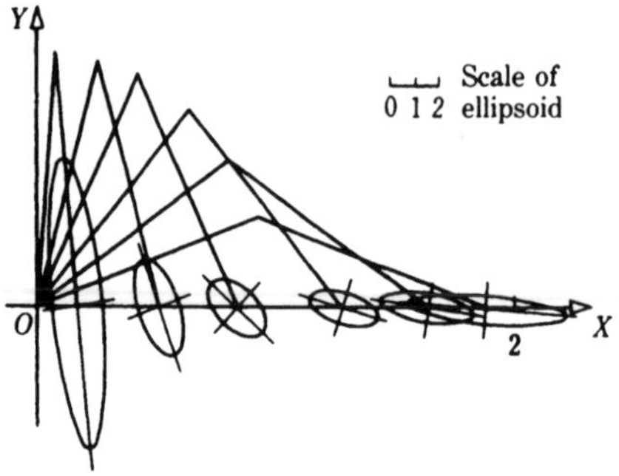

Figure 4.4
Manipulating-force ellipsoid.

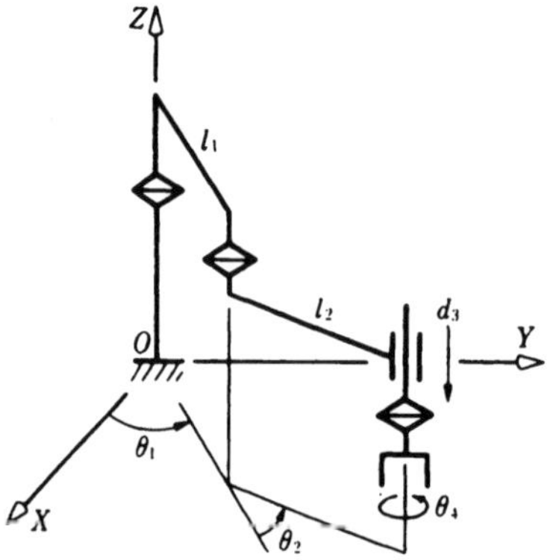

Figure 4.5
SCARA-type manipulator.

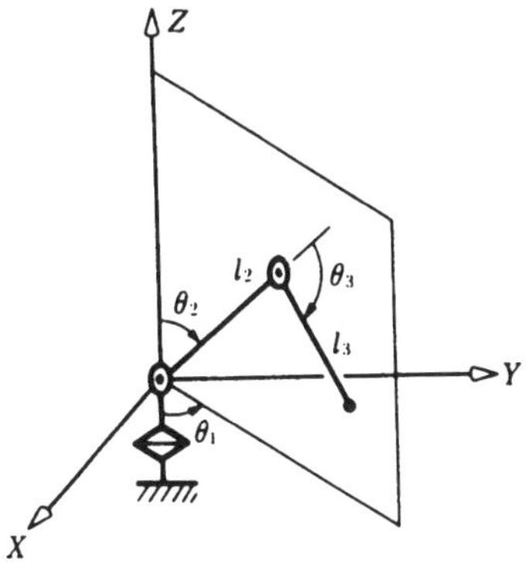

Figure 4.6
PUMA-type manipulator.

and α is the rotational angle of the hand about the Z axis. The Jacobian matrix for this case is

$$J = \begin{bmatrix} -l_1S_1 - l_2S_{12} & -l_2S_{12} & 0 & 0 \\ l_1C_1 + l_2C_{12} & l_2C_{12} & 0 & 0 \\ 0 & 0 & -1 & 0 \\ 1 & 1 & 0 & 1 \end{bmatrix}. \tag{4.25}$$

Hence,

$$w = l_1 l_2 |S_2|. \tag{4.26}$$

Therefore, as in the case of two-joint link mechanism in subsection 4.2.1, the best posture is given by $\theta_2 = \pm 90°$ for any given values of $l_1, l_2, \theta_1, \theta_3$, and θ_4. Also, under the constraint $l_1 + l_2 =$ constant, the manipulability measure attains its maximum value when $l_1 = l_2$.

4.2.3 PUMA-Type Robot Manipulator

Most commercially available PUMA-type robot manipulators have five or six degrees of freedom. Many of them have links with some displacements in the direction of the joint axis. However, we will consider only the main three joints shown in figure 4.6, neglecting the degrees of freedom placed at the wrist and neglecting the displacements in the direction of the joint axes. The joint vector is $\boldsymbol{q} = [\theta_1, \theta_2, \theta_3]^T$. Let the manipulation vector $\boldsymbol{r}$ be $[x, y, z]^T$. Then the Jacobian matrix is

$$J = \begin{bmatrix} -S_1(l_2S_2 + l_3S_{23}) & C_1(l_2C_2 + l_3C_{23}) & C_1l_3C_{23} \\ C_1(l_2S_2 + l_3S_{23}) & S_1(l_2C_2 + l_3C_{23}) & S_1l_3C_{23} \\ 0 & -(l_2S_2 + l_3S_{23}) & -l_3S_{23} \end{bmatrix}, \tag{4.27}$$

and the manipulability measure is

$$w = l_2l_3|(l_2S_2 + l_3S_{23})S_3|. \tag{4.28}$$

The best posture for given l_2 and l_3 is found as follows: First, θ_1 is not related to w and can have any value. Second, by assuming that $S_3 \neq 0$, we see from $\partial w/\partial\theta_2 = 0$ that

$$\tan\theta_2 = \frac{l_2 + l_3C_3}{l_3S_3}. \tag{4.29}$$

This means that the tip of the arm should be on the $X-Y$ plane, which is at the same height as the second joint. This can further be interpreted as maximizing the contribution of the angular velocity of the first joint to the manipulability measure.

Substituting equation 4.29 into equation 4.28 yields

$$w = l_2l_3\sqrt{l_2^2 + l_3^2 + 2l_2l_3C_3}\,|S_3|. \tag{4.30}$$

The value of θ_3 that maximizes the above w is given by

$$\cos\theta_3 = \frac{\sqrt{(l_2^2 + l_3^2)^2 + 12l_2^2l_3^2} - (l_2^2 + l_3^2)}{6l_2l_3}. \tag{4.31}$$

Figure 4.7 shows the best postures for the cases $l_3 = \gamma l_2$, where $\gamma = 0.5$, 1, 2. (Only those satisfying $0° \leq \theta_2 \leq 90°$ are shown in the figure.) If the manipulator is regarded as a two-joint mechanism consisting of θ_2 and θ_3,

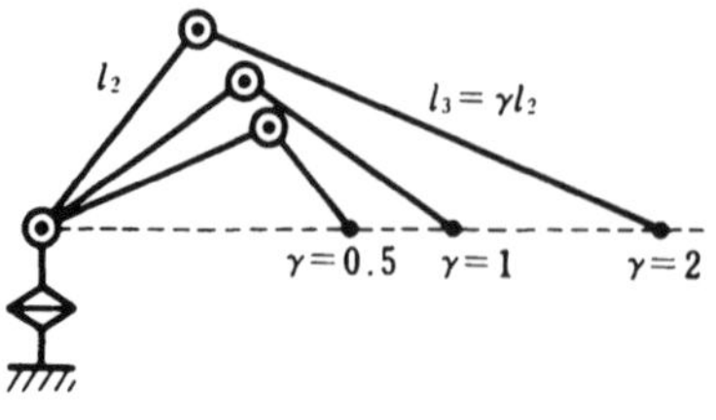

Figure 4.7
Optimal configurations for PUMA-type manipulator.

the optimal angle for θ_3 is 90°, as was discussed in subsection 4.2.1. In the present case, however, the optimal θ_3 is smaller than 90° because the contribution of θ_1 to w can be made larger by placing the tip of the arm farther from the first joint axis.

4.2.4 Orthogonal-, Cylindrical-, and Polar-Coordinate Manipulators

Only the three main degrees of freedom of manipulators and the hand position are considered in this subsection, as in the preceding subsection.

The manipulability measure w of an orthogonal-coordinate manipulator (figure 1.3a) is 1 everywhere in the workspace. The most manipulable posture for a cylindrical-coordinate manipulator (figure 1.3b) is attained when the arm is fully stretched out. Similarly, a polar-coordinate manipulator (figure 1.3c) is most manipulable when the arm is fully stretched out in the horizontal direction. Therefore, for cylindrical-coordinate and polar-coordinate manipulators, the best posture is achieved at the boundary of their workspace. Although this is inconvenient, it is true for all robotic mechanisms that have a prismatic joint whose axis is in the radial direction of a rotational joint. This is also intuitively understandable. For these manipulators, we will need considerations other than the manipulability measure, such as preferring a position near the center of the workspace, in order to determine the best working position.

4.2.5 Four-Joint Robotic Finger

Various robotic hands with multi-articulated fingers have been developed to achieve the dexterity and flexibility of human hands for tasks involving handling and assembling. In this subsection we will consider the four-joint finger shown in figure 4.8 from the viewpoint of the manipulability measure.

The Jacobian matrix relating $\boldsymbol{\theta} = [\theta_1,\theta_2,\theta_3,\theta_4]^T$ to $\boldsymbol{r} = [x,y,z]^T$ is

$$\boldsymbol{J}(\boldsymbol{\theta}) = \begin{bmatrix} 0 & -\tilde{a}_1 & -\tilde{a}_2 & -\tilde{a}_3 \\ C_1\tilde{a}_1 & S_1\tilde{b}_1 & S_1\tilde{b}_2 & S_1\tilde{b}_3 \\ S_1\tilde{a}_1 & -C_1\tilde{b}_1 & -C_1\tilde{b}_2 & -C_1\tilde{b}_3 \end{bmatrix}, \tag{4.32}$$

where

$\tilde{a}_1 = l_2S_2 + l_3S_{23} + l_4S_{234}$,

$\tilde{a}_2 = l_3S_{23} + l_4S_{234}$,

$\tilde{a}_3 = l_4S_{234}$,

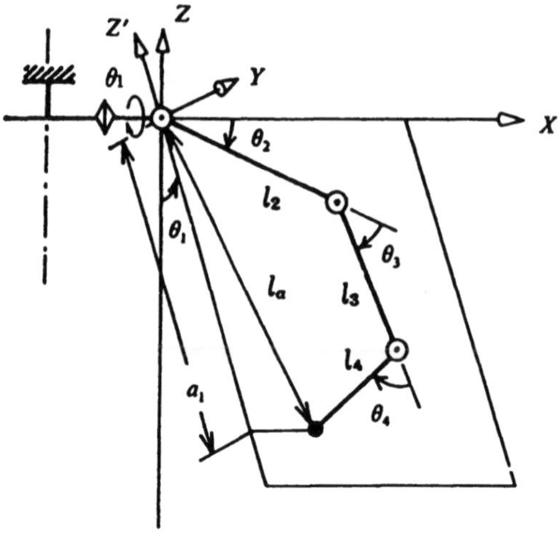

Figure 4.8
Four-joint finger.

$$\tilde{b}_1 = l_2 C_2 + l_3 C_{23} + l_4 C_{234},$$

$$\tilde{b}_2 = l_3 C_{23} + l_4 C_{234},$$

and

$$\tilde{b}_3 = l_4 C_{234},$$

From equation 4.8, the manipulability measure is calculated as

$$w = |\tilde{a}_1| \tilde{w}(\theta_2, \theta_3, \theta_4),$$

where

$$\tilde{w}(\theta_2, \theta_3, \theta_4) = \sqrt{\det \boldsymbol{J}\boldsymbol{J}^T}$$

and

$$\boldsymbol{J} = \begin{bmatrix} \tilde{a}_1 & \tilde{a}_2 & \tilde{a}_3 \\ \tilde{b}_1 & \tilde{b}_2 & \tilde{b}_3 \end{bmatrix}.$$

Note that $\tilde{w}(\theta_2, \theta_3, \theta_4)$ is the manipulability measure of the three-joint mechanism that consists of joints 2, 3, and 4 and moves in the $X-Z'$ plane shown in figure 4.8. The maximum value of $\tilde{w}(\theta_2, \theta_3, \theta_4)$ and the corresponding finger posture for a given distance l_a between joint 2 and the tip of the finger are shown in figure 4.9 for the case where $l_2 = l_3 = 0.4$ and

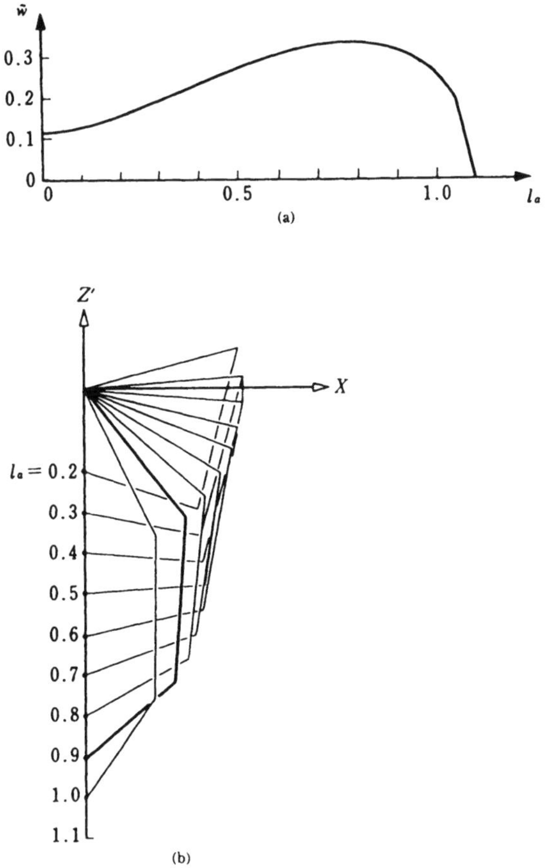

Figure 4.9
Maximum value of $\tilde{w}$ and corresponding best finger posture. (a) Maximum value of $\tilde{w}$ as a function of l_a. (b) Best finger posture.

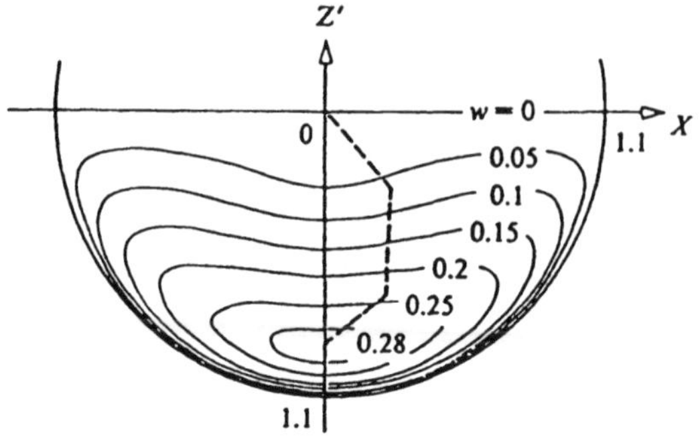

Figure 4.10
Maximum value of manipulability measure as a function of fingertip position.

$l_4 = 0.3$. (These postures are independent of the angle θ_2.) Figure 4.10 shows the maximum value of w as a function of the fingertip's position in the X–Z' plane (only the lower half-portion is shown, since the value in the upper half is symmetric with respect to the X axis). The best finger posture is shown in figure 4.10 by a broken line.

The finger postures illustrated in figure 4.9b are quite similar to those taken by human fingers during the manipulation of small, light objects.

4.3 Various Indices of Manipulability

Sections 4.1 and 4.2 discussed the manipulability measure, a typical index of manipulability induced from the manipulability ellipsoid. This section presents several other indices that are developed from the same ellipsoid. A remark is also made concerning global indices, which are required for the evaluation of a manipulator as a whole.

As was stated in section 4.1, the manipulability measure w_1 (w will be denoted as w_1 in this section) represents the volume of the manipulability ellipsoid. Other indices that might be induced from the manipulability ellipsoid are

$$w_2 = \sigma_m/\sigma_1, \tag{4.33a}$$

$$w_3 = \sigma_m, \tag{4.33b}$$

and

$$w_4 = (\sigma_1\sigma_2\cdots\sigma_m)^{1/m} = (w_1)^{1/m}. \tag{4.33c}$$

Index w_2 is the ratio of the minimum and maximum radii of the ellipsoid. The closer to unity this index is, the more spherical the ellipsoid is. In other words, w_2 is an index of the directional uniformity of the ellipsoid and is independent of its size. The reciprocal of w_2 is the condition number of the Jacobian matrix $\boldsymbol{J}$.[6] Index w_3 is the minimum radius of the ellipsoid.[7] This gives the upper bound of the magnitude of velocity at which the end effector can be moved in any direction. Index w_4 is the geometric mean of the radii $\sigma_1, \sigma_2, \ldots, \sigma_m$, and it is equal to the radius of the sphere whose volume is the same as that of the ellipsoid. It is also equal to the mth root of w_1.

The selection of an index among $w_1, \ldots, w_4$ depends on the purpose of evaluation, the ease of calculation, etc. Index w_1 or w_4 would be easy to calculate and would generally be good for a rather rough evaluation. Index w_2 would be suitable for the case where the uniformity of manipulating ability is important. Index w_3 is suited for the case where the minimum manipulating ability might be critical. However, w_2 and w_3 are usually more difficult to calculate than either w_1 or w_4.

The above indices are local ones in the sense that they are functions of the joint vector $\boldsymbol{q}$, implying that they are for evaluating a given particular arm configuration. When evaluating a manipulator as a whole, we need some global index. A simple way to produce a global index based on a local index is to choose a proper evaluation region S in the space of $\boldsymbol{q}$ and to define the index w_{i_g} by

$$w_{i_g} = \min_{\boldsymbol{q} \in S} w_i. \tag{4.34}$$

In this way, we can obtain a global index with a clear physical meaning.[8]

4.4 Dynamic Manipulability

4.4.1 Dynamic-Manipulability Ellipsoid and Dynamic-Manipulability Measure

The manipulability discussed in the preceding sections is based on kinematics; the manipulator dynamics are completely ignored. Therefore, although one can apply it to the conceptual design of arm mechanisms and to the avoidance of singularities without considering complicated dynamics of arms, it may not be suitable for the detailed design of arms or for high-speed, high-precision motion control. This section introduces the concepts of the dynamic-manipulability ellipsoid and the dynamic-manipulability measure for evaluating the manipulating ability, with the dynamics of the arm taken into consideration (ref. 3).

Assume that the manipulator dynamics is given by equation 3.62, i.e.,

$$M(q)\ddot{q} + h(q,\dot{q}) + g(q) = \tau. \tag{4.35}$$

Also assume that the relation between the end-effector position vector r and the joint vector q is given by equation 4.1, and that the relation between the end-effector velocity vector v and the joint velocity vector $\dot{q}$ is given by equation 4.2, i.e.,

$$v = J(q)\dot{q}. \tag{4.36}$$

Differentiating this with respect to time yields

$$\dot{v} = J(q)\ddot{q} + a_r(q,\dot{q}), \tag{4.37}$$

$$a_r(q,\dot{q}) = \dot{J}(q)\dot{q}. \tag{4.38}$$

The term $a_r(q,\dot{q})$ can be interpreted as the virtual acceleration caused by the nonlinear relationship between the two coordinate systems for q and r. Since

$$\begin{aligned} a_r &= JJ^+ a_r + (\mathrm{I} - JJ^+)a_r \\ &= JM^{-1}MJ^+ a_r + (\mathrm{I} - JJ^+)a_r, \end{aligned} \tag{4.39}$$

we obtain from equations 4.35 and 4.37

$$\dot{v} - (\mathrm{I} - J^+ J)a_r = JM^{-1}[\tau - h(q,\dot{q}) - g(q) + MJ^+ a_r]. \tag{4.40}$$

Introducing the new vectors

$$\tilde{\tau} = \tau - h(q,\dot{q}) - g(q) + MJ^+ a_r \tag{4.41a}$$

and

$$\tilde{\dot{v}} = \dot{v} - (\mathrm{I} - J^+ J)a_r, \tag{4.41b}$$

we can rewrite equation 4.40 as

$$\tilde{\dot{v}} = JM^{-1}\tilde{\tau}. \tag{4.42}$$

Note that equation 4.39 is a decomposition of a_r (part of the end-effector acceleration) into two acceleration components, one of which can be produced by the joint driving force and the other of which cannot. Note also that if the manipulator is not in a singular configuration, (that is, if rank $J = m$), then the end effector can be accelerated in any direction and the term $(\mathbf{I} - JJ^+)a_r$ in equations 4.40 and 4.41b vanishes, resulting in $\dot{\tilde{v}} = \dot{v}$.

The basic idea here is to quantify the degree of arbitrariness in changing the end-effector acceleration $\dot{\tilde{v}}$ under some constraint on the joint driving force $\tilde{\tau}$ on the basis of equation 4.42. We then adopt this "arbitrariness" quantity as a measure of the manipulability of the arm in the dynamic case. As the constraint, we consider the inequality $\|\tilde{\tau}\| \leqq 1$. The set of all end-effector accelerations $\dot{\tilde{v}}$ that the joint driving force can achieve such that $\|\tilde{\tau}\| \leqq 1$ is an ellipsoid in m-dimensional Euclidean space described by

$$\dot{\tilde{v}}^T (J^+)^T M^T M J^+ \dot{\tilde{v}} \leqq 1, \quad \dot{\tilde{v}} \in \mathrm{R}(J). \tag{4.43}$$

This ellipsoid is called the *dynamic-manipulability ellipsoid*, which will be abbreviated as DME hereafter. Let the singular-value decomposition of (JM^{-1}) be

$$JM^{-1} = U_d \Sigma_d V_d^T, \tag{4.44}$$

where

$$\Sigma_d = \left[\begin{array}{cccc|c} \sigma_{d1} & & & \mathbf{0} & \\ & \sigma_{d2} & & & \\ & & \ddots & & \mathbf{0} \\ \mathbf{0} & & & \sigma_{dm} & \end{array}\right]. \tag{4.45}$$

Let

$$U_d = [\boldsymbol{u}_{d1}, \boldsymbol{u}_{d2}, \ldots, \boldsymbol{u}_{dm}]. \tag{4.46}$$

Then the principal axes of the DME are

$$\sigma_{d1}\boldsymbol{u}_{d1}, \sigma_{d2}\boldsymbol{u}_{d2}, \ldots, \sigma_{dm}\boldsymbol{u}_{dm}.$$

Note that except at the singular configurations where the volume of the ellipsoid becomes zero (that is, except at configurations for which rank $J = m$), equation 4.43 can be replaced by

$$\dot{\tilde{v}}^T (J^+)^T M^T M J^+ \dot{\tilde{v}} \leqq 1. \tag{4.47}$$

A typical measure of dynamic manipulability corresponding to the manipulability measure would be the volume of DME. This is given by $c_m w_d$,

where

$$w_d = \sigma_{d1}\sigma_{d2}\cdots\sigma_{dm} \tag{4.48}$$

and c_m is the constant given by equation 4.7. Hence, we adopt w_d as an index and call it the *dynamic-manipulability measure* at configuration $\boldsymbol{q}$. The measure w_d has the following properties, which are analogous to those of the manipulability measure w:

(i) $w_d = \sqrt{\det[\boldsymbol{J}(\boldsymbol{M}^T\boldsymbol{M})^{-1}\boldsymbol{J}^T]}$. (4.49)

(ii) When $m = n$ (that is, when we consider nonredundant manipulators), w_d reduces to

$$w_d = \frac{|\det \boldsymbol{J}|}{|\det \boldsymbol{M}|}, \tag{4.50}$$

where the denominator represents the effect of manipulator dynamics on w_d and the numerator is equal to the manipulability measure that represents the kinematic effect.

(iii) The index w_d satisfies $w_d \geqq 0$ generally, and satisfies $w_d = 0$ if and only if rank $\boldsymbol{J}(\boldsymbol{q}) \neq m$ (i.e. the manipulator is in a singular configuration).

(iv) When $m = n$, w_d has the following physical interpretation as well as that of the ellipsoid's volume: The set of all accelerations $\tilde{\dot{\boldsymbol{v}}}$ achievable by a joint driving force $\tilde{\boldsymbol{\tau}}$ such that

$$|\tilde{\tau}_i| \leqq 1, \quad i = 1, 2, \ldots, n \tag{4.51}$$

is a parallelepiped in m-dimensional Euclidean space, with volume $2^m w_d$. In other words, the measure w_d is proportional to the volume of the parallelepiped.

So far, we have implicitly assumed that the maximum joint driving forces at all joints are 1 irrespective of $\boldsymbol{q}$, and that the weights of all components of the end-effector acceleration are the same. When these assumptions do not hold, each variable should be normalized as follows: Regard a state in which the manipulator is at rest ($\dot{\boldsymbol{q}} = \boldsymbol{0}$) as a standard one for considering the dynamic manipulability. The constraint on $\boldsymbol{\tau}$ is assumed to be given by

$$|\tau_i| \leqq \tau_{i\,\max}, \quad i = 1, 2, \ldots, n. \tag{4.52}$$

From $\dot{\boldsymbol{q}} = \boldsymbol{0}$ we have $\boldsymbol{h}(\boldsymbol{q},\dot{\boldsymbol{q}}) = \boldsymbol{0}$ and $\boldsymbol{a}_r(\boldsymbol{q},\dot{\boldsymbol{q}}) = \boldsymbol{0}$. Hence, from equation 4.41 we have

$$\tilde{\tau} = \tau - g(q), \tag{4.53}$$

$$\tilde{\dot{\nu}} = \dot{\nu}. \tag{4.54}$$

Now we take

$$|\tilde{\tau}_i| \leqq \tau_{i\,max} \tag{4.55}$$

as the constraint on $\tilde{\tau}$, where

$$\tilde{\tau}_{i\,max} = \tau_{i\,max} - |g_i(q)|. \tag{4.56}$$

Here we assume that $\tilde{\tau}_{i\,max} \geqq 0$ is always satisfied. This assumption is reasonable because $\tilde{\tau}_{i\,max} < 0$ means that the manipulator cannot support its own weight for certain arm configurations. Also, equation 4.56 corresponds to setting $\tilde{\tau}_{i\,max}$ by choosing the case where the gravitational force works in the worst direction. For the acceleration $\tilde{\dot{\nu}}$, we assume that the maximum desirable acceleration $\tilde{\dot{v}}_{j\,max}$ for each element $\tilde{\dot{v}}_j$ of $\tilde{\dot{\nu}}$ can be found by considering the set of tasks to be performed by the manipulator. If it is difficult to determine $\tilde{\dot{v}}_{j\,max}$, this value may be roughly selected as the weight of relative importance among the elements of $\tilde{\dot{\nu}}$.

Once the values $\tilde{\tau}_{i\,max}$ and $\tilde{\dot{v}}_{j\,max}$ are given, we can normalize the variable $\tilde{\tau}$ and $\tilde{\dot{\nu}}$ by

$$\hat{\tau} = [\hat{\tau}_1, \hat{\tau}_2, \ldots, \hat{\tau}_n]^T, \quad \hat{\tau}_i = \tilde{\tau}_i / \tilde{\tau}_{i\,max} \tag{4.57}$$

and

$$\hat{\dot{\nu}} = [\hat{\dot{v}}_1, \hat{\dot{v}}_2, \ldots, \hat{\dot{v}}_m]^T, \quad \hat{\dot{v}}_j = \tilde{\dot{v}}_j / \tilde{\dot{v}}_{j\,max}. \tag{4.58}$$

Then, from equation 4.42, we obtain

$$\hat{\dot{\nu}} = \hat{J}\hat{M}^{-1}\hat{\tau}, \tag{4.59}$$

where

$$\hat{J} = T_a J, \tag{4.60}$$

$$\hat{M} = T_\tau M, \tag{4.61}$$

$$T_a = \operatorname{diag}\left(\frac{1}{\tilde{\dot{v}}_{1\,max}}, \frac{1}{\tilde{\dot{v}}_{2\,max}}, \ldots, \frac{1}{\tilde{\dot{v}}_{m\,max}}\right), \tag{4.62}$$

$$T_\tau = \operatorname{diag}\left(\frac{1}{\tilde{\tau}_{1\,max}}, \frac{1}{\tilde{\tau}_{2\,max}}, \ldots, \frac{1}{\tilde{\tau}_{n\,max}}\right). \tag{4.63}$$

We can now define the DME and the dynamic-manipulability measure using the normalized Jacobian $\hat{J}$ and the normalized moment-of-inertia matrix $\hat{M}$ instead of J and M.

Even when the DME is defined on the basis of equation 4.59, as long as the manipulator is not in a singular configuration, any vector $\hat{\dot{v}}^*$ included in the DME is a realizable end-effector acceleration in the sense that the corresponding $\hat{\dot{v}}^*$ given by

$$\dot{v}^* = T_a^{-1}\hat{\dot{v}}^* \tag{4.64}$$

is achievable by some τ that satisfies equation 4.52.

As well as w_d, there are other useful indices of dynamic manipulability, such as the minimum singular value, σ_{dm}, or the reciprocal of the condition number, σ_{dm}/σ_{d1}. Similarly to the case of manipulability, σ_{dm} is the upper bound of the magnitude of acceleration with which the end effector can be moved in any direction. σ_{dm}/σ_{d1} is a measure of directional uniformity of realizable end-effector acceleration.

4.4.2 Two-Link Mechanism

We will now analyze the two-link mechanism shown in figure 4.11 from the viewpoint of dynamic manipulability. The following notations are used in the figure:

m_i the mass of link i,
$\tilde{I}_i$ the moment of inertia of link i about the center of mass,
l_i the length of link i,
l_{gi} the distance between the joint i and the center of mass of link i,

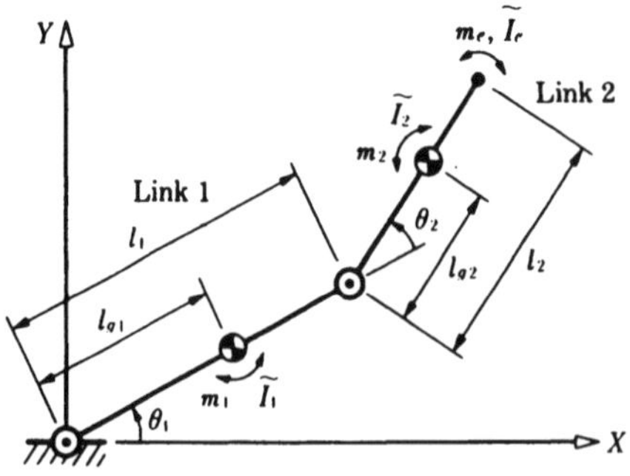

Figure 4.11
Two-link mechanism.

m_e the mass of the end effector and load,
$\tilde{I}_e$ the moment of inertia of the end effector and load.

It is assumed that the first joint driving torque, τ_1, acts between the base and link 1, and that the second joint driving torque, τ_2, acts between links 1 and 2. We let $r = [x, y]^T$, so that from subsection 3.3.1 we have

$$J = \begin{bmatrix} -l_1 S_1 - l_2 S_{12} & -l_2 S_{12} \\ l_1 C_1 + l_2 C_{12} & l_2 C_{12} \end{bmatrix}, \tag{4.65}$$

$$M = \begin{bmatrix} M_{11} & M_{12} \\ M_{21} & M_{22} \end{bmatrix}, \tag{4.66}$$

$$M_{11} = \tilde{I}_1 + \tilde{I}_2{}^* + m_1 l_{g1}{}^2 + m_2{}^*(l_1{}^2 + l_{g2}{}^{*2} + 2l_1 l_{g2}{}^* C_2), \tag{4.67a}$$

$$M_{12} = M_{21} = \tilde{I}_2{}^* + m_2{}^*(l_{g2}{}^{*2} + l_1 l_{g2}{}^* C_2), \tag{4.67b}$$

$$M_{22} = \tilde{I}_2{}^* + m_2{}^* l_{g2}{}^{*2}, \tag{4.67c}$$

where $m_2{}^*$, $l_{g2}{}^*$, and $\tilde{I}_2{}^*$ correspond to m_2, l_{g2}, and $\tilde{I}_2$, respectively, but since in this case the end effector and the load are regarded as part of link 2, these parameters become

$$m_2{}^* = m_2 + m_e, \tag{4.68a}$$

$$l_{g2}{}^* = (m_2 l_{g2} + m_e l_2)/(m_2 + m_e), \tag{4.68b}$$

$$\tilde{I}_2{}^* = \tilde{I}_2 + m_2(l_{g2}{}^* - l_{g2})^2 + \tilde{I}_e + m_e(l_2 - l_{g2}{}^*)^2. \tag{4.68c}$$

Since $m = n = 2$, we obtain from equation 4.50

$$w_d = \frac{l_1 l_2 |S_2|}{(\tilde{I}_1 + m_1 l_{g1}{}^2)(\tilde{I}_2{}^* + m_2{}^* l_{g2}{}^{*2}) + \tilde{I}_2{}^* m_2{}^* l_1{}^2 + m_2{}^{*2} l_{g2}{}^{*2} l_1{}^2 S_2{}^2}. \tag{4.69}$$

From now on we will assume that the link mechanism is at rest. The case where there is no gravity effect will be considered first. In this case, since $\tilde{\tau}_{i\max} = \tau_{i\max}$, by an argument similar to equation 4.18, T_a and T_t have only the effect of multiplying w_d by a scalar constant. Therefore, equation 4.69 is an adequate expression for evaluating dynamic manipulability.

If we let

$$\alpha = \frac{l_1 l_2}{(\tilde{I}_1 + m_1 l_{g1}{}^2 + m_2{}^* l_1{}^2)(\tilde{I}_2{}^* + m_2{}^* l_{g2}{}^{*2})} \tag{4.70}$$

and

$$\beta = \frac{m_2^{*2} l_{g2}^{*2} l_1^2}{(\hat{I}_1 + m_1 l_{g1}^2)(\hat{I}_2^* + m_2^* l_{g2}^{*2}) + \hat{I}_2^* m_2^* l_1^2}, \tag{4.71}$$

then equation 4.69 becomes

$$w_d = \frac{\alpha(1+\beta)|S_2|}{1+\beta S_2^2}. \tag{4.72}$$

Therefore, the relative shape of w_d as a function of $\boldsymbol{q}$ is uniquely determined by the parameter β, and the parameter α determines its scale.

Since the special case where $\beta = 0$ is of some interest, we will consider this case first. The condition $\beta = 0$ can be reduced to $l_{g2}^* = 0$ under the natural assumptions that $m_2^* \neq 0$ and $l_1 \neq 0$. The implication of $l_{g2}^* = 0$ is that the center of mass of the set of link 2, the end effector, and the load is located precisely at joint 2 (say, by the use of a counterbalance). When $l_{g2}^* = 0$, the value $|\det \boldsymbol{M}|$ is independent of θ_2, and the dynamic-manipulability measure w_d is equal to the manipulability measure $w = l_1 l_2 |S_2|$ times the scalar $1/|\det \boldsymbol{M}|$ (as was stated in the preceding subsection relating to equation 4.50). Therefore, the best arm posture from the viewpoint of w—that is, $\theta_2 = \pm 90°$—is also the best from the viewpoint of w_d.

Next we will consider the case where $\beta \neq 0$. Figure 4.12 shows the value of w_d as a function of θ_2 using β as a parameter. It can be seen from the figure that as β starts from zero and becomes larger, w_d approaches a trapezoidal shape, but it still attains its maximum α at $\theta_2 = 90°$ for β satisfying $0 \leqq \beta \leqq 1$. For $\beta > 1$, w_d attains its maximum at two values of θ_2, one of which is larger than 90° and one of which is smaller. As we have seen, the parameter β determines the relative shape of w_d and the parameter α determines its magnitude.

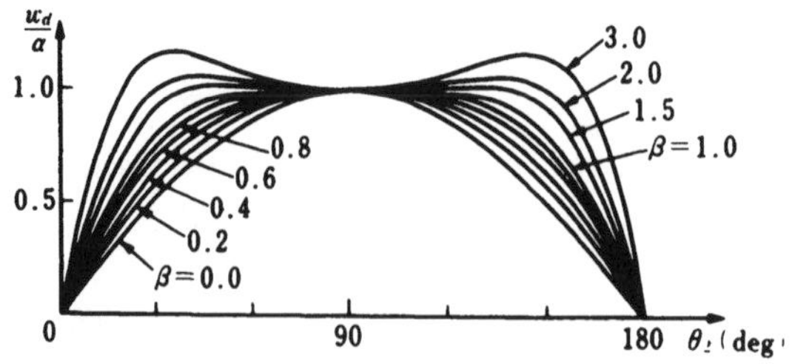

Figure 4.12
Dynamic-manipulability measure.

Now let us consider a numerical example. Let $l_1 = l_2 = 1.0$, $m_1 = 20$, $m_2 = 10, m_e = 5, l_{g1} = 0.5, l_{g2} = 0.3, \bar{I}_1 = 20/12, \bar{I}_2 = 10/12, \bar{I}_e = 0, \tau_{1\,\max} = 600$, $\tau_{2\,\max} = 200$ (units are m, kg, and sec), and $\tilde{\dot{v}}_{1\,\max} = \tilde{\dot{v}}_{2\,\max} = 1$ (the relative importance of acceleration in the X and Y directions is the same). Note that in determining the values of $\bar{I}_1$ and $\bar{I}_2$ we have assumed a uniform mass distribution over the links and have used the formula $I = ml^2/12$ for the moment of inertia I of a thin beam with uniform mass distribution and with mass m and length l. The DME and the dynamic-manipulability measure $\hat{w}_d$ as functions of the distance l_a between the origin and the arm tip are given in figure 4.13. From equation 4.71 we have $\beta = 0.78$, so $\hat{w}_d$ reaches a maximum when $\theta_2 = 90°$. As can be seen from the figure, however, the difference between $\hat{w}_d$ and the maximum value is not very large for a wide range of l_a. Hence, the mechanism with the given values of the inertial parameters could be judged to be a rather good design from the viewpoint of uniformity of the dynamic-manipulability measure over a wide area of the workspace.

Next we will consider the case where the gravitational force acts on the above mechanism in the $-Y$ direction. Let g be the gravitational acceleration constant. The gravity term $\boldsymbol{g}(\boldsymbol{q})$ is given by

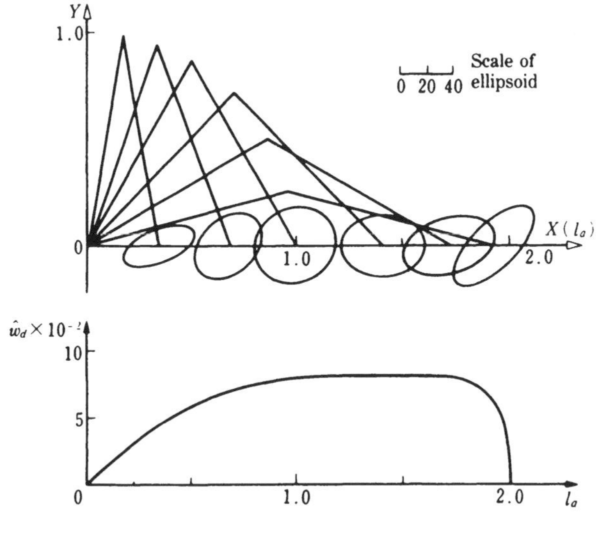

Figure 4.13
Dynamic-manipulability ellipsoid and dynamic-manipulability measure (without gravity).

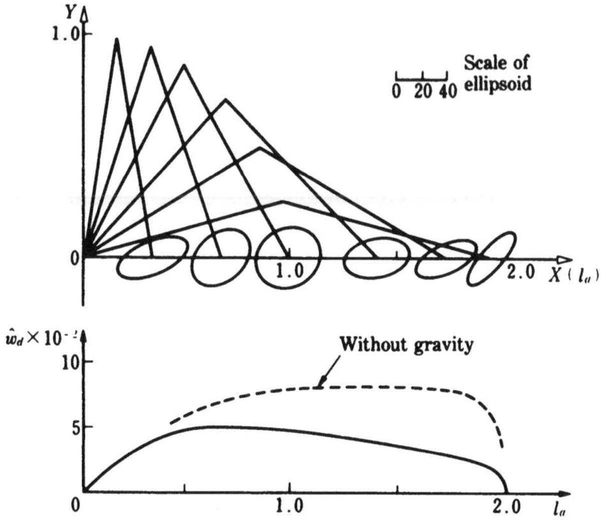

Figure 4.14
Dynamic-manipulability ellipsoid and dynamic-manipulability measure (with gravity; $l_{g1} = 0.5$, $l_{g2} = 0.3$).

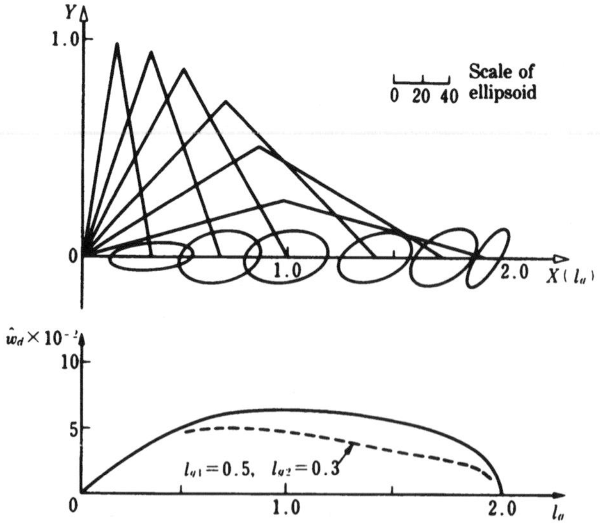

Figure 4.15
Dynamic-manipulability ellipsoid and dynamic-manipulability measure (with gravity; $l_{g1} = 0.4$, $l_{g2} = 0$).

$$g(q) = \begin{bmatrix} m_1 l_{g1} C_1 + m_2{}^*(l_1 C_1 + l_{g2} C_{12}) \\ m_2{}^* l_{g2}{}^* C_{12} \end{bmatrix} \hat{g}. \tag{4.73}$$

Figure 4.14 shows the DME and the dynamic-manipulability measure calculated from $\boldsymbol{J}$ and $\hat{\boldsymbol{M}}$ derived from equations 4.73, 4.56, and 4.61. Because of the effect of gravity, the dynamic-manipulability measure is rather small for stretched arm postures. Since this is usually not desirable, we consider a modification. If, for example, we can attain $l_{g1} = 0.4$ and $l_{g2}{}^* = 0$ by a change in the mass distribution of each link, then we see the change shown in figure 4.15. In comparison with the original design, the modified one has an improved dynamic-manipulability measure in the region $0.7 \leqq l_a \leqq 1.8$.

Exercises

4.1 Prove properties i–iv of the manipulability measure given in section 4.1.

4.2 Explain the relation between the arm posture and the manipulating-force ellipsoid given in figure 4.4 for the two-link mechanism shown in figure 4.2 by taking the human arm as an example.

4.3 Find the optimal arm posture with respect to the index w_2 given in equation 4.33a for the two-link mechanism shown in figure 4.2. Sketch the change of the optimal arm posture as the ratio of link lengths l_1 and l_2 changes.

4.4 Derive the principal axes of the manipulability ellipsoid and the manipulability measure for the parallel-drive two-link manipulator treated in subsection 3.3.3, and draw a figure corresponding to figure 4.3. Find the optimal arm posture with respect to the manipulability measure.

4.5 Derive the dynamic-manipulability measure for the two-link mechanism in subsection 4.4.2 with the drive mechanism replaced by a parallel drive. Compare the result with equation 4.69.

References

1. T. Yoshikawa, "Analysis and Control of Robot Manipulators with Redundancy," in *Robotics Research: The First International Symposium*, ed. M. Brady and R. Paul (MIT Press, 1984), pp. 735–747.

2. T. Yoshikawa, "Manipulability of Robotic Mechanisms," *International Journal of Robotics Research* 4, no. 2 (1985): 3–9.

3. T. Yoshikawa, "Dynamic Manipulability of Robotic Mechanisms," *Journal of Robotic Systems* 2, no. 1 (1985): 113–124.

4. A Kumar and K. J. Waldron, "The Workspace of a Mechanical Manipulator," *ASME Journal of Mechanical Design* 103 (1981): 665–672.

5. D. C. M. Yang and T. W. Lee, "Heuristic Combinational Optimization in the Design of Manipulator Workspace," *IEEE Transactions on Systems, Man, and Cybernetics* 14, no. 4 (1984): 571–580.

6. J. K. Salisbury and J. J. Craig, "Articulated Hands, Force Control and Kinematic Issues," *International Journal of Robotics Research* 1, no. 1 (1982): 4–17.

7. C. A. Klein, "Use of Redundancy in the Design of Robotic System," in *Robotics Research: The Second International Symposium*, ed. H. Hanafusa and H. Inoue (MIT Press, 1985), pp. 207–214.

8. T. Yoshikawa, "Analysis and Design of Articulated Robot Arms from the Viewpoint of Dynamic Manipulability," in *Robotics Research: The Third International Symposium*, ed. 0. Faugeras and G. Giralt (MIT Press, 1986), pp. 273–279.

5 Position Control

Control algorithms and the construction of control systems will be discussed in this chapter for tasks such as transferring the end effector of a manipulator from one position to another or making the end effector follow a given trajectory. Although the end effector may hold a load, it is assumed that the end effector and its load do not come in contact with any other environmental structure, and that they can move freely in three-dimensional space. The case where there is some contact with the environment will be treated in chapter 6.

First we will develop several methods for determining a desired trajectory that passes through given initial and final points and, intermediate points, if any. Then we will consider several control algorithms for realizing the desired trajectory: linear feedback control, two-stage control by linearization and servo compensation, decoupling control, and adaptive control.

5.1 Generating a Desired Trajectory

5.1.1 Joint-Variable Scheme

In this section we will consider methods to determine a desired trajectory of joint variables over time. A basic problem is how to select a trajectory between a given initial position ($\boldsymbol{r}_0$) and final position ($\boldsymbol{r}_f$) of the end effector with a time interval t_f allowed for moving between them. Various methods of solving this problem have been proposed.[1] A simple method based on polynomial functions of time[2,3] will be presented here. This method can be divided into two schemes, one in which the trajectory is considered in terms of joint variables and one in which it is considered in terms of position variables of the end effector. The present subsection will describe the joint-variable scheme. The other scheme will be developed in the next subsection.

Suppose we are given joint vectors $\boldsymbol{q}_0$ and $\boldsymbol{q}_f$, corresponding to $\boldsymbol{r}_0$ and $\boldsymbol{r}_f$ respectively. If only $\boldsymbol{r}_0$ and $\boldsymbol{r}_f$ are known, we determine $\boldsymbol{q}_0$ and $\boldsymbol{q}_f$ in advance by solving the inverse kinematics problem. We first choose an arbitrary joint variable, q_i, and represent it by ξ. We assume that the value of ξ at the initial time (0) is ξ_0 and that the value at the final time (t_f) is ξ_f:

$$\xi(0) = \xi_0, \quad \xi(t_f) = \xi_f. \tag{5.1}$$

We further assume that the velocity and the acceleration of ξ must satisfy the following boundary conditions:

$$\dot{\xi}(0) = \dot{\xi}_0, \quad \dot{\xi}(t_f) = \dot{\xi}_f, \tag{5.2}$$

$$\ddot{\xi}(0) = \ddot{\xi}_0, \quad \ddot{\xi}(t_f) = \ddot{\xi}_f. \tag{5.3}$$

Although there are many smooth functions that satisfy these constraints, we select polynomials of time t because of their ease of computation and simplicity of expression. Since the polynomials of the lowest order that satisfy the arbitrarily given boundary conditions 5.1–5.3 are of fifth order, we express $\xi(t)$ as a fifth-order polynomial:

$$\xi(t) = a_0 + a_1 t + a_2 t^2 + a_3 t^3 + a_4 t^4 + a_5 t^5. \tag{5.4}$$

Then the unknown coefficients a_1–a_5 that satisfy equations 5.1–5.3 are

$$a_0 = \xi_0, \tag{5.5a}$$

$$a_1 = \dot{\xi}_0, \tag{5.5b}$$

$$a_2 = \tfrac{1}{2}\ddot{\xi}_0, \tag{5.5c}$$

$$a_3 = \frac{1}{2t_f^3}[20\xi_f - 20\xi_0 - (8\dot{\xi}_f + 12\dot{\xi}_0)t_f - (3\ddot{\xi}_0 - \ddot{\xi}_f)t_f^2], \tag{5.5d}$$

$$a_4 = \frac{1}{2t_f^4}[30\xi_0 - 30\xi_f + (14\dot{\xi}_f + 16\dot{\xi}_0)t_f + (3\ddot{\xi}_0 - 2\ddot{\xi}_f)t_f^2], \tag{5.5e}$$

$$a_5 = \frac{1}{2t_f^5}[12\xi_f - 12\xi_0 - (6\dot{\xi}_f + 6\dot{\xi}_0)t_f - (\ddot{\xi}_0 - \ddot{\xi}_f)t_f^2], \tag{5.5f}$$

In particular, if $\ddot{\xi}_0 = \ddot{\xi}_f = 0$ and the relation shown in figure 5.1 is satisfied by ξ_0, ξ_f, $\dot{\xi}_0$, and $\dot{\xi}_f$—that is, if

$$\xi_f - \xi_0 = \frac{t_f}{2}(\dot{\xi}_0 + \dot{\xi}_f) \tag{5.6}$$

—then $a_0 = 0$, which implies that only a fourth-order polynomial is required for $\xi(t)$.

By using combinations of fourth-order polynomials and straight lines, trajectories for various cases can be determined fairly easily. Let us consider two such cases.

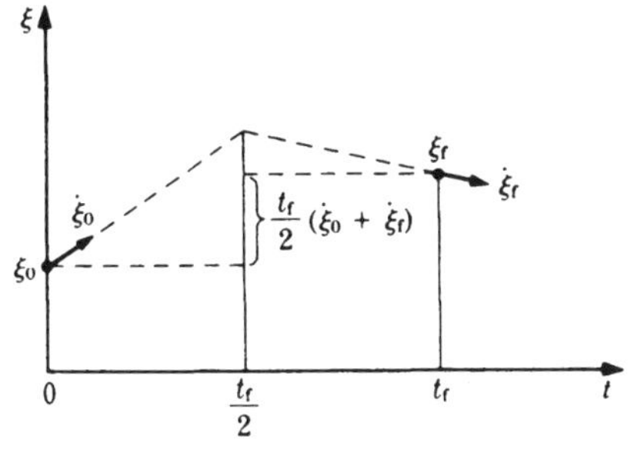

Figure 5.1
Boundary conditions $\dddot{\xi}_0 = \dddot{\xi}_f = 0$ and (5.6).

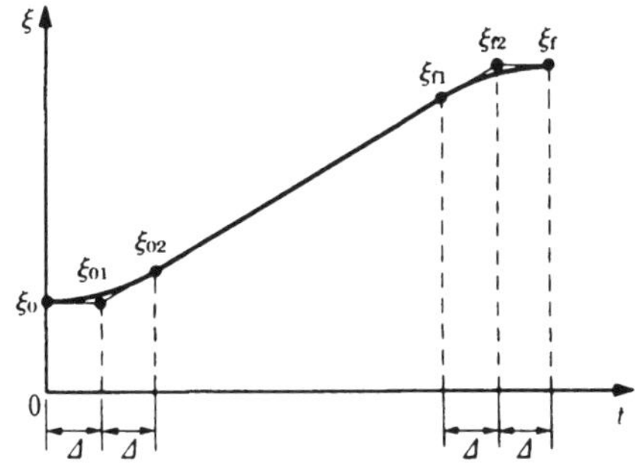

Figure 5.2
Trajectory with acceleration, constant velocity, and deceleration phases.

(1) Only the initial point ξ_0 and the final point ξ_f are known.

We develop a trajectory that starts from rest at ξ_0, passes through the phases of acceleration, constant velocity, and deceleration, and finally comes to a complete stop at ξ_f. For this purpose, we first choose the value of parameter Δ that denotes one-half of the acceleration and deceleration period. Second, we determine the auxiliary points ξ_{02} and ξ_{f1} shown in figure 5.2 by the following procedure: First two points ξ_{01} and ξ_{f2} at time $t = \Delta$ and $t = t_f - \Delta$ are taken as $\xi_{01} = \xi_0$ and $\xi_{f2} = \xi_f$. Then ξ_{01} and ξ_{f2} are connected by a straight line and ξ_{02} and ξ_{f1} are determined as the points on the straight line at time $t = 2\Delta$ and $t = t_f - 2\Delta$.

We determine the trajectory segments between ξ_0 and ξ_{02}, and between ξ_{f1} and ξ_f, by fourth-order polynomials such that their velocity coincides with the composition of straight lines connecting ξ_0, ξ_{01}, ξ_{f2}, and ξ_f at boundary points ξ_0, ξ_{02}, ξ_{f1}, and ξ_f, and such that their acceleration is zero

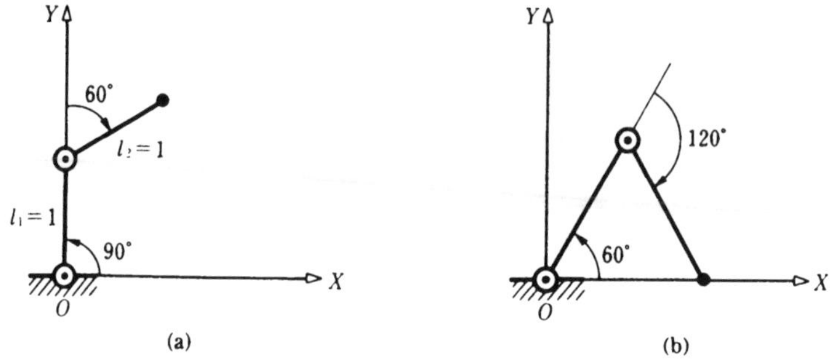

Figure 5.3
Two-link manipulator. (a) Initial position. (b) Final position.

at these boundary points. The trajectory segment between ξ_{02} and ξ_{f1} is specified by the straight line. Thus, the whole trajectory is given by the bold solid line in figure 5.2.

Example 5.1 Applying the above method to the two-link planar manipulator shown in figure 5.3, we generate a trajectory that starts from rest at the initial position in figure 5.3a and comes to a complete stop at the final position in figure 5.3b in 2 seconds. Suppose we choose $\Delta = 0.25$. Then the first joint angle, θ_1, is given by

$$\theta_1(t) = \begin{cases} 90 - 80t^3 + 80t^4, & 0 \leqq t \leqq 0.5 \\ 85 - 20(t - 0.5), & 0.5 < t \leqq 1.5 \\ 65 - 20(t - 1.5) + 80(t - 1.5)^3 - 80(t - 1.5)^4, & 1.5 < t \leqq 2.0 \end{cases}$$

and the second joint angle, θ_2, is given by

$$\theta_2(t) = \begin{cases} -60 - 160t^3 + 160t^4, & 0 \leqq t \leqq 0.5 \\ -70 - 40(t - 0.5), & 0.5 < t \leqq 1.5 \\ -110 - 40(t - 1.5) + 160(t - 1.5)^3 - 160(t - 1.5)^4, & 1.5 < t \leqq 2.0. \end{cases}$$

Figure 5.4 shows the resulting endpoint trajectory. □

(2) The initial point ξ_0, several intermediate points, and the final point ξ_f are given.

We determine a trajectory that starts from rest at initial position ξ_0, passes through intermediate positions ξ_1 and ξ_2, and stops at final position ξ_f. We first consider the case where it is not necessary to pass exactly through ξ_1

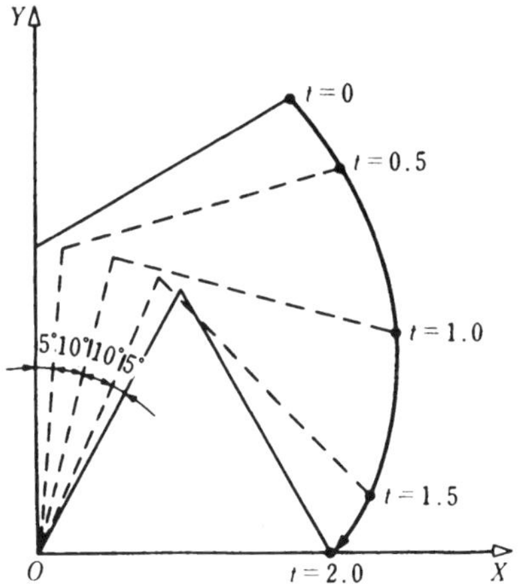

Figure 5.4
Endpoint trajectory.

and ξ_2. In this case, we specify auxiliary points $\xi_{02}, \xi_{11}, \xi_{12}, \ldots, \xi_{f1}$ as in figure 5.5. Note that the values at points ξ_{01} and ξ_0 are the same, that the values at ξ_{f2} and ξ_f are the same, and that ξ_{02} and ξ_{11} are on the straight line between ξ_{01} and ξ_1. Points $\xi_{12}, \ldots, \xi_{f1}$ are also determined in the same way. We then determine the trajectory segments for $\{\xi_0, \xi_{02}\}, \{\xi_{11}, \xi_{12}\}, \ldots,$ $\{\xi_{f1}, \xi_f\}$ by fourth-order polynomials, and those for $\{\xi_{02}, \xi_{11}\}$, $\{\xi_{12}, \xi_{21}\}$, and $\{\xi_{22}, \xi_{f1}\}$ by straight lines. The resulting trajectory is illustrated by a bold line in figure 5.5.

Next, we consider the case when the trajectory is required to pass exactly through ξ_1 and ξ_2. This case can be dealt with by increasing the number of auxiliary points. A scheme is shown in figure 5.6a. Auxiliary points are determined as follows: As figure 5.6b shows, ξ_{i2} $(i = 1,2)$ is the midpoint between A (the intersection of the line of $t = t_i - \Delta$ with the straight line between ξ_{i-1} (ξ_{01} when $i = 1$) and ξ_i) and B (the intersection of the line of $t = t_i - \Delta$ with straight line between ξ_i and ξ_{i+1} (ξ_{f2} when $i = 1$)). Point ξ_{i3} is determined similarly. We then determine the trajectory segments for $\{\xi_0, \xi_{02}\}, \{\xi_{11}, \xi_1\}, \{\xi_1, \xi_{14}\}, \ldots, \{\xi_{f1}, \xi_f\}$ by fourth-order polynomials, and those for $\{\xi_{02}, \xi_{11}\}$, $\{\xi_{14}, \xi_{21}\}$, and $\{\xi_{24}, \xi_{f1}\}$ by straight lines, as in the previous case.

In the basic problem of connecting ξ_0 and ξ_f by a polynomial, which was mentioned at the beginning of the section, if we consider the boundary

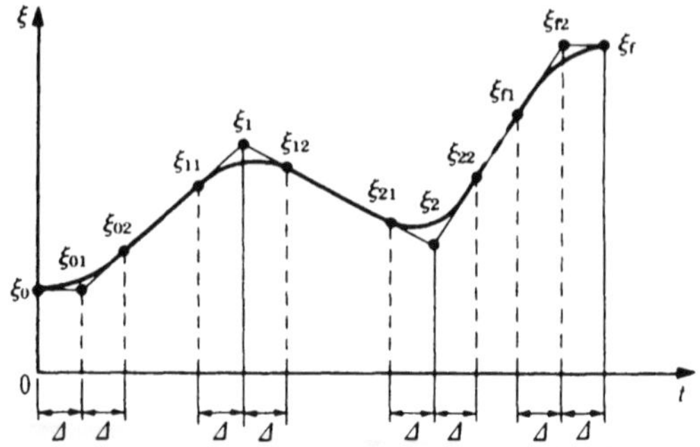

Figure 5.5
Trajectory passing near the intermediate points.

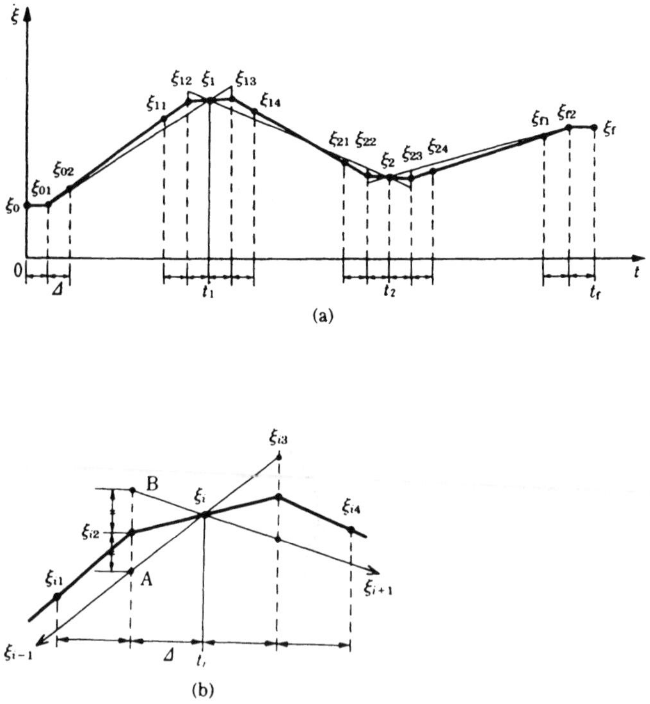

Figure 5.6
Trajectory passing through the intermediate points. (a) Intermediate points. (b) Determination of points ξ_{i2} and ξ_{i3}.

condition on position (equation 5.1) and that on velocity (equation 5.2), and do not take into account the continuity of acceleration (equation 5.3), then we can simplify the polynomials. More specifically, we may use a third-order polynomial,

$$\xi(t) = a_0 + a_1 t + a_2 t^2 + a_3 t^3, \tag{5.7}$$

instead of a fifth-order one. The constants in equation 5.7 are

$$a_0 = \xi_0, \tag{5.8a}$$

$$a_1 = \dot{\xi}_0, \tag{5.8b}$$

$$a_2 = \frac{1}{t_f^2}[3(\xi_f - \xi_0) - (2\dot{\xi}_0 + \dot{\xi}_f)t_f], \tag{5.8c}$$

and

$$a_3 = \frac{1}{t_f^3}[-2(\xi_f - \xi_0) + (\dot{\xi}_f + \dot{\xi}_0)t_f]. \tag{5.8d}$$

In particular, if ξ_0, ξ_f, $\dot{\xi}_0$, and $\dot{\xi}_f$ satisfy equation 5.6, then $a_3 = 0$, and so $\xi(t)$ becomes a second-order polynomial. Hence, for cases 1 and 2 treated above, we can also use second-order polynomials.

5.1.2 Scheme for Position Variables of End Effector

When a trajectory between $\boldsymbol{r}_0$ and $\boldsymbol{r}_f$ is generated by a joint variable scheme, as described in the preceding subsection, it is sometimes difficult to predict the motion of the end effector in space. There are also cases in which some specific end-effector trajectory is required. For example, in arc welding the electrode should follow a seam precisely. In such cases we wish to generate a trajectory between $\boldsymbol{r}_0$ and $\boldsymbol{r}_f$ in terms of the position variables of the end effector.

There are several ways to describe the position and orientation of the end effector using six variables. Once we choose one way, we can determine a trajectory by representing an arbitrarily selected variable of the six by ξ and then determining a trajectory of ξ by a sequence of polynomials of the form of equation 5.4 or equation 5.7.

A trajectory of an end effector obtained in this way is very simple and easy to visualize. For example, in case 1 of the preceding subsection the resulting trajectory moves on the straight line connecting $\boldsymbol{r}_0$ and $\boldsymbol{r}_f$ in the six-dimensional Euclidean space of end-effector position and orientation. The X, Y, and Z coordinates of the origin of the end-effector frame with respect to the reference frame are often used as the three variables for describing the translational position of the end effector. In this case, the position of the end effector literally moves along a straight line in space.

Example 5.2 Let us obtain a trajectory for the problem in example 5.1 not in terms of joint variables but in terms of end-effector position variables $\boldsymbol{r} = [x,y]^T$. Since the initial position $\boldsymbol{r}_0$ is $[\sqrt{3}/2, 3/2]^T$ and the final position $\boldsymbol{r}_f$ is $[1,0]^T$, the trajectory $\boldsymbol{r}(t) = [x(t), y(t)]^T$ is given by

$$x(t) = \begin{cases} \sqrt{3}/2 + 4(2-\sqrt{3})(t^3 - t^4)/3, & 0 \leqq t \leqq 0.5 \\ (5\sqrt{3}+2)/12 + (2-\sqrt{3})(t-0.5)/3, & 0.5 < t \leqq 1.5 \\ (10+\sqrt{3})/12 + (2-\sqrt{3})(t-1.5)/3 & \\ \quad -4(2-\sqrt{3})[(t-1.5)^3 - (t-1.5)^4]/3, & 1.5 < t \leqq 2.0 \end{cases}$$

$$y(t) = \begin{cases} 3/2 - 4t^3 + 4t^4, & 0 \leqq t \leqq 0.5 \\ 5/4 - (t-0.5), & 0.5 < t \leqq 1.5 \\ 1/4 - (t-1.5) + 4(t-1.5)^3 - 4(t-1.5)^4, & 1.5 < t \leqq 2.0. \end{cases}$$

Figure 5.7 shows the resulting endpoint trajectory. □

As for the end-effector orientation, if we take Euler angles or roll, pitch, and yaw angles, the end effector moves in a straight line with respect to

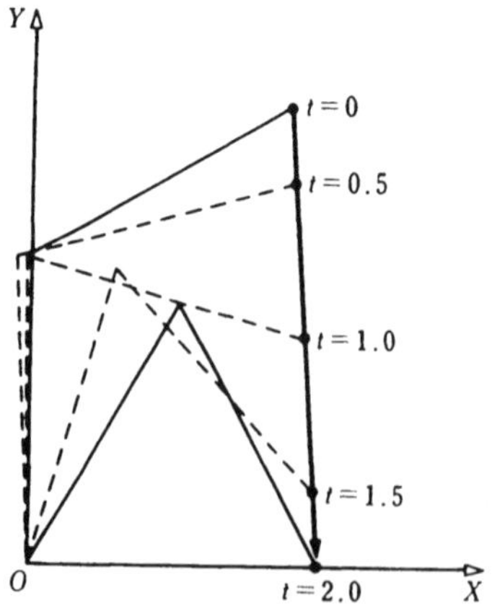

Figure 5.7
Endpoint trajectory.

these variables. However, the corresponding motion in the reference frame is difficult to understand intuitively, because it is given as a combination of three rotations about three different time-varying axes. The following two methods are effective in avoiding this difficulty. The first method is based on a representation of orientation by a rotation about a fixed axis, the second on a representation by rotations about two axes.

(1) Single-axis rotation method

In preparation, we give a representation of the relation between two frames Σ_A and Σ_B having the same origin by the pair $[\boldsymbol{k},\alpha]$, where $\boldsymbol{k} = [k_x,k_y,k_z]^T$ is the equivalent axis of rotation and α is the equivalent angle of rotation. We use this pair to obtain Σ_B from Σ_A by a single rotation about the fixed unit vector $\boldsymbol{k}$ by an angle α. Note that the pair $[\boldsymbol{k},\alpha]$ can also be represented by a three-dimensional vector $\alpha\boldsymbol{k}$ having direction $\boldsymbol{k}$ and magnitude α. Also note that the rotation matrix $\boldsymbol{R}(\boldsymbol{k},\alpha)$ corresponding to $[\boldsymbol{k},\alpha]$ is given by

$$\boldsymbol{R}(\boldsymbol{k},\alpha) = \begin{bmatrix} k_x^2 V_\alpha + C_\alpha & k_x k_y V_\alpha - k_z S_\alpha & k_x k_z V_\alpha + k_y S_\alpha \\ k_x k_y V_\alpha + k_z S_\alpha & k_y^2 V_\alpha + C_\alpha & k_y k_z V_\alpha - k_x S_\alpha \\ k_x k_z V_\alpha - k_y S_\alpha & k_y k_z V_\alpha + k_x S_\alpha & k_z^2 V_\alpha + C_\alpha \end{bmatrix}, \tag{5.9}$$

where $S_\alpha = \sin\alpha$, $C_\alpha = \cos\alpha$, and $V_\alpha = 1 - C_\alpha$.

The proof of equation 5.9 is as follows. First we note that

$$\boldsymbol{R}(\boldsymbol{k},\alpha) = [{}^A\boldsymbol{x}_B \; {}^A\boldsymbol{y}_B \; {}^A\boldsymbol{z}_B],$$

where ${}^A\boldsymbol{x}_B$, ${}^A\boldsymbol{y}_B$, and ${}^A\boldsymbol{z}_B$ are the unit vectors in the X, Y, and Z directions of Σ_B expressed in Σ_A. Letting $\boldsymbol{r}_1$ be an arbitrary vector in Σ_A and $\boldsymbol{r}_2$ be the vector obtained by rotating $\boldsymbol{r}_1$ about $\boldsymbol{k}$ by α, we have general equality

$$\boldsymbol{r}_2 = (\boldsymbol{k}^T\boldsymbol{r}_1)\boldsymbol{k} + C_\alpha[\boldsymbol{r}_1 - (\boldsymbol{k}^T\boldsymbol{r}_1)\boldsymbol{k}] + S_\alpha(\boldsymbol{k} \times \boldsymbol{r}_1). \tag{5.10}$$

Since when $\boldsymbol{r}_1 = [1,0,0]^T$ we have $\boldsymbol{r}_2 = {}^A\boldsymbol{x}_B$ from the definitions of $\boldsymbol{r}_1$ and $\boldsymbol{r}_2$, we obtain from equation 5.10

$$\boldsymbol{r}_2 = [k_x^2 V_\alpha + C_\alpha, k_x k_y V_\alpha + k_2 S_\alpha, k_x k_z V_\alpha - k_y S_\alpha]^T.$$

Hence the first column on the right-hand side of equation 5.9 is derived. The second and third columns are derived similarly.

Now the single-axis rotation method is given. Let the orientation of $\boldsymbol{r}_f$ with respect to the end-effector frame of $\boldsymbol{r}_0$ be $[\boldsymbol{k}_f,\alpha_f]$ when expressed by the above representation, $[\boldsymbol{k},\alpha]$. Then a trajectory from $\boldsymbol{r}_0$ to $\boldsymbol{r}_f$ can be given as one for which α changes from 0 to α_f about the fixed axis $\boldsymbol{k}_f$. We can specify the change of α by, for example, the solution of $\xi(t)$ in equation 5.4 with the following boundary conditions:

$$\xi(0) = 0, \quad \xi(t_f) = \alpha_f,$$

$$\dot{\xi}(0) = \dot{\alpha}_0, \quad \dot{\xi}(t_f) = \dot{\alpha}_f,$$

$$\ddot{\xi}(0) = \ddot{\alpha}_0, \quad \ddot{\xi}(t_f) = \ddot{\alpha}_f.$$

The trajectory for orientation is given by $[\boldsymbol{k}_f, \xi(t)]$, where $0 \leqq t \leqq t_f$. Since this trajectory is given by a rotation about an axis $\boldsymbol{k}_f$ which is fixed in the reference frame, it is easy to understand intuitively.

(2) Double-axis rotation method

This method, proposed by Paul (ref. 3), will be described here using a somewhat different formulation. Suppose the orientation of $\boldsymbol{r}_f$ with respect to $\boldsymbol{r}_0$ is given by (ϕ, θ, ψ) when expressed with Euler angles. Using equations 5.9 and 2.20, we can easily see that the orientation of $\boldsymbol{r}_f$ is also given by the rotation matrix $\boldsymbol{R}(\hat{\boldsymbol{k}}, \theta)\boldsymbol{R}(\hat{\boldsymbol{Z}}, \psi + \phi)$, where $\hat{\boldsymbol{k}} = [-\sin\phi, \cos\phi, 0]^T$ and where $\hat{\boldsymbol{Z}}$ is the Z axis after the transfer by $\boldsymbol{R}(\hat{\boldsymbol{k}}, \theta)$. Thus, we can realize a trajectory from $\boldsymbol{r}_0$ to $\boldsymbol{r}_f$ using $\boldsymbol{R}(\hat{\boldsymbol{k}}, \xi_\theta(t))\boldsymbol{R}(\hat{\boldsymbol{Z}}(t), \xi_{\psi+\phi}(t))$, where $\xi_\theta(t)$ and $\xi_{\psi+\phi}(t)$ are polynomials specified by equation 5.4 with appropriate boundary conditions and where $\hat{\boldsymbol{Z}}(t)$ is the Z axis at time t after the transfer by $\boldsymbol{R}(\hat{\boldsymbol{k}}, \xi_\theta(t))$. Simply put, this trajectory is a combination of two simultaneous rotations; one about the axis perpendicular to the approach vectors of $\boldsymbol{r}_0$ and $\boldsymbol{r}_f$ (which has a constant direction in the end-effector frame of $\boldsymbol{r}_0$) through an angle θ, and the other rotation through an angle $(\psi + \phi)$ about the approach vector at each instant. The axes of these two rotations are both easy to understand. In particular, when the last joint of a manipulator is revolute with its rotational axis coincident with the end-effector approach vector, this joint can perform the second rotation about $\hat{\boldsymbol{Z}}(t)$ by itself.

Although the double-axis rotation method is a little more complex than the single-axis rotation method, it makes it easier to understand the change of the approach vector.

Example 5.3 Suppose that we want to find a trajectory that transfers the end-effector orientation from rest at the initial orientation shown in figure 5.8a to the final orientation shown in figure 5.8b, coming to rest at time $t_f = 1$. First, we solve the problem by the single-axis rotation method. It is easily seen from figure 5.8 that the rotation matrix $\boldsymbol{R}$ representing the final

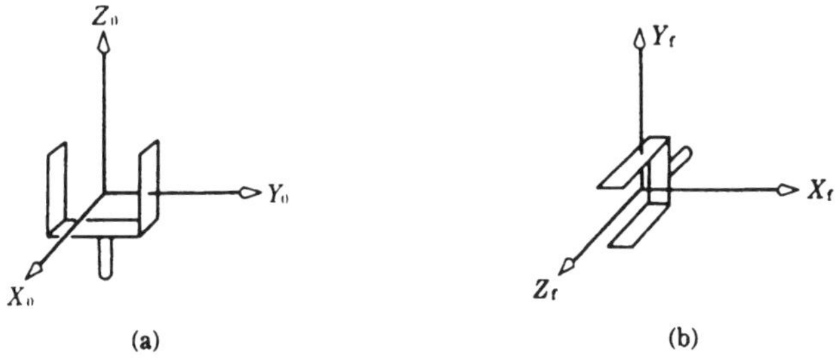

Figure 5.8
Initial and final orientations of the end effector. (a) Initial orientation. (b) Final orientation.

orientation with respect to the initial one is

$$\boldsymbol{R} = \begin{bmatrix} 0 & 0 & 1 \\ 1 & 0 & 0 \\ 0 & 1 & 0 \end{bmatrix}.$$

Comparing this matrix with equation 5.9, we get

$$\boldsymbol{k}_f = [1/\sqrt{3}, 1/\sqrt{3}, 1/\sqrt{3}]^T,$$

$$\alpha_f = 120°.$$

If we use a fifth-order polynomial (equation 5.4) for interpolation, the trajectory of orientation is given by

$$[\boldsymbol{k}_f, \alpha(t)], \quad 0 \leqq t \leqq 1$$

with

$$\alpha(t) = 1200t^3 - 1800t^4 + 720t^5.$$

An example of the rotation matrix representing the intermediate orientation at $t = 0.5$ of this trajectory is

$$\boldsymbol{R} = \begin{bmatrix} 2/3 & -1/3 & 2/3 \\ 2/3 & 2/3 & -1/3 \\ -1/3 & 2/3 & 2/3 \end{bmatrix}.$$

This orientation is shown in figure 5.9a. Next, we solve the problem by the double-axis rotation method. Euler angles for the initial and final orientations are $\boldsymbol{\phi}_0 = [0°,0°,0°]^T$ and $\boldsymbol{\phi}_f = [0°,90°,90°]^T$. Hence, the trajectory is given by

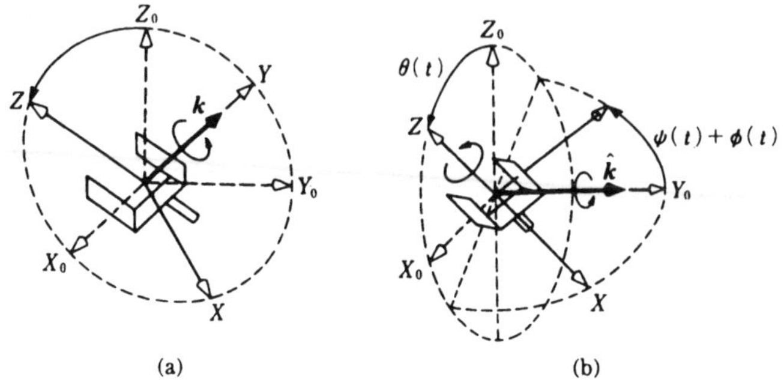

Figure 5.9
Intermediate orientation. (a) Single-axis rotation method. (b) Double-axis rotation method.

$$\boldsymbol{R}(\hat{\boldsymbol{k}},\xi_\theta(t))\boldsymbol{R}(\hat{\boldsymbol{Z}}(t),\xi_{\psi+\phi}(t)), \quad 0 \leqq t \leqq 1$$

where

$$\xi_\theta(t) = \xi_{\psi+\phi}(t) = 900t^3 - 1350t^4 + 540t^5.$$

The rotation matrix $\boldsymbol{R}$ for the intermediate orientation at time $t = 0.5$ for this case is calculated, from $\hat{\boldsymbol{k}} = [0,1,0]^T$ and $\xi_\theta(0.5) = \xi_{\psi+\phi}(0.5) = 45°$, to be

$$\boldsymbol{R} = \begin{bmatrix} 1/\sqrt{2} & 0 & 1/\sqrt{2} \\ 0 & 1 & 0 \\ -1/\sqrt{2} & 0 & 1/\sqrt{2} \end{bmatrix} \begin{bmatrix} 1/\sqrt{2} & -1/\sqrt{2} & 0 \\ 1/\sqrt{2} & 1/\sqrt{2} & 0 \\ 0 & 0 & 1 \end{bmatrix}$$
$$= \begin{bmatrix} 1/2 & -1/2 & 1/\sqrt{2} \\ 1/\sqrt{2} & 1/\sqrt{2} & 0 \\ -1/2 & 1/2 & 1/\sqrt{2} \end{bmatrix}.$$

This orientation is shown in figure 5.9b. Comparing this with figure 5.9a, we see that the approach vector is always perpendicular to the Y_0 axis, resulting in its shorter path. □

5.2 Linear Feedback Control

5.2.1 Effectiveness of Linear Feedback Control

Most manipulators in practical use today have a controller consisting of position and velocity feedback loops which are independent for each joint and receive a desired joint trajectory as its reference input. In spite of inherent nonlinear coupling among the joints of a manipulator, such a controller is usually fairly effective. The main two reasons for this seem to be the large reduction ratios between the actuators and the link mechanism and the large feedback gains in the control loops. An analytical argument supporting this will be developed in this subsection.

Suppose that the dynamics equation of a manipulator (equation 3.62) has a friction term added to the right-hand side. Then

$$\boldsymbol{\tau} = \boldsymbol{M}(\boldsymbol{q})\ddot{\boldsymbol{q}} + \boldsymbol{h}(\boldsymbol{q},\dot{\boldsymbol{q}}) + \boldsymbol{V}\dot{\boldsymbol{q}} + \boldsymbol{g}(\boldsymbol{q}), \tag{5.11}$$

where $\boldsymbol{V}$ is the joint friction coefficient matrix. The inertia matrix $\boldsymbol{M}(\boldsymbol{q})$ satisfies $\boldsymbol{M}(\boldsymbol{q}) = \boldsymbol{M}^T(\boldsymbol{q}) > \boldsymbol{0}$, where $\boldsymbol{M} > 0$ means that a square matrix $\boldsymbol{M}$ is positive definite (see appendix 4). Denoting the reduction ratio between the actuator displacement vector $\boldsymbol{q}_a$ and the joint vector $\boldsymbol{q}$ by a nonsingular matrix $\boldsymbol{G}_r$, we have

$$\boldsymbol{G}_r\boldsymbol{q} = \boldsymbol{q}_a. \tag{5.12}$$

We also assume that the dynamics equation of the actuators is

$$\boldsymbol{\tau}_m = \boldsymbol{M}_a\ddot{\boldsymbol{q}}_a + \boldsymbol{V}_a\dot{\boldsymbol{q}}_a + \boldsymbol{\tau}_a, \tag{5.13}$$

where $\boldsymbol{M}_a$ is the inertia matrix of the actuators, $\boldsymbol{V}_a$ is the frictional coefficient matrix, $\boldsymbol{\tau}_m$ is the force generated by the actuators, and $\boldsymbol{\tau}_a$ is the joint driving force transmitted to the link mechanism from the actuators. If we assume that $\boldsymbol{G}_r$ is constant, the relation between $\boldsymbol{\tau}_a$ and $\boldsymbol{\tau}$ is, by the principle of virtual work,

$$\boldsymbol{\tau} = \boldsymbol{G}_r^T\boldsymbol{\tau}_a. \tag{5.14}$$

Putting equations 5.11–5.14 together, we find that the dynamics equation for the whole system of the actuators and the link mechanism is

$$\begin{aligned}\boldsymbol{G}_r^T\boldsymbol{\tau}_m &= [\boldsymbol{G}_r^T\boldsymbol{M}_a\boldsymbol{G}_r + \boldsymbol{M}(\boldsymbol{q})]\ddot{\boldsymbol{q}} + \boldsymbol{h}(\boldsymbol{q},\dot{\boldsymbol{q}}) \\ &\quad + [\boldsymbol{G}_r^T\boldsymbol{V}_a\boldsymbol{G}_r + \boldsymbol{V}]\dot{\boldsymbol{q}} + \boldsymbol{g}(\boldsymbol{q}).\end{aligned} \tag{5.15}$$

Now we apply to this system a PD (proportional and differential) feedback law:

$$\boldsymbol{\tau}_m(t) = \boldsymbol{G}_r^{-T}\{-\boldsymbol{K}_v\dot{\boldsymbol{q}}(t) + \boldsymbol{K}_p[\boldsymbol{q}_d(t) - \boldsymbol{q}(t)]\}, \tag{5.16}$$

where $\boldsymbol{q}_d(t)$ is the desired trajectory for $\boldsymbol{q}(t)$.

When each joint has its own independent actuator with a large reduction ratio, the matrices M_a, V_a, and G_r are diagonal and the values of the diagonal elements of G_r are large. Further, we consider the case in which K_v and K_p are diagonal and the values of these diagonal elements are positive and large. Then the terms $M(q)$, $h(q,\dot{q})$, $V\dot{q}$, and $g(q)$ are small relative to other terms, so the dynamics equation of the closed-loop system consisting of equations 5.15 and 5.16 may be approximated by

$$[G_r^T M_a G_r]\ddot{q} + [G_r^T V_a G_r + K_v]\dot{q} + K_p[q - q_d] = 0. \tag{5.17}$$

This represents a set of independent second-order systems for each joint. We can adjust the response characteristics of these second-order systems by properly selecting gains K_v and K_p.

The above argument is dependent on various assumptions. Particularly, if the terms $M(q)$, $h(q,\dot{q})$, and $g(q)$ are not negligible in comparison with either of the terms $G_r^T M_a G_r$ and $G_r^T V_a G_r$, the above argument does not hold. Fast and accurate motion may not be possible without more sophisticated control algorithms like those given in later subsections. Note, however, that if we can at least compensate for the gravity term $g(q)$, we know that a closed-loop system with a PD feedback control law is stable under certain conditions. A typical condition is that the desired trajectory $q_d(t)$ is constant and the control mode is point-to-point control in which the end effector is required to stop at several desired points sequentially. This stability will be shown in the next subsection.

5.2.2 Stability of Proportional and Differential Feedback Control

Suppose that the control algorithm

$$\tau_m(t) = G_r^{-T}\{-K_v\dot{q}(t) + K_p[q_d - q(t)] + g(q)\} \tag{5.18}$$

is applied to the system of equation 5.15. We obtain this algorithm from equation 5.16 by adding gravity compensation. For simplicity we assume that $G_r^T V_a G_r + V \geqq 0$. We also assume that K_p and K_v are symmetric positive definite. Then, by using the Lyapunov stability theorem (appendix 4), we can prove that the constant equilibrium point q_d is asymptotically stable—that is, $q(t)$ converges to q_d after an infinite period of time.[4,5]

We first give another expression for the centrifugal and Coriolis force term $h(q,\dot{q})$ in equation 5.11. We saw in chapter 3 that this is generally given by equation 3.68. Noticing that

$$\sum_{j=1}^{n}\sum_{k=1}^{n}\frac{\partial M_{ij}}{\partial q_k}\dot{q}_j\dot{q}_k=\sum_{j=1}^{n}\sum_{k=1}^{n}\frac{\partial M_{ik}}{\partial q_j}\dot{q}_j\dot{q}_k,$$

we can easily see that $\boldsymbol{h}(\boldsymbol{q},\dot{\boldsymbol{q}})$ can be expressed as

$$\boldsymbol{h}(\boldsymbol{q},\dot{\boldsymbol{q}})=\hat{\boldsymbol{C}}(\boldsymbol{q},\dot{\boldsymbol{q}})\dot{\boldsymbol{q}}, \tag{5.19a}$$

where $\hat{\boldsymbol{C}}(\boldsymbol{q},\dot{\boldsymbol{q}})$ is an $n \times n$ matrix whose (i,j) element $\hat{C}_{ij}$ is

$$\hat{C}_{ij}=\frac{1}{2}\sum_{k=1}^{n}\left(\frac{\partial M_{ij}}{\partial q_k}+\frac{\partial M_{ik}}{\partial q_j}-\frac{\partial M_{jk}}{\partial q_i}\right)\dot{q}_k. \tag{5.19b}$$

We can also see that this $\hat{\boldsymbol{C}}(\boldsymbol{q},\dot{\boldsymbol{q}})$ has the property that the matrix $[\dot{\boldsymbol{M}}(\boldsymbol{q})-2\hat{\boldsymbol{C}}(\boldsymbol{q},\dot{\boldsymbol{q}})]$ becomes skew-symmetric. Hence, for any n-dimensional vector $\boldsymbol{x}$,

$$\boldsymbol{x}^T[\dot{\boldsymbol{M}}(\boldsymbol{q})-2\hat{\boldsymbol{C}}(\boldsymbol{q},\dot{\boldsymbol{q}})]\boldsymbol{x}=0. \tag{5.20}$$

Now we prove the convergence to $\boldsymbol{q}_{\mathrm{d}}$. Substituting equation 5.15 into equation 5.18 yields

$$\begin{aligned}&[\boldsymbol{G}_{\mathrm{r}}{}^T\boldsymbol{M}_{\mathrm{a}}\boldsymbol{G}_{\mathrm{r}}+\boldsymbol{M}(\boldsymbol{q})]\ddot{\boldsymbol{q}}+\boldsymbol{h}(\boldsymbol{q},\dot{\boldsymbol{q}})+[\boldsymbol{G}_{\mathrm{r}}{}^T\boldsymbol{V}_{\mathrm{a}}\boldsymbol{G}_{\mathrm{r}}+\boldsymbol{V}]\dot{\boldsymbol{q}}\\&\quad+\boldsymbol{K}_{\mathrm{v}}\dot{\boldsymbol{q}}-\boldsymbol{K}_{\mathrm{p}}(\boldsymbol{q}_{\mathrm{d}}-\boldsymbol{q})=\boldsymbol{0}.\end{aligned} \tag{5.21}$$

We let a scalar function $v(\boldsymbol{x})$ of $\boldsymbol{x}=[\boldsymbol{q}_{\mathrm{d}}{}^T-\boldsymbol{q}^T,\dot{\boldsymbol{q}}^T]^T$ be

$$v(\boldsymbol{x})=\frac{1}{2}\dot{\boldsymbol{q}}^T[\boldsymbol{G}_{\mathrm{r}}{}^T\boldsymbol{M}_{\mathrm{a}}\boldsymbol{G}_{\mathrm{r}}+\boldsymbol{M}(\boldsymbol{q})]\dot{\boldsymbol{q}}+\frac{1}{2}(\boldsymbol{q}_{\mathrm{d}}-\boldsymbol{q})^T\boldsymbol{K}_{\mathrm{p}}(\boldsymbol{q}_{\mathrm{d}}-\boldsymbol{q}). \tag{5.22}$$

Then $v(\boldsymbol{x})$ is positive definite. Using equation 5.21, the time derivative of $v(\boldsymbol{x})$ is

$$\begin{aligned}\dot{v}(\boldsymbol{x})&=\dot{\boldsymbol{q}}^T\{[\boldsymbol{G}_{\mathrm{r}}{}^T\boldsymbol{M}_{\mathrm{a}}\boldsymbol{G}_{\mathrm{r}}+\boldsymbol{M}(\boldsymbol{q})]\ddot{\boldsymbol{q}}+\tfrac{1}{2}\dot{\boldsymbol{M}}(\boldsymbol{q})\dot{\boldsymbol{q}}\}-\dot{\boldsymbol{q}}^T\boldsymbol{K}_{\mathrm{p}}(\boldsymbol{q}_{\mathrm{d}}-\boldsymbol{q})\\&=-\dot{\boldsymbol{q}}^T[\boldsymbol{G}_{\mathrm{r}}{}^T\boldsymbol{V}_{\mathrm{a}}\boldsymbol{G}_{\mathrm{r}}+\boldsymbol{V}+\boldsymbol{K}_{\mathrm{v}}]\dot{\boldsymbol{q}}+\dot{\boldsymbol{q}}^T\{\tfrac{1}{2}\dot{\boldsymbol{M}}(\boldsymbol{q})\dot{\boldsymbol{q}}-\boldsymbol{h}(\boldsymbol{q},\dot{\boldsymbol{q}})\}.\end{aligned}$$

On the other hand, using equation 5.20 we can easily see that the expression

$$\dot{\boldsymbol{q}}^T\{\tfrac{1}{2}\dot{\boldsymbol{M}}(\boldsymbol{q})\dot{\boldsymbol{q}}-\boldsymbol{h}(\boldsymbol{q},\dot{\boldsymbol{q}})\}=0$$

holds. Thus we have

$$\dot{v}(\boldsymbol{x})=-\dot{\boldsymbol{q}}^T[\boldsymbol{G}_{\mathrm{r}}{}^T\boldsymbol{V}_{\mathrm{a}}\boldsymbol{G}_{\mathrm{r}}+\boldsymbol{V}+\boldsymbol{K}_{\mathrm{v}}]\dot{\boldsymbol{q}}\leqq 0, \tag{5.23}$$

and so $v(\boldsymbol{x})$ is a Lyapunov function. From equation 5.23, any solution $\boldsymbol{q}(t)$ for $\dot{v}(\boldsymbol{x})=0$ must satisfy $\dot{\boldsymbol{q}}(t)=\boldsymbol{0}$. Such a solution that also satisfies equation 5.21 is uniquely determined by $\boldsymbol{q}(t)-\boldsymbol{q}_{\mathrm{d}}=\boldsymbol{0}$. Therefore, by theorem 2 of appendix 4, the equilibrium state $\boldsymbol{q}_{\mathrm{d}}$ is globally asymptotically stable.

When G_r and $g(q)$ are exactly known and the current values of q and $\dot{q}$ are measurable, this asymptotic stability is guaranteed by the control algorithm 5.18 even if there is no information at all about $M(q)$, $h(q,\dot{q})$, V, M_a, and V_a. However, if $g(q)$ is not known exactly, a steady-state error may occur. A way to cope with this error is to add an integral action term to equation 5.18:

$$\tau_m(t) = G_r^{-T}\left\{K_p[q_d - q(t)] - K_v\dot{q}(t) + \int_0^t K_i[q_d - q(\tau)]d\tau + g(q)\right\},$$

where K_i is the integral feedback gain matrix.

The result presented in this subsection does not guarantee anything about the quality of transient response other than asymptotic stability. In particular, when G_r is comparatively small, there may be a large change in transient response, depending on the arm configuration. Various control schemes have been proposed to cope with this problem (see refs. 2 and 6–14), and some of them will be discussed in later subsections. Although these schemes have not yet reached the point of common practice, they do have great potential.

5.3 Two-Stage Control by Linearization and Servo Compensation

5.3.1 Basic Concept of Two-Stage Control

Suppose that the dynamics of a manipulator are given by equation 5.11; that is,

$$\tau = M(q)\ddot{q} + h_N(q,\dot{q}), \tag{5.24}$$

where

$$h_N(q,\dot{q}) = h(q,\dot{q}) + V\dot{q} + g(q). \tag{5.25}$$

Observing that $[q^T,\dot{q}^T]^T$ may be taken as the state variables of this mechanical system, we consider a nonlinear-state feedback compensation described by

$$\tau = h_N(q,\dot{q}) + M(q)u_q, \tag{5.26}$$

where u_q is a new input vector. Then the resulting closed-loop system is

$$\ddot{q} = u_q, \tag{5.27}$$

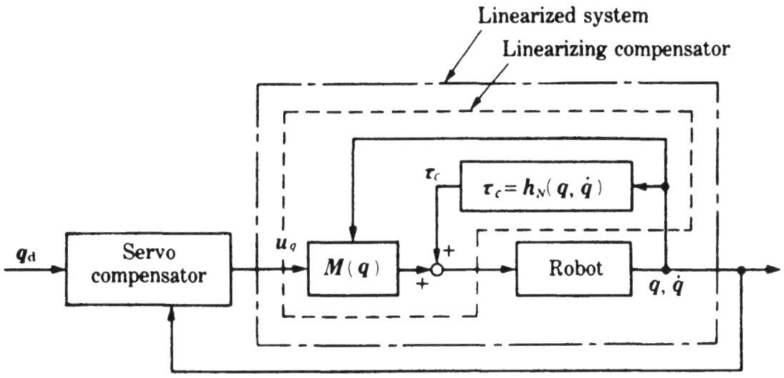

Figure 5.10
Two-stage control using joint variables.

which is linear and decoupled with respect to the joint variables. Thus, equation 5.26 is a linearizing compensation law.

Let us assume an ideal situation where equation 5.24 is an exact model of the manipulator without any modeling error and there exists no external disturbance to the system. Then we obtain $\boldsymbol{q}(t) = \boldsymbol{q}_d(t)$ by assigning the second derivative $\ddot{\boldsymbol{q}}_d(t)$ of a given desired trajectory $\boldsymbol{q}_d(t)$ as $\boldsymbol{u}_q$. This implies that the desired trajectory is perfectly achieved. In practice, however, some modeling error and some external disturbances are inevitable. The basic idea here is to reduce their effect on the control performance by installing a servo compensator to the linearized system (equation 5.27). Figure 5.10 is a schematic diagram of this two-stage approach of linearization and servo compensation.

Suppose that we adopt a servo compensator described by

$$\boldsymbol{u}_q = \ddot{\boldsymbol{q}}_d + \boldsymbol{K}_v(\dot{\boldsymbol{q}}_d - \dot{\boldsymbol{q}}) + \boldsymbol{K}_p(\boldsymbol{q}_d - \boldsymbol{q}). \quad (5.28)$$

Defining the error $\boldsymbol{e}$ as

$$\boldsymbol{e} = \boldsymbol{q}_d - \boldsymbol{q}, \quad (5.29)$$

we obtain, from equations 5.27 and 5.28,

$$\ddot{\boldsymbol{e}} + \boldsymbol{K}_v\dot{\boldsymbol{e}} + \boldsymbol{K}_p\boldsymbol{e} = \boldsymbol{0}. \quad (5.30)$$

Hence, if we set

$$\boldsymbol{K}_v = \mathrm{diag}(2\zeta\omega_c) \quad (5.31a)$$

and

$$K_p = \text{diag}(\omega_c^2), \tag{5.31b}$$

where $0 < \zeta \leq 1$ and $\omega_c > 0$, then equation 5.28 amounts to installing a PD feedback control loop for each q_i so that each component of e converges to zero with damping coefficient ζ. Therefore, we can expect that the effect of modeling error and disturbances, if there is any, will be reduced.

Example 5.4 Suppose that we wish to apply the above two-stage control concept using the servo compensator specified by equations 5.28 and 5.31 to the two-link manipulator in subsection 3.3.1. Letting $\theta_d = [\theta_{d1}, \theta_{d2}]^T$ and $u_q = [u_{q1}, u_{q2}]^T$ and using equations 5.28 and 5.31, we have

$$\begin{bmatrix} u_{q1} \\ u_{q2} \end{bmatrix} = \begin{bmatrix} \ddot{\theta}_{d1} + 2\zeta\omega_c(\dot{\theta}_{d1} - \dot{\theta}_1) + \omega_c^2(\theta_{d1} - \theta_1) \\ \ddot{\theta}_{d2} + 2\zeta\omega_c(\dot{\theta}_{d2} - \dot{\theta}_2) + \omega_c^2(\theta_{d2} - \theta_2) \end{bmatrix}.$$

From equations 5.26 and 3.39 we finally obtain the control algorithm:

$$\tau_1 = h_{122}\dot{\theta}_2^2 + 2h_{112}\dot{\theta}_1\dot{\theta}_2 + g_1 + M_{11}u_{q1} + M_{12}u_{q2},$$

$$\tau_2 = h_{211}\dot{\theta}_1^2 + g_2 + M_{21}u_{q1} + M_{22}u_{q2}. \ \square$$

So far we have considered an approach based on linearization in terms of joint variables. However, there are cases where it is more desirable to linearize and servo in terms of variables which are more directly related to the manipulator tasks, such as the position and orientation of the end effector. Hence we consider an n-dimensional output vector y given by

$$y = f_y(q), \tag{5.32}$$

and describe a two-stage control approach based on y. Differentiating equation 5.32, we have

$$\dot{y} = J_y(q)\dot{q}, \tag{5.33}$$

where $J_y(q) = \partial y/\partial q^T$. Assuming that the Jacobian matrix $J_y(q)$ is nonsingular in a certain region of q, we consider a nonlinear state feedback compensation

$$\tau = h_N(q,\dot{q}) + M(q)J_y^{-1}(q)[-\dot{J}_y(q)\dot{q} + u_y], \tag{5.34}$$

where u_y is a new input vector. The closed-loop system is

$$\ddot{y} = u_y, \tag{5.35}$$

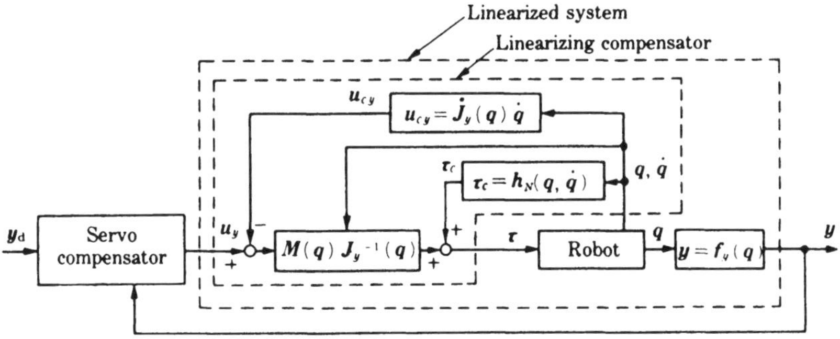

Figure 5.11
Two-stage control using output variables.

which is linear and decoupled with respect to y. Hence, as in the case of equation 5.27, by installing a servo compensator to the linear system 5.35, we obtain the control system shown in figure 5.11. If we futher adopt

$$u_y = \ddot{y}_d + K_v(\dot{y}_d - \dot{y}) + K_p(y_d - y) \tag{5.36}$$

as the servo compensator, by letting $e = y_d - y$ we find the same equation as 5.30.

Example 5.5 For the two-link manipulator in subsection 3.3.1, let us derive the state feedback law for linearizing the dynamics with respect to the end-effector position $y = [x,y]^T$. Since

$$y = \begin{bmatrix} l_1 C_1 + l_2 C_{12} \\ l_1 S_1 + l_2 S_{12} \end{bmatrix},$$

the Jacobian matrix $J_y(q)$ is

$$J_y(q) = \begin{bmatrix} -(l_1 S_1 + l_2 S_{12}) & -l_2 S_{12} \\ l_1 C_1 + l_2 C_{12} & l_2 C_{12} \end{bmatrix}$$

$$= \begin{bmatrix} -l_1 S_1 & -l_2 S_{12} \\ l_1 C_1 & l_2 C_{12} \end{bmatrix} \begin{bmatrix} 1 & 0 \\ 1 & 1 \end{bmatrix}.$$

Thus,

$$\dot{J}_y(q) = \begin{bmatrix} -l_1 C_1 \dot{\theta}_1 & -l_2 C_{12}(\dot{\theta}_1 + \dot{\theta}_2) \\ -l_1 S_1 \dot{\theta}_1 & -l_2 S_{12}(\dot{\theta}_1 + \dot{\theta}_2) \end{bmatrix} \begin{bmatrix} 1 & 0 \\ 1 & 1 \end{bmatrix}$$

and

$$-\dot{J}_y(q)\dot{q} = \begin{bmatrix} l_1 C_1 \dot{\theta}_1{}^2 + l_2 C_{12}(\dot{\theta}_1 + \dot{\theta}_2)^2 \\ l_1 S_1 \dot{\theta}_1{}^2 + l_2 S_{12}(\dot{\theta}_1 + \dot{\theta}_2)^2 \end{bmatrix}.$$

Letting $u_y = [u_{y1}, u_{y2}]^T$, we then have, from the above equation and 5.34,

$$\begin{aligned} \tau_1 = {} & h_{122}\dot{\theta}_2{}^2 + 2h_{112}\dot{\theta}_1\dot{\theta}_2 + g_1 \\ & + \{l_1[M_{11}l_2C_2 - M_{12}(l_2C_2 + l_1)]\dot{\theta}_1{}^2 \\ & \quad + l_2[M_{11}l_2 - M_{12}(l_2 + l_1C_2)](\dot{\theta}_1 + \dot{\theta}_2)^2 \\ & \quad + [M_{11}l_2C_{12} - M_{12}(l_2C_{12} + l_1C_1)]u_{y1} \\ & \quad + [M_{11}l_2S_{12} - M_{12}(l_2S_{12} + l_1S_1)]u_{y2}\} \\ & /l_1l_2S_2 \end{aligned}$$

and

$$\begin{aligned} \tau_2 = {} & h_{211}\dot{\theta}_1{}^2 + g_2 \\ & + \{l_1[M_{12}l_2C_2 - M_{22}(l_2C_2 + l_1)]\dot{\theta}_1{}^2 \\ & \quad + l_2[M_{12}l_2 - M_{22}(l_2 + l_1C_2)](\dot{\theta}_1 + \dot{\theta}_2)^2 \\ & \quad + [M_{12}l_2C_{12} - M_{22}(l_2C_{12} + l_1C_1)]u_{y1} \\ & \quad + [M_{12}l_2S_{12} - M_{22}(l_2S_{12} + l_1S_1)]u_{y2}\} \\ & /l_1l_2S_2. \end{aligned}$$

When $\theta_2 = 0$ (that is, when the manipulator is in a singular configuration), $S_2 = 0$. This means that τ_1 and τ_2 may become infinitely large. This is a difficulty we did not have in linearization with respect to the joint variables. We have to provide some measure to deal with this difficulty when we adopt a linearization with respect to the output variables. □

The two-stage control scheme is essentially the same as the computed torque method (refs. 2, 6) or the resolved acceleration control scheme (ref. 7). The idea of two-stage control by linearization and servo compensation has been studied by many researchers.[15–17]

When we want to use the two-stage control scheme, we need to consider several problems. One is the complexity of the algorithm, which usually requires digital computer processing. We therefore need to make the sampling rate high enough to minimize the deterioration of control performance due to computational delay. Another problem is the design of a robust servo compensator. We wish to design a servo compensator that makes the closed-loop system rugged against modeling errors of the manipulator dynamics and to external disturbances. These problems will be discussed in subsections 5.3.2, 5.3.3, and 5.4.2.

5.3.2 Structure of Control System

The problem of computing $\boldsymbol{\tau}$ from equation 5.26 for given $\boldsymbol{q}$, $\dot{\boldsymbol{q}}$, and $\boldsymbol{u}_q$ and the problem of computing $\boldsymbol{\tau}$ from equation 5.34 for given $\boldsymbol{q}$, $\dot{\boldsymbol{q}}$, and $\boldsymbol{J}_y^{-1}(\boldsymbol{q})$ $[-\dot{\boldsymbol{J}}_y(\boldsymbol{q})\dot{\boldsymbol{q}} + \boldsymbol{u}_y]$ are equivalent to the inverse dynamics problem of computing $\boldsymbol{\tau}$ from equation 5.24 for given $\boldsymbol{q}$, $\dot{\boldsymbol{q}}$, and $\ddot{\boldsymbol{q}}$. The computation scheme conceived earlier involved calculating all the terms on the right-hand side of equation 5.24 from their analytical expressions derived by the Lagrangian formulation. Since this requires a large amount of computation, it was regarded as impractical unless some simplification were to be employed. To cope with this difficulty, a computational scheme based on the Newton-Euler formulation was proposed. As was stated in chapter 3, whereas the Lagrangian approach requires a number of computations on the order of n^4, Newton-Euler computations are only of order n.

Even if we use the Newton-Euler approach, however, the amount of computation for the linearizing algorithm 5.34 depicted in figure 5.11 may still result in too large a sampling period for practical use. A large sampling period is generally undesirable from the viewpoint of steady-state error, stability, and response time. Two means of reducing this problem are calculating certain terms in advance and employing dual sampling rates in the controller.

The first means, which is applicable when $\boldsymbol{q}_d$ or $\boldsymbol{y}_d$ is given prior to the execution of control, is to calculate the terms $\boldsymbol{h}_N(\boldsymbol{q},\dot{\boldsymbol{q}})$, $\boldsymbol{M}(\boldsymbol{q})$, and $\boldsymbol{J}_y(\boldsymbol{q})$ in equation 5.34 in advance by replacing $\boldsymbol{q}$ with $\boldsymbol{q}_d$. This can be regarded as the linearization of the dynamics using the desired trajectory. The structure of control system for this case is shown in figure 5.12. Although the amount of on-line computation with this system is of course less than that of figure 5.11, the linearization is less accurate because of the difference between $\boldsymbol{q}$ and $\boldsymbol{q}_d$. This will result in degradation of control performance. If the improvement in performance due to the shorter sampling period is larger

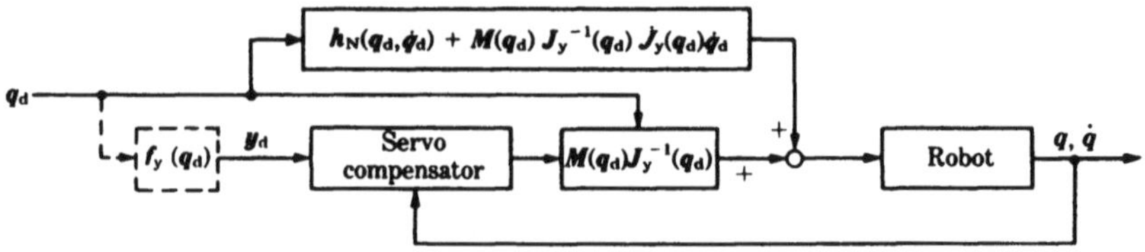

Figure 5.12
Linearization using the desired trajectory.

than the above degradation, then we can justify using the system of figure 5.12.

The second means is to distinguish the sampling period for linearization from that for servo compensation in the control system shown in figure 5.11 (ref. 8). This concept is based on the idea that the linearization, which requires a large amount of computation, may have a large sampling period provided that the servo compensation has a small enough sampling period to cover the error caused by the large sampling period of the linearization. For example, let

$$A = M(q)J_y^{-1}(q) \tag{5.37a}$$

and

$$b = -A\dot{J}_y(q)\dot{q} + h_N(q,\dot{q}). \tag{5.37b}$$

Then, from equations 5.34 and 5.36, we have

$$\tau = A[\ddot{y}_d + K_v(\dot{y}_d - \dot{y}) + K_p(y_d - y)] + b. \tag{5.38}$$

When the values A and b are given, very little computation is needed to obtain τ from equation 5.38. Thus, if we calculate A and b with a low sampling rate and calculate τ from equation 5.38 with a high sampling rate, we can expect a better control performance than if we do all the computation at only one sampling rate.[18] Figure 5.13 shows a block diagram for this dual-sampling-rate approach. Note that the linearizing compensation loop is outside the servo compensation loop.

5.3.3 Parallel Processing Scheme

So far we have discussed control systems under the implicit assumption that the necessary inverse-dynamics computation is done with only one

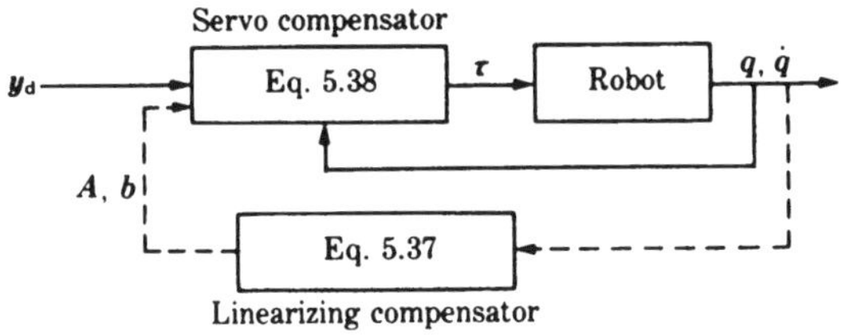

Figure 5.13
Dual-sampling-rate approach to two-stage control.

processor. However, it is of course possible to shorten the computation time for inverse dynamics by parallel processing using a multiple-processor system.

This approach was proposed for the first time by Luh and Lin.[19] A less theoretical, more intuitive algorithm will be presented below to illustrate the advantage of parallel processing. For a given n-link manipulator, we assign one microprocessor unit (MPU) to each joint. This means that we use n processors in all. Each processor is supposed to do all computations related to the assigned joint. On the other hand, the computation of equations 3.87′–3.95′ is decomposed into smaller subtasks as follows:

(1/i) $\xi_a = {}^{i-1}\boldsymbol{R}_i^{T\,i-1}\omega_{i-1}$,

(2/i) $${}^i\omega_i = \begin{cases} \xi_a + \boldsymbol{e}_z\dot{q}_i, & \text{if R} \\ \xi_a, & \text{if P} \end{cases}$$

(3/i) $$\xi_b = \begin{cases} \xi_a \times \boldsymbol{e}_z\dot{q}_i + \boldsymbol{e}_z\ddot{q}_i, & \text{if R} \\ \boldsymbol{0}, & \text{if P} \end{cases}$$

(4/i) $${}^i\dot{\omega}_i = \begin{cases} {}^{i-1}\boldsymbol{R}_i^{T\,i-1}\dot{\omega}_{i-1} + \xi_b, & \text{if R} \\ {}^{i-1}\boldsymbol{R}_i^{T\,i-1}\dot{\omega}_{i-1}, & \text{if P} \end{cases}$$

(5/i) $$\xi_c = \begin{cases} \boldsymbol{0}, & \text{if R} \\ 2\xi_a \times \boldsymbol{e}_z\dot{q}_i + \boldsymbol{e}_z\ddot{q}_i, & \text{if P} \end{cases}$$

(6/i) $\xi_d = {}^{i-1}\dot{\omega}_{i-1} \times {}^{i-1}\hat{\boldsymbol{p}}_i + {}^{i-1}\omega_{i-1} \times ({}^{i-1}\omega_{i-1} \times {}^{i-1}\hat{\boldsymbol{p}}_i)$,

(7/i) $${}^i\ddot{\boldsymbol{p}}_i = \begin{cases} {}^{i-1}\boldsymbol{R}_i^T[{}^{i-1}\ddot{\boldsymbol{p}}_{i-1} + \xi_d], & \text{if R} \\ {}^{i-1}\boldsymbol{R}_i^T[{}^{i-1}\ddot{\boldsymbol{p}}_{i-1} + \xi_d] + \xi_c, & \text{if P} \end{cases}$$

(8/i) $\xi_e = {}^i\omega_i \times ({}^i\omega_i \times {}^i\hat{\boldsymbol{s}}_i) + {}^i\dot{\omega}_i \times {}^i\hat{\boldsymbol{s}}_i$,

$$(9/i)\quad {}^i\hat{f}_i = m_i(\xi_e + {}^i\ddot{p}_i),$$

$$(10/i)\quad \xi_f = {}^iI_i{}^i\dot{\omega}_i,$$

$$(11/i)\quad \xi_g = {}^i\omega_i \times ({}^iI_i{}^i\omega_i),$$

$$(12/i)\quad {}^i\hat{n}_i = \xi_f + \xi_g,$$

$$(13/i)\quad \xi_p = {}^iR_{i+1}{}^{i+1}f_{i+1},$$

$$(14/i)\quad {}^if_i = \xi_p + {}^i\hat{f}_i,$$

$$(15/i)\quad \xi_q = {}^i\hat{n}_i + {}^i\hat{s}_i \times {}^i\hat{f}_i,$$

$$(16/i)\quad \xi_r = {}^i\hat{p}_{i+1} \times \xi_p,$$

$$(17/i)\quad {}^in_i = {}^iR_{i+1}{}^{i+1}n_{i+1} + \xi_q + \xi_r,$$

$$(18/i)\quad \tau_i = \begin{cases} e_z{}^T{}^in_i, & \text{if R} \\ e_z{}^T{}^if_i, & \text{if P.} \end{cases}$$

Among these subtasks, there exists a hierarchy that determines which subtasks must be done before a particular subtask is performed. This precedence relation is shown in figure 5.14. We want to develop an execution sequence for the subtasks that gives a short computation time under the constraint of the precedence relation.

The above decomposition was, in fact, organized in such a way that: (1) a subtask requiring information from other processors is done as late as possible (subtask (7/i) needs ${}^{i-1}\ddot{p}_{i-1}$, (13/i) needs ${}^{i+1}f_{i+1}$, and (17/i) needs ${}^{i+1}n_{i+1}$); (2) a subtask with a result needed by other processors is done as early as possible (MPU i can pass ${}^i\omega_i$ after (2/i), ${}^i\dot{\omega}_i$ after (4/i), and ${}^if_i$ after (14/i)); and (3) duplication of computation is avoided (ξ_a is used in (2/i) and (3/i), and ξ_p is used in (14/i) and (16/i)). We can therefore expect that the following simple algorithm will give a fairly good performance.

Algorithm I Processor i ($i = 1, 2, \ldots, n$) executes the subtasks in the order (1/i),(2/i),...,(18/i) as soon as data become available.

Example 5.6 Consider a six-link manipulator with all joints revolute. Assume that the initial values of ${}^0\omega_0$ and ${}^0\dot{\omega}_0$ are not necessarily $\mathbf{0}$, and that one multiplication in MPU takes 0.005 msec and one addition 0.004 msec. The computation time needed to execute each subtask is given in table 5.1. Using this table, we can determine the time history of the status

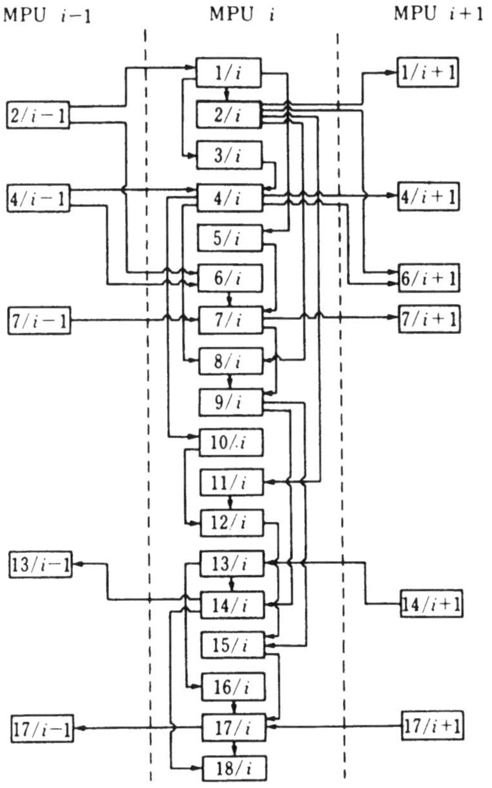

Figure 5.14
Precedence relation among subtasks.

of each processor for algorithm I, which is shown in figure 5.15. (The bold solid line means that the processor is on duty; blank space means waiting time.) We see that the total computation time of the above algorithm is 1.745 msec. Since the computation time is 5.790 msec when only one processor is used, the above parallel processing speeds up this computation by a factor of 3.3. □

We can also improve the above algorithm by changing the order of subtasks for the terminal processor, processor n, so that it computes the data necessary for processor $n-1$ as quickly as possible:

Algorithm II Processors 1 through $n-1$ use algorithm I. Processor n executes the subtasks in the order $(13/n), (16/n), (1/n), (2/n), (3/n), (5/n), (11/n)$.

Table 5.1
Computation time for each subtask.

Subtask	Multiplications	Additions	Computation time
(1/*i*)	8	5	0.060 ms
(2/*i*)	0	1	0.004
(3/*i*)	2	0	0.010
(4/*i*)	8	8	0.072
(5/*i*)	0	0	0
(6/*i*)	18	12	0.138
(7/*i*)	8	18	0.072
(8/*i*)	18	12	0.138
(9/*i*)	3	3	0.027
(10/*i*)	9	6	0.069
(11/*i*)	15	9	0.111
(12/*i*)	0	3	0.012
(13/*i*)	8	15	0.060
(14/*i*)	0	3	0.012
(15/*i*)	6	6	0.054
(16/*i*)	6	3	0.042
(17/*i*)	8	11	0.084
(18/*i*)	0	0	0
Total	117	95	0.965

(4/*n*), (6/*n*), ..., (10/*n*), (12/*n*), (14/*n*), (15/*n*), (17/*n*), (18/*n*) as soon as data become available.

Example 5.7 Consider the six-link manipulator in example 5.6. By drawing a figure similar to figure 5.15 it is easy to see that the total computation time of algorithm II is 1.604 msec, which is an 8 percent improvement from algorithm I. A lower bound of the computation time obtained by considering a critical path shown in figure 5.16, which is completely connected by the precedence relations, is 1.516 msec. Consequently, the difference between the computation time of algorithm II and that of the minimum-time algorithm is less than 6 percent. □

We can also consider algorithms that minimize the computation time without any restriction on the correspondence between processors and joints of a manipulator.[20]

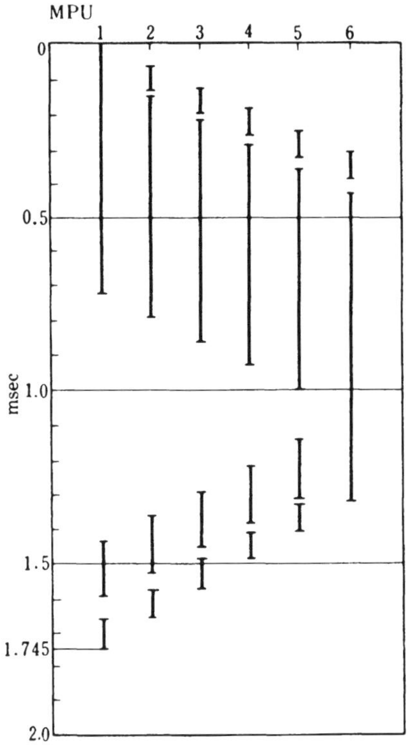

Figure 5.15
Processor status for Algorithm I.

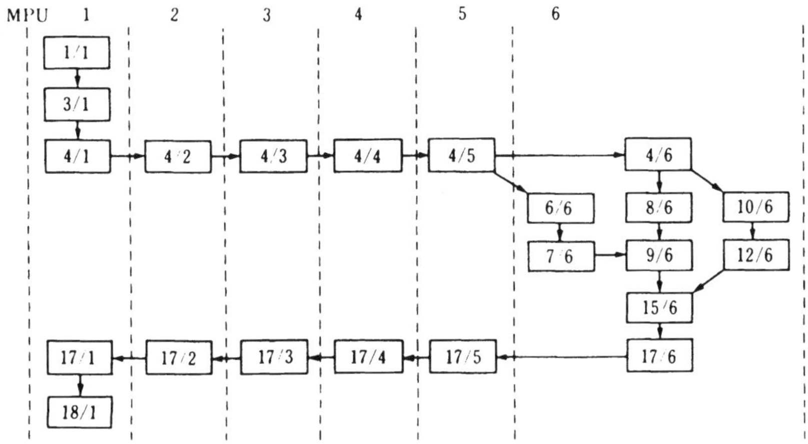

Figure 5.16
A critical path giving a lower bound of computation time for Algorithm II.

5.4 Design and Evaluation of Servo Compensators

5.4.1 Linear Servosystem Theory

In this section we will consider the foundations of design and evaluation for general linear time-invariant servosystems. First, we will consider the design of servo compensators from the viewpoint of step response in this section.

Let us consider the object with one degree of freedom shown in figure 5.17. This system is an armature-controlled d.c. motor connected to a load through a set of reduction gears. We want to control the angular velocity of the load. The dynamics equation of the system is derived as follows.

Electrically, the relation between the torque generated by the motor, τ_m, and the armature current, i, is

$$\tau_m = k_t i, \tag{5.39}$$

where k_t is the torque constant of the motor. The back electromotive-force voltage, v_b, is

$$v_b = k_b \dot{\theta}_m, \tag{5.40}$$

where θ_m is the rotational angle of the motor and k_b is the back electromotive-force constant. Regarding the armature circuit, we have

$$L\frac{di}{dt} + Ri + v_b = v, \tag{5.41}$$

where v is the input voltage, L the inductance, and R the resistance of the armature.

Mechanically, we have

$$\tau_m = J_m \ddot{\theta}_m + D_m \dot{\theta}_m + \tau_l, \tag{5.42}$$

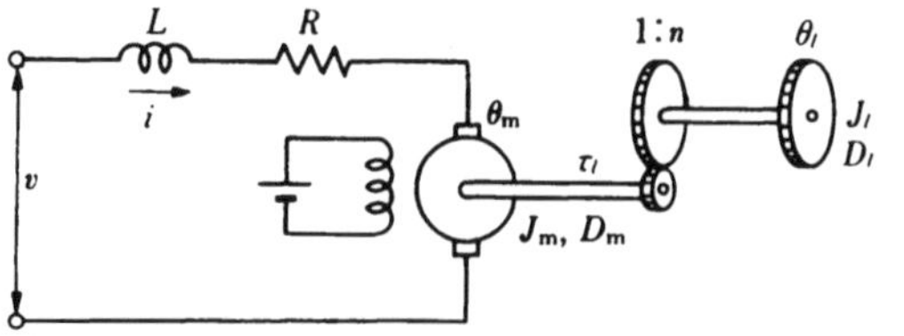

Figure 5.17
Direct-current servomotor and load.

where τ_l is the load torque on the motor, J_m is the moment of inertia, and D_m is the viscous-damping coefficient of the armature. Letting θ_l be the rotational angle, J_l the moment of inertia, D_l the viscous damping coefficient of the load, and n the gear ratio of the reduction system, we obtain

$$n\tau_l = J_l\ddot{\theta}_l + D_l\dot{\theta}_l. \tag{5.43}$$

From equations 5.39–5.43, we have the following relation between the input v and the output θ_l:

$$LJ\dddot{\theta}_l + (LD + RJ)\ddot{\theta}_l + (RD + n^2 k_t k_b)\dot{\theta}_l = nk_t v, \tag{5.44}$$

where

$$J = n^2 J_m + J_l, \tag{5.45}$$

$$D = n^2 D_m + D_l. \tag{5.46}$$

Hence, from equation 5.44, the transfer function from v to θ_l is

$$G(s) = \frac{nk_t}{s\{LJs^2 + (LD + RJ)s + (RD + n^2 k_t k_b)\}}, \tag{5.47}$$

which represents a third-order system containing an integrator. The inductance L of the armature is generally small. If we neglect L, then the transfer function 5.47 reduces to a second-order system containing an integrator:

$$G(s) = \frac{nk_t}{s\{RJs + (RD + n^2 k_t k_b)\}}. \tag{5.48}$$

With these transfer functions expressed in general forms, the controlled object is represented by

$$G(s) = \frac{a_2}{s(s + a_1)}, \tag{5.49}$$

or

$$G(s) = \frac{a_3}{s(s^2 + a_1 s + a_2)}, \tag{5.50}$$

where a_1, a_2, and a_3 are appropriate constants.

One basic structure for a servosystem that forces the output $y(t)$ of the above control object to follow the desired trajectory $r(t)$ is shown in figure 5.18. Transfer functions $G_1(s)$ and $G_2(s)$ are compensators to be designed.

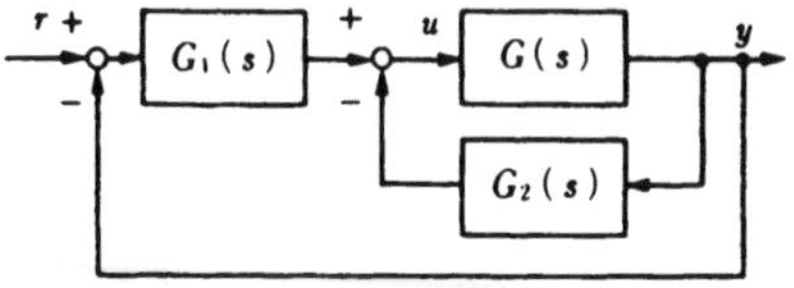

Figure 5.18
A basic servosystem structure.

When $G(s)$ is given by equation 5.49, it is very common to make $G_1(s)$ a proportional gain, that is, $G_1(s) = b_1$, and to make $G_2(s)$ a velocity feedback, that is, $G_2(s) = b_2 s$. In this case, the closed-loop transfer function becomes

$$G_f(s) = \frac{a_2 b_1}{s^2 + (a_1 + a_2 b_2)s + a_2 b_1}$$

$$= \frac{{\omega_c}^2}{s^2 + 2\zeta\omega_c s + {\omega_c}^2}, \quad (5.51)$$

which is a standard second-order form. The natural angular frequency and the damping coefficient are, respectively,

$$\omega_c \sqrt{a_2 b_1} \quad (5.52)$$

and

$$\zeta = \frac{a_1 + a_2 b_2}{2\sqrt{a_2 b_1}}. \quad (5.53)$$

Now let us transform the Laplace operator s into a new one defined by

$$\tilde{s} = s/\omega_c. \quad (5.54)$$

Then equation 5.51 becomes

$$G_f(s) = \frac{1}{\tilde{s}^2 + 2\zeta\tilde{s} + 1}. \quad (5.55)$$

Transform 5.54 changes the time scale from t to $\tilde{t} = \omega_c t$. The shape of the step response in the new time variable, $\tilde{t}$, is determined only by ζ. For example, if $\zeta < 1$, the step response is given by

$$y(\tilde{t}) = 1 - \frac{e^{-\zeta\tilde{t}}}{\sqrt{1-\zeta^2}} \sin\left(\sqrt{1-\zeta^2}\,\tilde{t} + \tan^{-1}\frac{\sqrt{1-\zeta^2}}{\zeta}\right). \quad (5.56)$$

The step responses for various values of ζ are shown in figure 5.19.

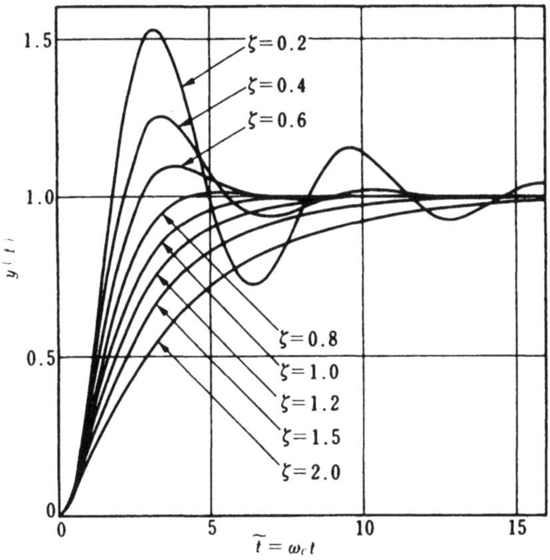

Figure 5.19
Step response of second-order system.

When designing the compensator, one good way is first to select a desirable shape of the step response from figure 5.19 and then to make ω_c as large as possible within the limits of hardware in order to have a quick response.

Now we will consider the case when $G(s)$ is given by equation 5.50. In figure 5.18, let us make $G_1(s)$ a proportional gain b_1, as in the case of the second-order system, and $G_2(s)$ a velocity and acceleration feedback $b_2 s + b_3 s^2$. Then the closed-loop transfer function is

$$G_f(s) = \frac{a_3 b_1}{s^3 + (a_1 + a_3 b_3)s^2 + (a_2 + a_3 b_2)s + a_3 b_1}. \tag{5.57}$$

As in the previous case, let us transform s into $\tilde{s}$ in the form

$$\tilde{s} = s/(a_3 b_1)^{1/3}, \tag{5.58}$$

and define scalars α and β by

$$\alpha = (a_1 + a_3 b_3)/(a_3 b_1)^{1/3}, \tag{5.59}$$

$$\beta = (a_2 + a_3 b_2)/(a_3 b_1)^{2/3}. \tag{5.60}$$

From equation 5.57 we obtain a standard form for third-order systems:

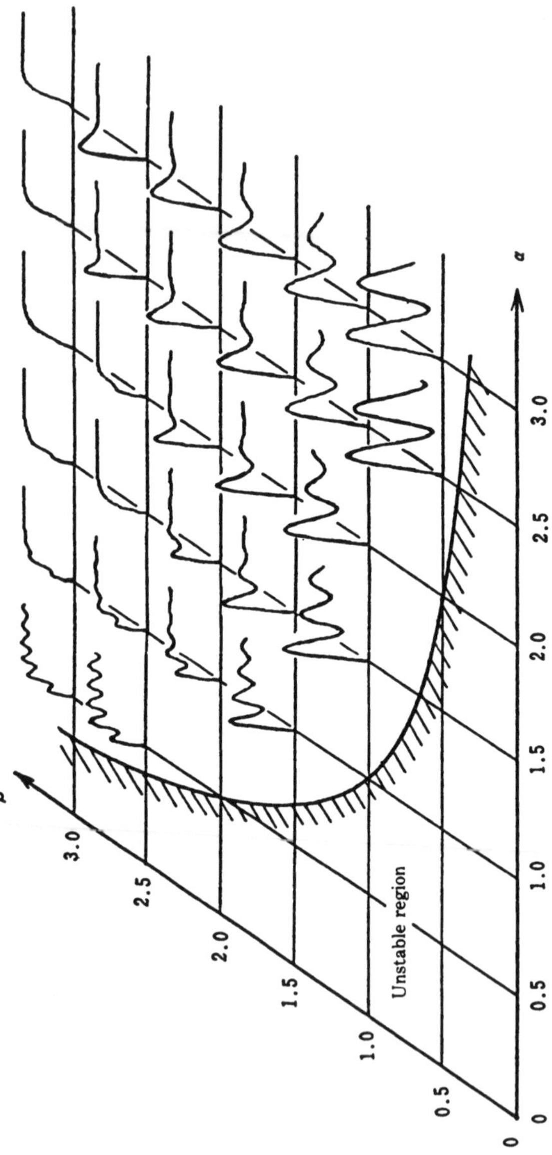

Figure 5.20
Step response of third-order system.

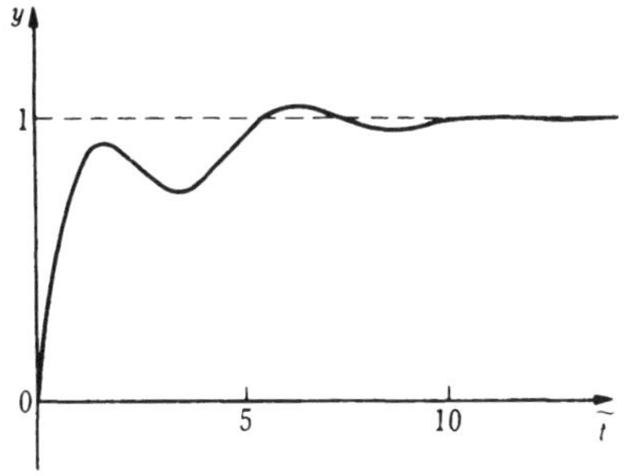

Figure 5.21
Step response of third-order system ($\alpha = 1.3$, $\beta = 2.0$).

$$G_f(s) = \frac{1}{\tilde{s}^3 + \alpha\tilde{s}^2 + \beta\tilde{s} + 1}. \tag{5.61}$$

The parameters α and β specify the shape of the step response of the third-order system (equation 5.61)[21] in the same way that ζ specified the shape of the step response of the second-order system (equation 5.55). The step responses for various combinations of α and β are shown in figure 5.20.

As in the second-order case, a possible design procedure for the third-order system is first to select a pair of α and β such that a desirable step response is obtained, and then to determine b_1 so that $a_3 b_1$ becomes as large as is practical. Parameters b_2 and b_3 are determined from α, β, and b_1. In figure 5.21 we see the step response for the case of $\alpha = 1.3$ and $\beta = 2.0$. Note that the response has a reverse motion before reaching the desired value of 1. This is one of the differences between third-order and second-order systems. This characteristic can be used to reduce the settling time.

5.4.2 Stability Margin and Sensitivity

In the preceding subsection we considered the design of compensators only from the viewpoint of step response, that is, the immediate response to the command signal. Another function expected of a servosystem is that it is not affected very much either by errors in the mathematical model of the controlled object or by external disturbances. This property is called *robustness*. As has always been recognized in the design of control systems, one advantage of closed-loop systems over open-loop ones is robustness. The design method of subsection 5.4.1 is robust enough for most situations; however, it is not always guaranteed. In this subsection, robustness will be

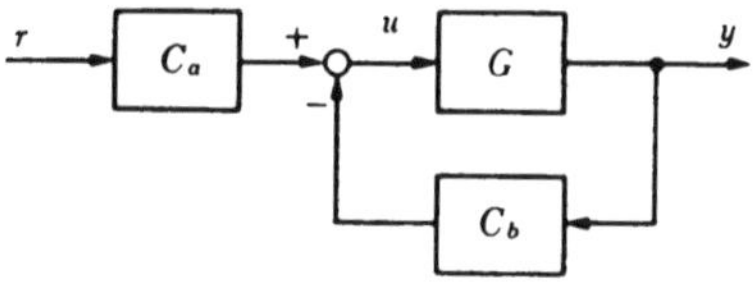

Figure 5.22
Servosystem with feedforward and feedback compensators.

discussed quantitatively and a method for using it in the analysis and design of servosystems will be presented.[22–24] For simplicity, we will consider only single-input, single-output systems.

Let us consider the servosystem shown as a block diagram in figure 5.22. G is the transfer function of the controlled object, and C_a and C_b are those of feedforward and feedback compensators. The scalar variables r, y, and u are the reference input, the controlled variable, and the controlling input, respectively. This block diagram is in a general form in the sense that current values of both the reference input and the controlled variable are available for determining the control input. For example, the control system in figure 5.18 is a special case of this general form, as we can see by using

$$C_a = G_1 \tag{5.62}$$

and

$$C_b = G_1 + G_2. \tag{5.63}$$

The response characteristic of this system with respect to the reference input is given by the transfer function from input r to output y:

$$G_{yr} = C_a G(1 + GC_b)^{-1}. \tag{5.64}$$

If we want to make G_{yr} equal to some desired transfer function, G_d, we only have to specify C_a as

$$C_a = G^{-1}G_d + C_b G_d. \tag{5.65}$$

If the controlled object, G, has unstable zeros, G_d must also have these zeros. Otherwise, $G^{-1}G_d$ turns out to be an unstable transfer function, causing an instability problem for the whole system.

Next, suppose that the transfer function G in figure 5.22 is perturbed and changes into $\tilde{G} = (1 + \Delta_G)G$. The transfer function G_{yr} from r to y changes into

$$\tilde{G}_{yr} = C_a\tilde{G}(1 + \tilde{G}C_b)^{-1}. \tag{5.66}$$

Thus, we have

$$(G_{yr} - \tilde{G}_{yr})\tilde{G}_{yr}{}^{-1} = S(G - \tilde{G})\tilde{G}^{-1} \tag{5.67}$$

and

$$S = (1 + GC_b)^{-1}. \tag{5.68}$$

Equation 5.67 implies that S is a ratio between the change rate of the transfer function for the controlled object, $(G - \tilde{G})\tilde{G}^{-1}$, and that for the closed-loop system, $(G_{yr} - \tilde{G}_{yr})\tilde{G}_{yr}{}^{-1}$. The ratio S is called the *sensitivity function.* While S is a function of the Laplace operator s, the absolute value of $S(j\omega)$, $|S(j\omega)|$, is more convenient for evaluating sensitivity. Using $|S(j\omega)|$ corresponds to evaluating sensitivity from the gain of the change rates of the transfer functions at each frequency.

On the other hand, the Small Gain Theorem gives a sufficient condition for the closed-loop system to be stable in spite of the change of G to $\tilde{G}$ (refs. 23, 24). Let us define T by

$$T = GC_b(1 + GC_b)^{-1}. \tag{5.69}$$

According to the Small Gain Theorem, if the original closed-loop system is stable, then the perturbed closed-loop system also remains stable for any perturbation Δ_G satisfying

$$|\Delta_G(j\omega)| < |T(j\omega)|^{-1} \tag{5.70}$$

for any ω. Hence, we can say that $|T|^{-1}$ expresses a stability margin. From equations 5.68 and 5.69 we have

$$S + T = 1, \tag{5.71}$$

and T is called the *complementary sensitivity function.*

In lieu of a rigorous proof of the Small Gain Theorem, an intuitive interpretation of equation 5.70 based on the Nyquist stability criterion is developed below. Focusing on the feedback loop consisting of G and C_b in figure 5.22, we assume that this part of the feedback loop is stable. Then, by the Nyquist stability criterion, the vector locus of the open-loop transfer function GC_b does not pass through the point $(-1 + 0j)$, as shown in figure 5.23. Let $d_1(\omega)$ be the distance between $(-1 + 0j)$ and the point P_a on the vector locus specified by $G(j\omega)C_b(j\omega)$ for a given ω. Then $d_1(\omega)$ is given by

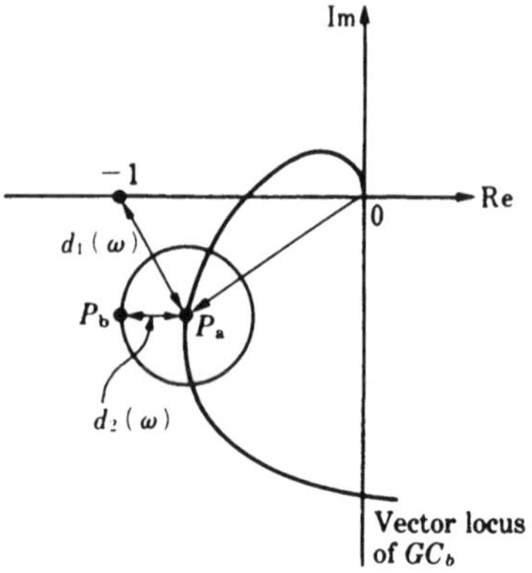

Figure 5.23
Interpretation of Small Gain Theorem.

$$d_1(\omega) = |1 + G(j\omega)C_b(j\omega)|, \tag{5.72}$$

and from the above argument it satisfies $d_1(\omega) > 0$. Now we assume that G changes to $\tilde{G} = (1 + \Delta_G)G$, and that the number of unstable zeros remains the same in spite of this change. The distance between P_a and the point P_b specified by $\tilde{G}(j\omega)C_b(j\omega)$ is given by

$$d_2(\omega) = |\Delta_G(j\omega)G(j\omega)C_b(j\omega)|. \tag{5.73}$$

Hence, if Δ_G satisfies equation 5.70, we have $d_2(\omega) < d_1(\omega)$ for all ω, which implies that the numbers of rotation about $(-1 + 0j)$ of GC_b and $\tilde{G}C_b$ are identical. Because of the Nyquist stability criterion, the stability property of the closed-loop system remains the same despite the change from G to $\tilde{G}$. Since the original system is assumed to be stable, the perturbed system is also stable.

Since the modeling error of the controlled object can be regarded as a perturbation Δ_G of G, the functions S and T may be interpreted as indices for the robustness of the control system against the modeling error of G (S representing the sensitivity aspect of the robustness and T representing the stability-margin aspect). Another interpretation of S and T is also possible: If we consider the control system shown in figure 5.24, obtained by adding a system disturbance d and a measurement disturbance d_n to the original system of figure 5.22, it is easy to show that S is the transfer function from d to y and $-T$ is that from d_n to y.

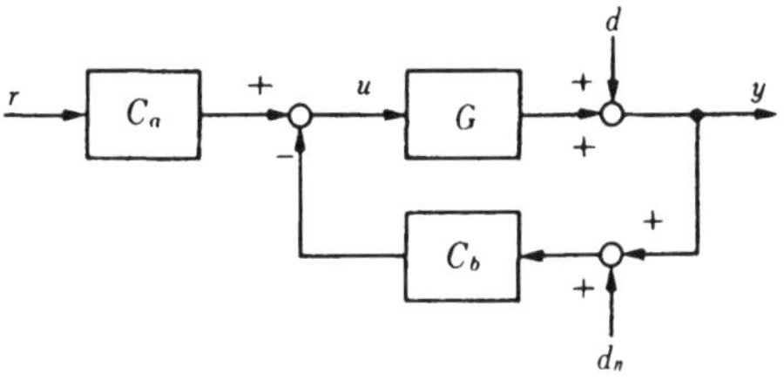

Figure 5.24
Servosystem with system noise and measurement noise.

Roughly speaking, for both of the above interpretations of S and T, it is desirable for both $|S|$ and $|T|$ to be small; however, because of the relation 5.71 it is impossible to make both of them arbitrarily small simultaneously. One reasonable compromise is to make $|S|$ small in a lower-frequency region and $|T|$ small in a higher-frequency region. At higher frequencies the modeling error is usually large, so it is desirable to have a large stability margin (in other words, a small $|T|$). At lower frequencies the modeling error is usually small, making it possible to give priority to reducing the sensitivity. Also, when we consider the interpretation of S and T as transfer functions from disturbances d and d_n to y, the system disturbance d usually consists of low-frequency components and d_n of high-frequency ones. Again we see that it is desirable to have small $|S|$ at low frequencies and small $|T|$ at high frequencies. Because S and T are functions of C_b but not of C_a, the robustness properties are determined by the feedback compensator C_b only, whereas the overall transfer function from r to y is determined by C_b and the feedforward compensator C_a.

Example 5.8 Consider the case when $G = 1/s^2$, $C_a = b_1$, and $C_b = b_1 + b_2 s$ in figure 5.24. This is identical to the case of figure 5.18 with $G_1(s) = b_1$ and $G_2(s) = b_2 s$. Let us examine this commonly used servosystem from the viewpoint of robustness. From equations 5.68 and 5.69 we have

$$S = \frac{s^2}{s^2 + b_2 s + b_1}$$

and

$$T = \frac{b_2 s + b_1}{s^2 + b_2 s + b_1}.$$

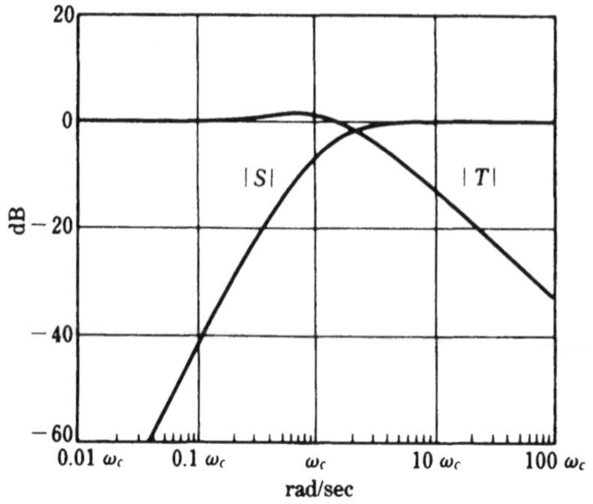

Figure 5.25
|S| and |T| for example 5.8.

The closed-loop transfer function G_{yr} is

$$G_{yr} = \frac{b_1}{s^2 + b_2 s + b_1}.$$

By supposing that $\zeta = 1$ and letting $\omega_c = \sqrt{b_1}$, we have

$$b_2 = 2\omega_c.$$

For this b_2, $|S|$ and $|T|$ are shown in figure 5.25 in units of decibels (dB). Note that the frequency ω_c is an index locating the boundary between the frequency region in which the sensitivity is the important design criterion and the region in which the stability margin is important. Thus, if we specify ω_c properly to take into consideration the extent of modeling error and the frequency of external disturbance, we can expect that the servosystem has an acceptable amount of robustness. □

5.5 Decoupling Control

5.5.1 Theory of Decoupling Control for Nonlinear Systems

In this section, we will first consider the theory of decoupling control for nonlinear systems; then we will develop its application to the control of a manipulator (ref. 9). This theory, used for achieving linearization of dynamics, decoupling among output variables, and arbitrary assignment of poles, also provides a theoretical grounding for linearizing compensation in two-stage control (see section 5.3).

Consider a nonlinear, time-varying system with n inputs and n outputs:

$$\dot{\boldsymbol{x}}(t) = \boldsymbol{a}(\boldsymbol{x},t) + \boldsymbol{B}(\boldsymbol{x},t)\boldsymbol{u}(t), \tag{5.74}$$

$$\boldsymbol{y}(t) = \boldsymbol{c}(\boldsymbol{x},t) + \boldsymbol{D}(\boldsymbol{x},t)\boldsymbol{u}(t), \tag{5.75}$$

where $\boldsymbol{x}$ is an n_s-dimensional state vector, $\boldsymbol{u}$ is an n-dimensional input vector, $\boldsymbol{y}$ is an n-dimensional output vector, and $\boldsymbol{a}(x,t)$, $\boldsymbol{c}(\boldsymbol{x},t)$, $\boldsymbol{B}(\boldsymbol{x},t)$, and $\boldsymbol{D}(\boldsymbol{x},t)$ are known vectors or matrices with appropriate dimensions. A design procedure is developed for which individual elements of the output $\boldsymbol{y}$ have arbitrarily assigned poles and no longer interact with one another by applying to the system a nonlinear time-varying state feedback law:

$$\boldsymbol{u}(t) = \boldsymbol{e}(\boldsymbol{x},t) + \boldsymbol{F}(\boldsymbol{x},t)\tilde{\boldsymbol{u}}(t), \tag{5.76}$$

where $\tilde{\boldsymbol{u}}(t)$ is a new n-dimensional vector.

Let the ith row vector of $\boldsymbol{D}(\boldsymbol{x},t)$ be $\boldsymbol{d}_i(\boldsymbol{x},t)$, let the ith element of $\boldsymbol{c}(\boldsymbol{x},t)$ be $c_i(\boldsymbol{x},t)$, and let the ith element of $\boldsymbol{y}$ be y_i. Also, let the jth derivative of y_i with respect to time be $y_i^{(j)}$. Then, by repeating the differentiation of y_i and the substitution of equation 5.74 until the coefficient of $\boldsymbol{u}$ becomes nonzero, we obtain, for a positive integer ν_i,

$$y_i^{(j)} = c_i^{[j]}(\boldsymbol{x},t), \quad j = 0, 1, \ldots, \nu_i - 1 \tag{5.77a}$$

$$y_i^{(\nu_i)} = c_i^{[\nu_i]}(\boldsymbol{x},t) + \boldsymbol{d}_i^{[\nu_i]}(\boldsymbol{x},t)\boldsymbol{u}, \tag{5.77b}$$

where $y_i^{(0)} = y_i$, $c_i^{[0]}(\boldsymbol{x},t) = c_i(\boldsymbol{x},t)$, $\boldsymbol{d}_i^{[0]}(\boldsymbol{x},t) = \boldsymbol{d}_i(\boldsymbol{x},t)$, and

$$c_i^{[j]}(\boldsymbol{x},t) = \frac{\partial}{\partial t} y_i^{(j-1)} + \left[\frac{\partial}{\partial \boldsymbol{x}^T} y_i^{(j-1)}\right] \boldsymbol{a}(\boldsymbol{x},t), \tag{5.78}$$

$$\boldsymbol{d}_i^{[j]}(\boldsymbol{x},t) = \left[\frac{\partial}{\partial \boldsymbol{x}^T} y_i^{(j-1)}\right] \boldsymbol{B}(\boldsymbol{x},t). \tag{5.79}$$

The integer ν_i may be written as

$$\nu_i = \min\{\, j : \boldsymbol{d}_i^{[j]}(\boldsymbol{x},t) \neq \boldsymbol{0}, \quad j = 1, 2, \ldots\}. \tag{5.80}$$

Assume that v_i is constant for any x and t in a region under consideration. Further, define

$$c^*(x,t) = \begin{bmatrix} c_1^{[v_1]}(x,t) \\ c_2^{[v_2]}(x,t) \\ \vdots \\ c_n^{[v_n]}(x,t) \end{bmatrix}, \tag{5.81}$$

$$D^*(x,t) = \begin{bmatrix} d_1^{[v_1]}(x,t) \\ d_2^{[v_2]}(x,t) \\ \vdots \\ d_n^{[v_n]}(x,t) \end{bmatrix}, \tag{5.82}$$

$$\alpha^*(x,t) = \text{col}\left[\sum_{k=0}^{v_i-1} \alpha_{ik} c_i^{[k]}(x,t)\right] = \text{col}\left[\sum_{k=0}^{v_i-1} \alpha_{ik} y_i^{(k)}\right], \tag{5.83}$$

and

$$\Lambda = \text{diag}[\lambda_1, \lambda_2, \ldots, \lambda_n], \tag{5.84}$$

where col[·] denotes a column vector, diag[·] denotes a diagonal matrix, and α_{ik} and λ_i are arbitrary constants. If $D^*(x,t)$ is nonsingular, then we can decouple the system with respect to the output by setting $e(x,t)$ and $F(x,t)$ of equation 5.76 as

$$e(x,t) = -D^{*-1}(x,t)[c^*(x,t) + \alpha^*(x,t)] \tag{5.85}$$

and

$$F(x,t) = D^{*-1}(x,t)\Lambda. \tag{5.86}$$

In fact, when equations 5.76, 5.85, and 5.86 are substituted into equations 5.74 and 5.75, we obtain

$$y_i^{(v_i)} + \alpha_{i(v_i-1)} y_i^{(v_i-1)} + \cdots + \alpha_{i0} y_i = \lambda_i \tilde{u}_i, \tag{5.87}$$

where $i = 1,2,\ldots,n$. Appropriate selection of α_{ik} and λ_i provides this single-input, single-output system with the desired pole placement and input gain.

Example 5.9 Let us derive a decoupling feedback law for the following two-input, two-output linear system:

$$\dot{x} = \begin{bmatrix} -2 & -1 & 0 \\ 2 & -4 & 0 \\ 0 & 1 & -2 \end{bmatrix} x + \begin{bmatrix} 1 & 0 \\ 0 & 1 \\ 0 & 0 \end{bmatrix} u,$$

$$y = \begin{bmatrix} 1 & 0 & 0 \\ 0 & 0 & 1 \end{bmatrix} x.$$

Since

$$y_1 = [1,0,0]x,$$

$$y_1^{(1)} = [-2,-1,0]x + [1,0]u,$$

$$y_2 = [0,0,1]x,$$

$$y_2^{(1)} = [0,1,-2]x,$$

$$y_2^{(2)} = [2,-6,4]x + [0,1]u.$$

We have $\nu_1 = 1$, and $\nu_2 = 2$. From equations 5.81 and 5.82,

$$c^*(x,t) = \begin{bmatrix} -2 & -1 & 0 \\ 2 & -6 & 4 \end{bmatrix} x$$

and

$$D^*(x,t) = \begin{bmatrix} 1 & 0 \\ 0 & 1 \end{bmatrix}.$$

Since D^* is nonsingular, we obtain from equations 5.76, 5.85, and 5.86 the feedback law:

$$u = -\left[\begin{array}{c|c|c} 2 - \alpha_{10} & 1 & 0 \\ \hline -2 & 6 - \alpha_{21} & -4 + 2\alpha_{21} - \alpha_{20} \end{array}\right] x + \begin{bmatrix} \lambda_1 & 0 \\ 0 & \lambda_2 \end{bmatrix} \tilde{u}.$$

Applying this law yields the decoupled dynamics:

$$y_1^{(1)} + \alpha_{10} y_1 = \lambda_1 \tilde{u}_1,$$

$$y_2^{(2)} + \alpha_{21} y_2^{(1)} + \alpha_{20} y_2 = \lambda_2 \tilde{u}_2.$$

If we further wish to assign a pole of -5 to the transfer function from $\tilde{u}_1$ to y_1, and two poles of $\{-6,-6\}$ to that from $\tilde{u}_2$ to y_2, then the arbitrary constants α_{ij} should be $\alpha_{10} = 5$, $\alpha_{21} = 12$, and $\alpha_{20} = 36$. □

5.5.2 Application to Manipulators

Now we will apply the above theory to manipulators (ref. 9). Let us consider a general n-link manipulator with its dynamics described by equation 5.11; that is,

$$M(\boldsymbol{q})\ddot{\boldsymbol{q}} + \boldsymbol{h}_N(\boldsymbol{q},\dot{\boldsymbol{q}}) = \boldsymbol{\tau}, \tag{5.88}$$

where $\boldsymbol{h}_N(\boldsymbol{q},\dot{\boldsymbol{q}})$ is a function defined by equation 5.25. We assume that the n-dimensional output vector $\boldsymbol{y}$ is given by equation 5.32:

$$\boldsymbol{y} = \boldsymbol{f}_y(\boldsymbol{q}). \tag{5.89}$$

We also assume that the dynamics of the actuators producing the joint driving force $\boldsymbol{\tau}$ are fast enough in comparison with those of the link mechanism that we can regard $\boldsymbol{\tau}$ as a directly operable input vector. In this case, $[\boldsymbol{q}^T,\dot{\boldsymbol{q}}^T]^T$ becomes a state vector and equation 5.74 is given by

$$\dot{\boldsymbol{x}} = \begin{bmatrix} \dot{\boldsymbol{q}} \\ -\boldsymbol{M}^{-1}(\boldsymbol{q})\boldsymbol{h}_N(\boldsymbol{q},\dot{\boldsymbol{q}}) \end{bmatrix} + \begin{bmatrix} \boldsymbol{0} \\ \boldsymbol{M}^{-1}(\boldsymbol{q}) \end{bmatrix}\boldsymbol{\tau}. \tag{5.90}$$

For the system given by equations 5.89 and 5.90, we have $v_i = 2\,(i = 1,2,\ldots, n)$ and

$$\boldsymbol{D}^* = \boldsymbol{J}_y(\boldsymbol{q})\boldsymbol{M}^{-1}(\boldsymbol{q}). \tag{5.91}$$

As was explained in subsection 2.5.6, arm configurations for which rank$\boldsymbol{J}_y(q) < n$ are called *singular configurations.* For any configuration except singular ones, $\boldsymbol{D}^*$ is nonsingular, and so decoupling is possible. Letting $\boldsymbol{J}_i(\boldsymbol{q})$ denote the ith row vector of $\boldsymbol{J}_y(\boldsymbol{q})$, we obtain from equations 5.76, 5.85, and 5.86 the state feedback law

$$\boldsymbol{\tau} = \boldsymbol{h}_N(\boldsymbol{q},\dot{\boldsymbol{q}}) + \boldsymbol{M}(\boldsymbol{q})\boldsymbol{J}_y^{-1}(\boldsymbol{q})\,\mathrm{col}[-\dot{\boldsymbol{J}}_i(\boldsymbol{q})\dot{\boldsymbol{q}} - \alpha_{i1}\dot{y}_i - \alpha_{i0}y_i + \lambda_i\tilde{u}_i], \tag{5.92}$$

which yields a decoupled system with the linear second-order property

$$\ddot{y}_i + \alpha_{i1}\dot{y}_i + \alpha_{i0}y_i = \lambda_i\tilde{u}_i, \quad i = 1,2,\ldots,n. \tag{5.93}$$

The constants α_{i1}, α_{i0}, and λ_i are to be determined by the designer using, for example, the approach of section 5.4.

The feedback control law (equation 5.92) for decoupling is equivalent to two-stage control in that both laws compensate for $\boldsymbol{h}_N(\boldsymbol{q},\dot{\boldsymbol{q}})$, the term for centrifugal, coriolis, frictional, and gravitational forces. The block diagram of the control law is given by figure 5.11 when the block of the servo compensator is specified by

$$u_y = \mathrm{col}[-\alpha_{i1}\dot{y}_i - \alpha_{i0}y_i + \lambda_i\tilde{u}_i].$$

5.5.3 Consideration of Actuator Dynamics

So far we have treated the joint driving force τ as the input, assuming that τ can be changed arbitrarily in any short period of time. This assumption holds, for example, for d.c. servomotors with negligible inductance, or for hydraulic cylinders or motors with negligible oil compressibility and little pipeline elasticity. When we consider the control of lightweight, high-speed, high-accuracy manipulators, however, there are cases where actuator dynamics are significant. Application of the decoupling control theory to such cases is discussed in this subsection.[25]

Let us assume again that equation 5.88 gives the dynamics of the manipulator. Let us also assume that the dynamics of the actuator are given by

$$\dot{p} = r(q,\dot{q},p) + G(q,\dot{q},p)u \tag{5.94}$$

and

$$\tau = l(q,p), \tag{5.95}$$

where u is an n-dimensional input signal vector to the actuators and p is an n-dimensional actuator state vector. The state p represents, for example, the armature current in a d.c. servomotor, or the operating pressure in a hydraulic actuator. In equations 5.94 and 5.95, $r(q,\dot{q},p)$ and $l(q,p)$ are n-dimensional vectors, and $G(q,\dot{q},p)$ is an $n \times n$ matrix. It is assumed that $G(q,\dot{q},p)$ and $\partial l(q,p)/\partial p^T$ are nonsingular in the required range of $(q,\dot{q},p)$. When individual elements of τ are generated by different actuators, $G(q,\dot{q},p)$ and $\partial l(q,p)/\partial p^T$ are generally diagonal, and so the above assumption is valid. Under these assumptions, we can employ $[q^T,\dot{q}^T,p^T]^T$ as the state vector of the total system, and equation 5.74 becomes

$$\frac{d}{dt}\begin{bmatrix} q \\ \dot{q} \\ p \end{bmatrix} = \begin{bmatrix} \dot{q} \\ M^{-1}(q)[l(q,p) - h_N(q,\dot{q})] \\ r(q,\dot{q},p) \end{bmatrix} + \begin{bmatrix} 0 \\ 0 \\ G(q,\dot{q},p) \end{bmatrix} u. \tag{5.96}$$

For the output given by equation 5.89, the value of ν_i given by equation 5.80 is $\nu_i = 3$ $(i = 1,2,\ldots,n)$ and we have

$$D^* = J(q)M^{-1}(q)\frac{\partial l}{\partial p^T}G(q,\dot{q},p) \tag{5.97}$$

and

$$c^* = J(q)M^{-1}(q)\left[\frac{\partial l}{\partial p^T}r(q,\dot{q},p) + \frac{\partial l}{\partial q^T}\dot{q} - \frac{dh_N(q,\dot{q})}{dt}\right]$$
$$+ \left[J(q)\frac{dM^{-1}(q)}{dt} + 2\dot{J}(q)M^{-1}(q)\right][l(q,p) - h_N(q,\dot{q})]$$
$$+ \ddot{J}(q)\dot{q}. \tag{5.98}$$

Since D^* is nonsingular (owing to the assumptions about the matrices on the right-hand side of equation 5.97), we can decouple the system using the state feedback law obtained from equations 5.97, 5.98, 5.85, 5.86, and 5.76. The resulting closed-loop system is

$$\dddot{y}_i + \alpha_{i2}\ddot{y}_i + \alpha_{i1}\dot{y}_i + \alpha_{i0}y_i = \lambda_i\tilde{u}_i, \quad i = 1,2,\ldots,n. \tag{5.99}$$

This is a linear third-order decoupled system for each output element. When the output y is the joint vector q itself, equations 5.97 and 5.98 simplify to

$$D^* = M^{-1}(q)\frac{\partial l}{\partial p^T}G(q,\dot{q},p) \tag{5.100}$$

and

$$c^* = M^{-1}(q)\left[\frac{\partial l}{\partial p^T}r(q,\dot{q},p) + \frac{\partial l}{\partial q^T}\dot{q} - \frac{dh_N(q,\dot{q})}{dt}\right]$$
$$+ \frac{dM^{-1}(q)}{dt}[l(q,p) - h_N(q,\dot{q})]. \tag{5.101}$$

Example 5.10 Let us consider a d.c.-servomotor-driven n-link manipulator with its mechanical elements modeled by equations 5.11–5.13. We will decouple the system dynamics with respect to the joint vector q, taking into consideration the dynamics of the electrical elements. Let i_j and v_j be the armature current and the input voltage of the jth motor, and let

$$i = [i_1,i_2,\ldots,i_n]^T$$

and

$$\boldsymbol{v} = [v_1, v_2, \ldots, v_n]^T.$$

Assume that the electric circuit of the motors is described by

$$\boldsymbol{\tau}_{\mathrm{m}} = \boldsymbol{K}_{\mathrm{t}} i, \quad \boldsymbol{K}_{\mathrm{t}} = \mathrm{diag}[k_{\mathrm{t}j}],$$

$$\boldsymbol{L}\frac{di}{dt} + \boldsymbol{R}i + \boldsymbol{v}_{\mathrm{b}} = \boldsymbol{v}, \quad \boldsymbol{L} = \mathrm{diag}[L_j], \quad \boldsymbol{R} = \mathrm{diag}[R_j],$$

$$\boldsymbol{v}_{\mathrm{b}} = \boldsymbol{K}_{\mathrm{b}}\dot{\boldsymbol{q}}_{\mathrm{a}}, \quad \boldsymbol{K}_{\mathrm{b}} = \mathrm{diag}[k_{\mathrm{b}j}],$$

where $k_{\mathrm{t}j}$, $k_{\mathrm{b}j}$, L_j, and R_j are the torque constant, the back electromotive-force constant, the inductance, and the resistance of the jth motor, respectively. If we assume that equation 5.88 represents the system of actuators and the arm given by equation 5.15, the dynamics of the actuator (equations 5.94 and 5.95) are given by

$$\frac{di}{dt} = -\boldsymbol{L}^{-1}(\boldsymbol{R}i + \boldsymbol{K}_{\mathrm{b}}\boldsymbol{G}_{\mathrm{r}}\dot{\boldsymbol{q}}) + \boldsymbol{L}^{-1}\boldsymbol{v}$$

and

$$\boldsymbol{G}_{\mathrm{r}}^T\boldsymbol{\tau}_{\mathrm{m}} = \boldsymbol{G}_{\mathrm{r}}^T\boldsymbol{K}_{\mathrm{t}}i.$$

From equations 5.100, 5.101, 5.85, 5.86, and 5.76, we can see that the feedback law

$$\begin{aligned}\boldsymbol{v} = {} & \boldsymbol{R}i + \boldsymbol{K}_{\mathrm{b}}\boldsymbol{G}_{\mathrm{r}}\dot{\boldsymbol{q}} \\ & + \boldsymbol{L}\boldsymbol{K}_{\mathrm{t}}^{-1}\boldsymbol{G}_{\mathrm{r}}^{-T}\Big\{\dot{\boldsymbol{M}}(\boldsymbol{q})\boldsymbol{M}^{-1}(\boldsymbol{q})[\boldsymbol{G}_{\mathrm{r}}^T\boldsymbol{K}_{\mathrm{t}}i - \boldsymbol{h}_N(\boldsymbol{q},\dot{\boldsymbol{q}})] \\ & \qquad + \frac{d\boldsymbol{h}_N(\boldsymbol{q},\dot{\boldsymbol{q}})}{dt} - \boldsymbol{M}(\boldsymbol{q})(\boldsymbol{\alpha}^* - \boldsymbol{\Lambda}\tilde{\boldsymbol{u}})\Big\}\end{aligned}$$

achieves the linearization and decoupling with respect to $\boldsymbol{q}$. □

5.6 Adaptive Control

The two-stage and decoupling control methods developed above require an accurate dynamic model of the manipulator being controlled. These control schemes are not always effective when the dynamics of the manipulator are not known exactly beforehand, or when they change because of uncertain factors (including the weight of an object grasped by the end effector and friction at the joints). One control scheme proposed to cope with such cases is *adaptive control*,[26] which uses some means to identify the unknown dynamics or to detect the change in the dynamics of the controlled object caused by changes in the environmental and/or the operational conditions. The parameters of the controller are adjusted on-line on the basis of the information gathered.

Various adaptive-control algorithms have been proposed to cope with the situation where the form of the dynamics equations of a manipulator is known but some of the dynamic parameters are not known exactly (refs. 10–12, 27, 28). An adaptive-control algorithm which is a modification of that in reference 11 will be developed in this section. This algorithm is composed of a two-stage-control law and a parameter-estimation law. The control and estimation laws are chosen so that the error between the desired and actual joint trajectories converges to zero. Although we assume that the unknown parameters are constant, this adaptive-control algorithm is practically valid also for the case when the parameters are piecewise constant or slowly varying with time.

We assume that the manipulator dynamics are described by equation 5.11—that is,

$$\boldsymbol{\tau} = \boldsymbol{M}(\boldsymbol{q})\ddot{\boldsymbol{q}} + \boldsymbol{h}_N(\boldsymbol{q},\dot{\boldsymbol{q}}), \tag{5.102a}$$

where $\boldsymbol{M}(\boldsymbol{q})$ is the inertia matrix satisfying $\boldsymbol{M}(\boldsymbol{q}) = \boldsymbol{M}^T(\boldsymbol{q}) > \boldsymbol{0}$ and where $\boldsymbol{h}_N(\boldsymbol{q},\dot{\boldsymbol{q}})$ is the vector defined by equation 5.25 which represents centrifugal, Coriolis, frictional, and gravitational forces. To indicate explicitly that these are functions of the parameter vector $\boldsymbol{\phi}$ consisting of the dynamic parameters and viscous friction coefficients, we write $\boldsymbol{M}(\boldsymbol{q})$ and $\boldsymbol{h}_N(\boldsymbol{q},\dot{\boldsymbol{q}})$ as $\boldsymbol{M}(\boldsymbol{q},\boldsymbol{\phi})$ and $\boldsymbol{h}_N(\boldsymbol{q},\dot{\boldsymbol{q}},\boldsymbol{\phi})$. Then we have

$$\boldsymbol{\tau} = \boldsymbol{M}(\boldsymbol{q},\boldsymbol{\phi})\ddot{\boldsymbol{q}} + \boldsymbol{h}_N(\boldsymbol{q},\dot{\boldsymbol{q}},\boldsymbol{\phi}). \tag{5.102b}$$

From equation 3.144, we know that the right-hand side of equation 5.102b can be expressed as a linear function of $\boldsymbol{\phi}$:

$$\boldsymbol{M}(\boldsymbol{q},\boldsymbol{\phi})\ddot{\boldsymbol{q}} + \boldsymbol{h}_N(\boldsymbol{q},\dot{\boldsymbol{q}},\boldsymbol{\phi}) = \boldsymbol{K}(\boldsymbol{q},\dot{\boldsymbol{q}},\ddot{\boldsymbol{q}})\boldsymbol{\phi}. \tag{5.103}$$

When we wish to remove the redundancy of parameters, we may replace $\boldsymbol{\phi}$ and $\boldsymbol{K}$ of equation 5.103 by $\boldsymbol{\phi}_d{}^*$ given by equation 3.124 and the corresponding $\boldsymbol{K}_d{}^*$, respectively. We will assume that this replacement is done, and $\boldsymbol{\phi}_d{}^*$ and $\boldsymbol{K}_d{}^*$ are denoted by $\boldsymbol{\phi}$ and $\boldsymbol{K}$ hereafter in this section. We will

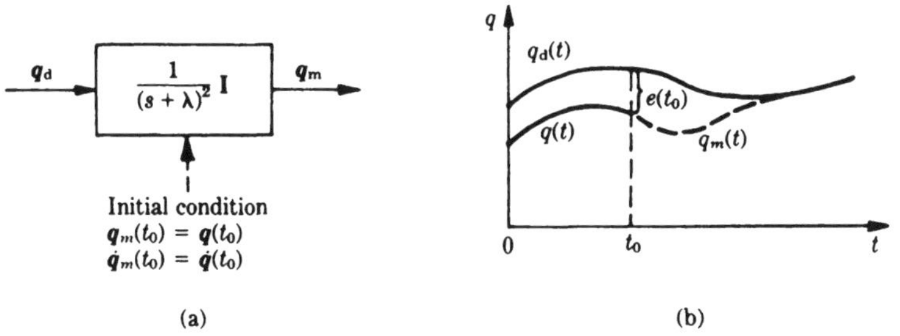

Figure 5.26
Modified desired trajectory $q_m(t)$ $(t > t_0)$ at time t_0. (a) Generator of modified desired trajectory. (b) Original and modified desired trajectories.

also assume that q and $\dot{q}$ are measurable, that the desired trajectory for q, $q_d(t)$, is known, and that its time derivatives $\dot{q}_d$ and $\ddot{q}_d$ exist and are finite. Under these assumptions, we can construct an adaptive-control system in which the error between q and q_d converges to $\mathbf{0}$.

First, assuming that an estimate $\hat{\phi}$ of ϕ is given, we consider the following control algorithm (similar to equations 5.26 and 5.28):

$$\tau = M(q,\hat{\phi})\ddot{q}_m + h_N(q,\dot{q},\hat{\phi}) + K_v\dot{e} + K_p e, \tag{5.104}$$

$$\ddot{q}_m = \ddot{q}_d + 2\lambda\dot{e} + \lambda^2 e, \tag{5.105}$$

where e is the tracking error given by

$$e = q_d - q, \tag{5.106}$$

λ is an appropriate positive constant, and K_v and K_p are square matrices (which may be functions of time and which will be determined later). The vector $\ddot{q}_m$ can be interpreted as a modified desired acceleration produced by applying a second-order filter to the original desired acceleration with the initial condition set to the current joint position and velocity as shown in figure 5.26a. In fact, let the current time be t_0, and let $q_m(t)$ $(t \geqq t_0)$ be given by

$$q_m(t) = q_d(t) - e^{-\lambda(t-t_0)}e(t_0) - (t - t_0)e^{-\lambda(t-t_0)}[\dot{e}(t_0) + \lambda e(t_0)]. \tag{5.107}$$

Then, by differentiating equation 5.107, we get

$$q_m(t_0) = q(t_0), \tag{5.108a}$$

$$\dot{q}_m(t_0) = \dot{q}(t_0), \tag{5.108b}$$

$$\ddot{q}_m(t_0) = \ddot{q}_d(t_0) + 2\lambda\dot{e}(t_0) + \lambda^2 e(t_0), \tag{5.108c}$$

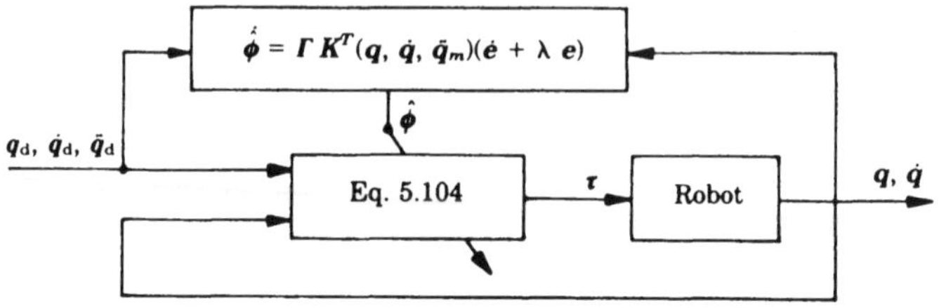

Figure 5.27
Block diagram of adaptive control system.

showing that $q_m(t)$ $(t \geqq t_0)$ is a modified desired joint trajectory that starts with the current position and velocity and converges to the original desired trajectory (see figure 5.26b). The last two terms on the right-hand side of equation 5.104, $K_v\dot{e} + K_p e$, are proportional and differential control terms to compensate for the performance deterioration due to the parameter-estimation errors.

For updating the estimate $\hat{\phi}$, we use the following parameter-estimation law based on the tracking error:

$$\dot{\hat{\phi}} = \Gamma K^T(q,\dot{q},\ddot{q}_m)(\dot{e} + \lambda e), \tag{5.109}$$

where Γ is a constant positive-definite symmetric matrix, and where $K(q,\dot{q},\ddot{q}_m)$ is given by equation 5.103 with $\ddot{q} = \ddot{q}_m$.

The resulting adaptive-control algorithm consists of the control law (equation 5.104) and the estimation law (equation 5.109). Figure 5.27 shows the block diagram of the adaptive control system.

We will now prove the convergence of the tracking error e to $\mathbf{0}$ as time tends to infinity by using the Lyapunov stability theory (see appendix 4). Noting that the vector $x = [e^T, \dot{e}^T, (\hat{\phi} - \phi)^T]^T$ is a state vector of the adaptive control system, we define a scalar function

$$v(x) = \tfrac{1}{2}(\dot{e} + \lambda e)^T M(q,\phi)(\dot{e} + \lambda e) + \tfrac{1}{2}e^T K_1 e$$
$$+ \tfrac{1}{2}(\hat{\phi} - \phi)^T \Gamma^{-1}(\hat{\phi} - \phi), \tag{5.110}$$

where K_1 is a constant symmetric positive-definite matrix. Obviously, $v(x)$ is a positive-definite function. Differentiating $v(x)$ with respect to time and using equation 5.106 and $\dot{\phi} = \mathbf{0}$, we have

$$\dot{v}(x) = (\dot{e} + \lambda e)^T M(q,\phi)(\ddot{q}_d - \ddot{q} + \lambda\dot{e}) + \tfrac{1}{2}(\dot{e} + \lambda e)^T \dot{M}(q,\phi)(\dot{e} + \lambda e)$$
$$+ e^T K_1 \dot{e} + (\hat{\phi} - \phi)^T \Gamma^{-1} \dot{\hat{\phi}}. \tag{5.111}$$

By equations 5.102b, 5.103, and 5.104,

$$\begin{aligned}\dot{v}(\boldsymbol{x}) = &-(\dot{e} + \lambda e)^T[\lambda \boldsymbol{M}(\boldsymbol{q},\boldsymbol{\phi}) - \tfrac{1}{2}\dot{\boldsymbol{M}}(\boldsymbol{q},\boldsymbol{\phi}) + \boldsymbol{K}_{\mathrm{v}}](\dot{e} + \lambda e)\\ &- \dot{e}^T(\boldsymbol{K}_{\mathrm{p}} - \lambda \boldsymbol{K}_{\mathrm{v}} - \boldsymbol{K}_1)e - \lambda e^T(\boldsymbol{K}_{\mathrm{p}} - \lambda \boldsymbol{K}_{\mathrm{v}})e\\ &- (\dot{e} + \lambda e)^T \boldsymbol{K}(\boldsymbol{q},\dot{\boldsymbol{q}},\ddot{\boldsymbol{q}}_m)(\hat{\boldsymbol{\phi}} - \boldsymbol{\phi}) + (\hat{\boldsymbol{\phi}} - \boldsymbol{\phi})^T \boldsymbol{\Gamma}^{-1}\dot{\hat{\boldsymbol{\phi}}}.\end{aligned} \tag{5.112}$$

Substituting equation 5.109 into equation 5.112 cancels the last two terms on the right-hand side.

If we can choose a velocity feedback gain $\boldsymbol{K}_{\mathrm{v}}$ satisfying either

$$\boldsymbol{K}_{\mathrm{v}} - \tfrac{1}{2}\dot{\boldsymbol{M}}(\boldsymbol{q},\boldsymbol{\phi}) + \lambda \boldsymbol{M}(\boldsymbol{q},\boldsymbol{\phi}) \geqq \boldsymbol{0} \tag{5.113a}$$

or

$$\boldsymbol{K}_{\mathrm{v}} - \tfrac{1}{2}\dot{\boldsymbol{M}}(\boldsymbol{q},\boldsymbol{\phi}) \geqq \boldsymbol{0}, \tag{5.113b}$$

then by choosing the position feedback gain $\boldsymbol{K}_{\mathrm{p}}$ such that

$$\boldsymbol{K}_{\mathrm{p}} = \lambda \boldsymbol{K}_{\mathrm{v}} + \boldsymbol{K}_1 \tag{5.114}$$

we obtain

$$\begin{aligned}\dot{v}(\boldsymbol{x}) = &-(\dot{e} + \lambda e)^T[\lambda \boldsymbol{M}(\boldsymbol{q},\boldsymbol{\phi}) - \tfrac{1}{2}\dot{\boldsymbol{M}}(\boldsymbol{q},\boldsymbol{\phi}) + \boldsymbol{K}_{\mathrm{v}}](\dot{e} + \lambda e) - \lambda e^T \boldsymbol{K}_1 e\\ &\leqq 0.\end{aligned} \tag{5.115}$$

Hence, $v(\boldsymbol{x})$ is a Lyapunov function.

By theorem 3 in appendix 4, $\boldsymbol{e}$ and $\dot{\boldsymbol{e}}$ converge to $\boldsymbol{0}$ as time tends to infinity. In other words, the joint trajectory $\boldsymbol{q}(t)$ converges to its desired trajectory, $\boldsymbol{q}_{\mathrm{d}}(t)$. Thus we have proved the validity of the adaptive-control algorithm consisting of the control law (equation 5.104 with conditions 5.113 and 5.114) and the estimation law (equation 5.109).

The above algorithm requires some *a priori* information on the bound for values of $[\dot{\boldsymbol{M}}(\boldsymbol{q},\boldsymbol{\phi})/2 - \lambda \boldsymbol{M}(\boldsymbol{q},\boldsymbol{\phi})]$ or $\dot{\boldsymbol{M}}(\boldsymbol{q},\boldsymbol{\phi})/2$ that may occur during the control. Even when this information is not available, however, the above adaptive-control approach is still valid with the following slight modification of the parameter-estimation law (equation 5.109) and the condition for choosing $\boldsymbol{K}_{\mathrm{v}}$ (equation 5.113): Since $\boldsymbol{M}(\boldsymbol{q},\boldsymbol{\phi})$ is linear in $\boldsymbol{\phi}$, so is $\dot{\boldsymbol{M}}(\boldsymbol{q},\boldsymbol{\phi})$. Hence, there exists a matrix $\boldsymbol{K}_M(\boldsymbol{q},\dot{\boldsymbol{q}},e,\dot{e})$ such that

$$\tfrac{1}{2}\dot{\boldsymbol{M}}(\boldsymbol{q},\boldsymbol{\phi})(\dot{e} + \lambda e) = K_M(\boldsymbol{q},\dot{\boldsymbol{q}},e,\dot{e})\boldsymbol{\phi}. \tag{5.116}$$

Using this relation, we can rewrite equation 5.112 as

$$\dot{v}(x) = -(\dot{e} + \lambda e)^T[\lambda M(q,\phi) - \tfrac{1}{2}\dot{M}(q,\hat{\phi}) + K_v](\dot{e} + \lambda e)$$
$$- \dot{e}^T(K_p - \lambda K_v - K_1)e - \lambda e^T(K_p - \lambda K_v)e$$
$$+ (\dot{e} + \lambda e)^T[K(q,\dot{q},\ddot{q}_m) + K_M(q,\dot{q},e,\dot{e})](\hat{\phi} - \phi)$$
$$+ (\hat{\phi} - \phi)^T \Gamma^{-1}\dot{\hat{\phi}}. \tag{5.117}$$

Suppose we use the parameter-estimation law

$$\dot{\hat{\phi}} = \Gamma[K(q,\dot{q},\ddot{q}_m) + K_M(q,\dot{q},e,\dot{e})]^T(\dot{e} + \lambda e) \tag{5.118}$$

instead of equation 5.109, and we choose a velocity feedback gain K_v such that

$$K_v - \tfrac{1}{2}\dot{M}(\dot{q},\hat{\phi}) \geqq 0, \tag{5.119}$$

instead of equation 5.113b. Then we have

$$v(x) = -(\dot{e} + \lambda e)^T[\lambda M(q,\phi) - \tfrac{1}{2}\dot{M}(q,\hat{\phi}) + K_v](\dot{e} + \lambda e) - \lambda e^T K_1 e \leqq 0. \tag{5.120}$$

Hence the tracking error e converges to $\mathbf{0}$, proving the validity of the modified adaptive-control algorithm consisting of the control law (equation 5.104 with conditions 5.119 and 5.114) and the estimation law (equation 5.118). A simple choice of K_v satisfying equation 5.119 is, of course,

$$K_v = \tfrac{1}{2}\dot{M}(\dot{q},\hat{\phi}).$$

Since equation 5.20 holds, we can replace $\dot{M}(q,\phi)/2$ in the development of this section by $\hat{C}(q,\dot{q},\phi)$ given by equation 5.19, with an additional argument ϕ to express its dependency on ϕ. This could be used to reduce the computational load in the above algorithms.

Example 5.11 Let us apply the above adaptive-control scheme to the two-link manipulator of figure 3.11. By regarding ϕ_d of equation 3.141 and K_d of equation 3.142 as the new ϕ and $K(\theta,\dot{\theta},\ddot{\theta})$, we obtain

$$\tau = M(\theta,\phi) + h(\theta,\dot{\theta},\phi) + g(\theta,\phi) = K(\theta,\dot{\theta},\ddot{\theta})\phi, \tag{5.121}$$

where

$$\boldsymbol{\phi} = \begin{bmatrix} \phi_{12} + l_1\phi_{21} \\ \phi_{13} \\ \phi_{17} + l_1{}^2\phi_{21} \\ \phi_{22} \\ \phi_{23} \\ \phi_{27} \end{bmatrix} = \begin{bmatrix} m_1\hat{s}_{1x} + l_1 m_2 \\ m_1\hat{s}_{1y} \\ \hat{I}_{1zz} + l_1{}^2 m_2 \\ m_2\hat{s}_{2x} \\ m_2\hat{s}_{2y} \\ \hat{I}_{2zz} \end{bmatrix} \tag{5.122}$$

and

$$\boldsymbol{K} = \begin{bmatrix} \hat{g}C_1 & -\hat{g}S_1 & \ddot{\theta}_1 & k_{1,2,2} & k_{1,2,3} & \ddot{\theta}_1 + \ddot{\theta}_2 \\ 0 & 0 & 0 & k_{2,2,2} & k_{2,2,3} & \ddot{\theta}_1 + \ddot{\theta}_2 \end{bmatrix}. \tag{5.123}$$

From equations 3.132 and 5.122, we have

$$\tfrac{1}{2}\dot{\boldsymbol{M}}(\boldsymbol{\theta},\boldsymbol{\phi}) = -h\begin{bmatrix} \dot{\theta}_2 & \dot{\theta}_2/2 \\ \dot{\theta}_2/2 & 0 \end{bmatrix}, \tag{5.124}$$

where

$$h = l_1(S_2\phi_{22} + C_2\phi_{23}). \tag{5.125}$$

With these preparations, from equations 5.104 and 5.105, the control law is

$$\boldsymbol{\tau} = \boldsymbol{K}(\boldsymbol{\theta},\dot{\boldsymbol{\theta}},\ddot{\boldsymbol{\theta}}_m)\hat{\boldsymbol{\phi}} + \boldsymbol{K}_{\mathrm{v}}\dot{\boldsymbol{e}} + \boldsymbol{K}_{\mathrm{p}}\boldsymbol{e}, \tag{5.126}$$

$$\ddot{\boldsymbol{\theta}}_m = \ddot{\boldsymbol{\theta}}_{\mathrm{d}} + 2\lambda\dot{\boldsymbol{e}} + \lambda^2\boldsymbol{e}, \tag{5.127}$$

where $\boldsymbol{\theta}_{\mathrm{d}}$ is the desired trajectory of $\boldsymbol{\theta}$, and $\boldsymbol{e} = \boldsymbol{\theta}_{\mathrm{d}} - \boldsymbol{\theta}$. First, consider the case where we have the *a priori* information

$$3 \leqq \phi_{22} = m_2\hat{s}_{2x} \leqq 6, \tag{5.128a}$$

$$-1 \leqq \phi_{23} = m_2\hat{s}_{2y} \leqq 1, \tag{5.128b}$$

$$|\dot{\theta}_i| \leqq 2\pi, \quad i = 1,2. \tag{5.128c}$$

For this case the velocity feedback gain $\boldsymbol{K}_{\mathrm{v}}$ in equation 5.126 can be determined as follows. For simplicity, let $\boldsymbol{K}_{\mathrm{v}} = k_{\mathrm{v}}\mathbf{I}$. Then the condition 5.113b becomes

$$\begin{bmatrix} k_{\mathrm{v}} + h\dot{\theta}_2 & h\dot{\theta}_2/2 \\ h\dot{\theta}_2/2 & k_{\mathrm{v}} \end{bmatrix} \geqq \mathbf{0}. \tag{5.129}$$

By Sylvester's criterion (theorem 4 in appendix 4), condition 5.129 is satisfied if and only if all its principal minors are non-negative:

$$k_v + h\dot{\theta}_2 \geqq 0, \quad k_v \geqq 0, \tag{5.130a}$$

$$k_v(k_v + h\dot{\theta}_2) - h^2\dot{\theta}_2{}^2/4 \geqq 0. \tag{5.130b}$$

Hence, we can choose any k_v such that

$$k_v \geqq 2\sqrt{37}\pi|l_1| \geqq -h\dot{\theta}_2. \tag{5.131}$$

If we let $\boldsymbol{K}_1 = k_1\mathbf{I}$ ($k_1 > 0$), from equation 5.114 the position feedback gain $\boldsymbol{K}_p$ in equation 5.126 is

$$\boldsymbol{K}_p = (\lambda k_v + k_1)\mathbf{I}. \tag{5.132}$$

With $\boldsymbol{\Gamma} = \gamma\mathbf{I}$ ($\gamma > 0$) in equation 5.109, the parameter-estimation law is given by

$$\dot{\hat{\boldsymbol{\phi}}} = \gamma\boldsymbol{K}^T(\boldsymbol{\theta},\dot{\boldsymbol{\theta}},\ddot{\boldsymbol{\theta}}_m)(\dot{\boldsymbol{e}} + \lambda\boldsymbol{e}). \tag{5.133}$$

The resulting adaptive controller consists of equations 5.126, 5.131, 5.132, and 5.133. Next, consider the case where no *a priori* information on the parameters (such as equation 5.128) is available. From equations 5.119 and 5.114, $\boldsymbol{K}_v$ and $\boldsymbol{K}_p$ in equation 5.126 are, for example, given by

$$\boldsymbol{K}_v = -\hat{h}\begin{bmatrix} \dot{\theta}_2 & \dot{\theta}_2/2 \\ \dot{\theta}_2/2 & 0 \end{bmatrix} \tag{5.134}$$

and

$$\boldsymbol{K}_p = \begin{bmatrix} -\lambda\hat{h}\dot{\theta}_2 + k_1 & -\hat{h}\dot{\theta}_2/2 \\ -\hat{h}\dot{\theta}_2/2 & k_1 \end{bmatrix}, \tag{5.135}$$

where

$$\hat{h} = l_1(S_2\hat{\phi}_{22} + C_2\hat{\phi}_{23}).$$

Substituting equations 5.124 and 5.125 into equation 5.116, we obtain

$$\boldsymbol{K}_M(\boldsymbol{\theta},\dot{\boldsymbol{\theta}},\boldsymbol{e},\dot{\boldsymbol{e}})\boldsymbol{\phi} = -\begin{bmatrix} \dot{\theta}_2 & \dot{\theta}_2/2 \\ \dot{\theta}_2/2 & 0 \end{bmatrix}(\dot{\boldsymbol{e}} + \lambda\boldsymbol{e})l_1[S_2,C_2]\begin{bmatrix} \phi_{22} \\ \phi_{23} \end{bmatrix}.$$

Thus, we have

$$\boldsymbol{K}_M(\boldsymbol{\theta},\dot{\boldsymbol{\theta}},\boldsymbol{e},\dot{\boldsymbol{e}}) = -\begin{bmatrix} \dot{\theta}_2 & \dot{\theta}_2/2 \\ \dot{\theta}_2/2 & 0 \end{bmatrix}(\dot{\boldsymbol{e}} + \lambda\boldsymbol{e})l_1[0,0,0,S_2,C_2,0].$$

From equation 5.118, the parameter-estimation law is

$$\dot{\hat{\boldsymbol{\phi}}} = \gamma[\boldsymbol{K}(\boldsymbol{\theta},\dot{\boldsymbol{\theta}},\ddot{\boldsymbol{\theta}}_m) + \boldsymbol{K}_M(\boldsymbol{\theta},\dot{\boldsymbol{\theta}},\boldsymbol{e},\dot{\boldsymbol{e}})]^T(\dot{\boldsymbol{e}} + \lambda\boldsymbol{e}). \tag{5.136}$$

The resulting adaptive controller consists of equations 5.126, 5.134, 5.135, and 5.136. □

Exercises

5.1 For the three-link manipulator shown in figure 5.28, use method 1 of subsection 5.1.1 to determine a trajectory to bring the manipulator state from rest at the initial position in figure 5.28a to a complete stop at the final position in figure 5.28b in 1 second. Assume that $\Delta = 0.2$ second.

5.2 Solve exercise 5.1 using the interpolation of end-effector position variables instead of joint variables.

5.3 Give an algorithm to determine $\boldsymbol{k}$ and α such that $\boldsymbol{R}(\boldsymbol{k},\alpha) = \boldsymbol{R}$ for any given value of the rotation matrix $\boldsymbol{R}$.

5.4 Using the single-axis rotation method, specify an orientation trajectory to bring the end effector from rest at the initial orientation of figure 5.29a to a complete stop at the final orientation of figure 5.29b in 2 seconds. Adopt the interpolation by a quintic polynomial function of time.

5.5 Solve exercise 5.4 using the double-axis rotation method. Using diagrams, show the difference between the mid orientations at time $t = 1$ for both the single-axis and the double-axis rotation method.

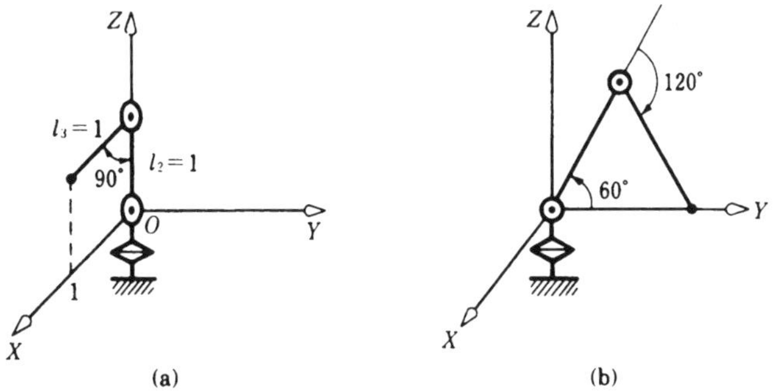

Figure 5.28
Three-link manipulator. (a) Initial position. (b) Final position.

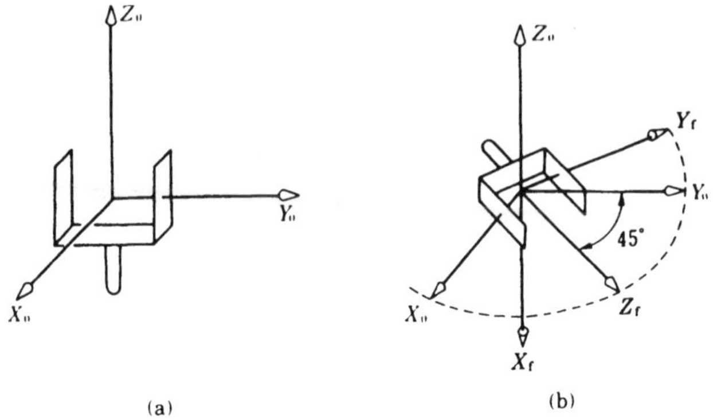

Figure 5.29
End-effector orientation. (a) Initial. (b) Final.

5.6 For the parallel-drive two-link manipulator treated in subsection 3.3.3, derive a state feedback law that linearizes the dynamics with respect to the end-effector position $\boldsymbol{y} = [x,y]^T$.

5.7 Rewrite the step response (equation 5.61) of a third-order system using parameters σ, ζ, and ω_c defined by

$$\tilde{s}^3 + \alpha\tilde{s}^2 + \beta\tilde{s} + 1 = (\tilde{s} + \sigma)(\tilde{s}^2 + 2\zeta\omega_c\tilde{s} + \omega_c{}^2).$$

Explain why the response for $\alpha = 1.3$ and $\beta = 2.0$ involves a backward motion before reaching the desired value 1.

5.8 Consider a nonlinear system with two-dimensional state vector $\boldsymbol{x} = [x_1,x_2]^T$:

$$\dot{\boldsymbol{x}} = \begin{bmatrix} -x_1{}^2 + x_2 \\ 2x_1 + x_2 \end{bmatrix}\boldsymbol{x} + \begin{bmatrix} 1 & x_2 \\ 0 & 1 \end{bmatrix}\boldsymbol{u},$$

$$\boldsymbol{y} = \begin{bmatrix} 1 & 0 \\ 0 & 1 \end{bmatrix}\boldsymbol{x}.$$

Give a state feedback law that decouples this system and allocates all poles at -3.

5.9 Design an adaptive controller for the parallel-drive two-link manipulator in figure 3.16.

References

1. M. Brady, "Trajectory Planning," in *Robot Motion*, ed. M. Brady et al. (MIT Press, 1982).

2. R. P. Paul, "Modeling, Trajectory Calculation and Servoing of a Computer Controlled Arm," Stanford Artificial Intelligence Laboratory memo AIM 177, 1972.

3. R. P. Paul, *Robot Manipulators: Mathematics, Programming, and Control* (MIT Press, 1981).

4. M. Takegaki and S. Arimoto, "A New Feedback Method for Dynamic Control of Manipulators," *ASME Journal of Dynamic Systems, Measurement, and Control* 102 (1981): 119–125.

5. S. Arimoto and F. Miyazaki, "Stability and Robustness of PID Feedback Control for Robot Manipulators of Sensory Capability," in *Robotics Research: The First International Symposium*, ed. M. Brady and R. Paul (MIT Press, 1984), pp. 783–799.

6. A. K. Bejczy, "Robot Arm Dynamics and Control," Jet Propulsion Laboratory, California Institute of Technology, report TM33-669, 1974.

7. J. Y. S. Luh, M. H. Walker, and R. P. C. Paul, "Resolved Acceleration Control of Mechanical Manipulators," *IEEE Transactions on Automatic Control* 25, no. 3 (1980): 468–474.

8. O. Khatib, "A Unified Approach for Motion and Force Control of Robot Manipulators," *IEEE Journal of Robotics and Automation* 3 (1987): 43–53.

9. E. Freund, "Fast Nonlinear Control with Arbitrary Pole-Placement for Industrial Robots and Manipulators," *International Journal of Robotics Research* 1, no. 1 (1982): 65–78.

10. J. J. Craig, P. Hsu, and S. Sastry, "Adaptive Control of Mechanical Manipulators," *International Journal of Robotics Research* 6, no. 2 (1987): 16–28.

11. J. J. Slotine and W. Li, "On the Adaptive Control of Robot Manipulators," *International Journal of Robotics Research* 6, no. 3 (1987): 49–59.

12. R. H. Middleton and G. C. Goodwin, "Adaptive Computed Torque Control for Rigid Link Manipulators," in Proceedings of the 25th IEEE Conference on Decision and Control (1986), pp. 68–73.

13. J. S. Albus, "A New Approach to Manipulator Control: The Cerebellar Model Articulation Controller (CMAC)," *ASME Journal of Dynamic Systems, Measurement, and Control* 97 (1975): 220–227.

14. S. Arimoto, S. Kawamura, and F. Miyazaki, "Bettering Operation of Robots by Learning," *Journal of Robotic Systems* 1, no. 2 (1984): 123–140.

15. E. G. Gilbert and I. J. Ha, "An Approach to Nonlinear Feedback Control with Applications to Robotics," in Proceedings of the 22nd IEEE Conference on Decision and Control (1983), pp. 134–138.

16. J. J. Craig, *Introduction to Robotics* (Addison-Wesley, 1986).

17. M. W. Spong and M. Vidyasagar, "Robust Linear Compensator Design for Nonlinear Robotic Control," *IEEE Journal of Robotics and Automation* 3, no. 1 (1987): 345–351.

18. T. Yoshikawa and M. Nose, "Study on Dynamic Control of Manipulators using Hierarchical Structure Method," *Transactions of the Institute of Systems, Control, and Information Engineers* 1, no. 7 (1988): 255–262 (in Japanese).

19. J. Y. S. Luh and C. S. Lin, "Scheduling of Parallel Computation for a Computer-Controlled Mechanical Manipulator," *IEEE Transactions on Systems, Man, and Cybernetics* 12, no. 2 (1982): 214–234.

20. H. Kasahara and S. Narita, "Parallel Processing of Robot-Arm Control Computation on a Multiprocessor System," *IEEE Journal of Robotics and Automation* 1, no. 2 (1985): 104–113.

21. D. Siljak, *Nonlinear Systems* (Wiley, 1968).

22. I. M. Horowiz, *Synthesis of Feedback Systems* (Academic, 1963).

23. M. J. Chen and C. A. Desoer, "Algebraic Theory for Robust Stability of Interconnected Systems; Necessary and Sufficient Conditions," *IEEE Transactions on Automatic Control* 29, no. 6 (1984): 511–519.

24. J. C. Doyle and G. Stein, "Multivariable Feedback Design: Concepts for Classical/Modern Synthesis," *IEEE Transactions on Automatic Control* 26, no. 1 (1981): 75–93.

25. T. Yoshikawa, "Multi-Variable Control of Robot Manipulators," *Advanced Robotics* 2, no. 2 (1987): 181–191.

26. Y. D. Landau, *Adaptive Control—The Model Reference Approach* (Marcel Dekker, 1979).

27. J. J. Slotine and W. Li, "Adaptive Manipulator Control: A Case Study," *IEEE Transactions on Automatic Control* 33, no. 11 (1988): 995–1003.

28. D. S. Bayard and J. T. Wen, "New Class of Control Laws for Robotic Manipulators, Part 2: Adaptive Case," *International Journal of Control* 47, no. 5 (1988): 1387–1406.

6 Force Control

Many of the tasks we wish to perform using manipulators require control not only of the position of a manipulator but also of the force exerted by its end effector on an object. Assembly, polishing, deburring, opening and closing a door, and turning a crank are typical examples of such tasks. Two methods have been developed for force control: impedance control and hybrid control.[1]

Impedance control[2,3] aims at controlling position and force by adjusting the mechanical impedance of the end effector to external forces generated by contact with the manipulator's environment. Mechanical impedance is roughly an extended concept of the stiffness of a mechanism against a force applied to it. Impedance control can further be divided into *passive-impedance* and *active-impedance* methods. In the passive-impedance method, the desired mechanical impedance of the end effector is achieved by using only mechanical elements, such as springs and dampers. The active-impedance method, on the other hand, realizes the desired mechanical impedance by driving joint actuators using feedback control based on measurements of end-effector position, velocity, contact force, and so on.

Hybrid control[4] uses two feedback loops for direct separate control of position and force. In this method, the directions in which the position is controlled and those in which the force is controlled are determined for a given task during operation. Current position in position-control directions and current force in force-control directions are measured. Corrections based on these measurements are applied by joint actuators in order to make them follow the desired position and force trajectories.

Procedures for implementing these two methods will be developed in this chapter.

6.1 Impedance Control

6.1.1 Passive-Impedance Method

Let us consider the task of inserting a peg into a hole with a tight clearance. If we wish to do this with a manipulator capable of position control only, then we need extremely accurate position control. Insertion of a peg requires the peg axis to line up almost exactly with the hole axis. If a significant discrepancy exists between the center axes of the peg and the hole in either distance or direction, then the insertion may not be accomplished, because of jamming or wedging. To overcome this difficulty using

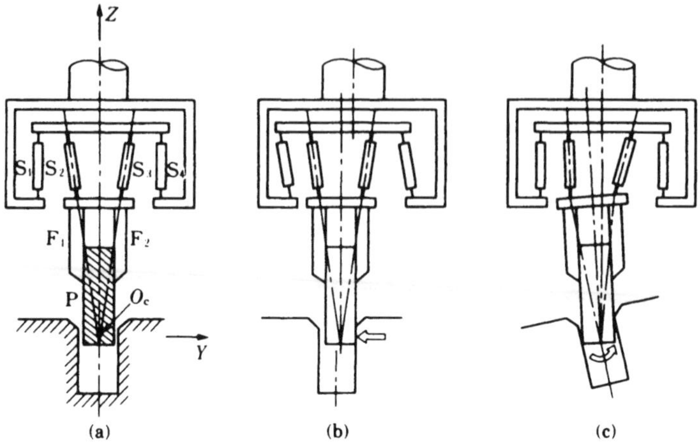

Figure 6.1
Conceptual sketch of RCC hand. (a) Structure. (b) Compliance to horizontal force. (c) Compliance to moment.

a mechanical device, the Remote Center Compliance (RCC) hand was developed.[5] This is a hand with great elasticity in certain directions, making it suitable for peg-in-hole tasks. A conceptual sketch of the mechanism is shown in figure 6.1a. Each of the four rigid parts S_1–S_4 has two springs, one at either end, illustrated by short solid lines. These springs can bend but are neither expandable nor compressible. The axes of S_1 and S_4 are parallel; however, those of S_2 and S_3 intersect at point O_c, near the end of peg P grasped by fingers F_1 and F_2.

Let us assume that the axes of the peg and the hole are parallel but do not coincide. When the hand moves down vertically toward the hole, it usually gets into the state shown in figure 6.1b, with the wall of the hole exerting a force on the peg. Owing to the horizontal force applied at the tip of the peg, the springs on S_1 and S_4 bend, but those on S_2 and S_3 do not. Consequently, the peg moves horizontally without changing orientation, and it slides into the hole. When the axes of the peg and the hole are not parallel, the hand usually pushes the peg into the hole until it jams (the state shown in figure 6.1c). Owing to the moment applied at the tip of the peg, S_2 and S_3 bend this time, turning the direction of the peg axis closer to that of the hole. Thus, the insertion can be accomplished just by moving the hand vertically downward.

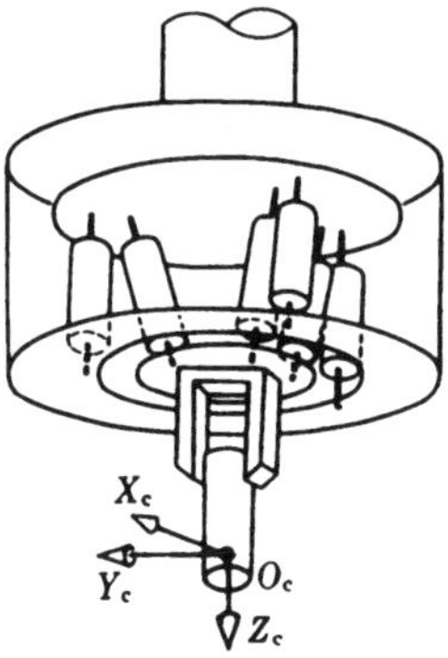

Figure 6.2
Three-dimensional RCC hand.

A three-dimensional version of the above mechanism is shown in figure 6.2. The axes of the three outer springs are parallel; those of the three inner springs intersect at point O_c, near the tip of the peg. When we assign a frame Σ_c with its origin at O_c and with its three axes parallel to those of the hand frame, as can be seen from the argument for the two-dimensional case, the relation between the external force exerted on the peg,

$$f = [f_x, f_y, f_z, n_x, n_y, n_z]^T,$$

and the differential displacement of the peg,

$$\varepsilon = [\varepsilon_x, \varepsilon_y, \varepsilon_z, \alpha_x, \alpha_y, \alpha_z]^T,$$

is statically given by

$$\varepsilon = \boldsymbol{K} f, \tag{6.1}$$

where

$$\boldsymbol{K} = \begin{bmatrix} k_{\mathrm{soft}} & & & & & \mathbf{0} \\ & k_{\mathrm{soft}} & & & & \\ & & k_{\mathrm{hard}} & & & \\ & & & k_{\mathrm{soft}} & & \\ & & & & k_{\mathrm{soft}} & \\ \mathbf{0} & & & & & k_{\mathrm{soft}} \end{bmatrix}$$

where k_{soft} are small stiffness coefficients and k_{hard} is a large one. When a translational force is applied at O_c, only a translational displacement occurs; when a moment is applied at O_c, only a rotational displacement results. Therefore, the point O_c is called the *compliance center*. A unique feature of this hand is that the compliance center is located near the tip of the peg and not inside the hand mechanism.

As is seen from the above example, the passive-impedance method does not require any force-control loop, and so the control system becomes simple. It generally lacks versatility, however, because different hardware must be designed for each different task. This limitation leads to the idea of changing the virtual mechanical impedance to make a manipulator versatile without continual hardware modifications. We can do this by driving the joint actuators using an appropriate feedback control law based on measurements of end-effector position and velocity, external force, and so on. This approach could be applied to various tasks just by changing the software of the controller feedback law. We will consider this active impedance approach in the following subsections.

6.1.2 Active-Impedance Method—One-Degree-of-Freedom Case

A simple one-degree-of-freedom system will serve to illustrate the active impedance method. We assume that the dynamics equation of the mechanical system shown in figure 6.3 is given by

$$m_a \ddot{x} + d_a \dot{x} + k_a x = f_u + F, \tag{6.2}$$

where m_a is the mass of body M, F is the external force, f_u is the driving force which we can apply, x is the displacement from the equilibrium of $F = f_u = 0$, k_a is the spring constant, and d_a is the damping coefficient. We

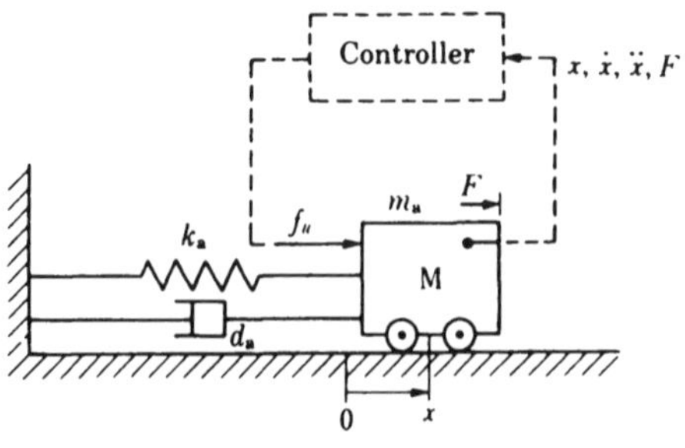

Figure 6.3
Active impedance control of one-degree-of-freedom system.

also assume that the desired impedance of the body to the external force is expressed by

$$m_d\ddot{x} + d_d(\dot{x} - \dot{x}_d) + k_d(x - x_d) = F, \tag{6.3}$$

where m_d, d_d, and k_d are the desired mass, damping coefficient, and spring constant, respectively, and x_d is the desired position trajectory.

When x, $\dot{x}$, and $\ddot{x}$ are measurable, we can use the control law

$$f_u = (m_a - m_d)\ddot{x} + (d_a - d_d)\dot{x} + (k_a - k_d)x + d_d\dot{x}_d + k_d x_d. \tag{6.4a}$$

Substituting equation 6.4a into equation 6.2 yields equation 6.3, showing that the closed-loop system has the desired impedance. When the external force F is measurable, the control law represented by equation 6.4a can be replaced by

$$f_u = (d_a - m_a m_d^{-1} d_d)\dot{x} + (k_a - m_a m_d^{-1} k_d)x - (1 - m_a m_d^{-1})F + m_a m_d^{-1}(d_d\dot{x}_d + k_d x_d). \tag{6.4b}$$

If it is allowable to have the original mass m_a as the desired mass m_d, then equations 6.4a and 6.4b reduce to a simple position and velocity feedback law:

$$f_u = (d_a - d_d)\dot{x} + (k_a - k_d)x + d_d\dot{x}_d + k_d x_d. \tag{6.5}$$

We have developed control laws to achieve the desired impedance (equation 6.3). A remaining problem is how to determine the coefficients m_d, d_d, and k_d of that equation. We first consider the case when the system makes no contact with other objects, or when we can regard the external force F to be zero because there is only a small perturbing force acting, if any. One procedure for this case is to let $m_d = m_a$, to make the natural frequency

$$\omega_c = \sqrt{\frac{k_d}{m_d}} \tag{6.6}$$

as large as possible for better transient response, and to let the damping coefficient

$$\zeta = \frac{d_d}{2\sqrt{m_d k_d}} \tag{6.7}$$

be around 0.7–1.0. As long as m_d, d_d, and k_d are positive, the steady-state

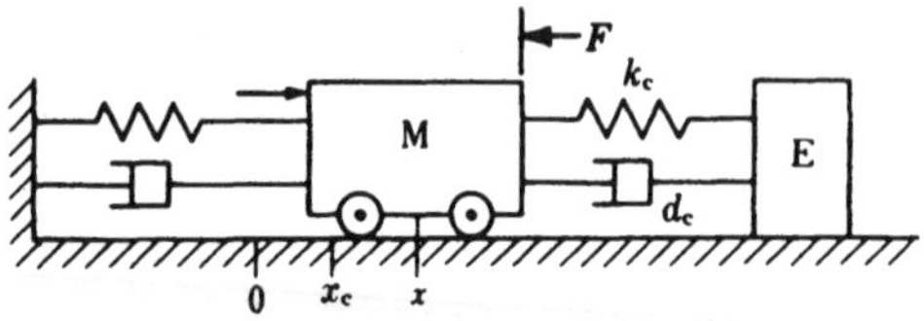

Figure 6.4
Contact with a fixed body.

position error and velocity error converge to zero for any desired trajectory x_d.

Next we consider the case when the body M is in contact with a fixed body E. We assume that the interaction through their place of contact can be modeled as in figure 6.4, or by

$$d_c\dot{x} + k_c(x - x_c) = -F, \tag{6.8}$$

where x_c is the equilibrium position for which $F = 0$. When either the contact surface on the side of body M or that of E is fairly elastic (or when both are), the value of k_c is small. When both surfaces are very stiff, k_c is large. The value of d_c also depends on the materials of the two bodies.

Substituting equation 6.8 into equation 6.3 yields

$$m_d\ddot{x} + (d_d + d_c)\dot{x} + (k_d + k_c)x = d_d\dot{x}_d + k_d x_d + k_c x_c. \tag{6.9}$$

The natural frequency is

$$\omega_c = \sqrt{\frac{k_d + k_c}{m_d}}, \tag{6.10}$$

and the damping coefficient is

$$\zeta = \frac{d_d + d_c}{2\sqrt{m_d(k_d + k_c)}}. \tag{6.11}$$

If we know the values of k_c and d_c, we can determine m_d, d_d, and k_d so that the above ω_c and ζ become acceptable. Unfortunately, the exact values of k_c and d_c are usually unknown. In particular, if the real value of k_c is larger than estimated and that of d_c is smaller, then the damping characteristic of the system described by equation 6.11 may be inadequate. For this reason we need to choose a fairly large d_d. If we further choose smaller k_d and m_d, there is less possibility of an excessively large contact force (which may cause damage to bodies M and E), and the body M will comply better with the constraint given by body E. An advantage of active impedance over passive impedance is that a system can always adjust to a desirable impedance by changing the values of m_d, k_d, and d_d during the performance of a given task and by considering contacts and noncontacts with other objects.

Example 6.1 The dynamics equation for the system shown in figure 6.3 is assumed to be given by

$$\ddot{x} + 0.1\dot{x} = f_u + F.$$

The interaction with another body is modeled as in figure 6.4 and is described by equation 6.8 with coefficients d_c and k_c such that

$$0 \leqq d_c \leqq 15 \tag{6.12}$$

and

$$500 \leqq k_c \leqq 2000. \tag{6.13}$$

For this system we wish to determine a desirable impedance (equation 6.3) to satisfy the specification that the natural frequency during contact should be between 30 and 50, the damping coefficient should be more than 0.5, m_d should be as close to 1 as possible, and k_d and d_d should be as small as possible. From equation 6.10 we have

$$30 \leqq \sqrt{\frac{k_d + k_c}{m_d}} \leqq 50,$$

or

$$900m_d \leqq k_d + 500, \tag{6.14a}$$

$$k_d + 2000 \leqq 2500m_d. \tag{6.14b}$$

From equation 6.11 we obtain

$$d_d \geqq \sqrt{m_d(k_d + k_c)} - d_c. \tag{6.15}$$

Equations 6.14 are satisfied by

$$m_d = 1, \qquad k_d = 400,$$

and the smallest d_d satisfying equation 6.15 is given by

$d_d = \sqrt{2400} \cong 49.$

Hence, a desirable impedance is described by

$\ddot{x} + 49(\dot{x} - \dot{x}_d) + 400(x - x_d) = F.$

By equation 6.5, the control algorithm achieving this impedance is

$f_u = -48.9\dot{x} - 400x + 49\dot{x}_d + 400x_d.$

We see that, from equation 6.11, the damping coefficient during contact is within the following limits:

$0.5 \leqq \zeta \leqq 1.07.$ □

While maintaining the desired impedance, it is still possible to adjust the force $f = -F$ applied by body M against body E to the desired value $f_d = -F_d$ in the steady state. For example, if we know x_c and k_c in equation 6.8, then we can achieve the desired force by just choosing the desired trajectory x_d in equation 6.3 to be

$$x_d = x_c - \frac{k_d + k_c}{k_d k_c} F_d. \tag{6.16}$$

This means that we have replaced the desired force with the corresponding desired position. When $k_c \gg k_d$, we can approximate equation 6.16 by $x_d = x_c - F_d/k_d$. Another way to achieve the desired force F_d is to replace the desired impedance (equation 6.3) with

$$m_d\ddot{x} + d_d(\dot{x} - \dot{x}_d) = F - F_d. \tag{6.17}$$

Both methods eventually drive the system to the steady state of $F = F_d$; that is, the applied force converges to the desired one.

6.1.3 Active-Impedance Method—General Case

In this subsection we will generalize the approach introduced above to manipulators with multiple degrees of freedom (ref. 2). As is shown in figure 6.5a, measurements of the manipulation vector $\boldsymbol{y}$ and the external force $\boldsymbol{F}$ acting on the end effector are used to drive the actuators at the joints through a feedback control law. By selecting this feedback law properly, we wish to develop a sytem that behaves like an end effector with a desired

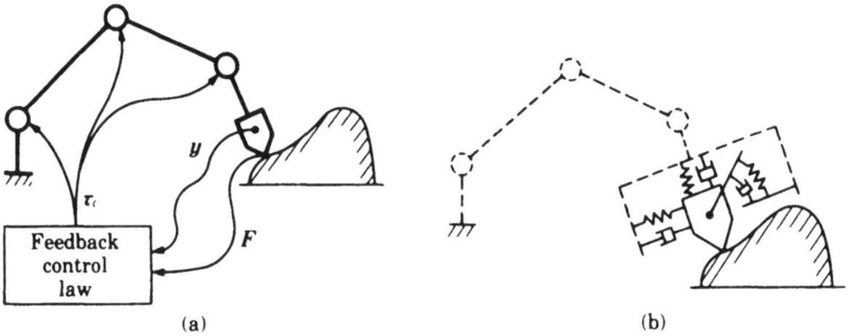

Figure 6.5
Active impedance method. (a) Feedback control system. (b) Mechanical impedance realized by (a).

mechanical impedence supported by an ideal arm that perfectly follows the desired trajectory without being affected by any external force. This system is shown pictorially in figure 6.5b.

Consider a six-link manipulator, and assume that the desired mechanical impedance for its end effector is described by

$$\boldsymbol{M}_d \ddot{\boldsymbol{y}} + \boldsymbol{D}_d \dot{\boldsymbol{y}}_e + \boldsymbol{K}_d \boldsymbol{y}_e = \boldsymbol{F}, \tag{6.18}$$

where $\boldsymbol{y}_e$ is the difference between the current value of an appropriate six-dimensional manipulation vector $\boldsymbol{y}$ and its desired value $\boldsymbol{y}_d$:

$$\boldsymbol{y}_e = \boldsymbol{y} - \boldsymbol{y}_d. \tag{6.19}$$

A typical example of $\boldsymbol{y}$ is the six-dimensional vector $\boldsymbol{r}$ expressing the position and orientation of the end effector. In equation 6.18, $\boldsymbol{F}$ represents the six-dimensional generalized force corresponding to $\boldsymbol{y}$. Physically, $\boldsymbol{F}$ is the external force exerted on the end effector by its environment. The 6×6 matrices $\boldsymbol{M}_d$, $\boldsymbol{D}_d$, and $\boldsymbol{K}_d$ are, respectively, the inertia matrix, the damping-coefficient matrix, and the stiffness matrix, all of which are symmetric and nonnegative definite. A simple way of choosing $\boldsymbol{M}_d$, $\boldsymbol{D}_d$, and $\boldsymbol{K}_d$ is to make them diagonal and to determine the diagonal elements by considerations similar to those in the one-degree-of-freedom case. Also taken into account are the directions in which large impedance is desirable and the directions in which small impedance is desirable.

The next step is to develop a control law that achieves the desired impedance (equation 6.18). Suppose that the dynamics of the manipulator are described by equation 5.24, or by

$$M(q)\ddot{q} + h_N(q,\dot{q}) = \tau. \tag{6.20}$$

The relation between y and q is

$$y = f_y(q). \tag{6.21}$$

Differentiating equation 6.21 yields

$$\dot{y} = J_y(q)\dot{q}, \tag{6.22}$$

where $J_y = \partial y/\partial q^T$. The joint torque equivalent to the external force F is given by

$$\tau_F = J_y^T(q)F. \tag{6.23}$$

Thus, the dynamic equation of the manipulator with external force F applied to it is found from equation 6.20 to be

$$M(q)\ddot{q} + h_N(q,\dot{q}) = \tau + J_y^T(q)F. \tag{6.24}$$

Assuming that $J_y(q)$ is nonsingular for any q in a region under consideration, we obtain from equations 6.22 and 6.24

$$M_y(q)\ddot{y} + h_{Ny}(q,\dot{q}) = J_y^{-T}(q)\tau + F, \tag{6.25}$$

where $J_y^{-T} = (J_y^T)^{-1}$ and

$$M_y(q) = J_y^{-T}(q)M(q)J_y^{-1}(q), \tag{6.26}$$

$$h_{Ny}(q,\dot{q}) = J_y^{-T}(q)h_N(q,\dot{q}) - M_y(q)\dot{J}_y(q)\dot{q}. \tag{6.27}$$

Now we apply a nonlinear feedback law of the form

$$\begin{aligned}\tau &= J_y^T(q)\{h_{Ny}(q,\dot{q}) - M_y(q)M_d^{-1}(D_d\dot{y}_e + K_d y_e) \\ &\qquad + [M_y(q)M_d^{-1} - I]F\} \\ &= h_N(q,\dot{q}) - M(q)J_y^{-1}(q)\dot{J}_y(q)\dot{q} \\ &\quad - M(q)J_y^{-1}(q)M_d^{-1}(D_d\dot{y}_e + K_d y_e) \\ &\quad + [M(q)J_y^{-1}(q)M_d^{-1} - J_y^T(q)]F.\end{aligned} \tag{6.28}$$

Then the closed-loop system becomes equal to equation 6.18.

If we do not require the inertia matrix M_d of the desired impedance (equation 6.18) to be a constant independent of q and allow it to be the current inertia matrix $M_y(q)$, that is, if the desired impedance is described by

$$\boldsymbol{M}_y(\boldsymbol{q})\ddot{\boldsymbol{y}} + \boldsymbol{D}_d\dot{\boldsymbol{y}}_e + \boldsymbol{K}_d\boldsymbol{y}_e = \boldsymbol{K}_{Fd}\boldsymbol{F}, \tag{6.29}$$

then the control law (equation 6.28) reduces to

$$\begin{aligned}\boldsymbol{\tau} = {} & \boldsymbol{h}_N(\boldsymbol{q},\dot{\boldsymbol{q}}) - \boldsymbol{M}(\boldsymbol{q})\boldsymbol{J}_y^{-1}(\boldsymbol{q})\dot{\boldsymbol{J}}_y(\boldsymbol{q})\dot{\boldsymbol{q}} \\ & - \boldsymbol{J}_y^T(\boldsymbol{q})\{\boldsymbol{D}_d\dot{\boldsymbol{y}}_e + \boldsymbol{K}_d\boldsymbol{y}_e - (\boldsymbol{K}_{Fd} - \mathbf{I})\boldsymbol{F}\}.\end{aligned} \tag{6.30}$$

The coefficient matrix $\boldsymbol{K}_{Fd}$ was introduced on the right-hand side of equation 6.29 to compensate for not being able to change $\boldsymbol{M}_y(\boldsymbol{q})$. For example, we can produce a large (or small) impedance in a given direction by letting $\boldsymbol{K}_{Fd}$ be a diagonal matrix and assigning a small (or large) positive value to the diagonal element corresponding to that direction.

Example 6.2 Consider the two-link manipulator treated in subsection 3.3.1. Suppose that the desired mechanical impedance is described by

$$\boldsymbol{M}_y(\boldsymbol{q})\ddot{\boldsymbol{y}} + \begin{bmatrix} D_{d1} & 0 \\ 0 & D_{d2} \end{bmatrix}\dot{\boldsymbol{y}}_e + \begin{bmatrix} K_{d1} & 0 \\ 0 & K_{d2} \end{bmatrix}\boldsymbol{y}_e = \begin{bmatrix} K_{Fd1} & 0 \\ 0 & K_{Fd2} \end{bmatrix}\boldsymbol{F}, \tag{6.31}$$

and that we wish to find the control law that produces this impedance. Using equation 6.30 and letting $\boldsymbol{y}_e = [y_{ex}, y_{ey}]^T$ and $F = [F_x, F_y]^T$, we obtain the following control law by an argument similar to that of example 5.5:

$$\begin{aligned}\tau_1 = {} & h_{122}\dot{\theta}_2^2 + 2h_{112}\dot{\theta}_1\dot{\theta}_2 + g_1 \\ & + \{l_1[M_{11}l_2C_2 - M_{12}(l_2C_2 + l_1)]\dot{\theta}_1^2 \\ & \quad + l_2[M_{11}l_2 - M_{12}(l_2 + l_1C_2)](\dot{\theta}_1 + \dot{\theta}_2)^2\}/l_1l_2S_2 \\ & + (l_1S_1 + l_2S_{12})\tilde{F}_x - (l_1C_1 + l_2C_{12})\tilde{F}_y,\end{aligned}$$

$$\begin{aligned}\tau_2 = {} & h_{211}\dot{\theta}_1^2 + g_2 \\ & + \{l_1[M_{12}l_2C_2 - M_{22}(l_2C_2 + l_1)]\dot{\theta}_1^2 \\ & \quad + l_2[M_{12}l_2 - M_{22}(l_2 + l_1C_2)](\dot{\theta}_1 + \dot{\theta}_2)^2\}/l_1l_2S_2 \\ & + l_2S_{12}\tilde{F}_x - l_2C_{12}\tilde{F}_y,\end{aligned}$$

where

$$\tilde{F}_x = D_{d1}\dot{y}_{ex} + K_{d1}y_{ex} - (K_{Fd1} - 1)F_x, \tag{6.32a}$$

$$\tilde{F}_y = D_{d2}\dot{y}_{ey} + K_{d2}y_{ey} - (K_{Fd2} - 1)F_y. \ \square \tag{6.32b}$$

The first term on the right-hand side of equation 6.30 compensates for the centrifugal and Coriolis forces of the manipulator dynamics; the second term compensates for the nonlinearity of transformation between $\ddot{\boldsymbol{y}}$ and $\ddot{\boldsymbol{q}}$. All these terms (except for the gravity force) are functions of $\dot{\boldsymbol{q}}$ and small when the manipulator moves at low speed. When these terms are neglected, the control law (equation 6.30) becomes

$$\boldsymbol{\tau} = -\boldsymbol{J}_y^T(\boldsymbol{q})[\boldsymbol{D}_{\mathrm{d}}\dot{\boldsymbol{y}}_{\mathrm{e}} + \boldsymbol{K}_{\mathrm{d}}\boldsymbol{y}_{\mathrm{e}} - (\boldsymbol{K}_{\mathrm{Fd}} - \mathbf{I})\boldsymbol{F}]. \tag{6.33}$$

This indicates that the impedance control is achievable to a certain degree by simple linear feedback of position error, velocity error, and external force. If the gravity force is not negligible, we only have to add the term $\boldsymbol{g}(\boldsymbol{q})$ to the right-hand side of equation 6.33 for compensation.

If we further consider the case when $\boldsymbol{D}_{\mathrm{d}} = \mathbf{0}$ and $\boldsymbol{K}_{\mathrm{Fd}} = \mathbf{I}$, then by letting $\boldsymbol{y}_{\mathrm{e}} = \boldsymbol{J}_y(\boldsymbol{q})\boldsymbol{q}_{\mathrm{e}}$ ($\boldsymbol{q}_{\mathrm{e}}$ is the joint error vector corresponding to $\boldsymbol{y}_{\mathrm{e}}$) under the assumption that $\boldsymbol{y}_{\mathrm{e}}$ is small, we obtain

$$\boldsymbol{\tau} = -\boldsymbol{J}_y^T(\boldsymbol{q})\boldsymbol{K}_{\mathrm{d}}\boldsymbol{J}_y(\boldsymbol{q})\boldsymbol{q}_{\mathrm{e}}. \tag{6.34}$$

The impedance control based on equation 6.34 is called *stiffness control* (ref. 3), because it makes the stiffness matrix expressed in the manipulation variables equal to the desired $\boldsymbol{K}_{\mathrm{d}}$. It is also called *compliance control*, because the inverse of a stiffness matrix is a compliance matrix. Finally, if we wish to achieve the desired force $\boldsymbol{F}_{\mathrm{d}}$ in the steady state, we adopt an approach similar to equation 6.16 or 6.17 in the one-degree-of-freedom case.

6.2 Hybrid Control

6.2.1 Hybrid Control via Feedback Compensation

The hybrid control method has been developed on the basic recognition that, in many tasks requiring the control of force, there are some directions in which position should be controlled and other directions in which force should be controlled. These directions may change during the task, but a single direction never requires both position and force control. This method fulfills both position and force control of a task simultaneously (ref. 4). The basic idea of the method is now illustrated by a simple example.

Example 6.3 Consider the two-link planar manipulator of figure 6.6. The task is to push the endpoint of the manipulator with a specified

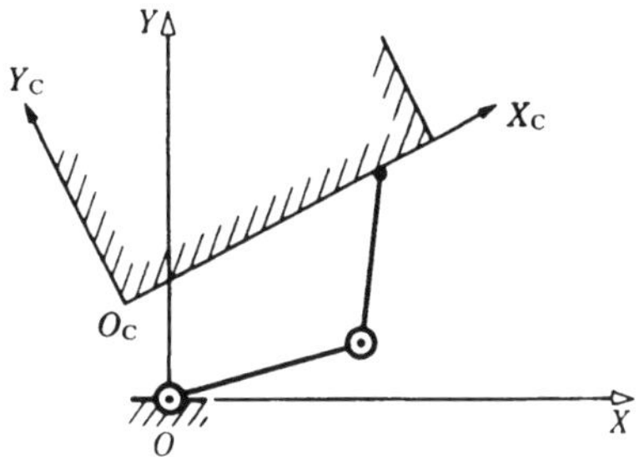

Figure 6.6
Example of hybrid control by feedback compensation.

force against the flat smooth surface of the shaded object, while moving the endpoint along the surface in a specified way. We assign a frame $\Sigma_C(O_C - X_C Y_C)$ such that the X_C axis is along the flat surface and the Y_C axis is normal to the surface. Thus, X_C is the position-control direction and Y_C is the force-control direction. We assume that a force sensor is attached to the endpoint to measure the pushing force, ${}^C\!f(t)$, expressed in frame Σ_C. We also assume that the position of the endpoint, ${}^C y(t)$, expressed in Σ_C, is measured by a position sensor. Denoting the desired values for ${}^C\!f(t)$ and ${}^C y(t)$ as ${}^C\!f_d(t)$ and ${}^C y_d(t)$, we obtain expressions for the errors that include consideration of their direction in Σ_C:

$$ {}^C y_e(t) = \begin{bmatrix} 1 & 0 \\ 0 & 0 \end{bmatrix} [{}^C y_d(t) - {}^C y(t)], \tag{6.35} $$

$$ {}^C\!f_e(t) = \begin{bmatrix} 0 & 0 \\ 0 & 1 \end{bmatrix} [{}^C\!f_d(t) - {}^C\!f(t)]. \tag{6.36} $$

Letting $\boldsymbol{J}_y$ denote the Jacobian matrix of ${}^C y$ with respect to $\boldsymbol{q}$, we can transform the above errors back to the joint coordinate space using the following equations:

$$ \boldsymbol{q}_e(t) \cong \boldsymbol{J}_y^{-1}\, {}^C y_e(t), \tag{6.37a} $$

$$ \dot{\boldsymbol{q}}_e(t) = \boldsymbol{J}_y^{-1}\, {}^C \dot{y}_e(t), \tag{6.37b} $$

$$ \boldsymbol{\tau}_e(t) = \boldsymbol{J}_y^{T}\, {}^C\!f_e(t). \tag{6.37c} $$

Note that equation 6.37a is an approximation in the case of small ${}^C y_e$. On the basis of these error expressions, we now calculate two joint driving forces, $\boldsymbol{\tau}_P$ and $\boldsymbol{\tau}_F$. Force $\boldsymbol{\tau}_P$ is to compensate for the position error and is given by an appropriate position control law; force τ_F is to compensate for the force error and is given by an appropriate force control law. Applying the sum of τ_P and τ_F to the joints, we can expect the result that the X_C directional component of the desired position ${}^C\boldsymbol{y}_d(t)$ and the Y_C directional component of the desired force ${}^C\boldsymbol{f}_d(t)$ are closely tracked. Although a variety of position and force control laws are applicable, a typical pair is the PD (proportional and differential) position control law

$$\boldsymbol{\tau}_P(t) = \boldsymbol{K}_{Pp}\boldsymbol{q}_e(t) + \boldsymbol{K}_{Pd}\dot{\boldsymbol{q}}_e(t), \tag{6.38}$$

and the I (integral) force control law

$$\boldsymbol{\tau}_F(t) = \boldsymbol{K}_{Fi}\int_0^t \boldsymbol{\tau}_e(t')\,dt', \tag{6.39}$$

where $\boldsymbol{K}_{Pp}$, $\boldsymbol{K}_{Pd}$, and $\boldsymbol{K}_{Fi}$ are feedback gain matrices. The joint driving torque is given by

$$\boldsymbol{\tau}(t) = \boldsymbol{\tau}_P(t) + \boldsymbol{\tau}_F(t). \tag{6.40}$$

Equations 6.35–6.40 constitute a hybrid control algorithm for the manipulator. Note that Raibert and Craig (ref. 4) adopt a PID (proportional, integral, and differential) position control law and a PI (proportional and integral) control law combined with a feedforward term from the desired force signal. □

Consider the X_C and Y_C directions in example 6.3 from the viewpoint of the constraint imposed on the endpoint by a given task. The Y_C axis is the direction in which the end-effector position is constrained. In other words, the environment restricts the possible positions along Y_C with the surface as a barrier. The X_C axis is the direction in which the force exerted on the object by the end effector is constrained. In example 6.3, this force is constrained to be zero because we assume that the surface is smooth and there is no friction force. Since these directions of position constraint and force constraint can be easily described by the coordinate frame Σ_C, Σ_C is called the *constraint frame* (refs. 6, 4); this explains the subscript C. In example 6.3, the frame Σ_C is fixed with respect to the reference frame. However, when the object surface is not flat, as in figure 6.7, the directions of the position and force constraints change according to where the endpoint is currently located. In such cases, it is convenient to define the constraint frame Σ_C by a moving frame with its origin at the current endpoint position, its X_C axis

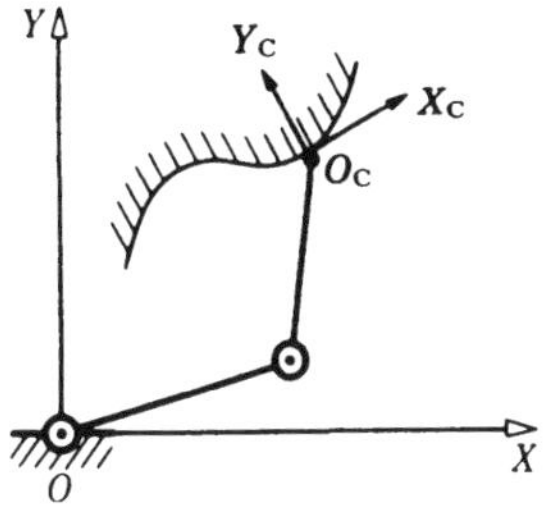

Figure 6.7
Constraint by a curved surface.

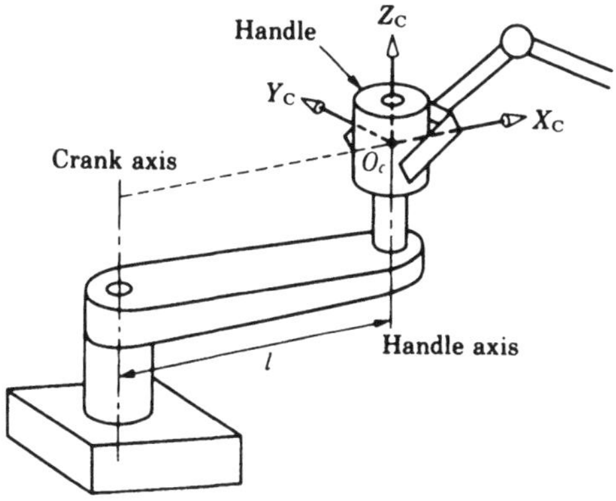

Figure 6.8
Turning a crank.

in the direction tangent to the surface, and its Y_C axis in the direction normal to the surface.

The concept of a constraint frame can, of course, be generalized to the case of three-dimensional space, as illustrated in the next example.

Example 6.4 Consider the task of turning a crank. As shown in figure 6.8, the hand of the manipulator firmly holds the handle, which rotates about the handle axis on the crank. A convenient choice for the constraint frame is one with its origin at an appropriate point on the handle axis, its Z_C axis parallel to the handle axis, its X_C in the direction radiating outward from the crank axis, and its Y_C axis such that the three axes form a right-hand coordinate frame. Having chosen this frame, we can describe the motion which the hand can make as a translation along the Y_C axis and a rotation about the Z_C axis. These are the two position-controlled directions in the six-dimensional space of the translational and rotational velocity vector. On the other hand, the hand can make no translation along the X_C or the Z_C axis. Also, no rotation is possible about the X_C or the Y_C axis. This means that the hand can apply force in these directions, so these four are the force-controlled directions. We can also look at the above argument from the viewpoint of the constraints posed by the task. There are four position constraints mentioned above and two force constraints, in the sense that no force can be produced along Y_C or about Z_C if we consider the ideal case of a frictionless, massless crank and handle. These are called *natural constraints*, because they are determined naturally by the given task. In contrast, there are also force commands in the four directions of position constraints and velocity commands in the two directions of force constraints which are artificially given by the designer. For this reason, they are called *artificial constraints*. With the hand velocity expressed in Σ_C denoted as ${}^C\boldsymbol{v} = [{}^Cv_x, {}^Cv_y, {}^Cv_z, {}^C\omega_x, {}^C\omega_y, {}^C\omega_z]^T$ and the force exerted on the handle by the hand as ${}^C\boldsymbol{f} = [{}^Cf_x, {}^Cf_y, {}^Cf_z, {}^Cn_x, {}^Cn_y, {}^Cn_z]^T$, the natural constraints for the task of turning a crank are described by

$$ {}^Cv_x = 0, \quad {}^Cv_z = 0, \quad {}^C\omega_x = 0, \quad {}^C\omega_y = 0, $$

$$ {}^Cf_y = 0, \quad {}^Cn_z = 0, $$

and the artificial constraints are described by

$$ {}^Cv_y = v_0, \quad {}^C\omega_z = \omega_0, $$

$$ {}^Cf_x = 0, \quad {}^Cf_z = 0, \quad {}^Cn_x = 0, \quad {}^Cn_y = 0, $$

where v_0 is determined from the desired rotational speed of the crank and ω_0 is given by the designer from the viewpoint of easy operation. Generally, ${}^Cf_x$, ${}^Cf_z$, ${}^Cn_x$, and ${}^Cn_y$ are given nonzero force commands, but in this case zero commands prevent the application of unnecessary force. □

Figure 6.9 is a block diagram of a general hybrid control system based on the above consideration. The function of the "position-error extraction" block is to retain position errors in the directions of position control and to neglect those in the directions of force control. The "force-error extraction" block has the complementary function of retaining force errors in the directions of force control. The "position (force) control law" block computes the joint driving force using the extracted errors. In the case of

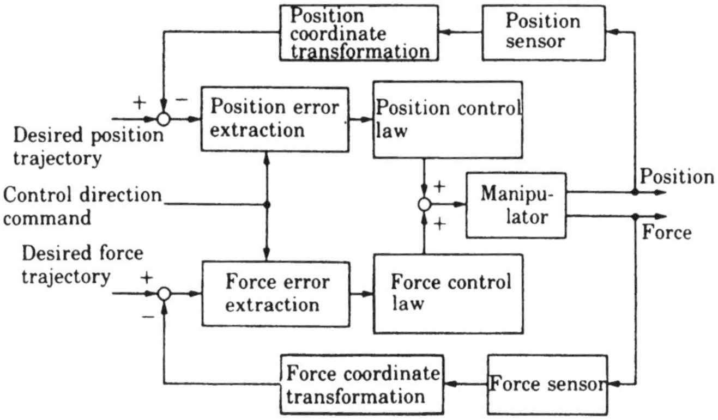

Figure 6.9
Block diagram of hybrid control system.

example 6.3, it calculates equations 6.37a, 6.37b, and 6.38 for position and equations 6.37c and 6.39 for force.

6.2.2 Dynamic Hybrid Control

In this subsection we will develop a hybrid control approach taking into consideration the dynamics of the manipulator.[7,8] First, the constraint on the end effector is described by a set of hypersurfaces in the end-effector coordinates. Second, on the basis of this constraint description and the manipulator dynamics, we derive the basic equations for what we will call *dynamic hybrid control*. These equations give the joint driving force needed to achieve the desired position and force trajectories. Finally, a basic structure of the dynamic hybrid control system is given. This control approach can also be regarded as an extension of two-stage control (section 5.3) to the case of force control.

(1) Description of end-effector constraint

We will express the constraint on the end effector caused by a contact with its environment by a set of hypersurfaces in the space of the position vector of the end effector. We assume that the environment is rigid, and therefore the hypersurfaces are independent of the force applied by the end effector.

Consider a manipulator with six degrees of freedom whose end-effector position with respect to a fixed reference frame is denoted by a six-dimensional vector $\boldsymbol{r}$. Assume that a given end-effector constraint can be expressed by a set of m hypersurfaces ($m \leqq 6$),

$$p_i(\boldsymbol{r}) = 0, \quad i = 1,2,\ldots,m \tag{6.41}$$

which are differentiable twice and mutually independent in a subset S of the six-dimensional Euclidean space R^6. When equation 6.41 is unilateral, in the sense of approaching from only one side as in the case of pushing a tool against the surface of an object, assume that $p_i(\boldsymbol{r}) > 0$ inside the object and $p_i(\boldsymbol{r}) < 0$ outside. Differentiating equation 6.41 with respect to time yields

$$\boldsymbol{E}_{\mathrm{F}}\dot{\boldsymbol{r}} = 0, \tag{6.42}$$

where

$$\boldsymbol{E}_{\mathrm{F}} = [\boldsymbol{e}_{7-m},\boldsymbol{e}_{8-m},\ldots,\boldsymbol{e}_6]^T, \tag{6.43}$$

$$\boldsymbol{e}_{6-m+i} = \frac{\partial p_i(\boldsymbol{r})}{\partial \boldsymbol{r}}, \quad i = 1,2,\ldots,m. \tag{6.44}$$

The rank of $\boldsymbol{E}_{\mathrm{F}}$ is m, owing to the assumed independence of equation 6.41. Differentiating equation 6.42 again, we obtain

$$\boldsymbol{E}_{\mathrm{F}}\ddot{\boldsymbol{r}} + \dot{\boldsymbol{E}}_{\mathrm{F}}\dot{\boldsymbol{r}} = \boldsymbol{0}. \tag{6.45}$$

To express the end-effector trajectory on the constraint surfaces given by equation 6.41, we assume that there exists a $(6-m)$-dimensional function

$$\boldsymbol{y}_{\mathrm{P}} = \boldsymbol{s}(\boldsymbol{r}) = [s_1(\boldsymbol{r}),s_2(\boldsymbol{r}),\ldots,s_{6-m}(\boldsymbol{r})]^T$$

such that $s_j(\boldsymbol{r})$ $(j = 1,2,\ldots,6-m)$ are scalar functions which are differentiable twice and $\{p_i(\boldsymbol{r}), i = 1,2,\ldots,m; s_j(\boldsymbol{r}), j = 1,2,\ldots,6-m\}$ are mutually independent in the region S. If we define

$$\boldsymbol{E}_{\mathrm{P}} = [\boldsymbol{e}_1,\boldsymbol{e}_2,\ldots,\boldsymbol{e}_{6-m}]^T, \tag{6.46}$$

where

$$\boldsymbol{e}_j = \frac{\partial s_j(\boldsymbol{r})}{\partial \boldsymbol{r}}, \quad j = 1, 2, \ldots, 6-m \tag{6.47}$$

then we have

$$\dot{\boldsymbol{y}}_{\mathrm{P}} = \boldsymbol{E}_{\mathrm{P}}\dot{\boldsymbol{r}}, \tag{6.48}$$

$$\ddot{\boldsymbol{y}}_{\mathrm{P}} = \boldsymbol{E}_{\mathrm{P}}\ddot{\boldsymbol{r}} + \dot{\boldsymbol{E}}_{\mathrm{P}}\dot{\boldsymbol{r}}. \tag{6.49}$$

For each $\boldsymbol{r}$ on the constraint surface, vectors $\boldsymbol{e}_1, \boldsymbol{e}_2, \ldots, \boldsymbol{e}_6$ are linearly independent of one other. The set $\{\boldsymbol{e}_1, \boldsymbol{e}_2, \ldots, \boldsymbol{e}_{6-m}\}$ represents the directions in which the end effector can move; the set $\{\boldsymbol{e}_{7-m}, \boldsymbol{e}_{8-m}, \ldots, \boldsymbol{e}_6\}$ represents the directions in which the end effector is constrained. Hence, the coordinate frame with its origin at the current position $\boldsymbol{r}$ and with $\{\boldsymbol{e}_1, \boldsymbol{e}_2, \ldots, \boldsymbol{e}_6\}$ as its basis could be called the *constraint frame*. This is a generalization of the constraint frame introduced in subsection 6.2.1. If we let $\boldsymbol{y}_{\mathrm{F}} = \boldsymbol{p}(\boldsymbol{r})$ and denote the six-dimensional generalized force vector corresponding to a generalized coordinate vector $\boldsymbol{y} = [\boldsymbol{y}_{\mathrm{P}}^T, \boldsymbol{y}_{\mathrm{F}}^T]^T$ as $\boldsymbol{f}_y = [\boldsymbol{f}_{\mathrm{P}}^T, \boldsymbol{f}_{\mathrm{F}}^T]^T$, the natural constraints in terms of the above constraint frame are given by $\dot{\boldsymbol{y}}_{\mathrm{F}} = \boldsymbol{0}$ and $\boldsymbol{f}_{\mathrm{P}} = \boldsymbol{0}$, and the artificial constraints are given by $\dot{\boldsymbol{y}}_{\mathrm{P}} = \dot{\boldsymbol{y}}_{\mathrm{Pd}}$ and $\boldsymbol{f} = \boldsymbol{f}_{\mathrm{Fd}}$. The values of $\dot{\boldsymbol{y}}_{\mathrm{Pd}}$ and $\boldsymbol{f}_{\mathrm{Fd}}$ are to be determined by the designer.

Let a 6×6 matrix $\boldsymbol{E}$ be

$$\boldsymbol{E} = \begin{bmatrix} \boldsymbol{E}_{\mathrm{P}} \\ \boldsymbol{E}_{\mathrm{F}} \end{bmatrix}. \tag{6.50}$$

Then we have

$$\boldsymbol{E}\dot{\boldsymbol{r}} = \begin{bmatrix} \dot{\boldsymbol{y}}_{\mathrm{P}} \\ \boldsymbol{0} \end{bmatrix} \tag{6.51}$$

and

$$\boldsymbol{E}\ddot{\boldsymbol{r}} = \begin{bmatrix} \ddot{\boldsymbol{y}}_{\mathrm{P}} \\ \boldsymbol{0} \end{bmatrix} - \dot{\boldsymbol{E}}\dot{\boldsymbol{r}}. \tag{6.52}$$

Obvious physical interpretations of the above equations are that the normal component of the velocity of the end effector to the constraint surface is zero and that the normal component of its acceleration to the constraint surface is determined only by the velocity $\dot{\boldsymbol{r}}$.

Example 6.5 Consider the case where the position of the end effector is constrained to a sphere of radius α with its approach vector directed to the center of sphere as shown in figure 6.10. Two examples of tasks of this kind are polishing a spherical surface with a whetstone and operating a ball-joint joystick. Take $[x, y, z, \phi, \theta, \psi]^T$ as the end-effector position vector $\boldsymbol{r}$, where $[x, y, z]^T$ is the translational position in the reference frame and $[\phi, \theta, \psi]^T$ is the orientation expressed by Euler angles with the configuration shown in figure 6.11 as the zero state. For simplicity, the region of interest, S, is taken as one such that $\alpha - |z| > \varepsilon$, where ε is a positive constant. The constraint

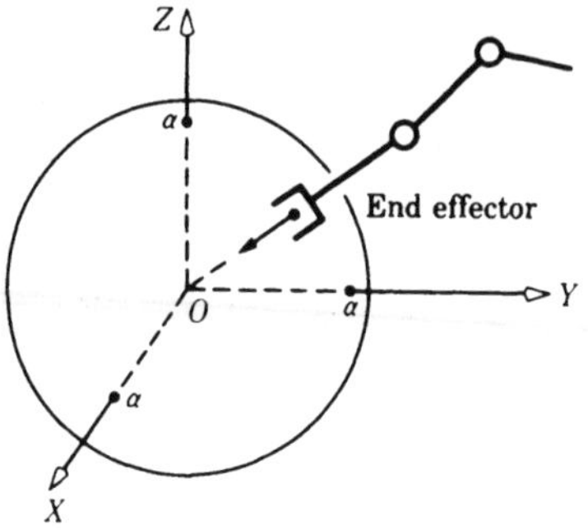

Figure 6.10
Constraint by a spherical surface.

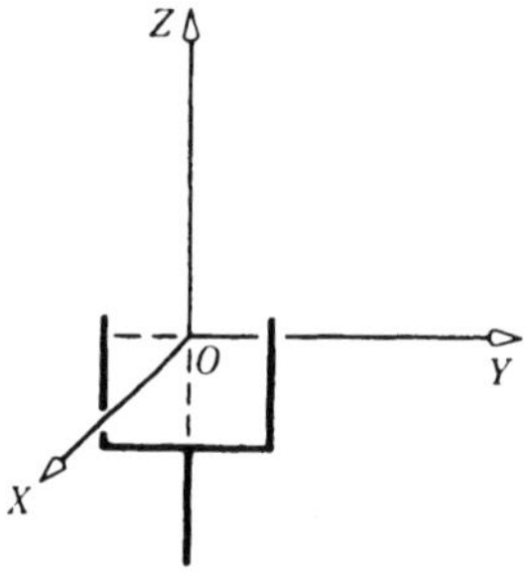

Figure 6.11
Reference orientation of hand.

hypersurfaces are

$$\alpha^2 - (x^2 + y^2 + z^2) = 0,$$

$$\phi - \operatorname{atan2}(-y, -x) = 0,$$

$$\theta - \operatorname{atan2}(\sqrt{\alpha^2 - z^2}, -z) = 0.$$

Differentiating these equations and using equation A1.8, we have

$$\boldsymbol{E}_{\mathbf{F}} = \begin{bmatrix} -x & -y & -z & 0 & 0 & 0 \\ y/(\alpha^2 - z^2) & -x/(\alpha^2 - z^2) & 0 & 1 & 0 & 0 \\ 0 & 0 & -1/\sqrt{(\alpha^2 - z^2)} & 0 & 1 & 0 \end{bmatrix}. \tag{6.53a}$$

If we let $\boldsymbol{y}_{\mathbf{P}} = \boldsymbol{s}(\boldsymbol{r}) = [\phi, \theta, \psi]^T$, then

$$E_P = \begin{bmatrix} 0 & 0 & 0 & 1 & 0 & 0 \\ 0 & 0 & 0 & 0 & 1 & 0 \\ 0 & 0 & 0 & 0 & 0 & 1 \end{bmatrix}. \tag{6.53b}$$

This y_P is an easily understandable variable for position control: ϕ and θ denote the translational position on the sphere, and ψ denotes the rotational position about the approach vector of the end effector. □

As was mentioned in subsection 2.5.2, the end-effector velocity $\dot{r}$ can also be expressed by a six-dimensional vector v, consisting of the translational velocity along each axis and the rotational velocity about each axis of the reference frame. The relation between $\dot{r}$ and v is

$$v = T_r \dot{r}, \tag{6.54}$$

where T_r is a 6×6 transformation matrix which is a function of r and which is assumed to be nonsingular in the subset S. For example, when Euler angles are used in r for representing the orientation, T_r is given by equation 2.86b.

(2) Motion of manipulator under constraint and constraining force

Consider a manipulator with n degrees of freedom, and denote its joint vector by q. Assume that the relation between the end-effector position r and the joint vector q is

$$r = f_r(q). \tag{6.55}$$

Differentiating equation 6.55 yields

$$\dot{r} = J_r \dot{q}, \quad J_r = \partial r / \partial q^T, \tag{6.56}$$

$$\ddot{r} = J_r \ddot{q} + \dot{J}_r \dot{q}. \tag{6.57}$$

Also assume that the dynamics of the arm are given by equation 5.24, or

$$M(q)\ddot{q} + h_N(q,\dot{q}) = \tau. \tag{6.58}$$

The motion of the joints (that is, $\ddot{q}$) and the constraining force will be found for the case when an arbitrary driving force command τ_c is applied to the manipulator at state $(q,\dot{q})$ and under the constraint 6.41. From equations 6.42 and 6.54 we have

$$E_F T_r^{-1} v = 0. \tag{6.59}$$

The six-dimensional generalized force corresponding to the generalized velocity $\boldsymbol{v}$ is given by the forces along and the torques about each axis of the reference frame. For simplicity, assume that the contact between the end effector and the object is frictionless. From the principle of virtual work, the force $\boldsymbol{f}$ exerted on the surface by the end effector, expressed in terms of the generalized force, satisfies $\boldsymbol{v}^T\boldsymbol{f} = 0$ for any realizable $\boldsymbol{v}$ under equation 6.59. Hence we have

$$\boldsymbol{f} = \hat{\boldsymbol{E}}_{\mathrm{F}}{}^T\boldsymbol{f}_{\mathrm{F}} \tag{6.60a}$$

and

$$\hat{\boldsymbol{E}}_{\mathrm{F}} = \boldsymbol{E}_{\mathrm{F}}\boldsymbol{T}_r{}^{-1}, \tag{6.60b}$$

where $\boldsymbol{f}_{\mathrm{F}}$ is an m-dimensional unknown vector. In equation 6.60a each column vector of $\hat{\boldsymbol{E}}_{\mathrm{F}}{}^T$ can be interpreted as a reference force vector normal to each constraint hypersurface. The vector $\boldsymbol{f}_{\mathrm{F}}$, therefore, represents the force $\boldsymbol{f}$ in terms of these reference force vectors. The force $-\boldsymbol{f}$ can be interpreted as the force that constrains the end effector to the surface. The joint force $\boldsymbol{\tau}_f$ equivalent to the constraining force $-\boldsymbol{f}$ is given by

$$\boldsymbol{\tau}_f = -(\boldsymbol{T}_r\boldsymbol{J}_r)^T\boldsymbol{f} = -\boldsymbol{J}_r{}^T\boldsymbol{E}_{\mathrm{F}}{}^T\boldsymbol{f}_{\mathrm{F}}. \tag{6.61}$$

Since $\boldsymbol{\tau}_c$ and $\boldsymbol{\tau}_f$ are applied to the joints, by substituting $\boldsymbol{\tau} = \boldsymbol{\tau}_c + \boldsymbol{\tau}_f$ into equation 6.58 we obtain

$$\boldsymbol{M}\ddot{\boldsymbol{q}} + \boldsymbol{J}_r{}^T\boldsymbol{E}_{\mathrm{F}}{}^T\boldsymbol{f}_{\mathrm{F}} = \boldsymbol{b}_1, \tag{6.62a}$$

where

$$\boldsymbol{b}_1 = \boldsymbol{\tau}_c - \boldsymbol{h}_N(\boldsymbol{q},\dot{\boldsymbol{q}}). \tag{6.62b}$$

Also, from equations 6.45 and 6.57 we obtain

$$\boldsymbol{E}_{\mathrm{F}}\boldsymbol{J}_r\ddot{\boldsymbol{q}} = \boldsymbol{b}_2, \tag{6.63a}$$

where

$$\boldsymbol{b}_2 = -\boldsymbol{E}_{\mathrm{F}}\dot{\boldsymbol{J}}_r\dot{\boldsymbol{q}} - \dot{\boldsymbol{E}}_{\mathrm{F}}\dot{\boldsymbol{r}}. \tag{6.63b}$$

Note that the vectors $\boldsymbol{b}_1$ and $\boldsymbol{b}_2$ can be calculated from the given values of $\boldsymbol{q}$ and $\dot{\boldsymbol{q}}$, i.e., the state of the manipulator. From equations 6.62a and 6.63a, we finally have

$$\ddot{\boldsymbol{q}} = \boldsymbol{M}^{-1}\{\boldsymbol{b}_1 + (\boldsymbol{E}_{\mathrm{F}}\boldsymbol{J}_r)^T\boldsymbol{K}(\boldsymbol{b}_2 - \boldsymbol{E}_{\mathrm{F}}\boldsymbol{J}_r\boldsymbol{M}^{-1}\boldsymbol{b}_1)\}, \tag{6.64}$$

$$f_F = -K(b_2 - E_F J_r M^{-1} b_1), \tag{6.65}$$

where

$$K = (E_F J_r M^{-1} J_r^T E_F^T)^{-1}. \tag{6.66}$$

(3) Calculation of joint driving force

Having just derived the manipulator motion and the constraining force for an arbitrary joint driving force τ_c, let us consider the inverse problem. Assume that the desired value for $\ddot{y}_P$ is $\ddot{y}_{Pd}$, and that the desired value for f_F is f_{Fd}.

Consider the following nonlinear state feedback law:

$$\tau_c = \tau_P + \tau_F, \tag{6.67}$$

$$\tau_P = M\ddot{q}_d + h_N(q,\dot{q}), \tag{6.68}$$

$$\ddot{q}_d = J_r^+ \left\{ E^{-1} \left(\begin{bmatrix} u_1 \\ 0 \end{bmatrix} - \dot{E} J_r \dot{q} \right) - \dot{J}_r \dot{q} \right\} + (I - J_r^+ J_r) k, \tag{6.69}$$

$$\tau_F = J_r^T E_F^T u_2, \tag{6.70}$$

where u_1 and u_2 are $(6 - m)$-dimensional and m-dimensional new input vectors. We can easily show using equations 6.64–6.66 that the closed-loop system is a linear system described by

$$\ddot{y}_P = u_1, \quad f_F = u_2. \tag{6.71}$$

Therefore, if the models given by equations 6.41 and 6.58 are exactly correct and if $y_P(0) = y_{Pd}(0)$ and $\dot{y}_P(0) = \dot{y}_{Pd}(0)$ at the initial time, $t = 0$, then the desired position and force trajectories will be perfectly produced by

$$u_1 = \ddot{y}_{Pd}, \quad u_2 = f_{Fd}. \tag{6.72}$$

The vector k in equation 6.69 is an arbitrary time function. This k represents the arbitrariness of the joint acceleration that appears when $n > 6$, i.e., when we consider redundant manipulators. If $n = 6$ and the rank of J_r is 6, then the second term on the right-hand side of equation 6.69 is $\mathbf{0}$.

It is a natural result of these arguments that the position and the force can be controlled simultaneously by applying the sum of the force τ_P to achieve the desired acceleration specified by $\ddot{y}_{Pd}$ and applying the force τ_F to achieve the desired force specified by f_{Fd} as the joint driving force. In order for this result to be achieved, the condition rank$\boldsymbol{J} = 6$ must be satisfied; that is, the manipulator must not be in a singular configuration.

The control law given by equations 6.67–6.70 corresponds to the linearizing compensation given by equation 5.34 in two-stage control, and equation 6.71 corresponds to the linearized system of equation 5.35.

When some friction force exists between the constraint surface and the end effector, and its exact value is known, then we can compensate for the friction force by including it in $\boldsymbol{h}_N(\boldsymbol{q},\dot{\boldsymbol{q}})$ of equation 6.68.

Example 6.6 Consider a task of following the surface of a sphere using a six-degree-of-freedom manipulator under the constraint described in example 6.5. Assume that the end effector should move from the initial position $\boldsymbol{y}_r(0) = [0, -\pi/2, 0]^T$ (which corresponds to the point of α on the X axis) in the direction of increasing ϕ with velocity $\hat{a}$, that the force should be applied in the direction of the center of the sphere with magnitude $\hat{f}$ without applying a moment, and that the condition rank$\boldsymbol{J}_r = 6$ is satisfied during the task. Substituting equations 6.60b, 6.53a, and 2.86b into 6.60a yields

$$\boldsymbol{f} = \begin{bmatrix} -x & -y & -z & 0 & 0 & 0 \\ y/(\alpha^2 - z^2) & -x/(\alpha^2 - z^2) & 0 & -C_\phi C_\theta / S_\theta & -S_\phi C_\theta / S_\theta & 1 \\ 0 & 0 & -1/\sqrt{\alpha^2 - z^2} & -S_\phi & C_\phi & 0 \end{bmatrix}^T \boldsymbol{f}_{\mathrm{F}}.$$

where $S_\theta = \sin\theta$, $C_\theta = \cos\theta$, $S_\phi = \sin\phi$, and $C_\phi = \cos\phi$. As was mentioned in (2), the columns of the coefficient matrix of $\boldsymbol{f}_{\mathrm{F}}$, $\hat{\boldsymbol{E}}_{\mathrm{F}}{}^T$, in the above equation express the reference-force vectors shown in figure 6.12. Each of them is a constraining force and causes no motion of the end effector; we can see this by considering the case of operating a ball-joint joystick, where the moment at the center is zero for each of the three reference forces shown in the figure. When we regard $\boldsymbol{y}_{\mathrm{P}}$ and $\boldsymbol{f}_{\mathrm{F}}$ as the controlled variables, the linearizing control law is given by equations 6.67–6.70, with $\boldsymbol{E}$ obtained from equation 6.53. The desired position and force trajectories are described in terms of $\boldsymbol{y}_{\mathrm{P}}$ and $\boldsymbol{f}_{\mathrm{F}}$ by

$$\boldsymbol{y}_{\mathrm{Pd}}(t) = \left[\frac{\hat{a}}{2\alpha} t^2, -\frac{\pi}{2}, 0\right]^T$$

and

$$\boldsymbol{f}_{\mathrm{Fd}}(t) = [\hat{f}/\alpha, 0, 0]^T.$$

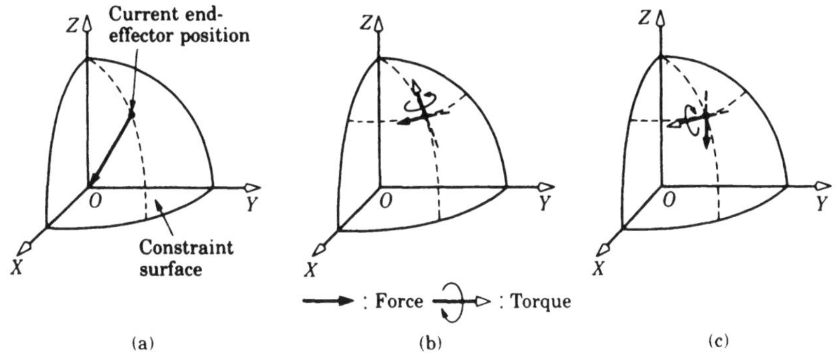

Figure 6.12
Reference force vectors represented by column vectors of $\hat{E}_F{}^T$. End-effector position: $\{x = \alpha/2, y = \alpha/2, z = \alpha/\sqrt{2}, \phi = -135°, \theta = 135°\}$. (a) First column vector. (b) Second column vector. (c) Third column vector.

Therefore, when we wish to achieve these desired trajectories in an open-loop manner, the joint driving force τ_c is given by equations 6.67 and 6.68, and

$$\ddot{q}_d = J_r^{-1}\left\{E^{-1}\left(\begin{bmatrix}\hat{a}/\alpha\\ 0\end{bmatrix} - \dot{E}J_r\dot{q}\right) - \dot{J}_r\dot{q}\right\},$$

$$\tau_F = -J_r^T E_F{}^T[\hat{f}/\alpha,0,0]^T. \ \square$$

(4) Basic structure of dynamic hybrid control system

If equations 6.41 and 6.58 are exactly correct, then the open-loop system in figure 6.13 can produce both the desired position and the desired force. However, because of modeling errors and unpredictable disturbances, the real response of this system may deviate from the desired one. To cope with this deviation, we have to add a servo compensator to the system. One basic configuration among various possible ones is given in figure 6.14, where two independent servo compensators (one for the position servo loop and one for the force servo loop) are installed. The specific design of the servo compensators could be carried out using any conventional design approach to servo systems, one instance being the approach based on the sensitivity and the stability margin described in subsection 5.4.2.

Example 6.7 Consider the two-link manipulator treated in subsection 3.3.1. Suppose we wish to design a hybrid control system for the case where

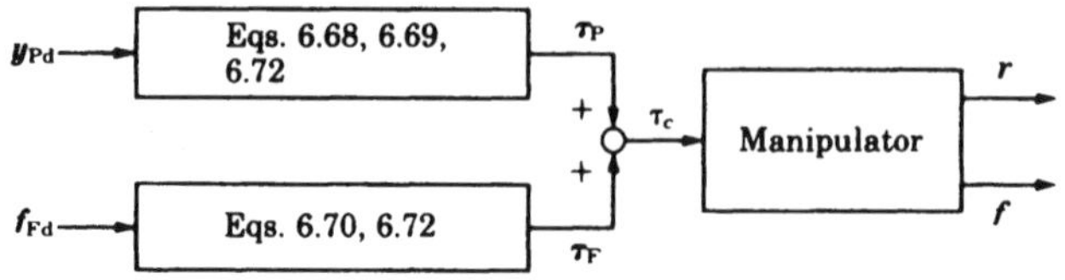

Figure 6.13
Open-loop dynamic hybrid control system.

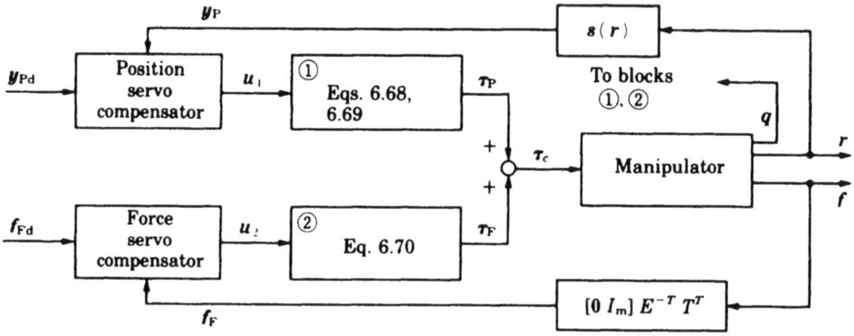

Figure 6.14
Dynamic hybrid control system.

the end-effector position vector $\boldsymbol{r} = [x,y]^T$ is constrained on a smooth curve as shown in figure 6.15. Obviously, $m = 1$. We adopt as y_P the distance along the curve from a fixed point on it. Using the tangent vector $\boldsymbol{e}_1$ and normal vector $\boldsymbol{e}_2$ shown in the figure, we find

$$\boldsymbol{E}_F = \boldsymbol{e}_2{}^T$$

and

$$\boldsymbol{E}_P = \boldsymbol{e}_1{}^T.$$

Thus, $\boldsymbol{E}$ is given by the 2×2 matrix $[\boldsymbol{e}_1,\boldsymbol{e}_2]^T$. The Jacobian matrix $\boldsymbol{J}_r$ is

$$\boldsymbol{J}_r = \begin{bmatrix} -l_1 S_1 - l_2 S_{12} & -l_2 S_{12} \\ l_1 C_1 + l_2 C_{12} & l_2 C_{12} \end{bmatrix},$$

and the arm dynamics are described by equation 3.39. Hence, from equations 6.67–6.70 the linearizing control law is given by

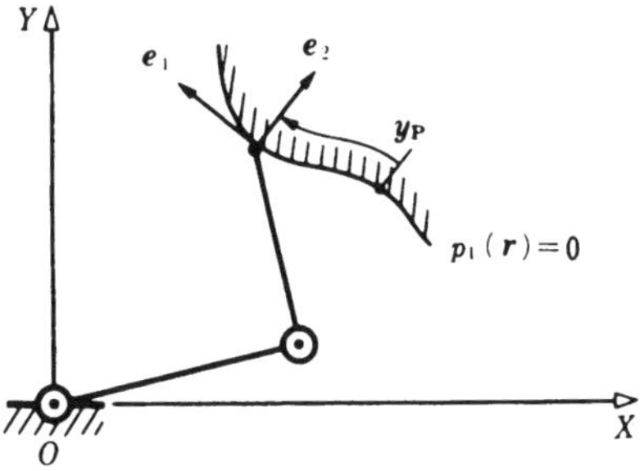

Figure 6.15
Constraint by a curve.

$$\tau_c = \begin{bmatrix} M_{11}\ddot{\theta}_{d1} + M_{12}\ddot{\theta}_{d2} + h_{122}\dot{\theta}_2{}^2 + 2h_{112}\dot{\theta}_1\dot{\theta}_2 + g_1 \\ M_{12}\ddot{\theta}_{d1} + M_{22}\ddot{\theta}_{d2} + h_{211}\dot{\theta}_1{}^2 + g_2 \end{bmatrix} - \boldsymbol{J}_r{}^T \boldsymbol{e}_2 u_2,$$

$$\ddot{\boldsymbol{\theta}}_d = \boldsymbol{J}_r{}^{-1}\left\{\boldsymbol{E}^{-1}\left(\begin{bmatrix} u_1 \\ 0 \end{bmatrix} - \dot{\boldsymbol{E}}\boldsymbol{J}_r\dot{\boldsymbol{\theta}}\right) - \dot{\boldsymbol{J}}_r\dot{\boldsymbol{\theta}}\right\}$$

and the closed-loop system is described by

$$\ddot{y}_P = u_1, \tag{6.73a}$$

$$f_F = u_2. \tag{6.73b}$$

One of the simplest servo compensators for this linearized system is

$$u_1 = \omega_{cP}{}^2(y_{Pd} - y_P) - 2\omega_{cP}\dot{y}_P, \tag{6.74a}$$

$$u_2 = \omega_{cF}\int_0^t (f_{Fd} - f_F)\,dt', \tag{6.74b}$$

where ω_{cP} and ω_{cF} are constant parameters. This means that we use a P control associated with velocity feedback for the position servo loop and an I control for the force servo loop. This also corresponds to using the servo system in figure 5.22, with the feedforward compensator C_{aP} and the feedback compensator C_{bP} for the position servo loop given by

$$C_{aP} = \omega_{cP}{}^2,$$

$$C_{bP} = \omega_{cP}{}^2 + 2\omega_{cP}s,$$

and with the feedforward compensator C_{aF} and the feedback compensator C_{bF} for the force servo loop given by

$$C_{aF} = \frac{\omega_{cF}}{s}$$

and

$$C_{bF} = \frac{\omega_{cF}}{s}.$$

After we implement equation 6.74, the transfer functions for position and force of the overall closed-loop system, G_{fP} and G_{fF}, become

$$G_{fP} = \frac{\omega_{cP}^2}{s^2 + 2\omega_{cP}s + \omega_{cP}^2}$$

and

$$G_{fF} = \frac{\omega_{cF}}{s + \omega_{cF}}.$$

Since these characteristics are quite reasonable, we have completed the design of a hybrid controller. The matrix E, which is necessary to compute τ_c, is determined when the constraint curve is given. For example, if the constraint curve is given as in figure 6.16, then, since it is described by

$$[(x + y) - (l_1 + l_2)]/\sqrt{2} = 0,$$

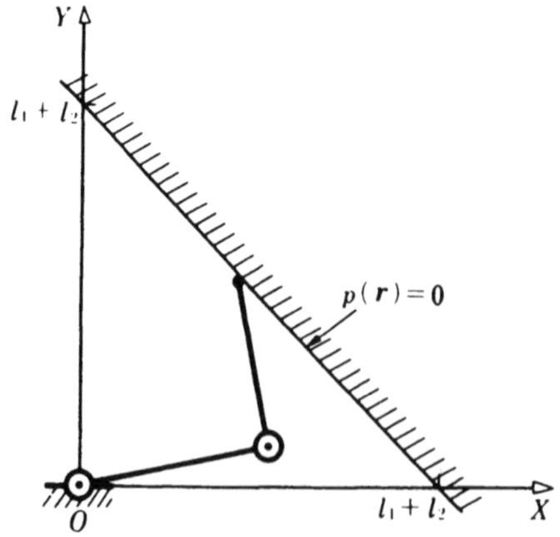

Figure 6.16
Example of constraint curve.

we have

$$E_F = e_2{}^T = [1/\sqrt{2}, 1/\sqrt{2}].$$

If we further let y_P be

$$y_P = s_1(r) = (y - x + l + l_2)/\sqrt{2},$$

then

$$E_P = e_1{}^T = [-1/\sqrt{2}, 1/\sqrt{2}].$$

Hence, we finally obtain

$$E = \begin{bmatrix} -1/\sqrt{2} & 1/\sqrt{2} \\ 1/\sqrt{2} & 1/\sqrt{2} \end{bmatrix}.$$

We can evaluate the sensitivity and the stability margin of the above servo systems using the curves of $|S|$ and $|T|$ introduced in subsection 5.4.2. The curves for the position control loop are identical to those in figure 5.25; those for the force control loop are shown in figure 6.17. Both loops have small sensitivity at low frequencies and large stability margin at high frequencies. Thus, we can expect to get good control performance by

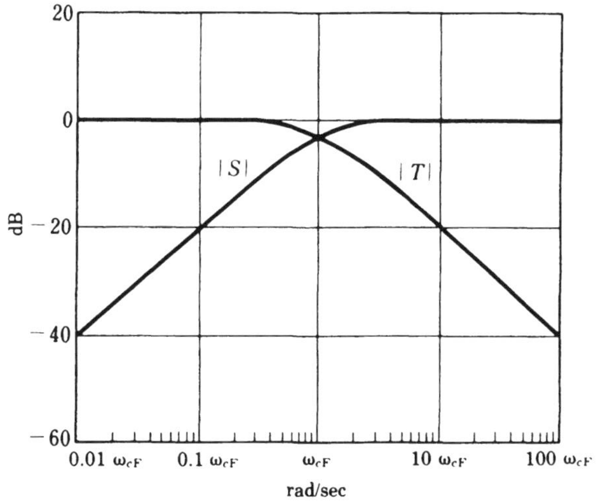

Figure 6.17
$|S|$ and $|T|$ for force-control loop.

adjusting the parameters w_{cP} and w_{cF}. Finally, by modifying only the feedforward compensators C_{aP} and C_{bP}, we can produce some other desired overall transfer characteristics without changing the sensitivity and stability-margin properties. □

In many tasks requiring force control, it is sufficient to operate manipulators at low velocity. In such cases, we can neglect the terms $\boldsymbol{h}_N(\boldsymbol{q},\dot{\boldsymbol{q}})$, $\dot{\boldsymbol{E}}\boldsymbol{J}_r\dot{\boldsymbol{q}}$, and $\dot{\boldsymbol{J}}_r\dot{\boldsymbol{q}}$ in equation 6.68 and 6.69 and develop the approximate linearizing control law

$$\boldsymbol{\tau}_c = \boldsymbol{M}(\boldsymbol{q})\boldsymbol{J}_r^{+}\boldsymbol{E}^{-1}\begin{bmatrix}\boldsymbol{u}_1\\ \boldsymbol{0}\end{bmatrix} - \boldsymbol{J}_r^{T}\boldsymbol{E}_{\mathrm{F}}^{T}\boldsymbol{u}_2. \tag{6.75}$$

This control law and a servo compensator like that given by equations 6.74 constitute a simplified hybrid controller.

Exercises

6.1 Determine a set of m_d, k_d, and d_d when the specification is

$5 \leqq d_c \leqq 10,$

$500 \leqq k_c \leqq 2500$

instead of equations 6.12 and 6.13.

6.2 Find a control law for the parallel-drive manipulator in subsection 3.3.3 when the desired mechanical impedance is given by equation 6.31.

6.3 Find a constraint frame for the task of polishing a sphere with a whetstone (figure 6.18). Determine the natural and artificial constraints.

6.4 Consider the two-link manipulator shown in figure 6.19. Both link lengths are 1. Give a detailed computational expression for each block of figure 6.9 for the task of moving the manipulator to follow the flat surface at an inclination of 45°. Assume that position sensors measure the joint angles θ_1 and θ_2, and that a force sensor measures the contact-force components in the X_H and Y_H directions of the hand coordinate frame $\Sigma_H(O_H - X_H Y_H)$. Assume also that $\boldsymbol{K}_{\mathrm{Pp}} = k_{\mathrm{Pp}}\mathbf{I}_2$, $\boldsymbol{K}_{\mathrm{Pd}} = k_{\mathrm{Pd}}\mathbf{I}_2$, and $\boldsymbol{K}_{\mathrm{Fi}} = k_{\mathrm{Fi}}\mathbf{I}_2$.

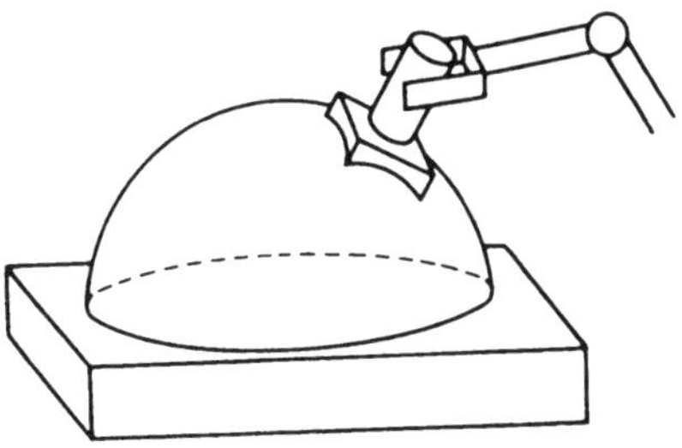

Figure 6.18
Polishing with a whetstone.

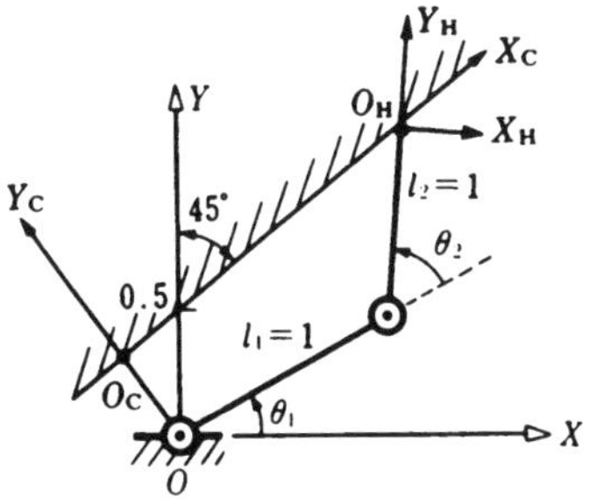

Figure 6.19
Hybrid control of two-link manipulator.

6.5 Find a set of constraint hypersurfaces for the task of turning a crank in example 6.4. A simple expression results from the use of the reference frame $\Sigma_0(O_0 - X_0 Y_0 Z_0)$ with its origin O_0 on the crank axis and its Z_0 axis parallel to the crank axis.

6.6 Find a set of constraint hypersurfaces for the task of turning a nut on a bolt (figure 6.20).

6.7 Consider the case, shown in figure 6.21, where the position of the end effector is constrained to an arbitrary smooth surface with its approach vector normal to the surface. Assume that the surface is described by $y = u(x,z)$, where $u(x,z)$ is a single-valued function that is differentiable three times. Find $\boldsymbol{E}_F$ and $\boldsymbol{E}_P$.

6.8 Consider a case of dynamic hybrid control where the constraint hypersurfaces change with time and are described by

$$p_i(\boldsymbol{r},t) = 0, \quad i = 1,2,\ldots,m$$

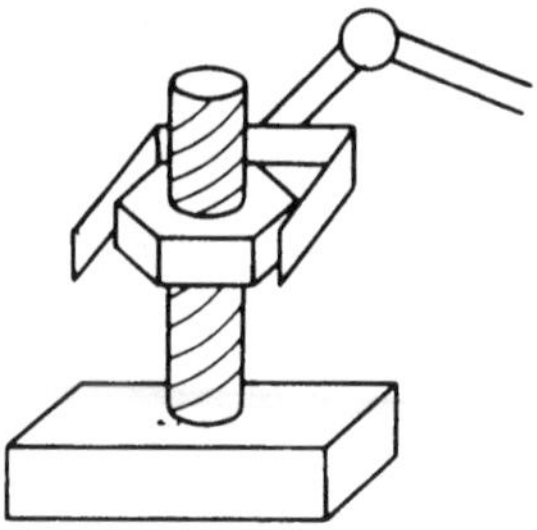

Figure 6.20
Turning a nut on a bolt.

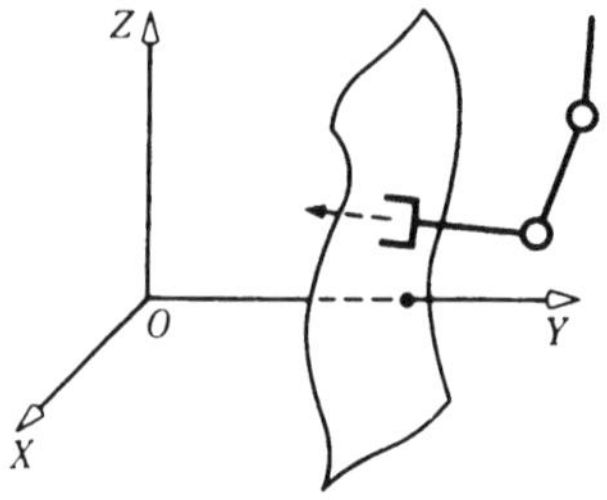

Figure 6.21
Constraint by an arbitrary surface.

instead of equation 6.41. What modification is necessary to the argument in (1)–(3) of subsection 6.2.2 to obtain a linearized system like that of equation 6.71?

References

1. D. E. Whitney, "Historical Perspective and State of the Art in Robot Force Control," in Proceedings of the 1985 IEEE International Conference on Robotics and Automation, pp. 262–268.

2. N. Hogan, "Impedance Control: An Approach to Manipulation, Parts I–III," *ASME Journal of Dynamic Systems, Measurement, and Control* 107, no. 1 (1985): 1–24.

3. J. K. Salisbury, "Active Stiffness Control of a Manipulator in Cartesian Coordinates," in Proceedings of the 19th IEEE Conference on Decision and Control (1980), pp. 95–100.

4. M. H. Raibert and J. J. Craig, "Hybrid Position/Force Control of Manipulators," *ASME Journal of Dynamic Systems, Measurement, and Control* 103, no. 2 (1981): 126–133.

5. D. E. Whitney, "Quasi-Static Assembly of Compliantly Supported Rigid Parts," *ASME Journal of Dynamic Systems, Measurement, and Control* 104, no. 1 (1982): 65–77.

6. M. T. Mason, "Compliance and Force Control for Computer Controlled Manipulators," *IEEE Transactions on Systems, Man, and Cybernetics* 11, no. 6 (1981): 418–432.

7. T. Yoshikawa, "Dynamic Hybrid Position/Force Control of Robot Manipulators—Description of Hand Constraints and Calculation of Joint Driving Force," *IEEE Journal of Robotics and Automation* 3, no. 5 (1987): 386–392.

8. T. Yoshikawa, T. Sugie, and M. Tanaka, "Dynamic Hybrid Control of Robot Manipulators—Controller Design and Experiment," *IEEE Journal of Robotics and Automation* 4, no. 6 (1988): 699–705.

7 Control of Redundant Manipulators

A manipulator is said to have redundancy if it has more degrees of freedom than are necessary to perform a given task. In this chapter, after a discussion about the advantages and disadvantages of redundant manipulators, a method of actively utilizing such redundancy will be given. This method will be applied to avoiding obstacles and avoiding singular configurations, and a numerical calculation method that is effective in the above approach will be described.

7.1 Redundant Manipulators

A human arm can be considered to have seven degrees of freedom. A hand requires a total of six degrees of freedom (three to hold an object at a certain position in space, and three more to orient it); therefore, the human arm has one redundant degree of freedom for this fundamental task of positioning and orienting the grasped object. This explains why we can move the elbow freely while grasping an object steadily in a certain position and orientation. This excess degree of freedom is the redundancy, and it gives the human arm great versatility and broad applicability.

The same argument applies to manipulators. Since six degrees of freedom are enough for full position and orientation control of an end effector, a manipulator with seven degrees of freedom can be said to be redundant. Even manipulators with six or fewer degrees of freedom are often regarded to have redundancy because the particular task to be performed requires fewer degrees of freedom than the manipulator has available. This is one of the main reasons why we need to consider the issue of redundancy.

What are the advantages of redundant manipulators? Generally sepaking, as in the case of the human arm, they excel in versatility and applicability. More specifically, they have the potential to avoid singularities, avoid obstacles, avoid structual limitations (e.g., angle limits of a rotational joint), carry out reasonable actions (e.g., low-energy-consuming motion, balanced motion among individual joint velocities, balanced configuration among joint driving forces), reach behind an object, crawl into concaves, and so on. Redundancy can also be used to make a manipulator more reliable in the sense that it can perform certain tasks even after a failure of some joints. This is important in certain application fields, such as space and the deep sea.

Of course, redundant manipulators have disadvantages too. They have more joints and actuators. Their structure is more complex, bulkier, and heavier. More complicated control algorithms are required, so the amount of necessary computation increases. Redundant manipulators will not be truly beneficial unless these disadvantages are offset by some advantages.

7.2 Task-Decomposition Approach

7.2.1 Decomposing a Task into Subtasks with Priority Order[1,2]

Most complicated tasks given to a manipulator can be formulated in such a way that the task is broken down into several subtasks with a priority order. Each subtask is performed using the degrees of freedom that remain after all the subtasks with higher priority have been implemented. A welding task, for instance, might be broken down into hand-position control and hand-orientation control, with hand positioning given first priority. A task of tracking a trajectory through a workspace with obstacles might be decomposed into controlling the position and orientation of the hand and avoiding obstacles, with the former given first priority. It is obvious that control problems of redundant manipulators can be approached via the subtask method by regarding a task to be done by a redundant manipulator as the subtask with first priority and regarding the reason for using the redundancy (singularity avoidance, joint limit avoidance, etc.) as the subtask with second priority.

We assume that each subtask is given in the form of either a desired trajectory of variables suitable for describing the subtask, or a certain criterion. The first form is suitable when the operator can give a trajectory that achieves the given subtask. The second form is used when the operator does not know the actual desired trajectory but knows how to evaluate the trajectory; for example, when the subtask is to keep the manipulator configuration away from singularities or to keep the joint angles within their limits, the configuration is evaluated using a criterion.

For ease of explanation, the discussion will be limited to simple cases in which the task is broken down into two subtasks and the first subtask is given in the form of a desired trajectory.

7.2.2 Basic Equations

Consider a manipulator with n degrees of freedom. The joint variable of the ith joint is q_i ($i = 1,2,\ldots,n$). The manipulator configuration is denoted by the vector $\boldsymbol{q} = [q_1,q_2,\ldots,q_n]^T$.

Assume that the first subtask can be described properly by an m_1-dimensional vector, $\boldsymbol{y}_1$, which is a function of $\boldsymbol{q}$:

$$\boldsymbol{y}_1 = \boldsymbol{f}_1(\boldsymbol{q}). \tag{7.1}$$

Assume also that the desired trajectory for $\boldsymbol{y}_1$ is given: $\boldsymbol{y}_{1\mathrm{d}}(t)$ ($0 \leqq t \leqq t_\mathrm{f}$; t_f is a terminal time). A vector (such as $\boldsymbol{y}_1$) which is suitable for describing a manipulation task is called a *manipulation vector*.

For the second subtask, consider the following two cases:

Case 1 An m_2-dimensional manipulation vector $\boldsymbol{y}_2$ is given by

$$\boldsymbol{y}_2 = \boldsymbol{f}_2(\boldsymbol{q}), \tag{7.2}$$

and the second subtask is specified by the desired trajectory $\boldsymbol{y}_{2\mathrm{d}}(t)$ ($0 \leqq t \leqq t_\mathrm{f}$) for $\boldsymbol{y}_2$.

Case 2 A criterion function

$$p = V(\boldsymbol{q}) \tag{7.3}$$

is given, and the second subtask is to keep this criterion as large as possible.

The problem we consider is first to obtain the joint velocity that achieves the first subtask of realizing $\boldsymbol{y}_1 = \boldsymbol{y}_{1\mathrm{d}}$ and then, if there is any ability left, to perform as much of the second subtask as possible at each time instant. The dynamics of the manipulator are not considered; that is, the problem is treated as purely kinematic. It is possible to formulate the problem in both case 1 and case 2 as an instantaneous optimal control problem in a mathematically more rigorous way, as we will do in subsection 7.2.5; however, we will first solve the problem in a rather heuristic way.

The general solution of the joint velocity that performs the first subtask will be given. Differentiating equation 7.1 with respect to time yields

$$\dot{\boldsymbol{y}}_1 = \boldsymbol{J}_1 \dot{\boldsymbol{q}}, \tag{7.4}$$

where $\boldsymbol{J}_j = d\boldsymbol{f}_j(\boldsymbol{q})/d\boldsymbol{q}^T$ ($j = 1, 2$) is the Jacobian matrix of $\boldsymbol{y}_j$ with respect to $\boldsymbol{q}$. When the desired trajectory $\boldsymbol{y}_{1\mathrm{d}}$ is given, from equation A2.22 in appendix 2, the general solution for $\dot{\boldsymbol{q}}$ of equation 7.4 is

$$\dot{\boldsymbol{q}} = \boldsymbol{J}_1^{+} \dot{\boldsymbol{y}}_{1\mathrm{d}} + (\mathbf{I} - \boldsymbol{J}_1^{+} \boldsymbol{J}_1)\boldsymbol{k}_1, \tag{7.5}$$

where $\boldsymbol{k}_1$ is an n-dimensional arbitrary constant vector.[3] The first term on the right-hand side of equation 7.5 is the joint velocity to achieve the desired trajectory, $\boldsymbol{y}_{1\mathrm{d}}(t)$. When there are multiple solutions for $\dot{\boldsymbol{q}}$ satisfying equation 7.4, this term gives a solution that minimizes $\|\dot{\boldsymbol{q}}\|$, the Euclidean norm of $\dot{\boldsymbol{q}}$. Also, even when there is no solution that satisfies equation 7.4, this term provides an approximate solution that minimizes the norm $\|\dot{\boldsymbol{y}}_{1\mathrm{d}} - \boldsymbol{J}_1\dot{\boldsymbol{q}}\|$, which is a kind of measure for approximation error. The second term on the right-hand side of equation 7.5 represents the redundancy left after performing the first subtask. Equation 7.5 is the basic equation for using a redundancy.

7.2.3 Second Subtask Given by Desired Trajectory

In this subsection we will consider case 1, where the second subtask is specified by the desired trajectory $\boldsymbol{y}_{2\mathrm{d}}(t)$ of the manipulation variable $\boldsymbol{y}_2$. What we have to do is select $\boldsymbol{k}_1$ in equation 7.5 so as to realize $\boldsymbol{y}_{2\mathrm{d}}$ as closely as possible. Differentiating equation 7.2, we have

$$\dot{\boldsymbol{y}}_2 = \boldsymbol{J}_2\dot{\boldsymbol{q}}. \tag{7.6}$$

Substituting $\dot{\boldsymbol{y}}_2 = \dot{\boldsymbol{y}}_{2\mathrm{d}}$ and equation 7.5 into 7.6, we obtain

$$\dot{\boldsymbol{y}}_{2\mathrm{d}} - \boldsymbol{J}_2\boldsymbol{J}_1^+\dot{\boldsymbol{y}}_{1\mathrm{d}} = \boldsymbol{J}_2(\mathbf{I} - \boldsymbol{J}_1^+\boldsymbol{J}_1)\boldsymbol{k}_1. \tag{7.7}$$

Letting $\tilde{\boldsymbol{J}}_2 = \boldsymbol{J}_2(\mathbf{I} - \boldsymbol{J}_1^+\boldsymbol{J}_1)$ and using equation A2.22, we obtain from equation 7.7

$$\boldsymbol{k}_1 = \tilde{\boldsymbol{J}}_2^+(\dot{\boldsymbol{y}}_{2\mathrm{d}} - \boldsymbol{J}_2\boldsymbol{J}_1^+\dot{\boldsymbol{y}}_{1\mathrm{d}}) + (\mathbf{I} - \tilde{\boldsymbol{J}}_2^+\tilde{\boldsymbol{J}}_2)\boldsymbol{k}_2, \tag{7.8}$$

where $\boldsymbol{k}_2$ is an n-dimensional arbitrary constant vector. Note that the relation

$$(\mathbf{I} - \boldsymbol{J}_1^+\boldsymbol{J}_1)\tilde{\boldsymbol{J}}_2^+ = \tilde{\boldsymbol{J}}_2^+ \tag{7.9}$$

holds (see ref. 4 and exercise 7.1). Therefore, from equations 7.5, 7.8, and 7.9,

$$\dot{\boldsymbol{q}}_{\mathrm{d}} = \boldsymbol{J}_1^+\dot{\boldsymbol{y}}_{1\mathrm{d}} + \tilde{\boldsymbol{J}}_2^+(\dot{\boldsymbol{y}}_{2\mathrm{d}} - \boldsymbol{J}_2\boldsymbol{J}_1^+\dot{\boldsymbol{y}}_{1\mathrm{d}}) + (\mathbf{I} - \boldsymbol{J}_1^+\boldsymbol{J}_1 - \tilde{\boldsymbol{J}}_2^+\tilde{\boldsymbol{J}}_2)\boldsymbol{k}_2 \tag{7.10a}$$

is the desired joint velocity that first realizes trajectory $\boldsymbol{y}_{1\mathrm{d}}$ and then realizes $\boldsymbol{y}_{2\mathrm{d}}$ as closely as possible using the remaining redundancy.

If $(\mathbf{I} - \boldsymbol{J}_1^+\boldsymbol{J}_1 - \tilde{\boldsymbol{J}}_2^+\tilde{\boldsymbol{J}}_2)$ is not zero, then some further redundancy is still left to perform a third subtask. When $\boldsymbol{y}_2 = \boldsymbol{q}$ (that is, when the second subtask provides the desired trajectory of the whole arm configuration), since $\boldsymbol{J}_2 = \mathbf{I}$ we have

$$\tilde{\boldsymbol{J}}_2^+ = (\mathbf{I} - \boldsymbol{J}_1^+\boldsymbol{J}_1)^+ = (\mathbf{I} - \boldsymbol{J}_1^+\boldsymbol{J}_1).$$

Hence, equation 7.10a simplifies to

$$\dot{q}_d = J_1^+ \dot{y}_{1d} + (\mathbf{I} - J_1^+ J_1)\dot{y}_{2d}, \tag{7.10b}$$

in which the term with k_2 disappears.

When the servo loop of each joint axis functions perfectly to produce the desired joint velocity, $y_{1d}(t)$ is followed exactly. Some deviation often occurs, however, between the desired subtask trajectory $y_{2d}(t)$ and the actually realized trajectory $y_2(t)$, because of the insufficient number of remaining degrees of freedom. One way to cope with such a situation is to modify the desired velocity $\dot{y}_{2d}$ to take the deviation into consideration. For example, we can define the modified velocity $\dot{y}_{2d}^*$ by

$$\dot{y}_{2d}^* = \dot{y}_{2d} + H_2(y_{2d} - y_2), \tag{7.11}$$

where H_2 is an appropriate diagonal gain matrix, and then replace $\dot{y}_{2d}$ in equation 7.10a or 7.10b with $\dot{y}_{2d}^*$.

7.2.4 Second Subtask Given by Criterion Function

In this subsection we will consider case 2, where the second subtask is specified by a criterion function. As in case 1, we select the value k_1 in equation 7.5 so as to make the criterion p given by equation 7.3 as large as possible. One natural approach is to determine k_1 by the following equations (ref. 3):

$$k_1 = \xi k_p, \tag{7.12}$$

$$\xi = [\xi_1, \xi_2, \ldots, \xi_n]^T, \tag{7.13}$$

$$\xi_l = \partial V(q)/\partial q_l, \tag{7.14}$$

where k_p is an appropriate positive constant. The desired joint velocity, $\dot{q}_d$, is given by

$$\dot{q}_d = J_1^+ \dot{y}_{1d} + (\mathbf{I} - J_1^+ J_1)\xi k_p. \tag{7.15}$$

Hence, we have

$$\dot{p} = \xi^T J_1^+ \dot{y}_{1d} + \xi^T(\mathbf{I} - J_1^+ J_1)\xi k_p. \tag{7.16}$$

Since $(\mathbf{I} - J_1^+ J_1)$ is nonnegative definite, the second term on the right-hand side of equation 7.16 is always nonnegative, causing the value of criterion p to increase.[5]

Mathematically, the vector $\boldsymbol{k}_1$ of equation 7.12 is the steepest gradient vector of the function $V(\boldsymbol{q})$; the vector $(\mathbf{I} - \boldsymbol{J}_1^+\boldsymbol{J}_1)\xi k_p$ corresponds to the orthogonal projection of $\boldsymbol{k}_1$ on the null space of $\boldsymbol{J}_1$. The constant k_p is chosen so as to make p increase as quickly as possible under the condition that $\dot{\boldsymbol{q}}_d$ does not become excessively large.

7.2.5 Formulation as Instantaneous Optimization Problem

The problem formulation in subsection 7.2.2 and the solutions in subsections 7.2.3 and 7.2.4 are rather intuitive. In this subsection it is shown that these results can be obtained as the rigorous solutions to some instantaneous optimization problems by adopting an appropriate criterion function for the second subtask.

For case 1, let the criterion function for the second subtask be

$$p_1 = \|\dot{\boldsymbol{y}}_{2d} - \dot{\boldsymbol{y}}_2 + \boldsymbol{H}_2(\boldsymbol{y}_{2d} - \boldsymbol{y}_2)\|. \tag{7.17}$$

The optimal solution, which minimizes equation 7.17 at each time instant under the constraint 7.5, is given by equations 7.10a and 7.11.

For case 2, using the original criterion $V(\boldsymbol{q})$ of equation 7.3, let the criterion function for the second subtask be

$$p_2 = k_p \frac{dV(\boldsymbol{q})}{dt} - \tfrac{1}{2}\|\dot{\boldsymbol{q}} - \boldsymbol{J}_1^+\dot{\boldsymbol{y}}_{1d}\|^2. \tag{7.18}$$

The optimal solution maximizing equation 7.18 at each time instant under the constraint 7.5 is given by equation 7.15. The first term of equation 7.18 attempts to increase the original criterion; the second term tries to minimize the difference between $\dot{\boldsymbol{q}}$ and the minimal norm solution $\boldsymbol{J}_1^+\dot{\boldsymbol{y}}_{1d}$ of the first subtask. The coefficient k_p represents the weight of importance of the first effort compared to the second effort.

7.3 Application to Avoiding Obstacles and Singularities

7.3.1 Avoiding Obstacles

Consider the three-link manipulator shown in figure 7.1, which moves in the $X-Y$ plane. The required task is to make the end effector follow a desired trajectory while avoiding collisions with the obstacle shown as the hatched area in the figure. We will solve this problem of avoiding the obstacle as an example of case 1 (see ref. 2).

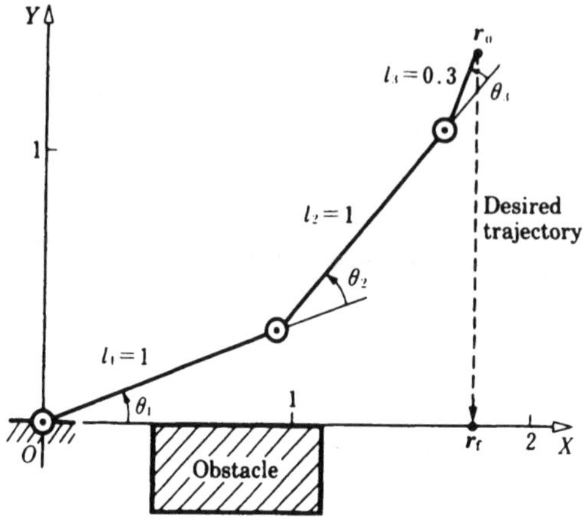

Figure 7.1
Three-link manipulator.

The link lengths are $l_1 = l_2 = 1$ and $l_3 = 0.3$, and there is no hardware limit on the rotation of any joint. At the beginning of the task, the initial configuration at time $t = 0$ is given by

$$q_0 = [20°, 30°, 20°]^T,$$

which corresponds to

$$r_0 = [x_0, y_0]^T \cong [1.69, 1.39]^T.$$

The end effector is required to move from initial position r_0 to final position $r_f = [x_0, 0]^T$ by time $t = 1$, along a straight line parallel to the Y axis. At the same time, the manipulator should avoid colliding with the hatched obstacle zone. This task is divided into a first subtask (moving along the desired trajectory) and a second subtask (avoiding the obstacle).

For the manipulation variable y_1 of the first subtask, we use the end-effector position r:

$$y_1 = \begin{bmatrix} l_1 C_1 + l_2 C_{12} + l_3 C_{123} \\ l_1 S_1 + l_2 S_{12} + l_3 S_{123} \end{bmatrix}. \tag{7.19}$$

Hence, the Jacobian matrix J_1 is given by

$$J_1 = \begin{bmatrix} -l_1 S_1 - l_2 S_{12} - l_3 S_{123} & -l_2 S_{12} - l_3 S_{123} & -l_3 S_{123} \\ l_1 C_1 + l_2 C_{12} + l_3 C_{123} & l_2 C_{12} + l_3 C_{123} & l_3 C_{123} \end{bmatrix}. \tag{7.20}$$

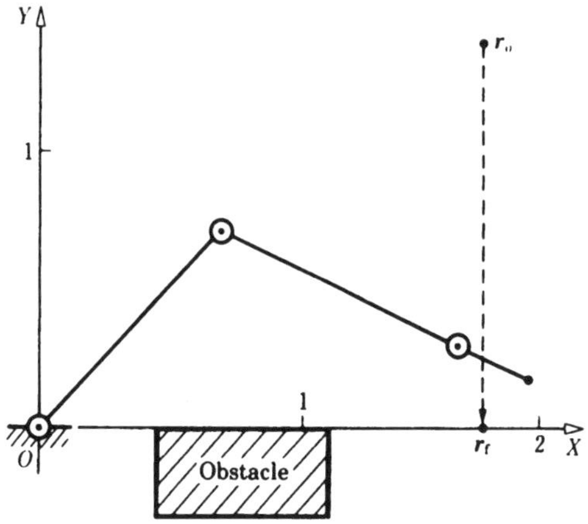

Figure 7.2
Obstacle and reference configuration taught for obstacle avoidance.

If we choose the desired trajectory using equation 5.7, then we have

$$y_{1d}(t) = \begin{bmatrix} x_0 \\ y_0 - (3 - 2t)t^2 y_0 \end{bmatrix}, \quad 0 \leqq t \leqq 1. \tag{7.21}$$

For the second subtask, we assume that a constant reference arm configuration, suitable for obstacle avoidance, has already been taught (say, by a human operator). Hence, the second subtask can be specified as trying to come as close to this configuration as possible. This means that the manipulation variable $\boldsymbol{y}_2$ for the second subtask is given by the joint vector $\boldsymbol{q}$. We assume that the reference arm configuration that plays the role of the desired trajectory for the second subtask has been given as

$$y_{2d} = \begin{bmatrix} 45^\circ \\ -70^\circ \\ 0^\circ \end{bmatrix}. \tag{7.22}$$

This reference configuration for collision avoidance is shown in figure 7.2.

Now that we have defined our terms, from equations 7.10b and 7.11 the desired joint velocity $\dot{\boldsymbol{q}}_d$ is given by

$$\dot{\boldsymbol{q}}_d = \boldsymbol{J}_1^+ \begin{bmatrix} 0 \\ -6(1 - t)ty_0 \end{bmatrix} + (\mathbf{I}_3 - \boldsymbol{J}_1^+ \boldsymbol{J}_1)\boldsymbol{H}_2(\boldsymbol{y}_{2d} - \boldsymbol{y}_2). \tag{7.23}$$

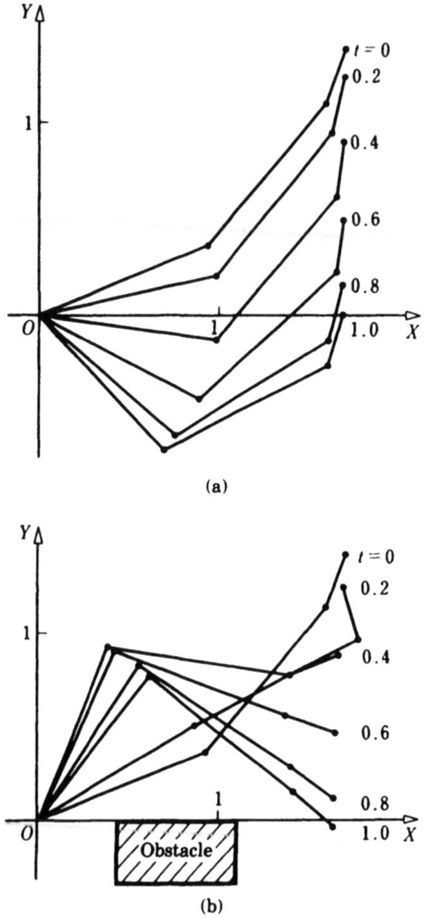

Figure 7.3
Simulation of obstacle avoidance. (a) Without using redundancy ($\boldsymbol{H}_2 = \mathbf{0}$). (b) Using redundancy ($\boldsymbol{H}_2 = 0.2\mathbf{I}_2$).

(The second term on the right hand side of this equation is needed because of the inconsistency between y_{2d} and $y_{1d}(t)$.)

The simulation results shown in figure 7.3 were obtained by assuming that the desired joint velocity of equation 7.23 occurs perfectly. Figure 7.3a depicts the case when $\boldsymbol{H}_2 = \mathbf{0}$, so $\dot{\boldsymbol{q}}$ has been chosen to minimize $\|\dot{\boldsymbol{q}}\|$, ignoring the obstacle avoidance. Figure 7.3b depicts the case when $\boldsymbol{H}_2 = 0.2\boldsymbol{I}_2$ (that is, when the redundancy is utilized). It is clear from the figure that collision with the obstacle has been avoided by the use of redundancy in the simulated case.

The above example treated a very simple obstacle. This approach to avoiding obstacles could also be adopted to cope with more complicated obstacles or time-varying obstacles by using several reference configurations taught beforehand and switching them in turn.

Another approach is to define a criterion function to express the proximity between the manipulator and obstacles[6] and to make it the criterion for the second subtask (ref. 2). This approach does not need any reference configuration, although it requires detailed information about the obstacles and a large amount of calculation.

7.3.2 Avoiding Singularities

As an example of case 2, where the second subtask is specified by a criterion function, let us consider the problem of making the end effector track a desired trajectory while avoiding singular configurations as much as possible (ref. 5).

A manipulator generally has certain configurations in which it can no longer move its end effector to change position or orientation in certain directions. These configurations are called singular configurations, as was discussed in subsection 2.5.6. It is undesirable not only for a manipulator to fall into such a singular configuration but also for it even to come close to one. Some joint velocities would become excessively large trying to maintain the desired trajectory. The manipulability measure was discussed in section 4.2 as a quantitative measure of the capability of a manipulator to move its end effector freely in any direction. This measure can also be regarded as an index of the distance from singular configurations. Hence, the manipulability measure can be used as the criterion when the second subtask is the avoidance of singularities.

Consider the same three-link manipulator as in the preceding subsection. The end-effector position $\boldsymbol{r}$ is again taken as the first manipulation variable,

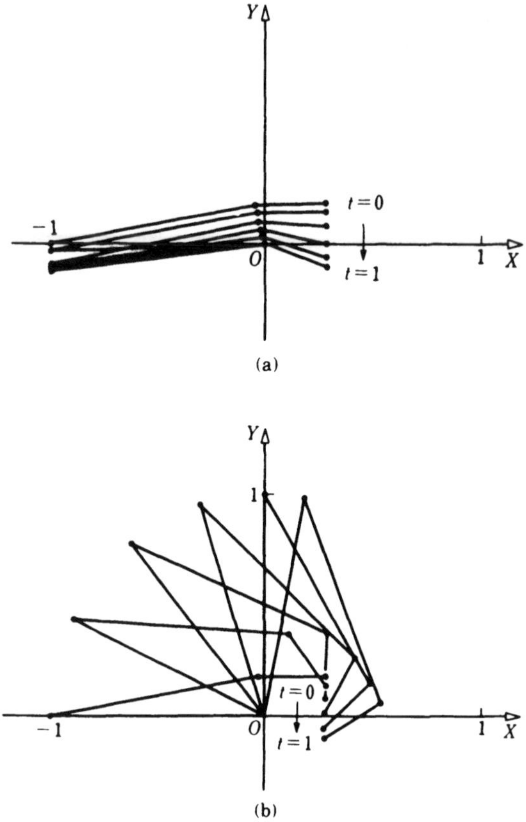

Figure 7.4
Simulation of singularity avoidance. (a) Without using redundancy ($k_p = 0$). (b) Using redundancy ($k_p = 20$).

y_1. The manipulability measure for $\boldsymbol{r}$ is taken as the criterion for the second subtask. Hence, using equation 4.8 and the Jacobian matrix $\boldsymbol{J}_1$ of equation 7.20, we have

$$V(\boldsymbol{q}) = \sqrt{\det \boldsymbol{J}_1 \boldsymbol{J}_1^T}.$$

Therefore, ξ_l of equation 7.14 is given by

$$\xi_l = \tfrac{1}{2}\sqrt{\det \boldsymbol{J}_1 \boldsymbol{J}_1^T} \sum_{i,j=1}^{2} q_{ij}(\boldsymbol{J}_{1il}\boldsymbol{J}_{1j}^T + \boldsymbol{J}_{1jl}\boldsymbol{J}_{1i}^T), \quad l = 1,2,3 \tag{7.24}$$

where q_{ij} is the (i,j) element of the inverse matrix of $(\boldsymbol{J}_1 \boldsymbol{J}_1^T)$, $\boldsymbol{J}_{1i}$ is the ith row vector of $\boldsymbol{J}_1$, and $\boldsymbol{J}_{1il}$ is the partial differential coefficient of $\boldsymbol{J}_{1i}$ with respect to θ_l. The vector $\boldsymbol{\xi}$ in equation 7.15 is obtained from equation 7.24.

Some results of computer simulation are shown in figure 7.4. The initial configuration is $\boldsymbol{q}_0 = [180°, 170°, -10°]^T$, which corresponds to the end-effector position $\boldsymbol{r}_0 = [x_0, y_0]^T = [0.28, 0.17]^T$. The desired trajectory is given by

$$y_{1d}(t) = \begin{bmatrix} x_0 \\ y_0 - (3 - 2t)t^2(y_0 + 0.1) \end{bmatrix}, \quad 0 \leqq t \leqq 1 \tag{7.25}$$

which is a straight line parallel to the Y axis going from $\boldsymbol{r}_0$ to the final position $\boldsymbol{r}_f = [x_0, -0.1]^T$. Equation 7.25 is, again, obtained from equation 5.7. Figure 7.4a shows the change of arm configuration for the case of $k_p = 0$ in equation 7.15; that is, the case where the simple pseudo-inverse control law is applied and no attempt is made to avoid singularity. Figure 7.4b is for the case where $k_p = 20$; the singularity is avoided by trying to keep the manipulability measure large. Figure 7.5 shows the change of manipula-

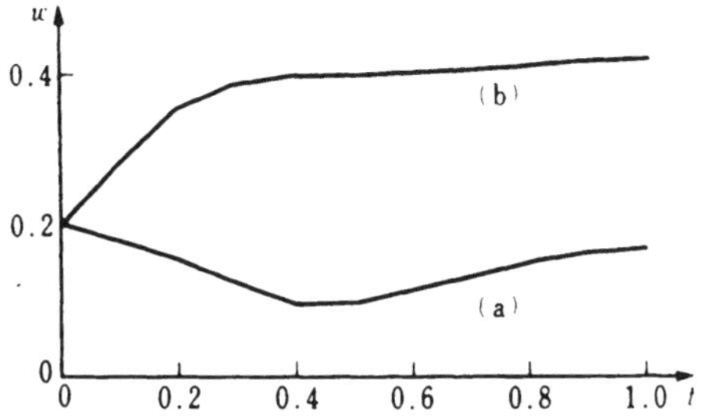

Figure 7.5
Trajectories of manipulability measure. (a) Without using redundancy ($k_p = 0$). (b) Using redundancy ($k_p = 20$).

bility measure in cases a and b of figure 7.4. As can be seen from the figure, the utilization of redundancy is quite effective in avoiding singularity.

7.4 Computational Method for Desired Joint Velocity

One of the difficulties in applying the method described above is the large amount of computation needed for obtaining the pseudo-inverse matrix. In this section, we will develop an efficient computational method for obtaining $\dot{\boldsymbol{q}}$ satisfying

$$\dot{\boldsymbol{q}} = \boldsymbol{J}^+ \dot{\boldsymbol{y}}_d + (\mathbf{I} - \boldsymbol{J}^+ \boldsymbol{J})\boldsymbol{k}, \tag{7.26}$$

which corresponds to equation 7.5, for given values of $\boldsymbol{J}$, $\dot{\boldsymbol{y}}_d$, and $\boldsymbol{k}$.

If the matrix $(\boldsymbol{J}\boldsymbol{J}^T)$ is nonsingular, $\dot{\boldsymbol{q}}$ can be obtained by the following procedure[7]: First, obtain the solution $\boldsymbol{\alpha}$ of

$$(\boldsymbol{J}\boldsymbol{J}^T)\boldsymbol{\alpha} = \dot{\boldsymbol{y}}_d - \boldsymbol{J}\boldsymbol{k} \tag{7.27}$$

by an appropriate method for solving linear algebraic equations, such as Gauss elimination. Then, calculate $\dot{\boldsymbol{q}}$ by

$$\dot{\boldsymbol{q}} = \boldsymbol{J}^T\boldsymbol{\alpha} + \boldsymbol{k}. \tag{7.28}$$

It is easy to check that $\dot{\boldsymbol{q}}$ calculated this way is equal to $\dot{\boldsymbol{q}}$ given by equation 7.26, since $\boldsymbol{J}^+ = \boldsymbol{J}^T(\boldsymbol{J}\boldsymbol{J}^T)^{-1}$.

At singular configurations, however, $(\boldsymbol{J}\boldsymbol{J}^T)$ becomes singular and the solution $\dot{\boldsymbol{q}}$ to equation 7.26 is not necessarily continuous with respect to the elements of $\boldsymbol{J}$. Because of the relationship of $\dot{\boldsymbol{q}}$ to $\boldsymbol{q}$ through $\boldsymbol{J}$, $\dot{\boldsymbol{q}}$ is also not necessarily continuous with respect to $\boldsymbol{q}$. One way to cope with this problem is to apply regularization, so that $(\boldsymbol{J}\boldsymbol{J}^T)$ is replaced by $(\boldsymbol{J}\boldsymbol{J}^T + k_s\mathbf{I})$ near singularities.[8] Thus, in place of equation 7.27 we use

$$(\boldsymbol{J}\boldsymbol{J}^T + k_s\mathbf{I})\boldsymbol{\alpha} = \dot{\boldsymbol{y}}_d - \boldsymbol{J}\boldsymbol{k}, \tag{7.29}$$

where k_s is a scalar continuous function of $\boldsymbol{q}$ that is positive near singularities and zero for other $\boldsymbol{q}$. For example, using the manipulability measure $w = \sqrt{\det \boldsymbol{J}\boldsymbol{J}^T}$, k_s can be assigned to be

$$k_s = \begin{cases} k_0(1 - w/w_0)^2, & w < w_0 \\ 0, & w \geqq w_0 \end{cases} \tag{7.30}$$

where k_0 and w_0 are appropriate positive constants. The parameter k_0

specifies the magnitude of regularization, and w_0 represents the threshold separating the vicinity of singularities from the other region.

Exercises

7.1 Show that the equality $B(CB)^+ = (CB)^+$ holds for any $n \times n$ symmetric and idempotent matrix B (i.e., $B^T = B$ and $BB = B$) and $m \times n$ matrix C (ref. 4). Using this relation, prove equation 7.9.

7.2 Show that the solution that minimizes equation 7.17 at each instant of time under the constraint 7.5 is given by equations 7.10a and 7.11.

7.3 Show that the solution that maximizes equation 7.18 at each instant of time under the constraint 7.5 is given by equation 7.15.

7.4 Calculate $\dot{\boldsymbol{q}}$ from equation 7.26 when

$$\boldsymbol{J} = \begin{bmatrix} 0 & 2 & 1 & 2 \\ 2 & 0 & 1 & 1 \\ 1 & 1 & 0 & 1 \end{bmatrix}, \quad \dot{\boldsymbol{y}}_d = \begin{bmatrix} 1 \\ 0 \\ 1 \end{bmatrix}, \quad \boldsymbol{k} = \begin{bmatrix} -1 \\ 0 \\ 1 \\ 1 \end{bmatrix}.$$

Also calculate the same value using equations 7.27 and 7.28.

7.5 Show that $\dot{\boldsymbol{q}}$ obtained from equation 7.28 using $\boldsymbol{\alpha}$ calculated from equation 7.29 is equal to $\dot{\boldsymbol{q}}$ minimizing

$$\|\boldsymbol{J}\dot{\boldsymbol{q}} - \dot{\boldsymbol{y}}_d\|^2 + k_s\|\dot{\boldsymbol{q}} - \boldsymbol{k}\|^2.$$

7.6 Decompose the task of writing letters on a sheet of paper with a ballpoint pen into several subtasks with priority order, and state the reasons for that decomposition. Do the same with the task of carrying a cup full of liquid.

7.7 Assume that the three-link manipulator shown in figure 7.1 has the following joint angle limits:

$$\theta_{i\,\mathrm{min}} \leqq \theta_i \leqq \theta_{i\,\mathrm{max}}, \quad i = 1,2,3.$$

Describe a formula for the desired joint velocity that makes the endpoint of the manipulator follow a given desired trajectory while keeping the joint angles within their limits as much as possible.

References

1. H. Hanafusa, T. Yoshikawa, and Y. Nakamura, "Analysis and Control of Articulated Robot Arms with Redundancy," in Proceedings of the 8th IFAC World Congress (1981), vol. XIV, pp. 78–83.

2. Y. Nakamura, H. Hanafusa, and T. Yoshikawa, "Task-Priority Based Redundancy Control of Robot Manipulators," *International Journal of Robotics Research* 6 (1987): 3–15.

3. A. Liégeois, "Automatic Supervisory Control of the Configuration and Behavior of Multibody Mechanisms," *IEEE Transactions on Systems, Man, and Cybernetics* 7, no. 12 (1977): 868–871.

4. A. A. Maciejewski and C. A. Klein, "Obstacle Avoidance for Kinematically Redundant Manipulators," *International Journal of Robotics Research* 4, no. 3 (1985): 109–117.

5. T. Yoshikawa, "Analysis and Control of Robot Manipulators with Redundancy," in *Robotics Research: The First International Symposium*, ed. M. Brady and R. Paul (MIT Press, 1984), pp. 735–747.

6. O. Khatib and J. F. LeMaitre, "Dynamic Control of Manipulators Operating in a Complex Environment," in Proceedings of the Third International CISM-IFToMM Symposium (1978), pp. 267–282.

7. C. A. Klein and C. H. Huang, "Review of Pseudoinverse Control for Use with Kinematically Redundant Manipulators," *IEEE Transactions on Systems, Man, and Cybernetics* 13, no. 3 (1983): 245–250.

8. Y. Nakamura and H. Hanafusa, "Inverse Kinematic Solutions with Singularity Robustness for Robot Manipulator Control," *ASME Journal of Dynamic Systems, Measurement, and Control* 108 (1986): 163–171.

Appendix 1 Function atan2

When we consider the problem of finding an angle θ for given consistent values of $\sin\theta$ and $\cos\theta$, it is obvious that there exists a unique solution in the region $-180° < \theta \leqq 180°$, or under a module of 360°. There has not, however, been a commonly used means for expressing this solution by a single function. Function atan2 provides such a means in the form of an extension of the function $\tan^{-1}\theta$. The name "atan2" comes from a subroutine name in computer programming languages that gives a unique solution of the arc tangent function.

Function atan2 is a scalar function of two scalar arguments defined by

$$\text{atan2}(a,b) = \arg(b + ja), \tag{A1.1}$$

where a and b are real numbers, j is the imaginary unit, and arg is the argument of a complex number (see figure A1.1). For notational convenience, we define atan2(0,0) to be indeterminate. Several properties and applications of this function are summarized in this appendix.

It is obvious that

$$\theta = \text{atan2}(\sin\theta, \cos\theta) \tag{A1.2}$$

and

$$\theta = \text{atan2}(k\sin\theta, k\cos\theta) \tag{A1.3}$$

for any positive scalar k.

It is also easy to show the following equalities:

$$\text{atan2}(-a,b) = -\text{atan2}(a,b), \tag{A1.4}$$

$$\tfrac{1}{2}\pi \pm \text{atan2}(a,b) = \text{atan2}(b, \mp a), \tag{A1.5}$$

$$\pi \pm \text{atan2}(a,b) = \pm\text{atan2}(-a, -b). \tag{A1.6}$$

For the differentiation of atan2, we have

$$\frac{\partial \text{atan2}(a,b)}{\partial a} = \frac{b}{a^2 + b^2}, \tag{A1.7a}$$

$$\frac{\partial \text{atan2}(a,b)}{\partial b} = \frac{-a}{a^2 + b^2}. \tag{A1.7b}$$

Hence, when a and b are differentiable functions of time t, we have

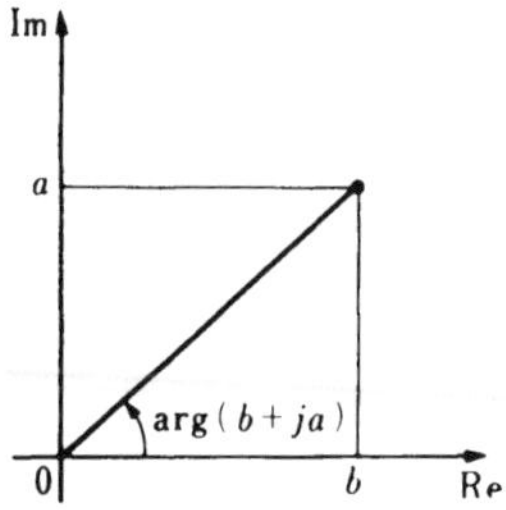

Figure A1.1
Argument of complex number.

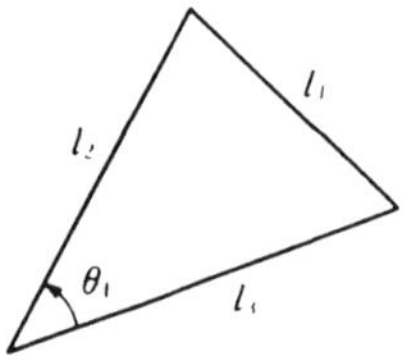

Figure A1.2
Cosine theorem.

$$\frac{d\mathrm{atan2}(a,b)}{dt} = \frac{\dot{a}b - a\dot{b}}{a^2 + b^2}, \quad \text{(A1.8)}$$

where $\dot{a} = da/dt$ and $\dot{b} = db/dt$.

As an application, the cosine theorem will be expressed using atan2. For the triangle shown in figure A1.2, assume that $l_1 \geqq 0$, $l_2 > 0$, and $l_3 > 0$. The cosine theorem tells us that

$$l_1{}^2 = l_2{}^2 + l_3{}^2 - 2l_2 l_3 \cos\theta_1. \quad \text{(A1.9)}$$

We let

$$\kappa = \sqrt{(l_1{}^2 + l_2{}^2 + l_3{}^2)^2 - 2(l_1{}^4 + l_2{}^4 + l_3{}^4)}, \quad \text{(A1.10)}$$

and then we have

$$2l_2 l_3 \sin\theta_1 = \pm\kappa.$$

Hence, we obtain from equation A1.3

$$\theta_1 = \pm\mathrm{atan2}(\kappa, l_2{}^2 + l_3{}^2 - l_1{}^2). \quad \text{(A1.11)}$$

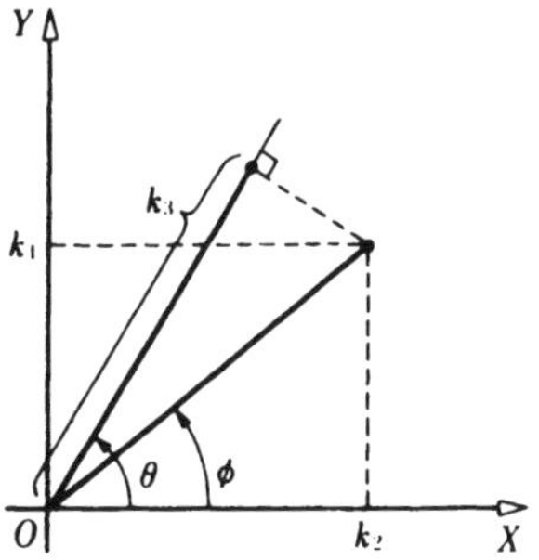

Figure A1.3
Geometric expression of $k_1\sin\theta + k_2\cos\theta = k_3$.

Although this expression has been derived under the assumption that $l_2 > 0$ and $l_3 > 0$, it is valid also for the case of $l_2 = 0$ or $l_3 = 0$ in the sense that θ_1 is indeterminate by the notational convention we have made. Note that the cosine theorem does not hold if the condition

$$(l_2 + l_3)^2 \geqq l_1{}^2 \geqq (l_2 - l_3)^2$$

is not satisfied.

As a second application, we derive the solution θ of

$$k_1\sin\theta + k_2\cos\theta = k_3, \tag{A1.12}$$

where k_1, k_2, and k_3 are known scalar constants satisfying $k_1{}^2 + k_2{}^2 \geqq k_3{}^2$. Geometrically, as shown in figure A1.3, the problem is to find angle θ between the X axis and a straight line such that k_3 is the distance between the origin and the foot of the normal drawn from point (k_1, k_2) to the straight line. Now we let

$$\phi = \text{atan2}(k_1, k_2). \tag{A1.13}$$

Since

$$k_3 = \sqrt{k_1{}^2 + k_2{}^2}\cos(\theta - \phi), \tag{A1.14}$$

we have

$$\sqrt{k_1{}^2 + k_2{}^2}\sin(\theta - \phi) = \pm\sqrt{k_1{}^2 + k_2{}^2 - k_3{}^2}. \tag{A1.15}$$

Thus, from equations A1.3, A1.14, and A1.15 we obtain

$$\theta - \phi = \pm\text{atan2}(\sqrt{k_1{}^2 + k_2{}^2 - k_3{}^2}, k_3). \tag{A1.16}$$

Therefore, the solution to equation A1.12 is given by

$$\theta = \operatorname{atan2}(k_1, k_2) \pm \operatorname{atan2}(\sqrt{k_1{}^2 + k_2{}^2 - k_3{}^2}, k_3). \tag{A1.17}$$

Function atan2 was first introduced into robotics by R. P. Paul in *Robot Manipulators: Mathematics, Programming, and Control* (MIT Press, 1981).

Appendix 2 Pseudo-Inverses

Inverses of matrices play an important role in linear algebra. They are particularly familiar as a means to express compactly the solution to a system of simultaneous linear equations. However, a matrix has an inverse only when it is square and nonsingular. The pseudo-inverse is a generalization of the inverse to the case of singular or even nonsquare matrices. In the field of robotics, pseudo-inverses are often used in the identification of manipulator dynamics and in the control of redundant manipulators. Although this appendix will deal only with matrices of real elements, the following arguments are also valid for matrices of complex elements with a little modification.

We start with the definition of the pseudo-inverse. For every finite $m \times n$ real matrix $\boldsymbol{A}$, there is a unique $n \times m$ real matrix $\boldsymbol{A}^+$ satisfying the following four conditions:

$$\boldsymbol{A}\boldsymbol{A}^+\boldsymbol{A} = \boldsymbol{A}, \tag{A2.1}$$

$$\boldsymbol{A}^+\boldsymbol{A}\boldsymbol{A}^+ = \boldsymbol{A}^+, \tag{A2.2}$$

$$(\boldsymbol{A}\boldsymbol{A}^+)^T = \boldsymbol{A}\boldsymbol{A}^+, \tag{A2.3}$$

$$(\boldsymbol{A}^+\boldsymbol{A})^T = \boldsymbol{A}^+\boldsymbol{A}. \tag{A2.4}$$

This $\boldsymbol{A}^+$ is called the *pseudo-inverse* of $\boldsymbol{A}$.

We first show the existence of $\boldsymbol{A}^+$ satisfying equations A2.1–A2.4. If $\boldsymbol{A} = \boldsymbol{0}$, then the obvious solution $\boldsymbol{A}^+ = \boldsymbol{0}$ satisfies these conditions. If we assume that $\boldsymbol{A} \neq \boldsymbol{0}$ and let $r = \operatorname{rank}\boldsymbol{A}$, then $\boldsymbol{A}$ can be expressed as the product of an $m \times r$ matrix $\boldsymbol{B}$ and an $r \times n$ matrix $\boldsymbol{C}$:

$$\boldsymbol{A} = \boldsymbol{B}\boldsymbol{C}. \tag{A2.5}$$

Using the above $\boldsymbol{B}$ and $\boldsymbol{C}$, we define an $n \times m$ matrix $\boldsymbol{D}$ by

$$\boldsymbol{D} = \boldsymbol{C}^T(\boldsymbol{C}\boldsymbol{C}^T)^{-1}(\boldsymbol{B}^T\boldsymbol{B})^{-1}\boldsymbol{B}^T. \tag{A2.6}$$

Then it is easy to show that $\boldsymbol{A}^+ = \boldsymbol{D}$ satisfies equations A2.1–A2.4. This completes the proof of the existence of $\boldsymbol{A}^+$.

Next we will show the uniqueness of $\boldsymbol{A}^+$. Let any two matrices satisfying equations A2.1–A2.4 be $\boldsymbol{A}_1{}^+$ and $\boldsymbol{A}_2{}^+$. Then

$$\begin{aligned}
\boldsymbol{A}_1{}^+ - \boldsymbol{A}_2{}^+ &= \boldsymbol{A}_1{}^+\boldsymbol{A}\boldsymbol{A}_1{}^+ - \boldsymbol{A}_2{}^+\boldsymbol{A}\boldsymbol{A}_2{}^+ \\
&= \boldsymbol{A}^T\boldsymbol{A}_1{}^{+T}\boldsymbol{A}_1{}^+ - \boldsymbol{A}_2{}^+\boldsymbol{A}_2{}^{+T}\boldsymbol{A}^T \\
&= (\boldsymbol{A}\boldsymbol{A}_2{}^+\boldsymbol{A})^T\boldsymbol{A}_1{}^{+T}\boldsymbol{A}_1{}^+ - \boldsymbol{A}_2{}^+\boldsymbol{A}_2{}^{+T}(\boldsymbol{A}\boldsymbol{A}_1{}^+\boldsymbol{A})^T
\end{aligned}$$

$$= A^T A_2^{+T} A^T A_1^{+T} A_1^{+} - A_2^{+} A_2^{+T} A^T A_1^{+T} A^T$$

$$= A^T A_2^{+T} A_1^{+} - A_2^{+} A_1^{+T} A^T$$

$$= A_2^{+} A A_1^{+} - A_2^{+} A A_1^{+} = 0, \tag{A2.7}$$

proving the uniqueness of A^+.

The pseudo-inverse has the following properties:

(i) $(A^+)^+ = A$. (A2.8)

(ii) $(A^T)^+ = (A^+)^T, (AA^T)^+ = (A^+)^T A^+$. (A2.9)

(iii) Let A be an $m \times n$ matrix and B be an $n \times p$ matrix. Then generally $(AB)^+$ is not equal to $B^+ A^+$. If, however, rank$A$ = rank$B = n$, then

$$(AB)^+ = B^+ A^+. \tag{A2.10}$$

(iv) $A^+ = (A^T A)^+ A^T = A^T (A A^T)^+$. (A2.11)

(v) If an $m \times n$ matrix A satisfies rank$A = m$, then

$$A^+ = A^T (A A^T)^{-1}. \tag{A2.12}$$

Also, if rank$A = n$, then

$$A^+ = (A^T A)^{-1} A^T. \tag{A2.13}$$

(vi) Let r = rank$A$, and let the singular-value decomposition (see appendix 3) of A be

$$A = U \Sigma V^T, \tag{A2.14}$$

where U and V are appropriate orthogonal matrices and Σ is the following $m \times n$ matrix:

$$\Sigma = \left[\begin{array}{cccc|c} \sigma_1 & & & \mathbf{0} & \\ & \sigma_2 & & & \\ & & \ddots & & \mathbf{0} \\ & \mathbf{0} & & \sigma_r & \\ \hline & & \mathbf{0} & & \mathbf{0} \end{array}\right] \begin{array}{l} \left.\vphantom{\begin{array}{c}1\\1\\1\\1\end{array}}\right\} r \\ \}\, m-r \end{array} \tag{A2.15}$$

(column blocks: r, $n-r$)

with

$\sigma_1 \geqq \sigma_2 \geqq \cdots \geqq \sigma_r > 0.$

Then A^+ is given by

$$A^+ = V\Sigma^+ U^T, \qquad \text{(A2.16)}$$

where Σ^+ is the $n \times m$ matrix defined by

$$\Sigma^+ = \left[\begin{array}{cccc|c} \sigma_1^{-1} & & \mathbf{0} & & \\ & \sigma_2^{-1} & & & \\ & & \ddots & & \mathbf{0} \\ & \mathbf{0} & & \sigma_r^{-1} & \\ \hline & & \mathbf{0} & & \mathbf{0} \end{array}\right] \begin{array}{l} \left.\vphantom{\begin{array}{c}1\\1\\1\\1\end{array}}\right\} r. \\ \}\, n - r \end{array} \qquad \text{(A2.17)}$$

$$\underbrace{\hphantom{xxxxxxxxxxxx}}_{r} \quad \underbrace{\hphantom{xx}}_{m-r}$$

Note that Σ^+ is the pseudo-inverse of Σ.

(vii) Let us consider a system of simultaneous linear equations given by

$$Ax = b, \qquad \text{(A2.18)}$$

where A is a known $m \times n$ matrix, b is a known m-dimensional vector, and x is an unknown n-dimensional vector. When A is square ($m = n$) and nonsingular, the solution to equation A2.18 is, as is well known, given by

$$x = A^{-1}b. \qquad \text{(A2.19)}$$

When A is not nonsingular, if A and b satisfy

$$b \in \mathrm{R}(A), \qquad \text{(A2.20)}$$

then equation A2.18 is solvable but the solution is not unique. Taking this into account, we now consider a more general problem of minimizing the Euclidean norm of error $(Ax - b)$:

$$\|Ax - b\| = \sqrt{(Ax - b)^T(Ax - b)}. \qquad \text{(A2.21)}$$

As is proved below, the general solution to this problem is

$$x = A^+b + (\mathrm{I} - A^+A)k, \qquad \text{(A2.22)}$$

where $\boldsymbol{k}$ is an arbitrary n-dimensional vector. If equation A2.18 has a solution, equation A2.22 is its general solution; if equation A2.18 has no solution, then equation A2.22 is the general form of its best approximate solution in the sense that it minimizes the norm (equation A2.21). Furthermore, if the best approximate solution is not unique, the one that minimizes its own norm $\|\boldsymbol{x}\|$ is given by

$$\boldsymbol{x} = \boldsymbol{A}^{+}\boldsymbol{b}. \tag{A2.23}$$

We will prove that equation A2.22 is the general solution to the problem of minimizing $\|\boldsymbol{A}\boldsymbol{x} - \boldsymbol{b}\|$. From equations A2.8–A2.11, we have

$$\boldsymbol{A}^{T}\boldsymbol{A}\boldsymbol{A}^{+} = \boldsymbol{A}^{T}. \tag{A2.24}$$

Using this relation, we can show that

$$\begin{aligned}
&\boldsymbol{b}^{T}[\mathbf{I} - (\boldsymbol{A}\boldsymbol{A}^{+})^{T}\boldsymbol{A}\boldsymbol{A}^{+}]\boldsymbol{b}\\
&\quad + [\boldsymbol{x} - \boldsymbol{A}^{+}\boldsymbol{b} - (\mathbf{I} - \boldsymbol{A}^{+}\boldsymbol{A})\boldsymbol{k}]^{T}\boldsymbol{A}^{T}\boldsymbol{A}[\boldsymbol{x} - \boldsymbol{A}^{+}\boldsymbol{b} - (\mathbf{I} - \boldsymbol{A}^{+}\boldsymbol{A})\boldsymbol{k}]\\
&\qquad = \boldsymbol{x}^{T}\boldsymbol{A}^{T}\boldsymbol{A}\boldsymbol{x} - 2\boldsymbol{x}^{T}\boldsymbol{A}^{T}\boldsymbol{b} + \boldsymbol{b}^{T}\boldsymbol{b}\\
&\qquad = \|\boldsymbol{A}\boldsymbol{x} - \boldsymbol{b}\|^{2}.
\end{aligned} \tag{A2.25}$$

Since the first term on the left-hand side of equation A2.25 is independent of $\boldsymbol{x}$, $\|\boldsymbol{A}\boldsymbol{x} - \boldsymbol{b}\|$ becomes minimum if and only if the second term is equal to zero, that is, if and only if

$$\boldsymbol{A}[\boldsymbol{x} - \boldsymbol{A}^{+}\boldsymbol{b} - (\mathbf{I} - \boldsymbol{A}^{+}\boldsymbol{A})\boldsymbol{k}] = \mathbf{0}. \tag{A2.26}$$

Hence, equation A2.22 is a solution to the problem for any $\boldsymbol{k}$. On the other hand, since equation A2.26 is equivalent to

$$\boldsymbol{A}[\boldsymbol{x} - \boldsymbol{A}^{+}\boldsymbol{b}] = \mathbf{0} \tag{A2.27}$$

by equation A2.1, any solution $\boldsymbol{x}^{*}$ to the problem must satisfy

$$\boldsymbol{A}\boldsymbol{x}^{*} = \boldsymbol{A}\boldsymbol{A}^{+}\boldsymbol{b}. \tag{A2.28}$$

Thus,

$$\begin{aligned}
\boldsymbol{x}^{*} &= \boldsymbol{A}^{+}\boldsymbol{b} + \boldsymbol{x}^{*} - \boldsymbol{A}^{+}\boldsymbol{b}\\
&= \boldsymbol{A}^{+}\boldsymbol{b} + \boldsymbol{x}^{*} - \boldsymbol{A}^{+}\boldsymbol{A}\boldsymbol{A}^{+}\boldsymbol{b}\\
&= \boldsymbol{A}^{+}\boldsymbol{b} + (\mathbf{I} - \boldsymbol{A}^{+}\boldsymbol{A})\boldsymbol{x}^{*}.
\end{aligned} \tag{A2.29}$$

Therefore, x^* can be expressed in the form of equation A2.22. This completes the proof.

The reader who wishes to learn more about pseudo-inverses is referred to the following:

A. Ben-Israel and T. N. E. Greville, *Generalized Inverses: Theory and Applications* (Wiley, 1974).

T. L. Boullion and P. L. Odell, *Generalized Inverse Matrices* (Wiley, 1971).

C. R. Rao and S. K. Mitra, *Generalized Inverse of Matrices and Its Applications* (Wiley, 1971).

Appendix 3 Singular-Value Decomposition

Suppose that we are given an $m \times n$ real matrix A. Then $A^T A$ is a nonnegative matrix whose eigenvalues (i.e., the solutions of $\det(\lambda \mathbf{I}_n - A^T A) = 0$) are nonnegative real numbers. We let the eigenvalues be $\lambda_1, \lambda_2, \ldots, \lambda_n$ ($\lambda_1 \geqq \lambda_2 \geqq \cdots \geqq \lambda_n \geqq 0$). We also let

$$\sigma_i = \sqrt{\lambda_i}, \quad i = 1, 2, \ldots, \min(m, n). \tag{A3.1}$$

Obviously we have $\sigma_1 \geqq \sigma_2 \geqq \cdots \geqq \sigma_{\min(m,n)} \geqq 0$. We can now express the matrix A as the product of three matrices:

$$A = U \Sigma V^T, \tag{A3.2}$$

where U is an $m \times m$ orthogonal matrix, V is an $n \times n$ orthogonal matrix, and Σ is an $m \times n$ matrix defined by

$$\Sigma = \begin{cases} \begin{bmatrix} \sigma_1 & & \mathbf{0} \\ & \ddots & \\ \mathbf{0} & & \sigma_n \\ \hline & \mathbf{0} & \end{bmatrix} & \text{if } m \geqq n \\ \left[\begin{array}{ccc|c} \sigma_1 & & \mathbf{0} & \\ & \ddots & & \mathbf{0} \\ \mathbf{0} & & \sigma_m & \end{array}\right] & \text{if } m < n. \end{cases} \tag{A3.3}$$

The right-hand side of equation A3.2 is called the *singular-value decomposition*, and σ_i ($i = 1, 2, \ldots, \min(m, n)$) are called *singular values*. The number of nonzero singular values is

$$r = \operatorname{rank} A. \tag{A3.4}$$

Since U and V are orthogonal, they satisfy

$$UU^T = U^T U = \mathbf{I}_m, \quad VV^T = V^T V = \mathbf{I}_n. \tag{A3.5}$$

Let us consider the meaning of the singular-value decomposition of A in relation to the linear transformation $y = Ax$. Letting $y_U = U^T y$ and $x_V = V^T x$, from equation A3.2 we have

$$y_U = \Sigma x_V. \tag{A3.6}$$

This implies that the transformation from x to y can be decomposed into three consecutive transformations: the orthogonal transformation from x

to x_V by V^T, which does not change length; the one from x_V to y_U, in which the ith element of x_V is multiplied by σ_i and becomes the ith element of y_U without changing its direction; and the orthogonal transform from y_U to y by U, which does not change length. Therefore, the singular-value decomposition highlights a basic property of linear transformation.

A scheme to obtain the singular-value decomposition follows. First, we calculate the singular values by equation A3.1. We note that, since the numbers of nonzero eigenvalues for A^TA and AA^T are the same, it is computationally more efficient to find the singular values using the eigenvalues of AA^T when $m < n$ and those of A^TA when $m > n$.

Next we obtain U and V. We define a diagonal matrix Σ_r using r nonzero singular values by

$$\Sigma_r = \begin{bmatrix} \sigma_1 & & 0 \\ & \ddots & \\ 0 & & \sigma_r \end{bmatrix}. \qquad \text{(A3.7)}$$

This is the $r \times r$ principal minor of Σ. We let the ith row vectors of U and V be u_i and v_i, respectively, and let

$$U_r = [u_1, u_2, \ldots, u_r]$$

and

$$V_r = [v_1, v_2, \ldots, v_r].$$

Then, from equation A3.2,

$$A = U_r \Sigma_r V_r^T.$$

Also, from equation A3.5,

$$U_r^T U_r = \mathrm{I}_r$$

and

$$V_r^T V_r = \mathrm{I}_r.$$

Hence, we have

$$A^T A V_r = V_r \Sigma_r^2, \qquad \text{(A3.8)}$$

$$U_r = A V_r \Sigma_r^{-1}. \qquad \text{(A3.9)}$$

Since equation A3.8 can be decomposed into

$$A^T A v_i = v_i \sigma_i^2, \quad i = 1,2,\ldots,r \tag{A3.10}$$

we see that v_i is the eigenvector of unit length for eigenvalue λ_i of $A^T A$. Thus we can determine V_r from the eigenvectors of $A^T A$ for eigenvalues $\lambda_1, \lambda_2, \ldots, \lambda_r$. The part of V other than V_r, which consists of vectors $v_{r+1}, v_{r+2}, \ldots, v_n$, is arbitrary as long as it satisfies equation A3.5. From the obtained V we can determine U_r by equation A3.9 and the other part of U by equation A3.5. Instead of equations A3.8 and A3.9, we can also use

$$AA^T U_r = U_r \Sigma_r^2 \tag{A3.8$'$}$$

and

$$V_r = A^T U_r \Sigma_r^{-1}. \tag{A3.9$'$}$$

A numerical example will illustrate the above sheme. Suppose that

$$A = \begin{bmatrix} 0 & 1 & -1 \\ -1 & 0 & 1 \\ 1 & -1 & 0 \\ 0 & 1 & -1 \end{bmatrix}.$$

Then

$$A^T A = \begin{bmatrix} 2 & -1 & -1 \\ -1 & 3 & -2 \\ -1 & -2 & 3 \end{bmatrix}.$$

Since

$$\det(\lambda \mathbf{I}_3 - A^T A) = \lambda(\lambda - 3)(\lambda - 5) = 0,$$

the eigenvalues of $A^T A$ are $\lambda_1 = 5$, $\lambda_2 = 3$, and $\lambda_3 = 0$, and the singular values of A are $\sigma_1 = \sqrt{5}$, $\sigma_2 = \sqrt{3}$, and $\sigma_3 = 0$. The eigenvectors v_i of $A^T A$ for λ_i $(i = 1, 2)$ are

$$v_1 = [0, 1/\sqrt{2}, -1/\sqrt{2}]^T$$

and

$$v_2 = [2/\sqrt{6}, -1/\sqrt{6}, -1/\sqrt{6}]^T.$$

Substituting $V_r = [v_1, v_2]$ into equation A3.9, we obtain

$$U_r = \begin{bmatrix} 2/\sqrt{10} & -1/\sqrt{10} & -1/\sqrt{10} & 2/\sqrt{10} \\ 0 & -1/\sqrt{2} & 1/\sqrt{2} & 0 \end{bmatrix}^T.$$

Hence, a singular-value decomposition of A is given by

$$\Sigma = \begin{bmatrix} \sqrt{5} & 0 & 0 \\ 0 & \sqrt{3} & 0 \\ 0 & 0 & 0 \\ 0 & 0 & 0 \end{bmatrix},$$

$$U = \begin{bmatrix} 2/\sqrt{10} & 0 & 1/\sqrt{2} & 1/\sqrt{10} \\ -1/\sqrt{10} & -1/\sqrt{2} & 0 & 2/\sqrt{10} \\ -1/\sqrt{10} & 1/\sqrt{2} & 0 & 2/\sqrt{10} \\ 2/\sqrt{10} & 0 & -1/\sqrt{2} & 1/\sqrt{10} \end{bmatrix},$$

and

$$V = \begin{bmatrix} 0 & 2/\sqrt{6} & 1/\sqrt{3} \\ 1/\sqrt{2} & -1/\sqrt{6} & 1/\sqrt{3} \\ -1/\sqrt{2} & -1/\sqrt{6} & 1/\sqrt{3} \end{bmatrix}.$$

The reader who wishes to learn more about singular-value decomposition is referred to the following:

V. C. Klema and A. J. Laub, "The Singular Value Decomposition: Its Computation and Some Applications," *IEEE Transactions on Automatic Control* 25, no. 2 (1980): 164–176.

G. E. Forsythe, M. A. Malcolm, and C. B. Moler, *Computer Methods for Mathematical Computations* (Prentice-Hall, 1977).

Appendix 4 Lyapunov Stability Theory

This appendix is a brief review of the stability theory by the Lyapunov method for a nonlinear autonomous system

$$\dot{\boldsymbol{x}} = \boldsymbol{f}(\boldsymbol{x}), \tag{A4.1}$$

where $\boldsymbol{x}$ is an n-dimensional state vector and $\boldsymbol{f}(\boldsymbol{x})$ is a nonlinear function of $\boldsymbol{x}$. In many cases the dynamics of a system are given not by equation A4.1 but by an nth-order differential equation

$$x^{(n)} = f(x,\dot{x},\ldots,x^{(n-1)}), \tag{A4.2}$$

where x is a scalar variable and $x^{(i)}$ is its ith time derivative. Even in that case, however, we can reduce the expression A4.2 into A4.1 by letting

$$\boldsymbol{x} = [x,\dot{x},\ddot{x},\ldots,x^{(n-1)}]^T \tag{A4.3}$$

and

$$\boldsymbol{f}(\boldsymbol{x}) = \begin{bmatrix} \dot{x} \\ \ddot{x} \\ \vdots \\ x^{(n-1)} \\ f(x,\dot{x},\ldots,x^{(n-1)}) \end{bmatrix}. \tag{A4.4}$$

We can reduce the expression A4.2 to A4.1. Thus, A4.1 is a fairly general expression for dynamics systems. In the following, we discuss the stability of the equilibrium point of system A4.1, that is, the equilibrium state $\hat{\boldsymbol{x}}$ such that

$$\boldsymbol{f}(\hat{\boldsymbol{x}}) = \boldsymbol{0}. \tag{A4.5}$$

Note, however, that there is no loss of generality even if we assume that the equilibrium point is at the origin $\boldsymbol{0}$, i.e., $\hat{\boldsymbol{x}} = \boldsymbol{0}$. We can say this because when $\hat{\boldsymbol{x}} \neq \boldsymbol{0}$ we can always transfer the equilibrium point to $\boldsymbol{0}$ by letting $\boldsymbol{x} - \hat{\boldsymbol{x}}$ be a new state vector $\boldsymbol{x}$ and expressing equation A4.1 in terms of the new state vector.

The stability of the origin $\boldsymbol{0}$ is defined as follows:

(i) The origin $\boldsymbol{0}$ is said to be stable if there exists a $\delta > 0$ for any given $\varepsilon > 0$ such that the solution $\boldsymbol{x}(t)$ to equation A4.1 with an arbitrary initial state $\boldsymbol{x}(0)$ such that $\|\boldsymbol{x}(0)\| < \delta$ satisfies $\|\boldsymbol{x}(t)\| < \varepsilon$ for all $t \geqq 0$.

(ii) The origin $\boldsymbol{0}$ is said to be asymptotically stable if it is stable and there

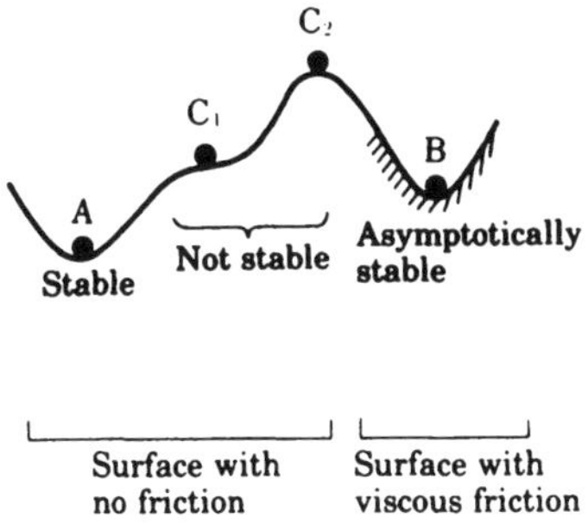

Figure A4.1
Stability of equilibrium point.

exists a $\delta' > 0$ such that the solution $\boldsymbol{x}(t)$ starting from any initial state $\boldsymbol{x}(0)$ satisfying $\|\boldsymbol{x}(0)\| < \delta'$ converges to $\mathbf{0}$ as time goes to infinity.
(iii) The origin $\mathbf{0}$ is globally asymptotically stable if it is stable and the solution $\boldsymbol{x}(t)$ starting from any initial point $\boldsymbol{x}(0)$ converges to $\mathbf{0}$ as time goes to infinity.

For example, consider the ball in figure A4.1 sliding on a curved surface with gravity acting downward. The equilibrium point A is stable (the ball continues to oscillate near the bottom because of the frictionless surface), B is asymptotically stable (the ball reaches the bottom and stops there after infinite length of time because of viscous friction), and C_1 and C_2 are not stable.

Before defining the Lyapunov function, we introduce the concept of positive-definite and positive-semidefinite functions of $\boldsymbol{x}$. Let us consider a scalar function $v(\boldsymbol{x})$ defined over a region Ω including the origin. The function $v(\boldsymbol{x})$ is said to be positive definite (or positive semidefinite) in Ω if $v(\mathbf{0}) = 0$ and $v(\boldsymbol{x}) > 0$ (or $v(\boldsymbol{x}) \geqq 0$) for any $\boldsymbol{x} \in \Omega$ such that $\boldsymbol{x} \neq \mathbf{0}$. Similarly, $v(\boldsymbol{x})$ is said to be negative definite (or negative semidefinite) in Ω if $v(\mathbf{0}) = 0$ and $v(\boldsymbol{x}) < 0$ (or $v(\boldsymbol{x}) \leqq 0$) for any $\boldsymbol{x} \in \Omega$ such that $\boldsymbol{x} \neq \mathbf{0}$.

The function $v(\boldsymbol{x})$ is called the *Lyapunov function* if $v(\boldsymbol{x})$ is positive definite in Ω, its partial derivative $\partial v(\boldsymbol{x})/\partial \boldsymbol{x}$ is continuous, and the time derivative

$$\dot{v}(\boldsymbol{x}) = \frac{dv(\boldsymbol{x}(t))}{dt} = \left(\frac{\partial v(\boldsymbol{x})}{\partial \boldsymbol{x}}\right)^T \boldsymbol{f}(\boldsymbol{x}) \tag{A4.6}$$

is negative semidefinite.

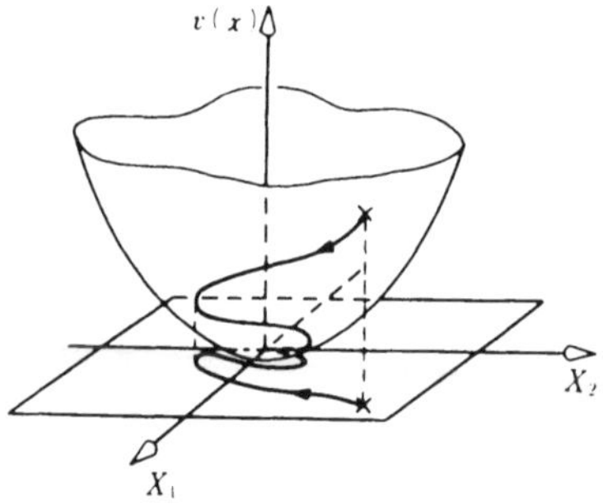

Figure A4.2
Lyapunov function.

Theorem 1 The equilibrium point **0** of system A4.1 is stable if and only if the following condition is satisfied in a neighborhood Ω of the origin:

(i) There exists a Lyapunov function.

The equilibrium point **0** is asymptotically stable if and only if condition i and the following condition are satisfied in Ω:

(ii) The time derivative of $v(\boldsymbol{x})$, $\dot{v}(\boldsymbol{x})$, is negative definite.

Condition ii can be replaced by the following:

(ii′) No solution $\boldsymbol{x}(t)$ to equation A4.1 for any initial condition $\boldsymbol{x}(0)$ such that $\boldsymbol{x}(0) \neq \mathbf{0}$ satifies $\dot{v}(\boldsymbol{x}(t)) = 0$ identically. □

This theorem is called *Lyapunov's stability theorem.*

Schematically, the Lyapunov function for the case of $n = 2$ is like the cup shown in figure A4.2. Condition i in the above theorem implies that the point $[\boldsymbol{x}^T(t), v(\boldsymbol{x}(t))]^T$ on the cup, which corresponds to a point $\boldsymbol{x}(t)$ of the trajectory of the system A4.1 on the X_1–X_2 plane, does not ascend as time passes. Condition ii implies that the point always descends until the point reaches the origin after an infinite length of time. Condition ii′ implies that, as shown in figure A4.3, although the point on the cup may not deecend but may move in a horizontal direction either at an instant of time or for a finite duration of time, it eventually starts to descend again.

The following theorem gives a condition for global asymptotic stability.

Theorem 2 The equilibrium point **0** of system A4.1 is globally asymptotically stable if and only if conditions i and ii and the following condition

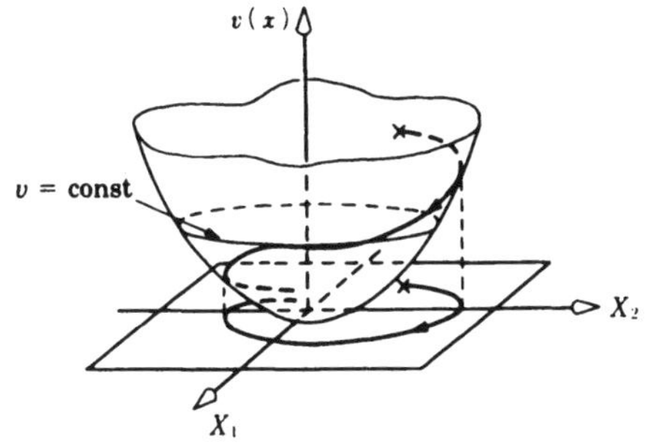

Figure A4.3
Condition ii′.

are satisfied in the whole space of $\boldsymbol{x}$:

(iii) The function $v(\boldsymbol{x})$ tends to infinity when $\|\boldsymbol{x}\|$ tends to infinity.

Condition ii can be replaced by condition ii′. □

The next result is a generalization of condition ii′. A subset S of the n-dimensional Euclidean space R^n of $\boldsymbol{x}$ is called an invariant set for A4.1 if the solution trajectory of A4.1 starting from arbitrary initial state $\boldsymbol{x}(0)$ in S remains in S all the time.

Theorem 3 Let us assume that there exists a Lyapunov function $v(\boldsymbol{x})$ for system A4.1 in the whole space of $\boldsymbol{x}$. Let E be the set of all states $\boldsymbol{x}$ satisfying $\dot{v}(\boldsymbol{x}) = 0$, and let M be the largest invariant set for A4.1 included in E. Then an arbitrary finite solution of A4.1 tends to M as time goes to infinity. In addition, if condition iii is satisfied for all $\boldsymbol{x}$, all solutions of A4.1 tend to M as time goes to infinity. □

A special case of theorem 3 where M consists only of the origin $\mathbf{0}$ corresponds to the case where condition ii′ holds in theorem 2.

As a candidate for a Lyapunov function, we often use a quadratic form $\boldsymbol{x}^T\boldsymbol{A}\boldsymbol{x}$, where $\boldsymbol{A}$ is a real symmetric matrix. When $\boldsymbol{A}$ is not symmetric, the matrix $\boldsymbol{B} = (\boldsymbol{A} + \boldsymbol{A}^T)/2$ is symmetric and satisfies $\boldsymbol{x}^T\boldsymbol{A}\boldsymbol{x} = \boldsymbol{x}^T\boldsymbol{B}\boldsymbol{x}$, so without any loss of generality we can assume that $\boldsymbol{A}$ is symmetric. The following classes of symmetric matrices are useful. An $n \times n$ real symmetric matrix $\boldsymbol{A}$ is said to be positive definite (positive semidefinite) if $\boldsymbol{x}^T\boldsymbol{A}\boldsymbol{x} > 0$ ($\geqq 0$) for any nonzero n-dimensional real vector $\boldsymbol{x}$. Similarly, $\boldsymbol{A}$ is said to be negative definite (negative semidefinite) if $-\boldsymbol{A}$ is positive definite (positive semidefinite).

The following theorem is useful for judging whether a given matrix $\boldsymbol{A}$ is positive definite (positive semidefinite) or not. Let the (i,j) element of $\boldsymbol{A}$ be $a(i,j)$, and let the principal minors be denoted by $A(i_1,i_2,\ldots,i_k)$:

$$A(i_1,i_2,\ldots,i_k) = \begin{vmatrix} a(i_1,i_1) & a(i_1,i_2) & \ldots & a(i_1,i_k) \\ a(i_2,i_1) & a(i_2,i_2) & \ldots & a(i_2,i_k) \\ \vdots & \vdots & & \vdots \\ a(i_k,i_1) & a(i_k,i_2) & \ldots & a(i_k,i_k) \end{vmatrix}, \tag{A4.7}$$

where $1 \leqq i_1 < i_2 < \cdots < i_k \leqq n$, $k = 1,2,\ldots,n$, and $|\cdot|$ denotes the determinant.

Theorem 4 (Sylvester's criterion)

(i) A symmetric matrix $\boldsymbol{A}$ is positive definite if and only if all the principal minors are positive, or, equivalently,

$$A(1,2,\ldots,k) > 0, \quad k = 1,2,\ldots,n. \tag{A4.8}$$

(ii) A symmetric matrix $\boldsymbol{A}$ is positive semidefinite if and only if all the principal minors are non-negative:

$$A(i_1,i_2,\ldots,i_k) \geqq 0, \tag{A4.9}$$

where $1 \leqq i_1 < i_2 < \cdots < i_k \leqq n$ and $k = 1,2,\ldots,n$. □

The reader who wish to learn more about Lyapunov stability theory is referred to J. La Salle and S. Lefschetz, *Stability by Lyapunov's Direct Method* (Academic, 1961).

Solutions to Selected Exercises

Chapter 1

1.1 Seven degrees of freedom. An example of the structural model is shown in figure E.1.

1.2 The singular configuration is shown in figure E.2.

1.3 Five degrees of freedom.

Chapter 2

2.1 If $\cos\theta \neq 0$, then $\phi = \operatorname{atan2}(\pm R_{21}, \pm R_{11})$, $\theta = \operatorname{atan2}(-R_{31}, \pm\sqrt{R_{32}^2 + R_{33}^2})$, and $\psi = \operatorname{atan2}(\pm R_{32}, \pm R_{33})$. If $\cos\theta = 0$, then ϕ is arbitrary, $\theta = -R_{31} \times 90°$, and $\psi = \operatorname{atan2}(R_{12}, R_{22}) + R_{31}\phi$.

2.2 From equations 2.23a and 2.23d, $\sin\psi = -\sin\phi R_{11} + \cos\phi R_{21}$; from equations 2.23b and 2.23e, $\cos\psi = -\sin\phi R_{12} + \cos\phi R_{22}$. Thus, $\psi = \operatorname{atan2}(-\sin\phi R_{11} + \cos\phi R_{21}, -\sin\phi R_{12} + \cos\phi R_{22})$.

2.5 $(\phi, 180°, 120° + \phi)$, where ϕ is arbitrary.

2.7 Transform T_p gives the image of an original point when a convex lens with focal distance f is placed on the X–Z plane.

2.11 $r_x = l_1 C_1 + l_2 C_{12}$, $r_y = l_1 S_1 + l_2 S_{12}$, $r_z = d_3$, $\alpha = \theta_1 + \theta_2 + \theta_4$.

2.16 $\tau = [0, -100(l_c + l_e), -100 l_e, 0, 0, 0]^T$.

2.17 ${}^A\boldsymbol{x}_B{}^T\,{}^A\boldsymbol{z}_B = {}^A\boldsymbol{x}_B{}^T({}^A\boldsymbol{x}_B \times {}^A\boldsymbol{y}_B) = {}^A\boldsymbol{y}_B{}^T({}^A\boldsymbol{x}_B \times {}^A\boldsymbol{x}_B) = 0$,

$$1 = {}^A\boldsymbol{z}_B{}^T\,{}^A\boldsymbol{z}_B = {}^A\boldsymbol{x}_B{}^T[{}^A\boldsymbol{y}_B \times ({}^A\boldsymbol{x}_B \times {}^A\boldsymbol{y}_B)]$$
$$= {}^A\boldsymbol{x}_B{}^T[({}^A\boldsymbol{y}_B{}^T\,{}^A\boldsymbol{y}_B){}^A\boldsymbol{x}_B - ({}^A\boldsymbol{y}_B{}^T\,{}^A\boldsymbol{x}_B){}^A\boldsymbol{y}_B] = 1 - ({}^A\boldsymbol{y}_B{}^T\,{}^A\boldsymbol{x}_B)^2.$$

Chapter 3

3.1
$$\boldsymbol{I} = \int_V [\boldsymbol{r}^T\boldsymbol{r}\mathbf{I}_3 - \boldsymbol{r}\boldsymbol{r}^T]\rho\, dv = \int_V [{}^B\boldsymbol{r}^T\,{}^B\boldsymbol{r}\mathbf{I}_3 - {}^V\boldsymbol{R}_B\,{}^B\boldsymbol{r}\,{}^B\boldsymbol{r}^T({}^V\boldsymbol{R}_B)^T]\rho\, dv$$
$$= {}^V\boldsymbol{R}_B\,{}^B\boldsymbol{I}({}^V\boldsymbol{R}_B)^T.$$

3.2
$$\tau_1 = (m_1 l_{g1}^2 + \tilde{I}_1 + m_2 d_2^2 + \tilde{I}_2)\ddot{\theta}_1 + 2m_2 d_2 \dot{d}_2 \dot{\theta}_1$$
$$+ (m_1 l_{g1} + m_2 d_2)C_1 g,$$
$$\tau_2 = m_2 \ddot{d}_2 - m_2 d_2 \dot{\theta}_1^2 + m_2 S_1 g.$$

Figure E.1
Seven-joint manipulator.

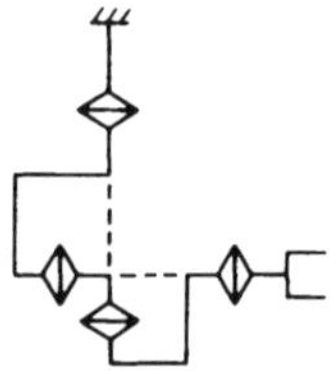

Figure E.2
Singular configuration of four-joint wrist.

3.7 $\tau_1 = (m_a l_{ga}^2 + \tilde{I}_a + m_c l_{gc}^2 + \tilde{I}_c + m_d l_a^2)\ddot{\theta}_1$
$\qquad - (l_{gc} l_b m_c - l_a l_{gd} m_d)\cos(\theta_1 - \theta_2)\ddot{\theta}_2$
$\qquad - (l_{gc} l_b m_c - l_a l_{gd} m_d)\sin(\theta_1 - \theta_2)\dot{\theta}_2^2$
$\qquad + (l_{ga} m_a + l_{gc} m_c + l_a m_d)g C_1,$

$\quad\tau_2 = (m_b l_{gb}^2 + \tilde{I}_b + m_c l_b^2 + m_d l_{gd}^2 + \tilde{I}_d)\ddot{\theta}_2$
$\qquad + (m_c l_{gc} l_b - m_d l_a l_{gd})\cos(\theta_1 - \theta_2)\ddot{\theta}_1$
$\qquad + (m_c l_{gc} l_b - m_d l_a l_{gd})\sin(\theta_1 - \theta_2)\dot{\theta}_1^2 - (m_b l_{gb} + m_c l_b - m_d l_{gd})g C_2.$

3.8 $\phi_d{}^* = [\phi_{d1}, \ldots, \phi_{d5}]^T$, where $\phi_{d1} = m_a l_{ga}^2 + \tilde{I}_a + m_c l_{gc}^2 + \tilde{I}_c + m_d l_a^2$,
$\phi_{d2} = m_b l_{gb}^2 + \tilde{I}_b + m_c l_b^2 + m_d l_{gd}^2 + \tilde{I}_d$, $\phi_{d3} = l_{gc} l_b m_c - l_a l_{gd} m_d$, $\phi_{d4} = m_a l_{ga} + m_c l_{gc} + m_d l_a$, $\phi_{d5} = m_b l_{gb} + m_c l_b - m_d l_{gd}$.

Chapter 4

4.3 The singular values are

$$\sigma_i = [(a_1 \pm \sqrt{a_1^2 + 4a_0})/2]^{1/2},$$

where

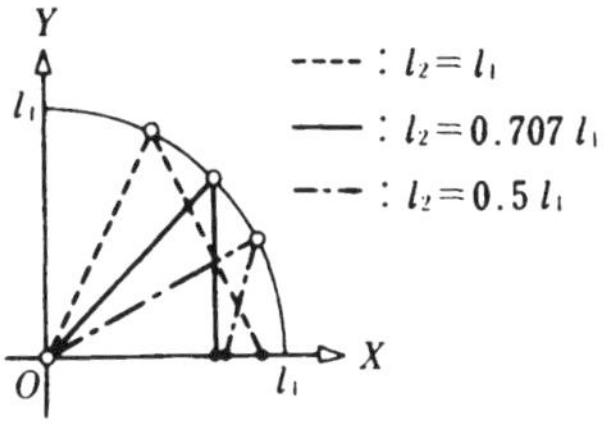

Figure E.3
Solution to exercise 4.3.

$$a_1 = l_1^2 + 2l_1l_2C_2 + 2l_2^2$$

and

$$a_0 = l_1^2l_2^2S_2^2.$$

The arm posture maximizing w_2 is given by θ_2 satisfying

$$C_2 = -2l_1l_2/(l_1^2 + 2l_2^2).$$

The optimal arm posture is shown in figure E.3 for various ratios of l_1 and l_2.

4.4 $w = |\det \boldsymbol{J}| = l_1l_2|\sin(\theta_2 - \theta_1)|$. The optimal arm posture is given by $\theta_2 - \theta_1 = \pm 90°$.

$$\sigma_i = \sqrt{\lambda_i},$$

where

$$\lambda_i = \{(l_1^2 + l_2^2) \pm [(l_1^2 + l_2^2)^2 - 4l_1^2l_2^2\sin^2(\theta_2 - \theta_1)]^{1/2}\}/2$$

($i = 1$ corresponds to $+$, and $i = 2$ corresponds to $-$).

Chapter 5

5.4 $\boldsymbol{k}_f = [-0.358, 0.358, 0.862]^T$, $\alpha_f = 81.6°$.

5.7 Let $\tilde{t} = (\sigma\omega_c^2)^{1/3}t$ and let $C = \sqrt{\sigma^2 - 2\sigma\zeta\omega_c + \omega_c^2}$. Then

$$y(\tilde{t}) = 1 - A\exp(-\sigma\tilde{t}) + AB\exp(-\zeta\omega_c\tilde{t})\sin(\sqrt{1-\zeta^2}\omega_c\tilde{t} + \theta),$$

where $A = \omega_c^2/C^2$, $B = \sigma C/(\omega_c^2\sqrt{1-\zeta^2})$, and $\sin\theta = (2\zeta\omega_c - \sigma)\sqrt{1-\zeta^2}/C$.

5.8 $\boldsymbol{u} = -[x_1{}^2 - 2x_1x_2 - 4x_2{}^2 + 3x_1 + x_2 + \lambda_1\tilde{u}_1 - \lambda_2 x_2\tilde{u}_2,$
$2x_1 + 4x_2 + \lambda_2\tilde{u}_2]^T.$

Chapter 6

6.1 $m_{\mathrm{d}} = 1.25,\ k_{\mathrm{d}} = 625,\ d_{\mathrm{d}} = 57.5.$

6.5 Let $\boldsymbol{r} = [x, y, z, \phi, \theta, \psi]^T$, where x, y, and z are the X, Y, and Z coordinates and ϕ, θ, and ψ are Euler angles of the end effector with respect to the reference frame. Then the constraint surfaces are given by $l^2 - x^2 - y^2 = 0$, $z - z_0 = 0$, $\theta - \theta_0 = 0$, and $\psi - \psi_0 = 0$, where z_0, θ_0, and ψ_0 are constants.

6.7 Letting $u_x = \partial u/\partial x$, $u_{xy} = \partial^2 u/(\partial x \partial y)$, etc., we have

$$\boldsymbol{E}_{\mathrm{F}} = \begin{bmatrix} -u_x & 1 & -u_z & 0 & 0 & 0 \\ -u_{xx} & 0 & -u_{xz} & 1 + u_z{}^2 & 0 & 0 \\ \delta_1 & 0 & \delta_2 & 0 & \delta_3 & 0 \end{bmatrix},$$

where

$$\delta_1 = (1 + u_x{}^2)u_{xz} - u_x u_z u_{xx},$$

$$\delta_2 = (1 + u_x{}^2)u_{zz} - u_x u_z u_{xz},$$

and

$$\delta_3 = (1 + u_x{}^2 + u_z{}^2)(1 + u_x{}^2)^{1/2}.$$

Matrix $\boldsymbol{E}_{\mathrm{P}}$ is, for example, given by

$$\boldsymbol{E}_{\mathrm{P}} = \begin{bmatrix} 1 & 0 & 0 & 0 & 0 & 0 \\ 0 & 0 & 1 & 0 & 0 & 0 \\ 0 & 0 & 0 & 0 & 0 & 1 \end{bmatrix}.$$

Chapter 7

7.1 Show that $A = CB$ and $A^+ = B(CB)^+$ satisfy equations A2.1–A2.4 in appendix 2. Use the fact that $(\mathbf{I} - \boldsymbol{J}_1{}^+ \boldsymbol{J}_1)$ is symmetric and idempotent.

7.2 Substitute equations 7.5 and 7.6 into equation 7.17, and let the derivative of p_1 with respect to $\boldsymbol{k}_1$ be equal to $\mathbf{0}$.

7.3 Substitute equations 7.5 and 7.6 into equation 7.18, and let derivative of p_2 with respect to $\boldsymbol{k}_1$ be equal to $\mathbf{0}$. Use

$$(\mathbf{I} - \boldsymbol{J}_1{}^+\boldsymbol{J}_1)^T(\mathbf{I} - \boldsymbol{J}_1{}^+\boldsymbol{J}_1) = (\mathbf{I} - \boldsymbol{J}_1{}^+\boldsymbol{J}_1).$$

7.7 A solution method is to specify the second subtask by the performance criterion

$$V(\boldsymbol{q}) = \sum_{i=1}^{3} \{1/(\theta_{i\,\mathrm{max}} - \theta_i)^2 + 1/(\theta_i - \theta_{i\,\mathrm{min}})^2\},$$

which is to be kept small, and to obtain $\dot{\boldsymbol{q}}_{\mathrm{d}}$ by the approach in subsection 7.2.4.

Index

Made in the USA
Columbia, SC
13 May 2024

35633371R00165